SEMIOTICS: *An Introductory Anthology*

Advances in Semiotics

THOMAS A. SEBEOK, GENERAL EDITOR

Semiotics: An Introductory Anthology
Edited with Introductions
by
Robert E. Innis

Indiana University Press
Bloomington

SEMIOTICS

An Introductory Anthology

Edited with Introductions

BY

Robert E. Innis

Indiana University Press

BLOOMINGTON

Manufactured in the United States of America

Library of Congress Cataloging in Publication Data
Main entry under title:

Semiotics, an introductory anthology.

(Advances in semiotics)
Includes index.
1. Semiotics—Addresses, essays, lectures. I. Innis,
Robert E. II. Series.
P99.S3873 1985   001.51   84-47700
ISBN 0-253-35162-6
ISBN 0-253-20344-9 (pbk.)

1   2   3   4   5   89 88 87 86 85

49, 015

CONTENTS

INTRODUCTION

In his *Foundations of the Theory of Signs* Charles Morris wrote: "Human civilization is dependent upon signs and systems of signs, and the human mind is inseparable from the functioning of signs—if indeed mentality is not to be identified with such functioning" (1). Later on in his famous little book Morris went on to say: "Indeed, it does not seem fantastic to believe that the concept of sign may prove as fundamental to the sciences of man as the concept of atom has been for the physical sciences or the concept of cell for the biological sciences" (42).

What is a sign? Why are there signs? Where do signs come from? How many types and kinds of signs are there? What is the basis for their classification? What are their respective powers? How do they stand to one another? What are the various uses to which they can be put? The discipline that tries to answer these questions in a systematic and comprehensive way is semiotics, the doctrine or general theory of signs. To put it bluntly, it deals with meanings and messages in all their forms and in all their contexts.

As Umberto Eco has put it in his *A Theory of Semiotics*: "Signification encompasses the whole of cultural life" (46) and the subject matter of semiotics is "co-extensive with the whole range of cultural phenomena, however pretentious that approach may at first seem" (6). Indeed, we can apply to 'signs' quite generally what Vygotsky, the great Russian semiotically influenced psychologist, wrote in his *Thought and Language* about "words," which are paradigmatic "semiotic objects":

A generalized reflection upon reality is the basic characteristic of words. This aspect of the word brings us to the threshold of a wider and deeper subject: the general problem of consciousness. Thought and language, which reflect reality in a way different from that of perception, are the key to the nature of human consciousness. Words play a central part in the historical growth of consciousness as a whole. A word is a microcosm of human consciousness (153).

Such a position is also echoed in Edward Sapir's contention, equally applicable to signs in all their forms, that "language is not a copy but a symbol of reality," and, as Susanne Langer has shown in a wide-ranging set of semiotically oriented philosophical investigations, "a symbol is any device whereby we are enabled to make an abstraction," a point with bearing on the functions performed by every type of sign.

The texts collected in this anthology are intended to serve the twofold purpose of making available in one place certain—but certainly not all—"classic" statements in semiotics dealing with the above questions and through them of introducing the vast set of problems and themes—philosophical, aesthetic, literary, culture-theoretical, biological, anthropological, and so forth—that fall under the purview of semiotics as the systematic and "scientific" study of all those factors that enter into semiosis, that is, into the production and interpretation of signs. Each one of the texts included here makes some contribution to delineating that vast interdisciplinary problem-space which semiotics takes as its domain, though it is not clear whether their respective answers and methodological procedures can ultimately be reconciled within one comprehensive framework.

More specifically, and in order of appearance, the materials included in this volume take up the following semiotic problems and themes. The texts from C. S. Peirce (1839–1914), extracted here from his *Collected Papers* and offered under the title of "Logic as Semiotic: The Theory of Signs" (they are identical in content and title with the Buchler selection published by Dover as *Philosophical Writings of Peirce*) mark out—with methodological sophistication and synthetic power—the systematic matrix of a general, quasi-formal semiotics which is not restricted to any one model of sign processes, although the predominant orientation is fundamentally "epistemological" and "logical," that is, directed toward the role of signs as "representational devices" principally in cognition. The Peircean categories and distinctions are an indispensable point of departure for all later sign theory and the generative source of one of semiotics' major traditions, represented in this volume especially by Morris, Thom, and Sebeok.

The texts from Ferdinand de Saussure's (1857–1913) *Course in General Linguistics*, the source of "structural linguistics" and effector of a theoretical revolution in linguistics as such, project a "semiology" (a term now largely restricted to French language discussions) as a science which "studies the life of signs within society." Presenting language as the analytical paradigm for all other sign-systems, these texts have supplied a categorical apparatus and methodological framework, quite different from the Peircean, which a major tradition has applied to a vast realm of materials ranging from photography and fashion to archaic kinship systems. The texts from Barthes and Lévi-Strauss in this reader explicitly situate themselves within the Saussurian conceptual space.

The chapter on "Verbal Interaction" from V. N. Vološinov's (1895–?)

Marxism and the Philosophy of Language, one of the first non-dogmatic fusions of "Marxist" inspired cultural and linguistic theory and semiotics, holds fast to the thesis that signs are "social forces" (Eco) and thematizes in the semiotic key and with aphoristic force the irretrievably social and creative nature of "utterances" as the primary unit of language and language study—a position directed against what Vološinov considers a blind spot in Saussurian structural linguistics and its tendencies to "abstract objectivism." Paralleling the work of his contemporary Vygotsky and his successor Luria, Vološinov delineates the dialogical, ideological, and subjectivity-constituting nature of semiosis in a fashion that intersects fruitfully with Peirce's positions and main themes.

"The Key Principle: The Sign-Character of Language," extracted from Karl Bühler's (1879–1963) "Axiomatization of the Language Sciences," which itself became part of this great semiotically oriented psycholinguist's masterwork *Sprachtheorie* (*Language Theory*)—described by Roman Jakobson in 1970 as "still for linguists probably the most inspiring among all the contributions to the psychology of language"—foregrounds the social steering elements of language, its use as a "tool" or "organon" (a position already present in Plato's *Cratylus*) in social exchange and coordination, and it details the implications of the great phonological revolution, glimpsed by Saussure and exploited by many others, for the theory of knowledge in particular and semiotics—called by him "sematology"—in general.

The selection from Susanne Langer (1895–   ) "Discursive and Presentational Forms," taken from her *Philosophy in a New Key*,—a book that has remained somewhat outside of the mainstream of semiotic work, often being relegated to a footnote—formulates with reliance on a wide range of references from symbolic logic to Gestalt theory of perception the syntactic and semantic divide between "discursive" and "presentational" forms as two different ways of symbolically transforming experience. Thus, this text opens up, without necessarily resolving, the problems of a semiotically oriented aesthetic theory, which has occupied many later thinkers.

Claude Lévi-Strauss's (1908–   ) essay, "Structural Analysis in Linguistics and in Anthropology," the first clear magisterial formulation of part of his great life project of a properly "structural"—i.e., semiotically inspired—anthropology, lays out the heuristic fertility of the structuralist linguistic model, deriving from Saussure's *Course*, for anthropological analysis and especially for the understanding of kinship structures, the logic of myth, and the nature of "primitive" thought, three of his (and his followers') great themes.

By reflecting upon the "logical paradoxes" of communication and by examining the ascension of logical levels in play and fantasy, activities that transcend segregation into "human" and "nonhuman," Gregory

Bateson (1904–1980) in his "A Theory of Play and Fantasy" is able to uncover some of the structural constants in the exchange of messages which constitutes, as he shows through copious examples and analogies, the essence of life and the theme of semiotics, a position recently emphasized by Thomas Sebeok.

The classic essay of Roman Jakobson (1896–1982), "Linguistics and Poetics," which for influence in post-Peircean and post-Saussurian semiotics is probably unparalleled, potentiates the functional matrix of language, systematized, as Jakobson points out, with semiotic intent by Bühler, and thematizes the distinctiveness of the "poetic" function of language, a topic dear to Russian and Prague Formalism and one with relevance not just to poetics and the theory of literature, but, as it turns out, to aesthetics as a whole.

The chapter from Charles Morris's (1901–1979) *Signification and Significance*, "Signs and the Act," which is heavily influenced by Morris's teacher G. H. Mead and his insistence upon the centrality of kinds of acts both in individual and social life, sketches a semiotics on a socio-behavioral basis, a position that is latent in Peirce, with his insistence on the ultimate significance of habits as the final "interpretants" of signs, but which is exploited in an ingenious and provocative way by one of the first Americans, after Peirce himself, to pursue with rigor and systematic intent the foundations of the theory of signs. His text must be looked on as belonging to the set of materials in this volume deriving from Peirce, Saussure, and Thom, the aim of which is to construct a categorical scheme for semiosis as such.

The applicability of Saussure's linguistico-semiotic schema is put to the test in Roland Barthes's (1915–1980) seminal essay, "Rhetoric of the Image," whose substantive import, apart from its methodological experiment in generalizing Saussurian categories to nonlinguistic domains, is illustrated in the peculiar "break" that photography—as distinctive form and instrument of modern "myth" making—has produced in the human perceptual system. Although focused upon photography, this essay forces us to rethink our immersion in images of all sorts and the matrices in which they are constructed.

A different approach to visual forms, this time focusing on painting, is furnished by Meyer Schapiro's (1904–   ) essay, "On Some Problems in the Semiotics of the Visual Arts: Field and Vehicle in Image-Signs." Here the primary concern is to establish—relying, in fact, on a subtle dialectic between semiotic and Gestalt categories—the signifying role of "field"— that is, ground of the image as "background"—and "vehicle"—that is, material character of the sense-bearing substance—in the production of a visual form. This concern with the semiotic logic of constructed perception intersects with the cognate themes of Langer and Barthes, though each one of them derives from a rather different intellectual tradition.

While Barthes takes as a given the possibility of expanding and generalizing the Saussurian categorical framework, which is based on the paradigmatic primacy of place of language and linguistics in the development of a general "semiology," Émile Benveniste (1902–1976), in his challenging and synthetic essay, "The Semiology of Language," subjects the viability and scope of the whole Saussurian project, and its later extensions, to a clear and disarming analysis—with full consciousness of the methodological and substantive import of such a critique.

The centrality of metaphor—as a sense- and meaning-constituting expression *par excellence*—and its semiotic import are taken up in Umberto Eco's (1931–) essay, "The Semantics of Metaphor," which not only clarifies a key topic in the so-called philosophy of language—where it has been subjected to intense and extensive analysis—but also reflects, as well as depends upon, the essential contours of Eco's nuanced, but ultimately Peircean, synthesis of semiotic theory as a whole and its "field-theory" of meaning, as found in his well-known *A Theory of Semiotics*.

The "neo-classical" (Sebeok) essay by René Thom (1923–), "From the Icon to the Symbol," takes up and rethinks the Peircean trichotomy of icons, indexes, and symbols, which has become quasi-definitive in distinguishing the ultimate and most useful classification of signs, by introducing a novel set of considerations into the foundations of sign theory, based on a general theory of structures and topological models which delineates the continuities—mirroring semiosic processes—between the inorganic and the organic.

Finally, in his "Zoosemiotic Components of Human Communication," an essay of remarkable synthetic power and heuristic fertility, Thomas Sebeok (1920–) explores the importance of nonanthroposemiotic systems of exchanging messages—already touched upon by Bateson in his essay reproduced in this volume and in his "Redundancy and Coding"—which connect human beings to the vast semiotic web constituted by organic life as such.

The present book is not, nor is it intended to be, a comprehensive sourcebook in semiotics. This would take a much larger volume or even a number of volumes and would involve rather different principles of organization and of editorial interventions. My task as editor of the volume has been to consult the wishes of many different people for an anthology that would bring together texts that would serve to introduce nonspecialists, both academic and otherwise, to the importance of the discipline and framework of semiotics and to illustrate its heuristic power and fertility. The aim has been to collect in one place crucial texts which grapple directly with semiotic issues so that they can be readily confronted with one another. After considering the vast range of suggested texts and authors, which totaled more than one hundred and fifty, and having to choose fifteen of them and put them into some sort of intelligible and useful order, I have tried to make a selection and ordering which, while certainly not all things to all men, might at least be something to most.

Accordingly and necessarily, this collection lies somewhere between an introduction and a sourcebook. As a teacher of the materials over many years, I have recognized in the wishes of others the desire to have selections that satisfied, each in its own way, the four criteria of (1) historical importance, (2) heuristic fertility, (3) exemplification of semiotic analysis, and (4) present relevance. The level of the selections is, as should be apparent, not "popular." The problem with too many "introductory" materials is that they are superficial, irretrievably "occasional," and they neither effectively initiate the beginner nor stimulate the teacher. I have tried to present selections that are capable of functioning as cell-forms which can grow into something even more complex in the course of analysis and discussion.

The issues mooted here are central topics, a kind of permanent core of semiotic concerns, although it is obvious that in an anthology containing only fifteen selections nothing like a survey of the state of the art can be attempted. There are, I am well aware, many notable and lamentable omissions from contemporary materials, such as: Lacan on the "semiotic" and "linguistic" transformation of Freudian psychoanalytic theory, Derrida's provocative and highly contentious "deconstructionist reading" and analysis of the history of philosophy and of our root models of articulation and sense-giving, Greimas's work on "structural semantics," Uspenskij's semiotic model of "poetics," Ricoeur's masterful attempts to weld phenomenology, structuralism, and hermeneutics together into a powerful interpretation theory, Apel's "semiotic transformation" of philosophy, Habermas's massive reconstruction of historical materialism on the basis of a theory of communicative action, Rossi-Landi's long pursuit of the "homologies" between semiotics and economics and his semiotic synthesis of materials on "ideology." The list starts to grow uncontrollably. Fortunately, we have a number of collections and accessible editions dealing with important contemporary materials, and I leave it to the choice of the instructor to determine what other things to assign.

I have also decided, for reasons of space and balance, not to include "pre-semiotic" texts, that is, those originating prior to Peirce and Saussure—ranging from Hippocrates to Freud (who anticipates, coincides with, and survives our principal "sources")—which bear upon our main problems. I hope to compensate for this ingratitude to the great thinkers of the past, as well as to supply a further pedagogical tool, in a volume of texts and commentaries *Forerunners of Semiotics*.

Nevertheless, the texts in this volume are by recognized "masters of the sign." They are meant to give one a real taste of semiotics and not present one with a menu. In light of the exclusions and in order to maximize the flexibility and appeal of the volume and to avoid the imposition of a specific focus, I have adhered to a strictly chronological order in presenting them. The texts can, of course, be read in any order.

Each text of the anthology is accompanied by a short introduction that outlines chief points, raises questions and objections, delineates parallels, and generally situates the texts with respect to the main problems of semiotics and with respect to one another. These introductions will make the job somewhat easier for those who want to become acquainted with semiotics directly from primary texts. At the same time the introductions can also facilitate the use of this volume with any number of secondary materials and surveys as well as supplementary volumes of readings. I have only included a short list of recommendations for further reading, the intention of which is both pedagogical and compensatory.

The following books offer penetrating and provocative introductions to the vast range of problems and issues of semiotics:

Umberto Eco's *A Theory of Semiotics* (Bloomington: Indiana University Press, 1976) is a full-fledged treatise, touching upon all the main topics of semiotics, both methodological and substantive. It is written at a fairly advanced level, has a dense and complicated internal structure, and shows both historical and philosophical sophistication of the first order. Its technical bibliography cites some important items from the European literature.

Terence Hawkes's *Structuralism and Semiotics* (Berkeley: University of California Press, 1977) is an intelligent, accurate, and relatively light-handed survey of the connection of semiotics with structuralism and their bearing upon many problems and issues in linguistics and anthropology and that vast domain encompassed by literature and literary theory. It has an annotated bibliography of one hundred and sixty-eight items and specific suggestions for reading them thematically.

James Bunn's *The Dimensionality of Signs, Tools, and Models* (Bloomington: Indiana University Press, 1981) offers a novel approach to the classification of signs and their respective functions, based on their belonging to one of the various Euclidian dimensions. It focuses upon their contribution to the processes of discovery and utilizes a wide range of stimulating and heuristically fertile examples. The notes are filled with references to materials which would not normally be looked at from a semiotic point of view.

Pierre Guiraud's *Semiology*, translated by George Gross (London and Boston: Routledge and Kegan Paul, 1975) is a compact and compressed survey in the French tradition of "introductions" to complex disciplines. It offers, within the space of a little over one hundred pages, a lot of stimulating analyses and clear models of semiotic procedures and categories.

John Deely's *Introducing Semiotic: Its History and Doctrine* (Bloomington: Indiana University Press, 1982) approaches semiotic problems from the point of view of the history of the foundations of logic and of philosophy. Particularly important are Deely's attempt to show the bearing upon semiotics of a framework derived from a semiotic transformation of Scholastic philosophy in the work of John Poinsot and his supplying of conceptual models for thematizing, in the semiotic mode, the domains of language, experience, and knowledge. The bibliography in this work is exceedingly helpful, especially for its "historical layering" of texts.

The enormous growth of semiotic literature cannot be charted in a work of this sort, and a representative bibliography would make a book in itself, and in fact has already done so: *Semiotik-Bibliographie I*, edited by Achim Eschbach and Wendelin Rader (Frankfurt: Syndikat, 1976). Perhaps, for us in the English-speaking world, the best mirrors of research are the extensive bibliographies found in the work of Thomas Sebeok. Since this book is not destined for specialists—it is not a research tool—and since, as I have noted here and will note again at various places, extensive bibliographies are available elsewhere, I have thought it more useful for the semiotic "common reader" to mention only several items which truly would be of immediate help for the independent reader, for the student, and for the classroom teacher.

The independent reader of the collection, who is approaching semiotics directly through classic texts, would also like to know just where to turn after the materials in the present book have been assimilated and would want some guidance in this regard, and I have at times perhaps suggested some unorthodox directions. The goal here, as in the selection of the texts themselves, has been, in light of the great demand for such a book, to supply a hard core of materials around which other materials could either be arranged or with which it could be integrated or radically confronted. I would like to note, however, that many of the selections contain extensive references to other materials, with which they are engaged or over against which they define their own set of problems, and they should be considered as contributions to the bibliographic structure of this book. Taken together they constitute a formidable list of further readings and span the historical and systematic space of semiotics as a whole. The assiduous reader and teacher will find plenty of indications of where to turn after working their way through the texts presented here.

I recommend that readers of the following texts and introductions keep constantly before their inner eyes (and ears) the strictures voiced by Plato in his only dialogue devoted explicitly and exclusively to language, the semiotic phenomenon *par excellence*. "Well, but surely . . . you do not suppose that you can learn, nor I explain, any subject of importance all in a moment; at any rate, not such a subject as language [or semiotics], which is, perhaps, the very greatest of all" (*Cratylus* 427). Indeed, by the end of this volume the reader might find himself echoing St. Augustine's complaint, originally expressed with regard to language, but with unmistakable relevance to the wider project undertaken here, that "discussing words with words [signs with signs] is as entangled as interlocking and rubbing the fingers with the fingers, in which case it may scarcely be distinguished, except by the one himself who does it, which fingers itch and which give aid to the itching" (*De Magistro* 372).

Ernst Cassirer, the philosopher of "symbolic forms," relying on the theoretical biologist Jakob von Uexküll's *Theory of Meaning* [*Bedeutungslehre*], remarked in his *An Essay on Man* that between the already semiotically defined receptor system and effector system which make up the particular "functional circles" of all organisms, human beings, though not exclusively, have interposed a third system of incredible differentiation and complexity, an artificial medium which he called, in accordance with his philosophical project, the symbolic system. The interposition of this new system of artificial signifying prostheses or extensions into human life does not just quantitatively enlarge but qualitatively transforms the functional circle of human beings.

In Cassirer's words:

> Physical reality seems to recede in proportion as man's symbolic activity advances. Instead of dealing with the things themselves man is in a sense constantly conversing with himself. He has so enveloped himself in linguistic forms, in artistic images, in mythical symbols or religious rites that he cannot see or know anything except by the interposition of this artificial medium (25).

Semiotics studies this sign-dependent and sign-constituted artificial medium and process in which human beings "weave the symbolic net, the tangled web of human experience."

If the drawn-out and self-involving character of the inquiry has been pointed out by Plato and Augustine and the scope by Cassirer, the payoff from engaging in these complicated and drawn-out inquiries was well put by Leibniz: "*Nemo autem vereri debet ne characterum contemplatio nos a rebus abducat, imo contra ad intima rerum ducet* [No one ought to be afraid that the contemplation of abstract characters (that is, signs and their formal structures) will lead us away from things. Rather, on the contrary, it will lead us right to their very heart]."

Acknowledgments

This book was assembled with the advice (if not the consent) of many who took the time to make suggestions as to format and to content. Although many of their suggestions were conveyed to me under conditions of anonymity, some suggestions were not so cloaked. I want to thank especially Milton Singer for his extensive, principled, and detailed recommendations, even though, for reasons beyond my control, I could only avail myself of part of them. The research staff at the University of Lowell libraries, in particular Ann Robinson, was very helpful in securing me materials and for tracking down references. I also owe a special thanks to Connie Brouillard of the duplicating staff for speedy and efficient copying, generally in triplicate. My wife, Marianne, has been a real source of help to me by discussing the format of the introductions and I am also most grateful to her for help with the proofs and with the indexing.

University of Lowell   ROBERT E. INNIS

SEMIOTICS: *An Introductory Anthology*

CHARLES S. PEIRCE

C. S. Peirce spent the greater part of his mature intellectual life developing a "semiotic" in the form of a methodologically aware, general, quasi-formal theory. His framework is "logical" in the sense ultimately derived from Scholastic philosophy, where logic was understood as the general theory of representation, that is, a theory of the ways a "mental product" is able to "reflect" or "mirror" veridically the world. Peirce's analysis of signs and of semiosis has become an indispensable starting point for a great deal of later reflection (see the texts by Morris, Eco, Thom, Benveniste in this book). Into it flowed, through Peirce's immense historical erudition, a vast amount of previous (especially Medieval) work dealing with semiotic themes, and out of it has emerged, with startling complexity and sophistication, practically all the problems and topics of the general theory of signs.

The semiotic focal point of Peirce's work—and of the texts reproduced here—is the fundamental trichotomy of the ways a sign can be related, via an "interpretant," to its object and what this threefold relationship tells us about the ultimate conditions of semiosis, the process of the production and interpretation of signs. Peirce saw semiosis as "unlimited" or "infinite" in principle, a point which Umberto Eco has taken up and made one of the keys to his synthesis of semiotic theory. As Peirce put it in a famous formulation, a "sign, or *representamen*, is something which stands to somebody for something in some respect or capacity," a definition echoed in the selection from Charles Morris, and which shows the internal complexity of the process of semiosis, each "factor"—sign, interpretant, object, interpreter, ground—being open to individual examination and variation. The core of this definition, with its specification of the complexly related components of a signifying structure and situation, is itself derived from the Scholastic formula *aliquid stat pro aliquo*, a theme Karl Bühler, in a different context, will also exploit.

Peirce divides the "standing for" relation (which is not, however, the only basis, as the text shows, for the classification of signs)—which always involves a mind or "quasi-mind" and hence an "intentional set" and processes of "abstraction"—into three classes, and hence he differentiates three fundamental "semantic" relationships between a sign and its object. *Indexes*, embodied and actuated in gestures, demonstratives, personal pronouns, field markers, and so forth, signify by existential or physical connection with their objects. *Icons*, under which Peirce includes not just "realistic" images but also such expressions as algebraic equations, graphs, diagrams, maps, and even metaphors, are based on "resemblance" between sign and object as well as on a putative sharing of "properties." *Symbols* signify without motivation, through conventions and rules, there being no immediate or direct bond between symbols and objects, a position exploited unmercifully by Saussure and his followers under the rubric of the "arbitrary character of the sign," which René Thom will trace to yet another root. Peirce's text here explores in detail the nature of this trichotomy—and other trichotomies, too—and broaches the network of problems of how our "speculative instruments" enable us to grasp the world through formally different ways.

For Peirce semiosis is the key anthropological fact. As he put it in a famous passage, which parallels themes of the great Russian semiotic psychologist, L. S. Vygotsky:

> There is no element whatever of man's consciousness that has not something corresponding to it in the word; and the reason is obvious. It is that the word or sign that man uses *is* the man himself. For, as the fact that every thought is a sign, taken in conjunction with the fact that life is a train of thought, proves that man is a sign; so, that every thought is an *external* sign, proves that man is an external sign. That is to say, the man and the external sign are identical, in the same sense in which the words *homo* and *man* are identical. Thus my language is the sum total of myself; for the man is the thought.

One of the consequences of this position, taken up by Umberto Eco in the section on the "subject" of semiotics in his *A Theory of Semiotics* and rather differently treated in the French semiotic tradition of Lacan, Derrida, Kristeva, and others, is that self-knowledge comes not from introspection, from an inquiry into a putative "inner world" of autonomous consciousness and sense-constituting acts—key themes in Husserlian phenomenology and "critical" philosophy—but from reflection upon the field of expressions in which one finds oneself, individually and socially. The self is "semiotically" defined as well as semiotically accessible. Peirce anticipated later analyses of this semiotic self, deriving from many later traditions, and they are necessary follow-ups to his own work. Indeed, because for Peirce "all thought . . . must necessarily be in signs" (CP 5.251), it follows that "whenever we think we have present to consciousness some feeling, image, conception, or other representation, which serves as a sign" (CP 5.283) and hence as support and medium of consciousness's activity. In this sense not only is the mind embedded in sign processes but it is structured as a sign process, for "even ideas are signs." Although this is the famous thesis of Locke, who foresaw its implications in his *An Essay Concerning Human Understanding*, it is also, as John Deely has shown in his stimulating *Introducing Semiotic* (Bloomington: Indiana University Press, 1982), the culminating focal point of an inner trajectory of Scholastic thought as it came to a head in the work of John Poinsot's *Tractatus de Signis*, but which is immanent in the central Medieval reflections upon the *verbum internum* or mental word.

Peirce's texts, therefore, and all the remaining texts in this collection, must be read not as exercises in classification for its own sake but as an account of the ultimate matrix wherein we construct both ourselves and our "picture" of the world. In his work the foundations of semiosis and the foundations of knowledge, both of the self and of the world, are indissolubly joined. This is the significance of an inquiry into, as Peirce put it, "that thought-sign that is myself."

Two selections from Peirce's *Collected Papers*, edited by Charles Hartshorne, Paul Weiss, and Arthur W. Burks (Cambridge: Harvard University Press, 1935–1966)—usually cited from this edition by volume and paragraph—are extremely useful: *Philosophical Writings of Peirce*, selected and edited with an introduction by Justus Buchler (New York: Dover, 1955) and *Charles S. Peirce: Selected Writings*, edited with an introduction and notes by Philip Wiener (New York: Dover, 1966). The materials on Peirce in general and on his semiotics in particular has grown to enormous proportions, and they will doubtlessly increase as the twenty-volume *Writings of Charles S. Peirce: A Chronological Edition* (Bloomington: Indiana University Press) have begun to appear—volume 1 in 1982 and volume 2 in 1984. See *A Comprehensive Bibliography and Index of the Published Works of Charles Sanders Peirce*, edited by members of the Texas Tech University Institute for Studies in Pragmaticism (Greenwich, Conn.: Johnson Associates, 1977). See also Christian J. W. Kloesel, "Bibliography of Charles Peirce 1976 through 1980," *The Monist* 65/2, April, 1982, pp. 246–276, where we find 648 items for these years alone. Despairing, I mention only the following, which, along with Cloesel, will lead one anywhere. Max H. Fisch, "Peirce's General Theory of Signs," in *Sight, Sound, and Sense*, edited by Thomas A. Sebeok (Bloomington: Indiana University Press, 1978) and his "The Range of Peirce's Relevance" (Part II), *The Monist* 65/2, April 1982, pp. 123–141 (the whole issue is devoted to Peirce). Paul Weiss and Arthur Burks, "Peirce's Sixty-six Signs," *The Journal of Philosophy* 42 (1945): 383–388, is a compact and schematic presentation, while Burks's "Icon, Index, Symbol," *Philosophy and Phenomenological Research* 9 (1949): 673–689, takes up the chief

Peircean trichotomy. Jay Zeman, "Peirce's Theory of Signs," in *A Perfusion of Signs*, edited by Thomas A. Sebeok, is clear and to the point. Milton Singer, "Signs of the Self: An Exploration in Semiotic Anthropology," *American Anthropologist* 82 (3), September 1980, 485–507, is a very stimulating broadening of the subject and has a fine bibliography dealing with anthropological implications. This theme is treated extensively and creatively in Singer's *Man's Glassy Essence: Explorations in Semiotic Anthropology* (Bloomington: Indiana University Press, 1984). See also *American Journal of Semiotics* 2/1–2 (1983), special double issue "Peirce's Semiotic and Its Audiences," edited by Kenneth Ketner.

Logic as Semiotic: The Theory of Signs

CHARLES S. PEIRCE

1. *What is a Sign? Three Divisions of Logic*

Logic, in its general sense, is, as I believe I have shown, only another name for *semiotic* (σημειωτική), the quasi-necessary, or formal, doctrine of signs. By describing the doctrine as "quasi-necessary," or formal, I mean that we observe the characters of such signs as we know, and from such an observation, by a process which I will not object to naming Abstraction, we are led to statements, eminently fallible, and therefore in one sense by no means necessary, as to what *must be* the characters of all signs used by a "scientific" intelligence, that is to say, by an intelligence capable of learning by experience. As to that process of abstraction, it is itself a sort of observation. The faculty which I call abstractive observation is one which ordinary people perfectly recognize, but for which the theories of philosophers sometimes hardly leave room. It is a familiar experience to every human being to wish for something quite beyond his present means, and to follow that wish by the question, "Should I wish

The first of the three selections in 1 is from ms. c. 1897 (*CP* 2.227–9), the third from ms. c. 1910 (*CP* 2.231–2). The second selection in 1, 3b, the second selection in 3c, and 3d are from mss. c. 1902, c. 1895, and c. 1893 (*CP* 2.274–302). 2 and 4 are from ms. c. 1903 (*CP* 2.243–52, 254–65). 3a is from the article "Sign" in Baldwin's *Dictionary of Philosophy and Psychology* 1902 (*CP* 2.304). The first selection in 3c is from the article "Index" in Baldwin's (*CP* 2.305, 306).

Reprinted by permission of the publishers from *The Collected Papers of Charles Sanders Peirce*, volumes I & II, edited by Charles Hartshorne and Paul Weiss, Cambridge, Mass.: The Belknap Press of Harvard University Press. Copyright © 1931, 1932, 1959, 1960 by the President and Fellows of Harvard College.

for that thing just the same, if I had ample means to gratify it?" To answer that question, he searches his heart, and in doing so makes what I term an abstractive observation. He makes in his imagination a sort of skeleton diagram, or outline sketch, of himself, considers what modifications the hypothetical state of things would require to be made in that picture, and then examines it, that is, *observes* what he has imagined, to see whether the same ardent desire is there to be discerned. By such a process, which is at bottom very much like mathematical reasoning, we can reach conclusions as to what *would be* true of signs in all cases, so long as the intelligence using them was scientific. The modes of thought of a God, who should possess an intuitive omniscience superseding reason, are put out of the question. Now the whole process of development among the community of students of those formulations by abstractive observation and reasoning of the truths which *must* hold good of all signs used by a scientific intelligence is an observational science, like any other positive science, notwithstanding its strong contrast to all the special sciences which arises from its aiming to find out what *must be* and not merely what *is* in the actual world.

A sign, or *representamen*, is something which stands to somebody for something in some respect or capacity. It addresses somebody, that is, creates in the mind of that person an equivalent sign, or perhaps a more developed sign. That sign which it creates I call the *interpretant* of the first sign. The sign stands for something, its *object*. It stands for that object, not in all respects, but in reference to a sort of idea, which I have sometimes called the *ground* of the representamen. "Idea" is here to be understood in a sort of Platonic sense, very familiar in everyday talk; I mean in that sense in which we say that one man catches another man's idea, in which we say that when a man recalls what he was thinking of at some previous time, he recalls the same idea, and in which when a man continues to think anything, say for a tenth of a second, in so far as the thought continues to agree with itself during that time, that is to have a *like* content, it is the same idea, and is not at each instant of the interval a new idea.

In consequence of every representamen being thus connected with three things, the ground, the object, and the interpretant, the science of semiotic has three branches. The first is called by Duns Scotus *grammatica speculativa*. We may term it *pure grammar*. It has for its task to ascertain what must be true of the representamen used by every scientific intelligence in order that they may embody any *meaning*. The second is logic proper. It is the science of what is quasi-necessarily true of the representamina of any scientific intelligence in order that they may hold good of any *object*, that is, may be true. Or say, logic proper is the formal science of the conditions of the truth of representations. The third, in imitation of Kant's fashion of preserving old associations of words in finding nomenclature for new conceptions, I call *pure rhetoric*. Its task is to ascertain the laws by which in every scientific intelligence one sign gives birth to another, and especially one thought brings forth another.

A *Sign*, or *Representamen*, is a First which stands in such a genuine triadic relation to a Second, called its *Object*, as to be capable of determining a Third, called its *Interpretant*, to assume the same triadic relation to its Object in which it stands itself to the same Object. The triadic relation is *genuine*, that is its three members are bound together by it in a way that does not consist in any complexus of dyadic relations. That is the reason the Interpretant, or Third, cannot stand in a mere dyadic relation to the Object, but must stand in such a relation to it as the Representamen itself does. Nor can the triadic relation in which the Third stands be merely similar to that in which the First stands, for this would make the relation of the Third to the First a degenerate Secondness merely. The Third must indeed stand in such a relation, and thus must be capable of determining a Third of its own; but besides that, it must have a second triadic relation in which the Representamen, or rather the relation thereof to its Object, shall be its own (the Third's) Object, and must be capable of determining a Third to this relation. All this must equally be true of the Third's Thirds and so on endlessly; and this, and more, is involved in the familiar idea of a Sign; and as the term Representamen is here used, nothing more is implied. A *Sign* is a Representamen with a mental Interpretant. Possibly there may be Representamens that are not Signs. Thus, if a sunflower, in turning toward the sun, becomes by that very act fully capable, without further condition, of reproducing a sunflower which turns in precisely corresponding ways toward the sun, and of doing so with the same reproductive power, the sunflower would become a Representamen of the sun. But *thought* is the chief, if not the only, mode of representation.

The Sign can only represent the Object and tell about it. It cannot furnish acquaintance with or recognition of that Object; for that is what is meant in this volume by the Object of a Sign; namely, that with which it presupposes an acquaintance in order to convey some further information concerning it. No doubt there will be readers who will say they cannot comprehend this. They think a Sign need not relate to anything otherwise known, and can make neither head nor tail of the statement that every sign must relate to such an Object. But if there be anything that conveys information and yet has absolutely no relation nor reference to anything with which the person to whom it conveys the information has, when he comprehends that information, the slightest acquaintance, direct or indirect—and a very strange sort of information that would be—the vehicle of that sort of information is not, in this volume, called a Sign.

Two men are standing on the seashore looking out to sea. One of them says to the other, "That vessel there carries no freight at all, but only passengers." Now, if the other, himself, sees no vessel, the first information he derives from the remark has for its Object the part of the sea that he does see, and informs him that a person with sharper eyes than his, or more trained in looking for such things, can see a vessel there; and then, that vessel having been thus introduced to his acquaintance, he is prepared to receive the information about it that it carries passengers exclusively. But the sentence as a whole has, for the person supposed, no other Object than that with which it finds him already acquainted. The Objects—for a Sign may have any number of them—may each be a single known existing thing or thing believed formerly to have existed or expected to exist, or a collection of such things, or a known quality or relation or fact, which single Object may be a collection, or whole of parts, or it may have some other mode of being, such as some act permitted whose being does not prevent its negation from being equally permitted, or something of a general nature desired, required, or invariably found under certain general circumstances.

2. Three Trichotomies of Signs

Signs are divisible by three trichotomies; first, according as the sign in itself is a mere quality, is an actual existent, or is a general law; secondly, according as the relation of the sign to its object consists in the sign's having some character in itself, or in some existential relation to that object, or in its relation to an interpretant; thirdly, according as its Interpretant represents it as a sign of possibility or as a sign of fact or a sign of reason.

I

According to the first division, a Sign may be termed a *Qualisign*, a *Sinsign*, or a *Legisign*.

A *Qualisign* is a quality which is a Sign. It cannot actually act as a sign until it is embodied; but the embodiment has nothing to do with its character as a sign.

A *Sinsign* (where the syllable *sin* is taken as meaning "being only once," as in *single, simple*, Latin *semel*, etc.) is an actual existent thing or event which is a sign. It can only be so through its qualities; so that it involves a qualisign, or rather, several qualisigns. But these qualisigns are of a peculiar kind and only form a sign through being actually embodied.

A *Legisign* is a law that is a Sign. This law is usually established by men. Every conventional sign is a legisign [but not conversely]. It is not a single object, but a general type which, it has been agreed, shall be significant. Every legisign signifies through an instance of its application, which may be termed a *Replica* of it. Thus, the word "the" will usually occur from fifteen to twenty-five times on a page. It is in all these occurrences one and the same word, the same legisign. Each single instance of it is a Replica. The Replica is a Sinsign. Thus, every Legisign requires Sinsigns. But these are not ordinary Sinsigns, such as are peculiar occurrences that are regarded as significant. Nor would the Replica be significant if it were not for the law which renders it so.

II

According to the second trichotomy, a Sign may be termed an *Icon*, an *Index*, or a *Symbol*.

An *Icon* is a sign which refers to the Object that it denotes merely by virtue of characters of its own, and which it possesses, just the same, whether any such Object actually exists or not. It is true that unless there really is such an Object, the Icon does not act as a sign; but this has nothing to do with its character as a sign. Anything whatever, be it quality, existent individual, or law, is an Icon of anything, in so far as it is like that thing and used as a sign of it.

An *Index* is a sign which refers to the Object that it denotes by virtue of being really affected by that Object. It cannot, therefore, be a Qualisign, because qualities are whatever they are independently of anything else. In so far as the Index is affected by the Object, it necessarily has some Quality in common with the Object, and it is in respect to these that it refers to the Object. It does, therefore, involve a sort of Icon, although an Icon of a peculiar kind; and it is not the mere resemblance of its Object, even in these respects which makes it a sign, but it is the actual modification of it by the Object.

A *Symbol* is a sign which refers to the Object that it denotes by virtue of a law, usually an association of general ideas, which operates to cause the Symbol to be interpreted as referring to that Object. It is thus itself a general type or law, that is, is a Legisign. As such it acts through a Replica. Not only is it general itself, but the Object to which it refers is of a general nature. Now that which is general has its being in the instances which it will determine. There must, therefore, be existent instances of what the Symbol denotes, although we must here understand by "existent," existent in the possibly imaginary universe to which the Symbol refers. The Symbol will indirectly, through the association or other law, be affected by those instances; and thus the Symbol will involve a sort of Index, although an Index of a peculiar kind. It will not, however, be by any means true that the slight effect upon the Symbol of those instances accounts for the significant character of the Symbol.

III

According to the third trichotomy, a Sign may be termed a *Rheme*, a *Dicisign* or *Dicent Sign* (that is, a proposition or quasiproposition), or an *Argument*.

A *Rheme* is a Sign which, for its Interpretant, is a Sign of qualitative Possibility, that is, is understood as representing such and such a kind of possible Object. Any Rheme, perhaps, will afford some information; but it is not interpreted as doing so.

A *Dicent Sign*, is a Sign, which, for its Interpretant, is a Sign of actual existence. It cannot, therefore, be an Icon, which affords no ground for an interpretation of it as referring to actual existence. A Dicisign necessarily involves, as a part of it, a Rheme, to describe the fact which it is interpreted as indicating. But this is a peculiar kind of Rheme; and while it is essential to the Dicisign, it by no means constitutes it.

An *Argument* is a Sign which, for its Interpretant, is a Sign of law. Or we may say that a Rheme is a sign which is understood to represent its object in its characters merely; that a Dicisign is a sign which is understood to represent its object in respect to actual existence; and that an Argument is a Sign which is understood to represent its Object in its character as Sign. Since these definitions touch upon points at this time much in dispute, a word may be added in defence of them. A question often put is: What is the essence of a Judgment? A judgment is the mental act by which the judger seeks to impress upon himself the truth of a proposition. It is much the same as an act of asserting the proposition, or going before a notary and assuming formal responsibility for its truth, except that those acts are intended to affect others, while the judgment is only intended to affect oneself. However, the logician, as such, cares not what the psychological nature of the act of judging may be. The question for him is: What is the nature of the sort of sign of which a principal variety is called a proposition, which is the matter upon which the act of judging is exercised? The proposition need not be asserted or judged. It may be contemplated as a sign capable of being asserted or denied. This sign itself retains its full meaning whether it be actually asserted or not. The peculiarity of it, therefore, lies in its mode of meaning; and to say this is to say that its peculiarity lies in its relation to its interpretant. The proposition professes to be really affected by the actual existent or real law to which it refers. The argument makes the same pretension, but that is not the principal pretension of the argument. The rheme makes no such pretension.

3. Icon, Index, and Symbol

A. SYNOPSIS

A sign is either an *icon*, an *index*, or a *symbol*. An *icon* is a sign which would possess the character which renders it significant, even though its object had no existence; such as a lead-pencil streak as representing a geometrical line. An *index* is a sign which would, at once, lose the character which makes it a sign if its object were removed, but would not lose that character if there were no interpretant. Such, for instance, is a piece of mould with a bullet-hole in it as sign of a shot; for without the shot there would have been no hole; but there is a hole there, whether anybody has the sense to attribute it to a shot or not. A *symbol* is a sign which would lose the character which renders it a sign if there were no interpretant. Such is any utterance of speech which signifies what it does only by virtue of its being understood to have that signification.

B. ICON

. . . While no Representamen actually functions as such until it actually determines an Interpretant, yet it becomes a Representamen as soon as it is fully capable of doing this; and its Representative Quality is not necessarily dependent upon its ever actually determining an Interpretant, nor even upon its actually having an Object.

An *Icon* is a Representamen whose Representative Quality is a Firstness of it as a First. That is, a quality that it has *qua* thing renders it fit to be a representamen. Thus, anything is fit to be a *Substitute* for anything that it is like. (The conception of "substitute" involves that of a purpose, and thus of genuine thirdness.) Whether there are other kinds of substitutes or not we shall see. A Representamen by Firstness alone can only have a similar Object. Thus, a Sign by Contrast denotes its object only by virtue of a contrast, or Secondness, between two qualities. A sign by Firstness is an image of its object and, more strictly speaking, can only be an *idea*. For it must produce an Interpretant idea; and an external object excites an idea by a reaction upon the brain. But most strictly speaking, even an idea, except in the sense of a possibility, or Firstness, cannot be an Icon. A possibility alone is an Icon purely by virtue of its quality; and its object can only be a Firstness. But a sign may be *iconic*, that is, may represent its object mainly by its similarity, no matter what its mode of being. If a substantive be wanted, an iconic representamen may be termed a *hypoicon*. Any material image, as a painting, is largely conventional in its mode of representation; but in itself, without legend or label it may be called a *hypoicon*.

Hypoicons may be roughly divided according to the mode of Firstness of which they partake. Those which partake of simple qualities, or First Firstnesses, are *images*; those which represent the relations, mainly dyadic, or so regarded, of the parts of one thing by analogous relations in their own parts, are *diagrams*; those which represent the representative character of a representamen by representing a parallelism in something else, are *metaphors*.

The only way of directly communicating an idea is by means of an icon; and every indirect method of communicating an idea must depend for its establishment upon the use of an icon. Hence, every assertion must contain an icon or set of icons, or else must contain signs whose meaning is only explicable by icons. The idea which the set of icons (or the equivalent of a set of icons) contained in an assertion signifies may be termed the *predicate* of the assertion.

Turning now to the rhetorical evidence, it is a familiar fact that there are such representations as icons. Every picture (however conventional its method) is essentially a representation of that kind. So is every diagram, even although there be no sensuous resemblance between it and its object, but only an analogy between the relations of the parts of each. Particularly deserving of notice are icons in which the likeness is aided by conventional rules. Thus, an algebraic formula is an icon, rendered such by the rules of commutation, association, and distribution of the symbols. It may seem at first glance that it is an arbitrary classification to call an algebraic expression an icon; that it might as well, or better, be regarded as a compound conventional sign. But it is not so. For a great distinguishing property of the icon is that by the direct observation of it other truths concerning its object can be discovered than those which suffice to determine its construction. Thus, by means of two photographs a map can be drawn, etc. Given a conventional or other general sign of an object, to deduce any other truth than that which it explicitly signifies, it is necessary, in all cases, to replace that sign by an icon. This capacity of revealing unexpected truth is precisely that wherein the utility of algebraical formulae consists, so that the iconic character is the prevailing one.

That icons of the algebraic kind, though usually very simple ones, exist in all ordinary grammatical propositions is one of the philosophic truths that the Boolean logic brings to light. In all primitive writing, such as the Egyptian hieroglyphics, there are icons of a non-logical kind, the ideographs. In the earliest form of speech, there probably was a large element of mimicry. But in all languages known, such representations have been replaced by conventional auditory signs. These, however, are such that they can only be explained by icons. But in the syntax of every language there are logical icons of the kind that are aided by conventional rules. . . .

Photographs, especially instantaneous photographs, are very instructive, because we know that they are in certain respects exactly like the objects they represent. But this resemblance is due to the photographs having been produced under such circumstances that they were physically forced to correspond point by point to nature. In that aspect, then, they belong to the second class of signs, those by physical connection. The case is different if I surmise that zebras are likely to be obstinate, or otherwise disagreeable animals, because they seem to have a general resemblance to donkeys, and donkeys are self-willed. Here the donkey serves precisely as a probable likeness of the zebra. It is true we suppose that resemblance has a physical cause in heredity; but then, this hereditary affinity is itself only an inference from the likeness between the two animals, and we have not (as in the case of the photograph) any independent knowledge of the circumstances of the production of the two species. Another example of the use of a likeness is the design an artist draws of a statue, pictorial composition, architectural elevation, or piece of decoration, by the contemplation of which he can ascertain whether what he proposes will be beautiful and satisfactory. The question asked is thus answered almost with certainty because it relates to how the artist will himself be affected. The reasoning of mathematicians will be found to turn chiefly upon the use of likenesses, which are the very hinges of the gates of their science. The utility of likenesses to mathematicians consists in their suggesting in a very precise way, new aspects of supposed states of things. . . .

Many diagrams resemble their objects not at all in looks; it is only in respect to the relations of their parts that their likeness consists. Thus, we may show the relation between the different kinds of signs by a brace, thus:

$$\text{Signs:} \left\{ \begin{array}{l} \text{Icons,} \\ \text{Indices,} \\ \text{Symbols.} \end{array} \right.$$

This is an icon. But the only respect in which it resembles its object is that the brace shows the classes of *icons, indices,* and *symbols* to be related to one another and to the general class of signs, as they really are, in a general way. When, in algebra, we write equations under one another in a regular array, especially when we put resembling letters for corresponding coefficients, the array is an icon. Here is an example:

$$a_1x + b_1y = n_1,$$
$$a_2x + b_2y = n_2.$$

This is an icon, in that it makes quantities look alike which are in analogous relations to the problem. In fact, every algebraical equation is an icon, in so far as it *exhibits*, by means of the algebraical signs (which are not themselves icons), the relations of the quantities concerned.

It may be questioned whether all icons are likenesses or not. For example, if a drunken man is exhibited in order to show, by contrast, the excellence of temperance, this is certainly an icon, but whether it is a likeness or not may be doubted. The question seems somewhat trivial.

C. INDEX

[An index is] a sign, or representation, which refers to its object not so much because of any similarity or analogy with it, nor because it is associated with general characters which that object happens to possess, as because it is in dynamical (including spatial) connection both with the individual object, on the one hand, and with the senses of memory of the person for whom it serves as a sign, on the other hand. . . . While demonstrative and personal pronouns are, as ordinarily used, "genuine indices," relative pronouns are "degenerate indices"; for though they may, accidentally and indirectly, refer to existing things, they directly refer, and need only refer, to the images in the mind which previous words have created.

Indices may be distinguished from other signs, or representations, by three characteristic marks: first, that they have no significant resemblance to their objects; second, that they refer to individuals, single units, single collections of units, or single continua; third, that they direct the attention to their objects by blind compulsion. But it would be difficult, if not impossible, to instance an absolutely pure index, or to find any sign absolutely devoid of the indexical quality. Psychologically, the action of indices depends upon association by contiguity, and not upon association by resemblance or upon intellectual operations.

An *Index* or *Seme* (σῆμα) is a Representamen whose Representative character consists in its being an individual second. If the Secondness is an existential relation, the Index is *genuine*. If the Secondness is a reference, the Index is *degenerate*. A genuine Index and its Object must be existent individuals (whether things or facts), and its immediate Interpretant must be of the same character. But since every individual must have characters, it follows that a genuine Index may contain a Firstness, and so an Icon as a constituent part of it. Any individual is a degenerate Index of its own characters.

Subindices or *Hyposemes* are signs which are rendered such principally by an actual connection with their objects. Thus a proper name, personal demonstrative, or relative pronoun or the letter attached to a diagram, denotes what it does owing to a real connection with its object, but none of these is an Index, since it is not an individual.

Let us examine some examples of indices. I see a man with a rolling gait. This is a probable indication that he is a sailor. I see a bowlegged man in corduroys, gaiters, and a jacket. These are probable indications that he is a jockey or something of the sort. A sundial or a clock *indicates* the time of day. Geometricians mark letters against the different parts of their diagrams and then use these letters to indicate those parts. Letters are similarly used by lawyers and others. Thus, we may say: If A and B are married to one another and C is their child while D is brother of A, then D is uncle of C. Here A, B, C, and D fulfill the office of relative pronouns, but are more convenient since they require no special collocation of words. A rap on the door is an index. Anything which focusses the attention is an index. Anything which startles us is an index, in so far as it marks the junction between two portions of experience. Thus a tremendous thunderbolt indicates that *something* considerable happened, though we may not know precisely what the event was. But it may be expected to connect itself with some other experience.

. . . A low barometer with a moist air is an index of rain; that is we suppose that the forces of nature establish a probable connection between the low barometer with moist air and coming rain. A weathercock is an index of the direction of the wind; because in the first place it really takes the self-same direction as the wind, so that there is a real connection between them, and in the second place we are so constituted that when we see a weathercock pointing in a certain direction it draws our attention to that direction, and when we see the weathercock veering with the wind, we are forced by the law of mind to think that direction is connected with the wind. The pole star is an index, or pointing finger, to show us which way is north. A spirit-level, or a plumb bob, is an index of the vertical direction. A yard-stick might seem, at first sight, to be an icon of a yard; and so it would be, if it were merely intended to show a yard as near as it can be seen and estimated to be a yard. But the very purpose of a yard-stick is to show a yard nearer than it can be estimated by its appearance. This it does in consequence of an accurate mechanical comparison made with the bar in London called the yard. Thus it is a real connection which gives the yardstick its value as a representamen; and thus it is an *index*, not a mere *icon*.

When a driver to attract the attention of a foot passenger and cause him to save himself, calls out "Hi!" so far as this is a significant word, it is, as will be seen below, something more than an index; but so far as it is simply intended to act upon the hearer's nervous system and to rouse him to get out of the way, it is an index, because it is meant to put him in real connection with the object, which is his situation relative to the approaching horse. Suppose two men meet upon a country road and one of them says to the other, "The chimney of that house is on fire." The other looks about him and descries a house with green blinds and a verandah having a smoking chimney. He walks on a few miles and meets a second traveller. Like a Simple Simon he says, "The chimney of that house is on fire." "What house?" asks the other. "Oh, a house with green blinds and a verandah," replies the simpleton. "Where is the house?" asks the stranger. He desires some *index* which shall connect his apprehension with the house meant. Words alone cannot do this. The demonstrative pronouns, "this" and "that," are indices. For they call upon the hearer to use his powers of observation, and so establish a real connection between his mind and the object; and if the demonstrative pronoun does that—without which its meaning is not understood—it goes to establish such a connection; and so is an index. The relative pronouns, *who* and *which*, demand observational activity in much the same way, only with them the

observation has to be directed to the words that have gone before. Lawyers use A, B, C, practically as very effective relative pronouns. To show
how effective they are, we may note that Messrs. Allen and Greenough,
in their admirable (though in the edition of 1877 [?], too small) Latin
Grammar, declare that no conceivable syntax could wholly remove the
ambiguity of the following sentence, "A replied to B that he thought C
(his brother) more unjust to himself than to his own friend." Now, any
lawyer would state that with perfect clearness, by using A, B, C, as relatives, thus:

A replied to B that he $\left\{ \begin{array}{c} A \\ B \end{array} \right\}$, thought C (his $\left\{ \begin{array}{c} A\text{'s} \\ B\text{'s} \end{array} \right\}$, brother) more un-

just to himself, $\left\{ \begin{array}{c} A \\ B \\ C \end{array} \right\}$ than to his $\left\{ \begin{array}{c} A\text{'s} \\ B\text{'s} \\ C\text{'s} \end{array} \right\}$ own friend. The terminations

which in any inflected language are attached to words "governed" by
other words, and which serve to show which the governing word is, by
repeating what is elsewhere expressed in the same form, are likewise *indices* of the same relative pronoun character. Any bit of Latin poetry illustrates this, such as the twelve-line sentence beginning, "*Jam satis terris.*"
Both in these terminations and in the A, B, C, a likeness is relied upon to
carry the attention to the right object. But this does not make them icons,
in any important way; for it is of no consequence how the letters A, B, C,
are shaped or what the terminations are. It is not merely that one occurrence of an A is like a previous occurrence that is the important circum-
stance, but that *there is an understanding that like letters shall stand for
the same thing*, and this acts as a force carrying the attention from one
occurrence of A to the previous one. A possessive pronoun is two ways an
index: first it indicates the possessor, and, second, it has a modification
which syntactically carries the attention to the word denoting the thing
possessed.

Some indices are more or less detailed directions for what the hearer is
to do in order to place himself in direct experiential or other connection
with the thing meant. Thus, the Coast Survey issues "Notices to Mari-
ners," giving the latitude and longitude, four or five bearings of prominent objects, etc., and saying *there* is a rock, or shoal, or buoy, or light-
ship. Although there will be other elements in such directions, yet in the
main they are indices.

Along with such indexical directions of what to do to find the object
meant, ought to be classed those pronouns which should be entitled *selective* pronouns [or quantifiers] because they inform the hearer how he
is to pick out one of the objects intended, but which grammarians call by
the very indefinite designation of *indefinite* pronouns. Two varieties of
these are particularly important in logic, the *universal selectives*, such as
quivis, quilibet, quisquam, ullus, nullus, nemo, quisque, uterque, and in

English, *any, every, all, no, none, whatever, whoever, everybody, anybody, nobody.* These mean that the hearer is at liberty to select any instance he likes within limits expressed or understood, and the assertion is intended to apply to that one. The other logically important variety consists of the *particular selectives, quis, quispiam, nescio quis, aliquis, quidam,* and in English, *some, something, somebody, a, a certain, some or other, a suitable, one.*

Allied to the above pronouns are such expressions as *all but one, one or two, a few, nearly all, every other one,* etc. Along with pronouns are to be classed adverbs of place and time, etc.

Not very unlike these are, *the first, the last, the seventh, two-thirds of, thousands of,* etc.

Other indexical words are prepositions, and prepositional phrases, such as, "on the right (or left) of." Right and left cannot be distinguished by any general description. Other prepositions signify relations which may, perhaps, be described; but when they refer, as they do oftener than would be supposed, to a situation relative to the observed, or assumed to be experientially known, place and attitude of the speaker relatively to that of the hearer, then the indexical element is the dominant element.

Icons and indices assert nothing. If an icon could be interpreted by a sentence, that sentence must be in a "potential mood," that is, it would merely say, "Suppose a figure has three sides," etc. Were an index so interpreted, the mood must be imperative, or exclamatory, as "See there!" or "Look out!" But the kind of signs which we are now coming to consider are, by nature, in the "indicative," or, as it should be called, the *declarative* mood. Of course, they can go to the expression of any other mood, since we may declare assertions to be doubtful, or mere interrogations, or imperatively requisite.

D. SYMBOL

A Symbol is a Representamen whose Representative character consists precisely in its being a rule that will determine its Interpretant. All words, sentences, books, and other conventional signs are Symbols. We speak of writing or pronouncing the word "man"; but it is only a *replica*, or embodiment of the word, that is pronounced or written. The word itself has no existence although it has a real being, *consisting in* the fact that existents *will* conform to it. It is a general mode of succession of three sounds or representamens of sounds, which becomes a sign only in the fact that a habit, or acquired law, will cause replicas of it to be interpreted as meaning a man or men. The word and its meaning are both general rules; but the word alone of the two prescribes the qualities of its replicas in themselves. Otherwise the "word" and its "meaning" do not differ, unless some special sense be attached to "meaning."

A Symbol is a law, or regularity of the indefinite future. Its Interpretant must be of the same description; and so must be also the complete immediate Object, or meaning. But a law necessarily governs, or "is embodied in" individuals, and prescribes some of their qualities. Consequently, a constituent of a Symbol may be an Index, and a constituent may be an Icon. A man walking with a child points his arm up into the air and says, "There is a balloon." The pointing arm is an essential part of the symbol without which the latter would convey no information. But if the child asks, "What is a balloon," and the man replies, "It is something like a great big soap bubble," he makes the image a part of the symbol. Thus, while the complete object of a symbol, that is to say, its meaning, is of the nature of a law, it must *denote* an individual, and must *signify* a character. A *genuine* symbol is a symbol that has a general meaning. There are two kinds of degenerate symbols, the *Singular Symbol* whose Object is an existent individual, and which signifies only such characters as that individual may realize; and the *Abstract Symbol*, whose only Object is a character.

Although the immediate Interpretant of an Index must be an Index, yet since its Object may be the Object of an Individual [Singular] Symbol, the Index may have such a Symbol for its indirect Interpretant. Even a genuine Symbol may be an imperfect Interpretant of it. So an *icon* may have a degenerate Index, or an Abstract Symbol, for an indirect Interpretant, and a genuine Index or Symbol for an imperfect Interpretant.

A *Symbol* is a sign naturally fit to declare that the set of objects which is denoted by whatever set of indices may be in certain ways attached to it is represented by an icon associated with it. To show what this complicated definition means, let us take as an example of a symbol the word "loveth." Associated with this word is an idea, which is the mental icon of one person loving another. Now we are to understand that "loveth" occurs in a sentence; for what it may mean by itself, if it means anything, is not the question. Let the sentence, then, be "Ezekiel loveth Huldah." Ezekiel and Huldah must, then, be or contain indices; for without indices it is impossible to designate what one is talking about. Any mere description would leave it uncertain whether they were not mere characters in a ballad; but whether they be so or not, indices can designate them. Now the effect of the word "loveth" is that the pair of objects denoted by the pair of indices Ezekiel and Huldah is represented by the icon, or the image we have in our minds of a lover and his beloved.

The same thing is equally true of every verb in the declarative mood; and indeed of every verb, for the other moods are merely declarations of a fact somewhat different from that expressed by the declarative mood. As for a noun, considering the meaning which it has in the sentence, and not as standing by itself, it is most conveniently regarded as a portion of a symbol. Thus the sentence, "every man loves a woman" is equivalent to "whatever is a man loves something that is a woman." Here "whatever" is a universal selective index, "is a man" is a symbol, "loves" is a symbol, "something that" is a particular selective index, and "is a woman" is a symbol. . . .

The word *Symbol* has so many meanings that it would be an injury to the language to add a new one. I do not think that the signification I attach to it, that of a conventional sign, or one depending upon habit (acquired or inborn), is so much a new meaning as a return to the original meaning. Etymologically, it should mean a thing thrown together, just as ἔμβολον (embolum) is a thing thrown into something, a bolt, and παράβολον (parabolum) is a thing thrown besides, collateral security, and ὑπόβολον (hypobolum) is a thing thrown underneath, an antenuptial gift. It is usually said that in the word *symbol* the throwing together is to be understood in the sense of "to conjecture"; but were that the case, we ought to find that *sometimes* at least it meant a conjecture, a meaning for which literature may be searched in vain. But the Greeks used "throw together" (συμβάλλειν) very frequently to signify the making of a contract or convention. Now, we do find symbol (σύμβολον) early and often used to mean a convention or contract. Aristotle calls a noun a "symbol," that is, a conventional sign. In Greek, watchfire is a "symbol," that is, a signal agreed upon; a standard or ensign is a "symbol," a watchword is a "symbol," a badge is a "symbol"; a church creed is called a "symbol," because it serves as a badge or shibboleth; a theatre ticket is called a "symbol"; any ticket or check entitling one to receive anything is a "symbol." Moreover, any expression of sentiment was called a "symbol." Such were the principal meanings of the word in the original language. The reader will judge whether they suffice to establish my claim that I am not seriously wrenching the word in employing it as I propose to do.

Any ordinary word, as "give," "bird," "marriage," is an example of a symbol. It is *applicable to whatever may be found to realize the idea connected with the word*; it does not, in itself, identify those things. It does not show us a bird, nor enact before our eyes a giving or a marriage, but supposes that we are able to imagine those things, and have associated the word with them.

A regular progression of one, two, three may be remarked in the three orders of signs, Icon, Index, Symbol. The Icon has no dynamical connection with the object it represents; it simply happens that its qualities resemble those of that object, and excite analogous sensations in the mind for which it is a likeness. But it really stands unconnected with them. The index is physically connected with its object; they make an organic pair, but the interpreting mind has nothing to do with this connection, except remarking it, after it is established. The symbol is connected with its object by virtue of the idea of the symbol-using mind, without which no such connection would exist.

Every physical force reacts between a pair of particles, either of which may serve as an index of the other. On the other hand, we shall find that every intellectual operation involves a triad of symbols.

A symbol, as we have seen, cannot indicate any particular thing; it denotes a kind of thing. Not only that, but it is itself a kind and not a single thing. You can write down the word "star," but that does not make you the creator of the word, nor if you erase it have you destroyed the word. The word lives in the minds of those who use it. Even if they are all asleep, it exists in their memory. So we may admit, if there be reason to do so, that generals are mere words without at all saying, as Ockham supposed, that they are really individuals.

Symbols grow. They come into being by development out of other signs, particularly from icons, or from mixed signs partaking of the nature of icons and symbols. We think only in signs. These mental signs are of mixed nature; the symbol-parts of them are called concepts. If a man makes a new symbol, it is by thoughts involving concepts. So it is only out of symbols that a new symbol can grow. *Omne symbolum de symbolo.* A symbol, once in being, spreads among the peoples. In use and in experience, its meaning grows. Such words as *force, law, wealth, marriage*, bear for us very different meanings from those they bore to our barbarous ancestors. The symbol may, with Emerson's sphynx, say to man,

Of thine eye I am eyebeam.

4. *Ten Classes of Signs*

The three trichotomies of Signs result together in dividing Signs into TEN CLASSES OF SIGNS, of which numerous subdivisions have to be considered. The ten classes are as follows:

First: A Qualisign [*e.g.*, a feeling of "red"] is any quality in so far as it is a sign. Since a quality is whatever it is positively in itself, a quality can only denote an object by virtue of some common ingredient or similarity; so that a Qualisign is necessarily an Icon. Further, since a quality is a mere logical possibility, it can only be interpreted as a sign of essence, that is, as a Rheme.

Second: An Iconic Sinsign [*e.g.*, an individual diagram] is any object of experience in so far as some quality of it makes it determine the idea of an object. Being an Icon, and thus a sign by likeness purely, of whatever it may be like, it can only be interpreted as a sign of essence, or Rheme. It will embody a Qualisign.

Third: A Rhematic Indexical Sinsign [*e.g.*, a spontaneous cry] is any object of direct experience so far as it directs attention to an Object by which its presence is caused. It necessarily involves an Iconic Sinsign of a peculiar kind, yet is quite different since it brings the attention of the interpreter to the very Object denoted.

Fourth: A Dicent Sinsign [*e.g.*, a weathercock] is any object of direct experience, in so far as it is a sign, and, as such, affords information concerning its Object. This it can only do by being really affected by its Object; so that it is necessarily an Index. The only information it can afford is of actual fact. Such a Sign must involve an Iconic Sinsign to embody the information and a Rhematic Indexical Sinsign to indicate the Object to which the information refers. But the mode of combination, or *Syntax*, of these two must also be significant.

Fifth: An Iconic Legisign [*e.g.*, a diagram, apart from its factual individuality] is any general law or type, in so far as it requires each instance of it to embody a definite quality which renders it fit to call up in the mind the idea of a like object. Being an Icon, it must be a Rheme. Being a Legisign, its mode of being is that of governing single Replicas, each of which will be an Iconic Sinsign of a peculiar kind.

Sixth: A Rhematic Indexical Legisign [*e.g.*, a demonstrative pronoun] is any general type or law, however established, which requires each instance of it to be really affected by its Object in such a manner as merely to draw attention to that Object. Each Replica of it will be a Rhematic Indexical Sinsign of a peculiar kind. The Interpretant of a Rhematic Indexical Legisign represents it as an Iconic Legisign; and so it is, in a measure—but in a very small measure.

Seventh: A Dicent Indexical Legisign [*e.g.*, a street cry] is any general type or law, however established, which requires each instance of it to be really affected by its Object in such a manner as to furnish definite information concerning that Object. It must involve an Iconic Legisign to signify the information and a Rhematic Indexical Legisign to denote the subject of that information. Each Replica of it will be a Dicent Sinsign of a peculiar kind.

Eighth: A Rhematic Symbol or Symbolic Rheme [*e.g.*, a common noun] is a sign connected with its Object by an association of general ideas in such a way that its Replica calls up an image in the mind, which image, owing to certain habits or dispositions of that mind, tends to produce a general concept, and the Replica is interpreted as a Sign of an Object that is an instance of that concept. Thus, the Rhematic Symbol either is, or is very like, what the logicians call a General Term. The Rhematic Symbol, like any Symbol, is necessarily itself of the nature of a general type, and is thus a Legisign. Its Replica, however, is a Rhematic Indexical Sinsign of a peculiar kind, in that the image it suggests to the mind acts upon a Symbol already in that mind to give rise to a General Concept. In this it differs from other Rhematic Indexical Sinsigns, including those which are Replicas of Rhematic Indexical Legisigns. Thus, the demonstrative pronoun "that" is a Legisign, being a general type; but it is not a Symbol, since it does not signify a general concept. Its Replica draws attention to a single Object, and is a Rhematic Indexical Sinsign. A

Replica of the word "camel" is likewise a Rhematic Indexical Sinsign, being really affected, through the knowledge of camels, common to the speaker and auditor, by the real camel it denotes, even if this one is not individually known to the auditor; and it is through such real connection that the word "camel" calls up the idea of a camel. The same thing is true of the word "phoenix." For although no phoenix really exists, real descriptions of the phoenix are well known to the speaker and his auditor; and thus the word is really affected by the Object denoted. But not only are the Replicas of Rhematic Symbols very different from ordinary Rhematic Indexical Sinsigns, but so likewise are Replicas of Rhematic Indexical Legisigns. For the thing denoted by "that" has not affected the replica of the word in any such direct and simple manner as that in which, for example, the ring of a telephone-bell is affected by the person at the other end who wants to make a communication. The Interpretant of the Rhematic Symbol often represents it as a Rhematic Indexical Legisign; at other times as an Iconic Legisign; and it does in a small measure partake of the nature of both.

Ninth: A Dicent Symbol, or ordinary Proposition, is a sign connected with its object by an association of general ideas, and acting like a Rhematic Symbol, except that its intended interpretant represents the Dicent Symbol as being, in respect to what it signifies, really affected by its Object, so that the existence or law which it calls to mind must be actually connected with the indicated Object. Thus, the intended Interpretant looks upon the Dicent Symbol as a Dicent Indexical Legisign; and if it be true, it does partake of this nature, although this does not represent its whole nature. Like the Rhematic Symbol, it is necessarily a Legisign. Like the Dicent Sinsign it is composite inasmuch as it necessarily involves a Rhematic Symbol (and thus is for its Interpretant an Iconic Legisign) to express its information and a Rhematic Indexical Legisign to indicate the subject of that information. But its Syntax of these is significant. The Replica of the Dicent Symbol is a Dicent Sinsign of a peculiar kind. This is easily seen to be true when the information the Dicent Symbol conveys is of actual fact. When that information is of a real law, it is not true in the same fullness. For a Dicent Sinsign cannot convey information of law. It is, therefore, true of the Replica of such a Dicent Symbol only in so far as the law has its being in instances.

Tenth: An Argument is a sign whose interpretant represents its object as being an ulterior sign through a law, namely, the law that the passage from all such premises to such conclusions tends to the truth. Manifestly, then, its object must be general; that is, the Argument must be a Symbol. As a Symbol it must, further, be a Legisign. Its Replica is a Dicent Sinsign.

The affinities of the ten classes are exhibited by arranging their designations in the triangular table here shown, which has heavy boundaries between adjacent squares that are appropriated to classes alike in only

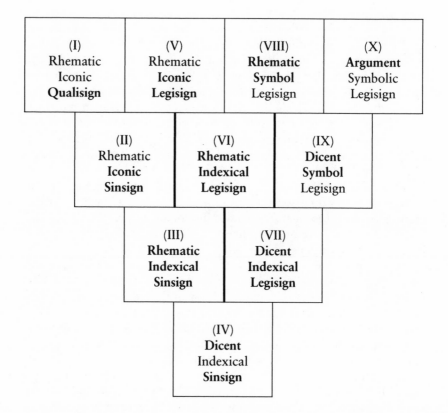

one respect. All other adjacent squares pertain to classes alike in two respects. Squares not adjacent pertain to classes alike in one respect only, except that each of the three squares of the vertices of the triangle pertains to a class differing in all three respects from the classes to which the squares along the opposite side of the triangle are appropriated. The lightly printed designations are superfluous.

In the course of the above descriptions of the classes, certain subdivisions of some of them have been directly or indirectly referred to. Namely, beside the normal varieties of Sinsigns, Indices, and Dicisigns, there are others which are Replicas of Legisigns, Symbols, and Arguments, respectively. Beside the normal varieties of Qualisigns, Icons, and Rhemes, there are two series of others; to wit, those which are directly involved in Sinsigns, Indices, and Dicisigns, respectively, and also those which are indirectly involved in Legisigns, Symbols, and Arguments, respectively. Thus, the ordinary Dicent Sinsign is exemplified by a weathercock and its veering and by a photograph. The fact that the latter is known to be the effect of the radiations from the object renders it an index and highly informative. A second variety is a Replica of a Dicent Indexical Legisign. Thus any given street cry, since its tone and theme identifies the individual, is not a symbol, but an Indexical Legisign; and any individual instance of it is a Replica of it which is a Dicent Sinsign. A third variety is a Replica of a Proposition. A fourth variety is a Replica of an Argument. Beside the normal variety of the Dicent Indexical Legisign, of which a street cry is an example, there is a second variety, which is that sort of proposition which has the name of a well-known individual as its predicate; as if one is asked, "Whose statue is this?" the answer may be, "It is Farragut." The meaning of this answer is a Dicent Indexical Legisign. A third variety may be a premiss of an argument. A Dicent Symbol, or ordinary proposition, insofar as it is a premiss of an Argument, takes on a new force, and becomes a second variety of the Dicent Symbol. It would not be worth while to go through all the varieties; but it may be well to consider the varieties of one class more. We may take the Rhematic Indexical Legisign. *The* shout of "Hullo!" is an example of the ordinary variety—meaning, not an individual shout, but this shout "Hullo!" in general—this type of shout. A second variety is a constituent of a Dicent Indexical Legisign; as the word "that" in the reply, "that is Farragut." A third variety is a particular application of a Rhematic Symbol; as the exclamation "Hark!" A fourth and fifth variety are in the peculiar force a general word may have in a proposition or argument. It is not impossible that some varieties are here overlooked. It is a nice problem to say to what class a given sign belongs; since all the circumstances of the case have to be considered. But it is seldom requisite to be very accurate; for if one does not locate the sign precisely, one will easily come near enough to its character for any ordinary purpose of logic.

FERDINAND DE SAUSSURE

The generality of Peirce's starting point in "logic" as a general theory of inquiry and in his trichotomy of signifying relationships is matched by the specificity of Saussure's taking the linguistic sign and linguistics as his "semiological" model. Later semiotic theory has not only inherited as a given the Peircean triad—which itself is an echo of the Medieval division of signs into mimetic, deictic, and conventional—but it has also been bequeathed by Saussure what has become a practically unavoidable way of speaking about signs in general, though the original context was linguistic. The linguistic sign, Saussure pointed out, is a "double entity," a Janus-faced thing, both sides or faces of which are absolutely necessary for it to function as a sign. Taking, not without detriment to later work in the tradition deriving from him, the "word" as his fundamental unit, Saussure asserted that "the linguistic sign unites, not a thing and a name, but a concept and a sound-image." This "sound-image," to use a terminology somewhat different from Saussure's, is a concrete psychologically realized token of an abstract type, and the "concept" is the "meaning," Peirce's "interpretant," which is the "thought-sign" generated by another sign.

Now by a "sign" Saussure means the indissoluble *union* of the two components, not the "sound-image"—or visual image if we are talking about graphic signs—alone, a temptation to which linguistic theory and general sign theory has been prone. Saussure's great proposal—which, as Bühler points out in his text, is nevertheless tainted by the adoption of an "association" theory of meaning—was "to retain the word *sign* [*signe*] to designate the whole and to replace *concept* and *sign-image* respectively by *signified* [*signifié*] and *signifier* [*signifiant*]," a terminological choice which has spread far and wide beyond the domain in which Saussure himself used it and is now used to analyze systems of signs in every medium whatsoever. See, thus, Barthes's essay on the "Rhetoric of the Image" (also his *The Fashion System*) and Schapiro's use of this terminology, too. As, however, Benveniste's essay and other cognate texts will show—see especially the essay by Lévi-Strauss—the range of application as well as the peculiarity of the framework in which it is found give rise to problems and profound solutions alike. Here one can also profitably compare Langer's rather different formulations.

For Saussure, signs, as the union of signifier and signified, signify through differential opposition, one of the key ideas of his "semiologically" oriented language theory which has been exploited widely in many different domains. Both sides of the sign are for him in the deepest sense fundamentally diacritical, a theme Eco, himself echoing Hjelmslev, will exploit quite generally under the rubric of "segmentation." Just as the signifier is not a "thing," a substantial entity, but a relational structure, so signifieds likewise are defined through relations of opposition, not through being referred to "extra-semiotic" entities or "the world." Both are defined by and within a system of contrasts from other signifiers and signifieds. They are "form," not "substance." Since a sign functions only within a system—that is, within a code, one of the chief semiotic categories—and a system is a set of *formally structured* oppositions and differences, Saussure has become one of the sources not just of "structural linguistics," but a participant in that vast and still disputed movement called "structuralism," which extends from linguistics, through literary theory, anthropology, history, and psychology, to psychoanalysis, and even beyond.

Saussure's differential definition of the sign parallels his concept of the phoneme as itself a differential unity in the constitution of the linguistic sign. Although Saussure only just glimpsed the heuristic power of the great phonological analogy—something exploited extensively by Bühler, Jakobson, Merleau-Ponty, and others—he did see that "our system of phonemes is the instrument we play in order to articulate the words of language" and he foresaw, at least implicitly, the possibility of searching for nonlinguistic elements, analogous to phonemes and the higher unities built on them, that would constitute the vast set of differential oppositions making up the signifying domains of painting, architecture, music, dance, film, and other systems, an idea which has now generated a large and uneven literature under the rubric of secondary modeling systems, a theme predominant in the Russian semiotic tradition, a representative selection from which can be found in Daniel P. Lucid, *Soviet Semiotics* (Baltimore: The Johns Hopkins University Press, 1977). The ultimate value of this framework and its generalizability are matters of some dispute. By no means does a "semiotic" approach to nonlinguistic domains have to restrict itself to the Saussurian categorial matrix—Langer, Nelson Goodman, and the essay by Meyer Schapiro are prime examples of alternative frameworks—although French language work has, with mixed though extremely interesting results, tended to do so, for temperamental as well as linguistic reasons.

One of Saussure's most famous distinctions, which bears directly upon

Vološinov's project, is that between *langue* and *parole*. *Langue* is the linguistic *system*—the objective "code"—upon which the concrete speakers depend to produce utterances in the process of speech or *parole*. While *langue* is social, *parole* is individual. This distinction, which is based on Durkheim's analyses of the objectivity of social "facts" and their realization in individual consciousnesses, has had a very checkered history (see Bühler, Lévi-Strauss, Jakobson, Barthes, Benveniste, plus many essays of Paul Ricoeur) and was subjected to severe, and essentially modifying, criticism in Vološinov's account of the centrality of "verbal interaction" which pivots around the "utterance," as the primary object of a "philosophy" of language.

Although Saussure's work was not essentially "epistemological" in orientation, there is, however, a Saussurian epistemology. Saussure put at the heart of his work the extremely problematical thesis, which was also taken up by Hjelmslev in his *Prolegomena to a Theory of Language*, that experience is an undifferentiated and amorphous continuum until it is "cut" by the diacritical act of speech and codified in the system of differences which make up language [*langue*]. This idea, which is not exactly challenged but certainly modified by Langer's (and Gestalt theory's) account of perception itself as articulation of form, was given classic expression in Hjelmslev's notion, exploited by Umberto Eco, of an abstract "form of content," which became *forms* of content in Eco's project. The key idea—also formulated within a very different context by John Deely in his *Introducing Semiotic*—is that each language or sign system, including the system of conceptual signs or ideas, is a kind of invisible, diaphanous field of forces or coordinate system. In each system the lines of distinctions are not drawn in the same places in the continuum of experience. Language is not a neutral system of transparent filters which pass on to us distinctions and structures existing external to it. Language—and all sign and symbol systems as such—is constitutive.

Writing in his *Roman Jakobson's Approach to Language: Phenomenological Structuralism* (Bloomington: Indiana University Press, 1976), Elmar Holenstein noted that "the universe of language may not be a closed system; the universe of signs certainly is" (159). Signification, the genesis of "sense" or meaning, as Eco put it, "encompasses the whole of cultural life, even at the lower threshold of semiotics," which is perceptual consciousness itself. When confronted with the problem of the "genesis of perceptual signification" semiotics comes to "regard perception itself as the result of a preceding semiotic act." By focusing on the semiotic structure of consciousness quite generally—by seeing it, in Karl Bühler's phrase, as a *Sinngefüge*, a meaning-structure—semiotics approaches the whole problem-space of what has come to be known as "transcendental" philosophy, that branch of philosophy, stemming from Kant and passing through Husserl, that focuses on the modes of consciousness and the structures of "givenness."

In the words of Holenstein:

> Traditional transcendental philosophers . . . organized the data of the world largely in psychological terms. Structuralism offers the tools and material for a semiotic apprehension of the transcendental approach. Transcendental philosophy proceeds from the observation that all consciousness is 'consciousness of something' and that the world can in principle be given to us only in a subjective mode of appearance as perceived, remembered, imagined, thought, or otherwise conscious world. Structuralism draws our attention to the root-like attachment of the world's subjective constitution to sign systems (5).

Here is an important point of intersection between Peircean and Saussurian semiotics, and other texts in this collection—those of Barthes, Langer, Thom, Bühler, and Bateson—will bear directly upon this most important of themes. Semiosis, once again, points toward subjectivity.

The literature on Saussure and the ensuing "structuralist" movement is vast. Three collections of materials supplement and overlap the present volume. *Structuralism*, edited with an introduction by Jacques Ehrmann (Garden City, N.Y.: Doubleday-Anchor, 1970); *The Structuralists: From Marx to Lévi-Strauss*, edited with an introduction by Richard T. De George and Fernande M. De George (Garden City, N.Y.: Doubleday-Anchor, 1972); and *Introduction to Structuralism*, edited and introduced by Michael Lane (New York: Basic Books, 1970). The Ehrmann and Lane volumes have fine bibliographies and will lead one to the other primary and secondary materials. For beginners a good place to start on the relation between semiotics and structuralism is the handy little compendium by Terence Hawkes, *Structuralism and Semiotics* (Berkeley and Los Angeles: University of California Press, 1977). In addition to introducing the structuralist contributions to literary theory the book contains a superb and extremely useful annotated bibliography. See also the useful book *Saussure* by Jonathan Culler (New York: Penguin, 1977) and his earlier *Structuralist Poetics: Structuralism, Linguistics, and the Study of Literature* (Ithaca, N.Y.: Cornell University Press, 1975). In the latter volume we find fine discussions of Barthes and Jakobson, among many others.

The Linguistic Sign

FERDINAND DE SAUSSURE

The Object of Linguistics

DEFINITION OF LANGUAGE

What is both the integral and concrete object of linguistics? The question is especially difficult; later we shall see why; here I wish merely to point up the difficulty.

Other sciences work with objects that are given in advance and that can then be considered from different viewpoints; but not linguistics. Someone pronounces the French word *nu* 'bare': a superficial observer would be tempted to call the word a concrete linguistic object; but a more careful examination would reveal successively three or four quite different things, depending on whether the word is considered as a sound, as the expression of an idea, as the equivalent of Latin *nudum*, etc. Far from it being the object that antedates the viewpoint, it would seem that it is the viewpoint that creates the object; besides, nothing tells us in advance that one way of considering the fact in question takes precedence over the others or is in any way superior to them.

Moreover, regardless of the viewpoint that we adopt, the linguistic phenomenon always has two related sides, each deriving its values from the other. For example:

1) Articulated syllables are acoustical impressions perceived by the ear, but the sounds would not exist without the vocal organs; an *n*, for example, exists only by virtue of the relation between the two sides. We simply cannot reduce language to sound or detach sound from oral articulation; reciprocally, we cannot define the movements of the vocal organs without taking into account the acoustical impression.

2) But suppose that sound were a simple thing: would it constitute speech? No, it is only the instrument of thought; by itself, it has no existence. At this point a new and redoubtable relationship arises: a sound, a complex acoustical-vocal unit, combines in turn with an idea to form a

Reprinted from *Course in General Linguistics*, by Ferdinand de Saussure, edited by Charles Bally and Albert Sechehaye, in collaboration with Albert Riedlinger, translated from the French by Wade Baskin. New York: Philosophical Library, 1959. Reprinted by permission of the publisher; British edition, Peter Owen Ltd., reprinted by permission.

complex physiological-psychological unit. But that is still not the complete picture.

3) Speech has both an individual and a social side, and we cannot conceive of one without the other. Besides:

4) Speech always implies both an established system and an evolution; at every moment it is an existing institution and a product of the past. To distinguish between the system and its history, between what it is and what it was, seems very simple at first glance; actually the two things are so closely related that we can scarcely keep them apart. Would we simplify the question by studying the linguistic phenomenon in its earliest stages—if we began, for example, by studying the speech of children? No, for in dealing with speech, it is completely misleading to assume that the problem of early characteristics differs from the problem of permanent characteristics. We are left inside the vicious circle.

From whatever direction we approach the question, nowhere do we find the integral object of linguistics. Everywhere we are confronted with a dilemma: if we fix our attention on only one side of each problem, we run the risk of failing to perceive the dualities pointed out above; on the other hand, if we study speech from several viewpoints simultaneously, the object of linguistics appears to us as a confused mass of heterogeneous and unrelated things. Either procedure opens the door to several sciences—psychology, anthropology, normative grammar, philology, etc.—which are distinct from linguistics, but which might claim speech, in view of the faulty method of linguistics, as one of their objects.

As I see it there is only one solution to all the foregoing difficulties: *from the very outset we must put both feet on the ground of language and use language as the norm of all other manifestations of speech.* Actually, among so many dualities, language alone seems to lend itself to independent definition and provide a fulcrum that satisfies the mind.

But what is language [*langue*]? It is not to be confused with human speech [*langage*], of which it is only a definite part, though certainly an essential one. It is both a social product of the faculty of speech and a collection of necessary conventions that have been adopted by a social body to permit individuals to exercise that faculty. Taken as a whole, speech is many-sided and heterogeneous; straddling several areas simultaneously—physical, physiological, and psychological—it belongs both to the individual and to society; we cannot put it into any category of human facts, for we cannot discover its unity.

Language, on the contrary, is a self-contained whole and a principle of classification. As soon as we give language first place among the facts of speech, we introduce a natural order into a mass that lends itself to no other classification.

One might object to that principle of classification on the ground that

since the use of speech is based on a natural faculty whereas language is
something acquired and conventional, language should not take first
place but should be subordinated to the natural instinct.

That objection is easily refuted.

First, no one has proved that speech, as it manifests itself when we
speak, is entirely natural, i.e. that our vocal apparatus was designed for
speaking just as our legs were designed for walking. Linguists are far from
agreement on this point. For instance Whitney, to whom language is one
of several social institutions, thinks that we use the vocal apparatus as the
instrument of language purely through luck, for the sake of convenience:
men might just as well have chosen gestures and used visual symbols instead of acoustical symbols. Doubtless his thesis is too dogmatic; language is not similar in all respects to other social institutions (see p. 73 f.
and p. 75 f.); moreover, Whitney goes too far in saying that our choice
happened to fall on the vocal organs; the choice was more or less imposed by nature. But on the essential point the American linguist is right:
language is a convention, and the nature of the sign that is agreed upon
does not matter. The question of the vocal apparatus obviously takes a
secondary place in the problem of speech.

One definition of *articulated speech* might confirm that conclusion. In
Latin, *articulus* means a member, part, or subdivision of a sequence; applied to speech, articulation designates either the subdivision of a spoken
chain into syllables or the subdivision of the chain of meanings into significant units; *gegliederte Sprache* is used in the second sense in German.
Using the second definition, we can say that what is natural to mankind is
not oral speech but the faculty of constructing a language, i.e. a system of
distinct signs corresponding to distinct ideas.

Broca discovered that the faculty of speech is localized in the third left
frontal convolution; his discovery has been used to substantiate the attribution of a natural quality to speech. But we know that the same part
of the brain is the center of *everything* that has to do with speech, including writing. The preceding statements, together with observations that
have been made in different cases of aphasia resulting from lesion of the
centers of localization, seem to indicate: (1) that the various disorders of
oral speech are bound up in a hundred ways with those of written speech;
and (2) that what is lost in all cases of aphasia or agraphia is less the faculty of producing a given sound or writing a given sign than the ability to
evoke by means of an instrument, regardless of what it is, the signs of a
regular system of speech. The obvious implication is that beyond the
functioning of the various organs there exists a more general faculty
which governs signs and which would be the linguistic faculty proper.
And this brings us to the same conclusion as above.

To give language first place in the study of speech, we can advance a
final argument: the faculty of articulating words—whether it is natural or

not—is exercised only with the help of the instrument created by a collectivity and provided for its use; therefore, to say that language gives unity to speech is not fanciful.

PLACE OF LANGUAGE IN THE FACTS OF SPEECH

In order to separate from the whole of speech the part that belongs to language, we must examine the individual act from which the speaking-circuit can be reconstructed. The act requires the presence of at least two persons; that is the minimum number necessary to complete the circuit. Suppose that two people, A and B, are conversing with each other:

Suppose that the opening of the circuit is in A's brain, where mental facts (concepts) are associated with representations of the linguistic sounds (sound-images) that are used for their expression. A given concept unlocks a corresponding sound-image in the brain; this purely *psychological* phenomenon is followed in turn by a *physiological* process: the brain transmits an impulse corresponding to the image to the organs used in producing sounds. Then the sound waves travel from the mouth of A to the ear of B: a purely *physical* process. Next, the circuit continues in B, but the order is reversed: from the ear to the brain, the physiological transmission of the sound-image; in the brain, the psychological association of the image with the corresponding concept. If B then speaks, the new act will follow—from his brain to A's—exactly the same course as the first act and pass through the same successive phases, which I shall diagram as follows:

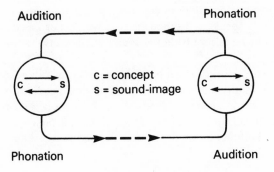

The preceding analysis does not purport to be complete. We might also single out the pure acoustical sensation, the identification of that sensation with the latent sound-image, the muscular image of phonation, etc. I have included only the elements thought to be essential, but the drawing brings out at a glance the distinction between the physical (sound waves), physiological (phonation and audition), and psychological parts (word-images and concepts). Indeed, we should not fail to note that the word-image stands apart from the sound itself and that it is just as psychological as the concept which is associated with it.

The circuit that I have outlined can be further divided into:

(*a*) an outer part that includes the vibrations of the sounds which travel from the mouth to the ear, and an inner part that includes everything else;

(*b*) a psychological and a nonpsychological part, the second including the physiological productions of the vocal organs as well as the physical facts that are outside the individual;

(*c*) an active and a passive part: everything that goes from the associative center of the speaker to the ear of the listener is active, and everything that goes from the ear of the listener to his associative center is passive;

(*d*) finally, everything that is active in the psychological part of the circuit is executive ($c \rightarrow s$), and everything that is passive is receptive ($s \rightarrow c$).

We should also add the associative and co-ordinating faculty that we find as soon as we leave isolated signs; this faculty plays the dominant role in the organization of language as a system.

But to understand clearly the role of the associative and co-ordinating faculty, we must leave the individual act, which is only the embryo of speech, and approach the social fact.

Among all the individuals that are linked together by speech, some sort of average will be set up: all will reproduce—not exactly of course, but approximately—the same signs united with the same concepts.

How does the social crystallization of language come about? Which parts of the circuit are involved? For all parts probably do not participate equally in it.

The nonpsychological part can be rejected from the outset. When we hear people speaking a language that we do not know, we perceive the sounds but remain outside the social fact because we do not understand them.

Neither is the psychological part of the circuit wholly responsible: the executive side is missing, for execution is never carried out by the collectivity. Execution is always individual, and the individual is always its master: I shall call the executive side *speaking* [*parole*].

Through the functioning of the receptive and co-ordinating faculties, impressions that are perceptibly the same for all are made on the minds of speakers. How can that social product be pictured in such a way that language will stand apart from everything else? If we could embrace the sum of word-images stored in the minds of all individuals, we could identify the social bond that constitutes language. It is a storehouse filled by the members of a given community through their active use of speaking, a grammatical system that has a potential existence in each brain, or, more specifically, in the brains of a group of individuals. For language is not complete in any speaker; it exists perfectly only within a collectivity.

In separating language from speaking we are at the same time separating: (1) what is social from what is individual; and (2) what is essential from what is accessory and more or less accidental.

Language is not a function of the speaker; it is a product that is passively assimilated by the individual. It never requires premeditation, and reflection enters in only for the purpose of classification, which we shall take up later.

Speaking, on the contrary, is an individual act. It is wilful and intellectual. Within the act, we should distinguish between: (1) the combinations by which the speaker uses the language code for expressing his own thought; and (2) the psychophysical mechanism that allows him to exteriorize those combinations.

Note that I have defined things rather than words; these definitions are not endangered by certain ambiguous words that do not have identical meanings in different languages. For instance, German *Sprache* means both "language" and "speech"; *Rede* almost corresponds to "speaking" but adds the special connotation of "discourse." Latin *sermo* designates both "speech" and "speaking," while *lingua* means "language," etc. No word corresponds exactly to any of the notions specified above; that is why all definitions of words are made in vain; starting from words in defining things is a bad procedure.

To summarize, these are the characteristics of language:

(1) Language is a well-defined object in the heterogeneous mass of speech facts. It can be localized in the limited segment of the speaking-circuit where an auditory image becomes associated with a concept. It is the social side of speech, outside the individual who can never create nor modify it by himself; it exists only by virtue of a sort of contract signed by the members of a community. Moreover, the individual must always serve an apprenticeship in order to learn the functioning of language; a child assimilates it only gradually. It is such a distinct thing that a man deprived of the use of speaking retains it provided that he understands the vocal signs that he hears.

(2) Language, unlike speaking, is something that we can study separately. Although dead languages are no longer spoken, we can easily as-

similate their linguistic organisms. We can dispense with the other elements of speech; indeed, the science of language is possible only if the other elements are excluded.

(3) Whereas speech is heterogeneous, language, as defined, is homogeneous. It is a system of signs in which the only essential thing is the union of meanings and sound-images, and in which both parts of the sign are psychological.

(4) Language is concrete, no less so than speaking; and this is a help in our study of it. Linguistic signs, though basically psychological, are not abstractions; associations which bear the stamp of collective approval—and which added together constitute language—are realities that have their seat in the brain. Besides, linguistic signs are tangible; it is possible to reduce them to conventional written symbols, whereas it would be impossible to provide detailed photographs of acts of speaking [*actes de parole*]; the pronunciation of even the smallest word represents an infinite number of muscular movements that could be identified and put into graphic form only with great difficulty. In language, on the contrary, there is only the sound-image, and the latter can be translated into a fixed visual image. For if we disregard the vast number of movements necessary for the realization of sound-images in speaking, we see that each sound-image is nothing more than the sum of a limited number of elements or phonemes that can in turn be called up by a corresponding number of written symbols. The very possibility of putting the things that relate to language into graphic form allows dictionaries and grammars to represent it accurately, for language is a storehouse of sound-images, and writing is the tangible form of those images.

PLACE OF LANGUAGE IN HUMAN FACTS: SEMIOLOGY

The foregoing characteristics of language reveal an even more important characteristic. Language, once its boundaries have been marked off within the speech data, can be classified among human phenomena, whereas speech cannot.

We have just seen that language is a social institution; but several features set it apart from other political, legal, etc. institutions. We must call in a new type of facts in order to illuminate the special nature of language.

Language is a system of signs that express ideas, and is therefore comparable to a system of writing, the alphabet of deaf-mutes, symbolic rites, polite formulas, military signals, etc. But it is the most important of all these systems.

A *science that studies the life of signs within society* is conceivable; it would be a part of social psychology and consequently of general psychology; I shall call it *semiology*[1] (from Greek *sēmeîon* 'sign'). Semiology would show what constitutes signs, what laws govern them. Since the science does not yet exist, no one can say what it would be; but it has a right to existence, a place staked out in advance. Linguistics is only a part of the general science of semiology; the laws discovered by semiology will be applicable to linguistics, and the latter will circumscribe a well-defined area within the mass of anthropological facts.

To determine the exact place of semiology is the task of the psychologist.[2] The task of the linguist is to find out what makes language a special system within the mass of semiological data. This issue will be taken up again later; here I wish merely to call attention to one thing: if I have succeeded in assigning linguistics a place among the sciences, it is because I have related it to semiology.

Why has semiology not yet been recognized as an independent science with its own object like all the other sciences? Linguists have been going around in circles: language, better than anything else, offers a basis for understanding the semiological problem; but language must, to put it correctly, be studied in itself; heretofore language has almost always been studied in connection with something else, from other viewpoints.

There is first of all the superficial notion of the general public: people see nothing more than a name-giving system in language, thereby prohibiting any research into its true nature.

Then there is the viewpoint of the psychologist, who studies the sign-mechanism in the individual; this is the easiest method, but it does not lead beyond individual execution and does not reach the sign, which is social.

Or even when signs are studied from a social viewpoint, only the traits that attach language to the other social institutions—those that are more or less voluntary—are emphasized; as a result, the goal is by-passed and the specific characteristics of semiological systems in general and of language in particular are completely ignored. For the distinguishing characteristic of the sign—but the one that is least apparent at first sight—is that in some way it always eludes the individual or social will.

In short, the characteristic that distinguishes semiological systems from all other institutions shows up clearly only in language where it manifests itself in the things which are studied least, and the necessity or specific value of a semiological science is therefore not clearly recognized. But to me the language problem is mainly semiological, and all developments derive their significance from that important fact. If we are to discover the true nature of language we must learn what it has in common with all other semiological systems; linguistic forces that seem very important at first glance (e.g., the role of the vocal apparatus) will receive only secondary consideration if they serve only to set language apart from the other systems. This procedure will do more than to clarify the linguistic problem. By studying rites, customs, etc. as signs, I believe that we shall throw new light on the facts and point up the need for including them in a science of semiology and explaining them by its laws.

Nature of the Linguistic Sign

SIGN, SIGNIFIED, SIGNIFIER

Some people regard language, when reduced to its elements, as a naming-process only—a list of words, each corresponding to the thing that it names. For example:

This conception is open to criticism at several points. It assumes that ready-made ideas exist before words; it does not tell us whether a name is vocal or psychological in nature (*arbor*, for instance, can be considered from either viewpoint); finally, it lets us assume that the linking of a name and a thing is a very simple operation—an assumption that is anything but true. But this rather naive approach can bring us near the truth by showing us that the linguistic unit is a double entity, one formed by the associating of two terms.

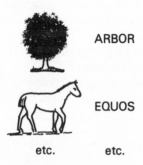

ARBOR

EQUOS

etc.　　　　　etc.

We have seen in considering the speaking-circuit (p. 31) that both terms involved in the linguistic sign are psychological and are united in the brain by an associative bond. This point must be emphasized.

The linguistic sign unites, not a thing and a name, but a concept and a sound-image.[3] The latter is not the material sound, a purely physical thing, but the psychological imprint of the sound, the impression that it makes on our senses. The sound-image is sensory, and if I happen to call it "material," it is only in that sense, and by way of opposing it to the other term of the association, the concept, which is generally more abstract.

The psychological character of our sound-images becomes apparent when we observe our own speech. Without moving our lips or tongue, we can talk to ourselves or recite mentally a selection of verse. Because we regard the words of our language as sound-images, we must avoid speaking of the "phonemes" that make up the words. This term, which suggests vocal activity, is applicable to the spoken word only, to the realization of the inner image in discourse. We can avoid that misunderstanding by speaking of the *sounds* and *syllables* of a word provided we remember that the names refer to the sound-image.

The linguistic sign is then a two-sided psychological entity that can be represented by the drawing:

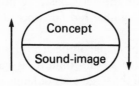

The two elements are intimately united, and each recalls the other. Whether we try to find the meaning of the Latin word *arbor* or the word that Latin uses to designate the concept "tree," it is clear that only the associations sanctioned by that language appear to us to conform to reality, and we disregard whatever others might be imagined.

Our definition of the linguistic sign poses an important question of terminology. I call the combination of a concept and a sound-image a *sign*, but in current usage the term generally designates only a sound-image, a word, for example (*arbor*, etc.). One tends to forget that *arbor* is called a sign only because it carries the concept "tree," with the result that the idea of the sensory part implies the idea of the whole.

Ambiguity would disappear if the three notions involved here were designated by three names, each suggesting and opposing the others. I propose to retain the word *sign* [*signe*] to designate the whole and to replace *concept* and *sound-image* respectively by *signified* [*signifié*] and *signifier* [*signifiant*]; the last two terms have the advantage of indicating the opposition that separates them from each other and from the whole of which they are parts. As regards *sign*, if I am satisfied with it, this is simply because I do not know of any word to replace it, the ordinary language suggesting no other.

The linguistic sign, as defined, has two primordial characteristics. In enunciating them I am also positing the basic principles of any study of this type.

PRINCIPLE I: THE ARBITRARY NATURE OF THE SIGN

The bond between the signifier and the signified is arbitrary. Since I mean by sign the whole that results from the associating of the signifier with the signified, I can simply say: *the linguistic sign is arbitrary*.

The idea of "sister" is not linked by any inner relationship to the succession of sounds s-ö-r which serves as its signifier in French; that it could be represented equally by just any other sequence is proved by differences among languages and by the very existence of different languages: the signified "ox" has as its signifier b-ö-f on one side of the border and o-k-s (Ochs) on the other.

No one disputes the principle of the arbitrary nature of the sign, but it is often easier to discover a truth than to assign to it its proper place. Principle I dominates all the linguistics of language; its consequences are numberless. It is true that not all of them are equally obvious at first glance; only after many detours does one discover them, and with them the primordial importance of the principle.

One remark in passing: when semiology becomes organized as a science, the question will arise whether or not it properly includes modes of expression based on completely natural signs, such as pantomime. Supposing that the new science welcomes them, its main concern will still be the whole group of systems grounded on the arbitrariness of the sign. In fact, every means of expression used in society is based, in principle, on collective behavior or—what amounts to the same thing—on convention. Polite formulas, for instance, though often imbued with a certain natural expressiveness (as in the case of a Chinese who greets his emperor by bowing down to the ground nine times), are nonetheless fixed by rule; it is this rule and not the intrinsic value of the gestures that obliges one to use them. Signs that are wholly arbitrary realize better than the others the ideal of the semiological process; that is why language, the most complex and universal of all systems of expression, is also the most characteristic; in this sense linguistics can become the master-pattern for all branches of semiology although language is only one particular semiological system.

The word *symbol* has been used to designate the linguistic sign, or more specifically, what is here called the signifier. Principle I in particular weighs against the use of this term. One characteristic of the symbol is that it is never wholly arbitrary; it is not empty, for there is the rudiment of a natural bond between the signifier and the signified. The symbol of justice, a pair of scales, could not be replaced by just any other symbol, such as a chariot.

The word *arbitrary* also calls for comment. The term should not imply that the choice of the signifier is left entirely to the speaker (we shall see below that the individual does not have the power to change a sign in any way once it has become established in the linguistic community); I mean that it is unmotivated, i.e. arbitrary in that it actually has no natural connection with the signified.

In concluding let us consider two objections that might be raised to the establishment of Principle I:

　1) *Onomatopoeia* might be used to prove that the choice of the sig-

nifier is not always arbitrary. But onomatopoeic formations are never organic elements of a linguistic system. Besides, their number is much smaller than is generally supposed. Words like French *fouet* 'whip' or *glas* 'knell' may strike certain ears with suggestive sonority, but to see that they have not always had this property we need only examine their Latin forms (*fouet* is derived from *fāgus* 'beech-tree,' *glas* from *classicum* 'sound of a trumpet'). The quality of their present sounds, or rather the quality that is attributed to them, is a fortuitous result of phonetic evolution.

As for authentic onomatopoeic words (e.g. *glug-glug, tick-tock*, etc.), not only are they limited in number, but also they are chosen somewhat arbitrarily, for they are only approximate and more or less conventional imitations of certain sounds (cf. English *bow-wow* and French *ouaoua*). In addition, once these words have been introduced into the language, they are to a certain extent subjected to the same evolution—phonetic, morphological, etc.—that other words undergo (cf. *pigeon*, ultimately from Vulgar Latin *pīpiō*, derived in turn from an onomatopoeic formation): obvious proof that they lose something of their original character in order to assume that of the linguistic sign in general, which is unmotivated.

2) *Interjections*, closely related to onomatopoeia, can be attacked on the same grounds and come no closer to refuting our thesis. One is tempted to see in them spontaneous expressions of reality dictated, so to speak, by natural forces. But for most interjections we can show that there is no fixed bond between their signified and their signifier. We need only compare two languages on this point to see how much such expressions differ from one language to the next (e.g. the English equivalent of French *aïe!* is *ouch!*). We know, moreover, that many interjections were once words with specific meanings (cf. French *diable!* 'darn!' *mordieu!* 'golly!' from *mort Dieu* 'God's death,' etc.).[4]

Onomatopoeic formations and interjections are of secondary importance, and their symbolic origin is in part open to dispute.

PRINCIPLE II: THE LINEAR NATURE OF THE SIGNIFIER

The signifier, being auditory, is unfolded solely in time from which it gets the following characteristics: (a) it represents a span, and (b) the span is measurable in a single dimension; it is a line.

While Principle II is obvious, apparently linguists have always neglected to state it, doubtless because they found it too simple; nevertheless, it is fundamental, and its consequences are incalculable. Its importance equals that of Principle I; the whole mechanism of language depends upon it. In contrast to visual signifiers (nautical signals, etc.) which can offer simultaneous groupings in several dimensions, auditory signifiers have at their command only the dimension of time. Their elements are presented in succession; they form a chain. This feature becomes readily apparent when they are represented in writing and the spatial line of graphic marks is substituted for succession in time.

Sometimes the linear nature of the signifier is not obvious. When I accent a syllable, for instance, it seems that I am concentrating more than one significant element on the same point. But this is an illusion; the syllable and its accent constitute only one phonational act. There is no duality within the act but only different oppositions to what precedes and what follows.

Immutability and Mutability of the Sign

IMMUTABILITY

The signifier, though to all appearances freely chosen with respect to the idea that it represents, is fixed, not free, with respect to the linguistic community that uses it. The masses have no voice in the matter, and the signifier chosen by language could be replaced by no other. This fact, which seems to embody a contradiction, might be called colloquially "the stacked deck." We say to language: "Choose!" but we add: "It must be this sign and no other." No individual, even if he willed it, could modify in any way at all the choice that has been made; and what is more, the community itself cannot control so much as a single word; it is bound to the existing language.

No longer can language be identified with a contract pure and simple, and it is precisely from this viewpoint that the linguistic sign is a particularly interesting object of study; for language furnishes the best proof that a law accepted by a community is a thing that is tolerated and not a rule to which all freely consent.

Let us first see why we cannot control the linguistic sign and then draw together the important consequences that issue from the phenomenon.

No matter what period we choose or how far back we go, language always appears as a heritage of the preceding period. We might conceive of an act by which, at a given moment, names were assigned to things and a contract was formed between concepts and sound-images; but such an act has never been recorded. The notion that things might have happened like that was prompted by our acute awareness of the arbitrary nature of the sign.

No society, in fact, knows or has ever known language other than as a product inherited from preceding generations, and one to be accepted as such. That is why the question of the origin of speech is not so important as it is generally assumed to be. The question is not even worth asking; the only real object of linguistics is the normal, regular life of an existing idiom. A particular language-state is always the product of historical forces, and these forces explain why the sign is unchangeable, i.e. why it resists any arbitrary substitution.

Nothing is explained by saying that language is something inherited and leaving it at that. Can not existing and inherited laws be modified from one moment to the next?

To meet that objection, we must put language into its social setting and frame the question just as we would for any other social institution. How are other social institutions transmitted? This more general question includes the question of immutability. We must first determine the greater or lesser amounts of freedom that the other institutions enjoy; in each instance it will be seen that a different proportion exists between fixed tradition and the free action of society. The next step is to discover why in a given category, the forces of the first type carry more weight or less weight than those of the second. Finally, coming back to language, we must ask why the historical factor of transmission dominates it entirely and prohibits any sudden widespread change.

There are many possible answers to the question. For example, one might point to the fact that succeeding generations are not superimposed on one another like the drawers of a piece of furniture, but fuse and interpenetrate, each generation embracing individuals of all ages—with the result that modifications of language are not tied to the succession of generations. One might also recall the sum of the efforts required for learning the mother language and conclude that a general change would be impossible. Again, it might be added that reflection does not enter into the active use of an idiom—speakers are largely unconscious of the laws of language; and if they are unaware of them, how could they modify them? Even if they were aware of these laws, we may be sure that their awareness would seldom lead to criticism, for people are generally satisfied with the language they have received.

The foregoing considerations are important but not topical. The following are more basic and direct, and all the others depend on them.

(1) *The arbitrary nature of the sign.* Above, we had to accept the theoretical possibility of change; further reflection suggests that the arbitrary nature of the sign is really what protects language from any attempt to modify it. Even if people were more conscious of language than they are, they would still not know how to discuss it. The reason is simply that any subject in order to be discussed must have a reasonable basis. It is possible, for instance, to discuss whether the monogamous form of marriage is more reasonable than the polygamous form and to advance arguments to support either side. One could also argue about a system of symbols, for the symbol has a rational relationship with the thing signified (see p. 38); but language is a system of arbitrary signs and lacks the necessary basis, the solid ground for discussion. There is no reason for preferring *soeur* to *sister*, *Ochs* to *boeuf*, etc.

(2) *The multiplicity of signs necessary to form any language.* Another important deterrent to linguistic change is the great number of signs that

must go into the making of any language. A system of writing comprising twenty to forty letters can in case of need be replaced by another system. The same would be true of language if it contained a limited number of elements; but linguistic signs are numberless.

(3) *The over-complexity of the system.* A language constitutes a system. In this one respect (as we shall see later) language is not completely arbitrary but is ruled to some extent by logic; it is here also, however, that the inability of the masses to transform it becomes apparent. The system is a complex mechanism that can be grasped only through reflection; the very ones who use it daily are ignorant of it. We can conceive of a change only through the intervention of specialists, grammarians, logicians, etc.; but experience shows us that all such meddlings have failed.

(4) *Collective inertia toward innovation.* Language—and this consideration surpasses all the others—is at every moment everybody's concern; spread throughout society and manipulated by it, language is something used daily by all. Here we are unable to set up any comparison between it and other institutions. The prescriptions of codes, religious rites, nautical signals, etc., involve only a certain number of individuals simultaneously and then only during a limited period of time; in language, on the contrary, everyone participates at all times, and that is why it is constantly being influenced by all. This capital fact suffices to show the impossibility of revolution. Of all social institutions, language is least amenable to initiative. It blends with the life of society, and the latter, inert by nature, is a prime conservative force.

But to say that language is a product of social forces does not suffice to show clearly that it is unfree; remembering that it is always the heritage of the preceding period, we must add that these social forces are linked with time. Language is checked not only by the weight of the collectivity but also by time. These two are inseparable. At every moment solidarity with the past checks freedom of choice. We say *man* and *dog*. This does not prevent the existence in the total phenomenon of a bond between the two antithetical forces—arbitrary convention by virtue of which choice is free and time which causes choice to be fixed. Because the sign is arbitrary, it follows no law other than that of tradition, and because it is based on tradition, it is arbitrary.

MUTABILITY

Time, which insures the continuity of language, wields another influence apparently contradictory to the first: the more or less rapid change of linguistic signs. In a certain sense, therefore, we can speak of both the immutability and the mutability of the sign.[5]

In the last analysis, the two facts are interdependent: the sign is exposed to alteration because it perpetuates itself. What predominates in all change is the persistence of the old substance; disregard for the past is only relative. That is why the principle of change is based on the principle of continuity.

Change in time takes many forms, on any one of which an important chapter in linguistics might be written. Without entering into detail, let us see what things need to be delineated.

First, let there be no mistake about the meaning that we attach to the word change. One might think that it deals especially with phonetic changes undergone by the signifier, or perhaps changes in meaning which affect the signified concept. That view would be inadequate. Regardless of what the forces of change are, whether in isolation or in combination, they always result in *a shift in the relationship between the signified and the signifier*.

Here are some examples. Latin *necāre* 'kill' became *noyer* 'drown' in French. Both the sound-image and the concept changed; but it is useless to separate the two parts of the phenomenon; it is sufficient to state with respect to the whole that the bond between the idea and the sign was loosened, and that there was a shift in their relationship. If instead of comparing Classical Latin *necāre* with French *noyer*, we contrast the former term with *necare* of Vulgar Latin of the fourth or fifth century meaning 'drown' the case is a little different; but here again, although there is no appreciable change in the signifier, there is a shift in the relationship between the idea and the sign.[6]

Old German *dritteil* 'one-third' became *Drittel* in Modern German. Here, although the concept remained the same, the relationship was changed in two ways: the signifier was changed not only in its material aspect but also in its grammatical form; the idea of *Teil* 'part' is no longer implied; *Drittel* is a simple word. In one way or another there is always a shift in the relationship.

In Anglo-Saxon the preliterary form *fot* 'foot' remained while its plural **fōti* became *fēt* (Modern English *feet*). Regardless of the other changes that are implied, one thing is certain: there was a shift in their relationship; other correspondences between the phonetic substance and the idea emerged.

Language is radically powerless to defend itself against the forces which from one moment to the next are shifting the relationship between the signified and the signifier. This is one of the consequences of the arbitrary nature of the sign.

Unlike language, other human institutions—customs, laws, etc.—are all based in varying degrees on the natural relations of things; all have of necessity adapted the means employed to the ends pursued. Even fashion in dress is not entirely arbitrary; we can deviate only slightly from the conditions dictated by the human body. Language is limited by nothing in the choice of means, for apparently nothing would prevent the associating of any idea whatsoever with just any sequence of sounds.

To emphasize the fact that language is a genuine institution, Whitney quite justly insisted upon the arbitrary nature of signs; and by so doing, he placed linguistics on its true axis. But he did not follow through and see that the arbitrariness of language radically separates it from all other institutions. This is apparent from the way in which language evolves. Nothing could be more complex. As it is a product of both the social force and time, no one can change anything in it, and on the other hand, the arbitrariness of its signs theoretically entails the freedom of establishing just any relationship between phonetic substance and ideas. The result is that each of the two elements united in the sign maintains its own life to a degree unknown elsewhere, and that language changes, or rather evolves, under the influence of all the forces which can affect either sounds or meanings. The evolution is inevitable; there is no example of a single language that resists it. After a certain period of time, some obvious shifts can always be recorded.

Mutability is so inescapable that it even holds true for artificial languages. Whoever creates a language controls it only so long as it is not in circulation; from the moment when it fulfills it mission and becomes the property of everyone, control is lost. Take Esperanto as an example; if it succeeds, will it escape the inexorable law? Once launched, it is quite likely that Esperanto will enter upon a fully semiological life; it will be transmitted according to laws which have nothing in common with those of its logical creation, and there will be no turning backwards. A man proposing a fixed language that posterity would have to accept for what it is would be like a hen hatching a duck's egg: the language created by him would be borne along, willy-nilly, by the current that engulfs all languages.

Signs are governed by a principle of general semiology: continuity in time is coupled to change in time; this is confirmed by orthographic systems, the speech of deaf-mutes, etc.

But what supports the necessity for change? I might be reproached for not having been as explicit on this point as on the principle of immutability. This is because I failed to distinguish between the different forces of change. We must consider their great variety in order to understand the extent to which they are necessary.

The causes of continuity are *a priori* within the scope of the observer, but the causes of change in time are not. It is better not to attempt giving an exact account at this point, but to restrict discussion to the shifting of relationships in general. Time changes all things; there is no reason why language should escape this universal law.

Let us review the main points of our discussion and relate them to the principles set up in the Introduction.

1) Avoiding sterile word definitions, within the total phenomenon

represented by speech we first singled out two parts: language and speaking. Language is speech less speaking. It is the whole set of linguistic habits which allow an individual to understand and to be understood.

2) But this definition still leaves language outside its social context; it makes language something artificial since it includes only the individual part of reality; for the realization of language, a community of speakers [*masse parlante*] is necessary. Contrary to all appearances, language never exists apart from the social fact, for it is a semiological phenomenon. Its social nature is one of its inner characteristics. Its complete definition confronts us with two inseparable entities, as shown in this drawing:

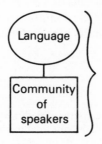

But under the conditions described language is not living—it has only potential life; we have considered only the social, not the historical, fact.

3) The linguistic sign is arbitrary; language, as defined, would therefore seem to be a system which, because it depends solely on a rational principle, is free and can be organized at will. Its social nature, considered independently, does not definitely rule out this viewpoint. Doubtless it is not on a purely logical basis that group psychology operates; one must consider everything that deflects reason in actual contacts between individuals. But the thing which keeps language from being a simple convention that can be modified at the whim of interested parties is not its social nature; it is rather the action of time combined with the social force. If time is left out, the linguistic facts are incomplete and no conclusion is possible.

If we considered language in time, without the community of speakers—imagine an isolated individual living for several centuries—we probably would notice no change; time would not influence language. Conversely, if we considered the community of speakers without considering time, we would not see the effect of the social forces that influence language. To represent the actual facts, we must then add to our first drawing a sign to indicate passage of time:

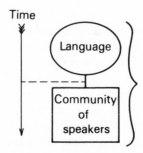

Language is no longer free, for time will allow the social forces at work on it to carry out their effects. This brings us back to the principle of continuity, which cancels freedom. But continuity necessarily implies change, varying degrees of shifts in the relationship between the signified and the signifier.

NOTES

1. *Semiology* should not be confused with *semantics*, which studies changes in meaning, and which Saussure did not treat methodically.

2. Cf. A. Naville, *Classification des Sciences* (2nd. ed.), p. 104. [Editorial note to French edition.]

3. The term sound-image may seem to be too restricted inasmuch as beside the representation of the sounds of a word there is also that of its articulation, the muscular image of the phonational act. But for F. de Saussure language is essentially a depository, a thing received from without (see p. [33 of this book]).

4. Cf. English *goodness*! and *zounds*! (from *God's wounds*). [Translator's note.]

5. It would be wrong to reproach F. de Saussure for being illogical or paradoxical in attributing two contradictory qualities to language. By opposing two striking terms, he wanted only to emphasize the fact that language changes in spite of the inability of speakers to change it. One can also say that it is intangible but not unchangeable. [Editorial note to French edition.]

6. From May to July of 1911, Saussure used interchangeably the old terminology (*idea* and *sign*) and the new (*signified* and *signifier*). [Translator's note.]

V. N. VOLOŠINOV

Part II of the book from which this selection is taken is entitled "Toward a Marxist Philosophy of Language," and in it Vološinov confronts, and tries to mediate between, what he calls "two trends of thought in the philosophy of language," to wit, individualistic subjectivism and abstract objectivism. In his words, the first trend, represented paradigmatically in the work of Wilhelm von Humboldt, incorporates these four basic principles:

1. Language is an activity, an unceasing process of creation (energeia) realized in individual speech acts;

2. The laws of language creativity are the laws of individual psychology;

3. Creativity of language is meaningful creativity, analogous to creative art;

4. Language as a ready-made product (ergon), as a stable system (lexicon, grammar, phonetics) is, so to speak, the inert crust, the hardened lava of language creativity, of which linguistics makes an abstract construct in the interests of the practical teaching of language as a ready-made instrument.

The second trend, abstract objectivism, he summarizes in the following basic principles which are antitheses to the foregoing.

1. Language is a stable, immutable system of normatively identical linguistic forms which the individual consciousness finds ready-made and which is incontestable for that consciousness.

2. The laws of language are the specifically linguistic laws of connection between linguistic signs within a given, closed linguistic system. These laws are objective with respect to any subjective consciousness.

3. Specifically linguistic connections have nothing in common with ideological values (artistic, cognitive, or other). Language phenomena are not grounded in ideological motives. No connection of a kind natural and comprehensible to the consciousness or of an artistic kind obtains between the word and its meaning.

4. Individual acts of speaking are, from the viewpoint of language, merely fortuitous refractions and variations or plain and simple distortions

of normatively identical forms; but precisely these acts of individual discourse explain the historical changeability of linguistic forms, a changeability that in itself, from the standpoint of the language system, is irrational and senseless. There is no connection, no sharing of motives, between the system of language and its history. They are alien to one another.

The two chapters following the chapter from which I have taken Vološinov's own summaries are devoted to his attempt to modify, and mediate between, these antithetical positions. Vološinov argues, against abstract objectivism, that although from the point of view of analysis it is possible to look upon language as a system of normatively identical forms, "this system cannot serve as a basis for understanding and explaining linguistic facts as they really exist and come into being." The key to these facts is the *utterance*—the paradigmatic speech act—which is not individual but thoroughly social. Utterances are the generative source of "the stream of verbal communication" which is concerned with understanding and not with recognition. As Vološinov put it, "what is important for the speaker about a linguistic form is not that it is a stable and self-equivalent signal, but that it is an always changeable and adaptable sign." This consideration is definitive for the speaker's point of view. The linguist, on Vološinov's reckoning, treats, however, the sign and the system in which it is embedded in the way a "philologist" treats an alien tongue.

It is, however, in his criticism and transformation of individualistic subjectivism that Vološinov works out his own position and develops his account of "verbal interaction," with which the text presented here deals. It gives us the heart of his own "Marxist" theory of language and presents us with theses and formulations that merit the closest consideration. Put in its bluntest terms, Vološinov's main point is this: "The immediate social situation and the broader social milieu wholly determine—and determine from within, so to speak—the structure of an utterance." Now, in his account of "inner speech," a topic which he also discussed, along with his great Russian compatriot, L. S. Vygotsky, Vološinov had noted that "expression organizes experience" and that "there is no such thing as experience outside of embodiment in signs." Hence, once again, the focal point of subjectivity becomes sociality and once again semiotics—as the science which studies "signs as social forces"—penetrates, *via*, to be sure, a rather circuitous route, into consciousness itself. "Outside objectification, outside embodiment in some particular material (the material of gesture, inner word, outcry) consciousness is a fiction."

All of Vološinov's text circles around these issues, thematizing the various aspects of the social matrix of utterances and heading toward his main conclusion that "verbal interaction is the basic reality of language." Vološinov hence takes up, in transformed fashion, Saussure's great dichotomy between *langue* and *parole*. He forces us to think about consciousness neither as source nor as product but as process, as a set or web of relationships, a "moving totality" which shifts and changes. Signs "segment" the world and the self. Now, one of the key themes in Marxist thought and in semiotic thought, too, is that all segmentation is "motivated" and often by interests which are not, materially speaking, "interest-free," but rather are embodiments of pragmatic motivations which govern the various power- and meaning-relations in social process. The function of a sign is to "reflect" and "refract" a meaning, which is never immediately present as a mere physical object but always "filtered" through a semiotic medium which, in the last analysis, is identical with consciousness itself. Not only is consciousness a distinctively social product, but, as social, it is a distinctively semiotic product: "The logic of consciousness is the logic of ideological communication, of the semiotic interaction of a social group." Indeed, "individual consciousness is not the architect of the ideological superstructure, but only a tenant lodging in the social edifice of ideological signs." Consciousness, in short, is not to be found through "introspection" but through an investigation of the "external," dialogical matrix of expressions in which it is embodied and embedded. Once again, the science of signs and the science of subjectivity intersect.

The best places to follow up the Vološinov material are the two books by Vološinov himself, which should be read in their entirety. *Freudianism: A Marxist Critique*, translated by I. R. Titunik and edited in collaboration with Neal H. Bruss (New York: Academic Press, 1976), has a good introduction by Titunik, and two appendices, one containing Vološinov's essay "Discourse in Life and Discourse in Art (Concerning Sociological Poetics)" and another containing Bruss's stimulating essay "V. N. Vološinov and the Structure of Language in Freudianism." *Marxism and the Philosophy of Language*, translated by Ladislav Matejka and I. R. Titunik (New York: Seminar Press, 1973), contains a good introduction and two appendices: "On the First Russian Prolegomena to Semiotics" by Matejka and "The Formal Method and the Sociological Method (M. M. Baxtin, P. N. Medvedev, V. N. Vološinov) in Russian Theory and the Study of Literature" by Titunik. For background and original texts see *Readings in Russian Poetics: Formalist and Structuralist Views*, edited by Ladislav Matejka and Krystyna Pomorska (Cambridge: MIT Press, 1971) and Victor Erlich, *Russian Formalism: History-Doctrine* third edition (New Haven and London: Yale University Press, 1981). It is important to see Vološinov in the wider context in which he worked.

Verbal Interaction

V. N. VOLOŠINOV

Individualistic subjectivism and its theory of expression. Criticism of the theory of expression. The sociological structure of experience and expression. The problem of behavioral ideology. The utterance as the basic unit in the generative process of speech. Approaches to the solution of the problem of the actual mode of existence of language. The utterance as a whole entity and its forms.

The second trend of thought in the philosophy of language was associated, as we saw, with rationalism and neoclassicism. The first trend—individualistic subjectivism—is associated with *romanticism*. Romanticism, to a considerable degree, was a reaction against the alien word and the categories of thought promoted by the alien word. More particularly and more immediately, romanticism was a reaction against the last resurgences of the cultural power of the alien word—the epochs of the Renaissance and neoclassicism. The romanticists were the first philologists of native language, the first to attempt a radical restructuring of linguistic thought. Their restructuring was based on experience with native language as the medium through which consciousness and ideas are generated. True, the romanticists remained philologists in the strict sense of the word. It was, of course, beyond their power to restructure a mode of thinking about language that had taken shape and had been sustained over the course of centuries. Nevertheless, new categories were introduced into that thinking, and these new categories were precisely what gave the first trend its specific characteristics. Symptomatically, even recent representatives of individualistic subjectivism have been specialists in modern languages, chiefly the Romance languages (Vossler, Leo Spitzer, Lorch, et al.)

However, individualistic subjectivism also took the monologic utterance as the ultimate reality and the point of departure for its thinking about language. To be sure, it did not approach the monologic utterance from the viewpoint of the passively understanding philologist but, rather, approached it from within, from the viewpoint of the person speaking and expressing himself.

Reprinted from *Marxism and the Philosophy of Language*, by V. N. Vološinov, translated by Ladislav Matejka and I. R. Titunik. New York and London: Seminar Press. Copyright © 1973, by Seminar Press, Inc. Reprinted by permission of the publisher.

What does the monologic utterance amount to, then, in the view of individualistic subjectivism? We have seen that it is a purely individual act, the expression of an individual consciousness, its ambitions, intentions, creative impulses, tastes, and so on. The category of expression for individualistic subjectivism is the highest and broadest category under which the speech act—the utterance—may be subsumed.

But what is expression?

Its simplest, rough definition is: something which, having in some way taken shape and definition in the psyche of an individual, is outwardly objectified for others with the help of external signs of some kind.

Thus there are two elements in expression: that inner something which is *expressible*, and its *outward objectification* for others (or possibly for oneself). Any theory of expression, however complex or subtle a form it may take, inevitably presupposes these two elements—the whole event of expression is played out between them. Consequently, any theory of expression inevitably presupposes that the expressible is something that can somehow take shape and exist apart from expression; that it exists first in one form and then switches to another form. This would have to be the case; otherwise, if the expressible were to exist from the very start in the form of expression, with quantitative transition between the two elements (in the sense of clarification, differentiation, and the like), the whole theory of expression would collapse. The theory of expression inevitably presupposes a certain dualism between the inner and outer elements and the explicit primacy of the former, since each act of objectification (expression) goes from inside out. Its sources are within. Not for nothing were idealistic and spiritualistic grounds the only grounds on which the theory of individualistic subjectivism and all theories of expression in general arose. Everything of real importance lies within; the outer element can take on real importance only by becoming a vessel for the inner, by becoming expression of spirit.

To be sure, by becoming external, by expressing itself outwardly, the inner element does undergo alteration. After all, it must gain control of outer material that possesses a validity of its own apart from the inner element. In this process of gaining control, of mastering outer material and making it over into a compliant medium of expression, the experiential, expressible element itself undergoes alteration and is forced to make a certain compromise. Therefore, idealistic grounds, the grounds on which all theories of expression have been established, also contain provision for the radical negation of expression as something that deforms the purity of the inner element.[1] In any case, all the creative and organizing forces of expression are within. Everything outer is merely passive material for manipulation by the inner element. Expression is formed basically within and then merely shifts to the outside. The understanding, interpretation, and explanation of an ideological phenomenon, it would follow from this argument, must also be directed inward; it must traverse a route the reverse of that for expression. Starting from outward objectification, the explanation must work down into its inner, organizing bases. That is how individualistic subjectivism understands expression.

The theory of expression underlying the first trend of thought in philosophy of language is fundamentally untenable.

The experiential, expressible element and its outward objectification are created, as we know, out of one and the same material. After all, there is no such thing as experience outside of embodiment in signs. Consequently, the very notion of a fundamental, qualitative difference between the inner and the outer element is invalid to begin with. Furthermore, the location of the organizing and formative center is not within (i.e., not in the material of inner signs) but outside. It is not experience that organizes expression, but the other way around—*expression organizes experience.* Expression is what first gives experience its form and specificity of direction.

Indeed, from whichever aspect we consider it, expression-utterance is determined by the actual conditions of the given utterance—above all, by its *immediate social situation.*

Utterance, as we know, is constructed between two socially organized persons, and in the absence of a real addressee, an addressee is presupposed in the person, so to speak, of a normal representative of the social group to which the speaker belongs. The *word is oriented toward an addressee,* toward *who* that addressee might be: a fellow-member or not of the same social group, of higher or lower standing (the addressee's hierarchical status), someone connected with the speaker by close social ties (father, brother, husband, and so on) or not. There can be no such thing as an abstract addressee, a man unto himself, so to speak. With such a person, we would indeed have no language in common, literally and figuratively. Even though we sometimes have pretensions to experiencing and saying things *urbi et orbi,* actually, of course, we envision this "world at large" through the prism of the concrete social milieu surrounding us. In the majority of cases, we presuppose a certain typical and stabilized *social purview* toward which the ideological creativity of our own social group and time is oriented, i.e., we assume as our addressee a contemporary of our literature, our science, our moral and legal codes.

Each person's inner world and thought has its stabilized *social audience* that comprises the environment in which reasons, motives, values, and so on are fashioned. The more cultured a person, the more closely his inner audience will approximate the normal audience of ideological creativity; but, in any case, specific class and specific era are limits that the ideal of addressee cannot go beyond.

Orientation of the word toward the addressee has an extremely high significance. In point of fact, *word is a two-sided act.* It is determined equally by *whose* word it is and *for whom* it is meant. As word, it is pre-cisely *the product of the reciprocal relationship between speaker and lis-tener, addresser and addressee*. Each and every word expresses the "one" in relation to the "other." I give myself verbal shape from another's point of view, ultimately, from the point of view of the community to which I belong. A word is a bridge thrown between myself and another. If one end of the bridge depends on me, then the other depends on my ad-dressee. A word is territory shared by both addresser and addressee, by the speaker and his interlocutor.

But what does being the speaker mean? Even if a word is not entirely his, constituting, as it were, the border zone between himself and his ad-dressee—still, it does in part belong to him.

There is one instance of the situation wherein the speaker is the un-doubted possessor of the word and to which, in this instance, he has full rights. This instance is the physiological act of implementing the word. But insofar as the act is taken in purely physiological terms, the category of possession does not apply.

If, instead of the physiological act of implementing sound, we take the implementation of word as sign, then the question of proprietorship be-comes extremely complicated. Aside from the fact that word as sign is a borrowing on the speaker's part from the social stock of available signs, the very individual manipulation of this social sign in a concrete utter-ance is wholly determined by social relations. The stylistic individualiza-tion of an utterance that the Vosslerites speak about represents a reflec-tion of social interrelationships that constitute the atmosphere in which an utterance is formed. *The immediate social situation and the broader social milieu wholly determine—and determine from within, so to speak—the structure of an utterance.*

Indeed, take whatever kind of utterance we will, even the kind of utter-ance that is not a referential message (communication in the narrow sense) but the verbal expression of some need—for instance, hunger—we may be certain that it is socially oriented in its entirety. Above all, it is determined immediately and directly by the participants of the speech event, both explicit and implicit participants, in connection with a spe-cific situation. That situation shapes the utterance, dictating that it sound one way and not another—like a demand or request, insistence on one's rights or a plea for mercy, in a style flowery or plain, in a confident or hesitant manner, and so on.

The immediate social situation and its immediate social participants determine the "occasional" form and style of an utterance. The deeper layers of its structure are determined by more sustained and more basic social connections with which the speaker is in contact.

Even if we were to take an utterance still in process of generation "in the soul," it would not change the essence of the matter, since the structure of experience is just as social as is the structure of its outward objectification. The degree to which an experience is perceptible, distinct, and formulated is directly proportional to the degree to which it is socially oriented.

In fact, not even the simplest, dimmest apprehension of a feeling—say, the feeling of hunger not outwardly expressed—can dispense with some kind of ideological form. Any apprehension, after all, must have inner speech, inner intonation and the rudiments of inner style: one can apprehend one's hunger apologetically, irritably, angrily, indignantly, etc. We have indicated, of course, only the grosser, more egregious directions that inner intonation may take; actually, there is an extremely subtle and complex set of possibilities for intoning an experience. Outward expression in most cases only continues and makes more distinct the direction already taken by inner speech and the intonation already embedded in it.

— Which way the intoning of the inner sensation of hunger will go depends upon the hungry person's general social standing as well as upon the immediate circumstances of the experience. These are, after all, the circumstances that determine in what evaluative context, within what social purview, the experience of hunger will be apprehended. The immediate social context will determine possible addressees, friends or foes, toward whom the consciousness and the experience of hunger will be oriented: whether it will involve dissatisfaction with cruel Nature, with oneself, with society, with a specific group within society, with a specific person, and so on. Of course, various degrees of perceptibility, distinctiveness, and differentiation in the social orientation of an experience are possible; but without some kind of evaluative social orientation there is no experience. Even the cry of a nursing infant is "oriented" toward its mother. There is the possibility that the experience of hunger may take on political coloring, in which case its structure will be determined along the lines of a potential political appeal or a reason for political agitation. It may be apprehended as a form of protest, and so on.

With regard to the potential (and sometimes even distinctly sensed) addressee, a distinction can be made between two poles, two extremes between which an experience can be apprehended and ideologically structured, tending now toward the one, now toward the other. Let us label these two extremes the "*I-experience*" and the "*we-experience*."

The "I-experience" actually tends toward extermination: the nearer it approaches its extreme limit, the more it loses its ideological structuredness and, hence, its apprehensible quality, reverting to the physiological reaction of the animal. In its course toward this extreme, the experience relinquishes all its potentialities, all outcroppings of social orientation, and, therefore, also loses its verbal delineation. Single experiences or whole groups of experiences can approach this extreme, relinquishing, in doing so, their ideological clarity and structuredness and testifying to the inability of the consciousness to strike social roots.[2]

⁰The "we-experience" is not by any means a nebulous herd experience; it is differentiated. Moreover, ideological differentiation, the growth of consciousness, is in direct proportion to the firmness and reliability of the social orientation. The stronger, the more organized, the more differentiated the collective in which an individual orients himself, the more vivid and complex his inner world will be.

The "we-experience" allows of different degrees and different types of ideological structuring.

Let us suppose a case where hunger is apprehended by one of a disparate set of hungry persons whose hunger is a matter of chance (the man down on his luck, the beggar, or the like). The experience of such a declassé loner will be colored in some specific way and will gravitate toward certain particular ideological forms with a range potentially quite broad: humility, shame, enviousness, and other evaluative tones will color his experience. The ideological forms along the lines of which the experience would develop would be either the individualistic protest of a vagabond or repentant, mystical resignation.

Let us now suppose a case in which the hungry person belongs to a collective where hunger is not haphazard and does bear a collective character—but the collective of these hungry people is not itself tightly bound together by material ties, each of its members experiencing hunger on his own. This is the situation most peasants are in. Hunger is experienced "at large," but under conditions of material disparateness, in the absence of a unifying economic coalition, each person suffers hunger in the small, enclosed world of his own individual economy. Such a collective lacks the unitary material frame necessary for united action. A resigned but unashamed and undemeaning apprehension of one's hunger will be the rule under such conditions—"everyone bears it, you must bear it, too." Here grounds are furnished for the development of the philosophical and religious systems of the nonresistor or fatalist type (early Christianity, Tolstoyanism).

A completely different experience of hunger applies to a member of an objectively and materially aligned and united collective (a regiment of soldiers; workers in their association within the walls of a factory; hired hands on a large-scale, capitalist farm; finally, a whole class once it has matured to the point of "class unto itself"). The experience of hunger this time will be marked predominantly by overtones of active and self-confident protest with no basis for humble and submissive intonation. These are the most favorable grounds for an experience to achieve ideological clarity and structuredness.[3]

All these types of expression, each with its basic intonations, come rife with corresponding terms and corresponding forms of possible utterances. The social situation in all cases determines which term, which metaphor, and which form may develop in an utterance expressing hunger out of the particular intonational bearings of the experience.

A special kind of character marks the individualistic *self-experience*. It does not belong to the "I-experience" in the strict sense of the term as defined above. The individualistic experience is fully differentiated and structured. Individualism is a special ideological form of the "we-experience" of the bourgeois class (there is also an analogous type of individualistic self-experience for the feudal aristocratic class). The individualistic type of experience derives from a steadfast and confident social orientation. Individualistic confidence in oneself, one's sense of personal value, is drawn not from within, not from the depths of one's personality, but from the outside world. It is the ideological interpretation of one's social recognizance and tenability by rights, and of the objective security and tenability provided by the whole social order, of one's individual livelihood. The structure of the conscious, individual personality is just as social a structure as is the collective type of experience. It is a particular kind of interpretation, projected into the individual soul, of a complex and sustained socioeconomic situation. But there resides in this type of individualistic "we-experience," and also in the very order to which it corresponds, an inner contradication that sooner or later will demolish its ideological structuredness.

An analogous structure is presented in solitary self-experience ("the ability and strength to stand alone in one's rectitude"), a type cultivated by Romain Rolland and, to some extent, by Tolstoj. The pride involved in this solitude also depends upon "we." It is a variant of the "we-experience" characteristic of the modern-day West European intelligentsia. Tolstoj's remarks about there being different kinds of thinking— "for oneself" and "for the public"—merely juxtapose two different conceptions of "public." Tolstoj's "for oneself" actually signifies only another social conception of addressee peculiar to himself. There is no such thing as thinking outside orientation toward possible expression and, hence, outside the social orientation of that expression and of the thinking involved.

Thus the personality of the speaker, taken from within, so to speak, turns out to be wholly a product of social interrelations. Not only its outward expression but also its inner experience are social territory. Consequently, the whole route between inner experience (the "expressible") and its outward objectification (the "utterance") lies entirely across social territory. When an experience reaches the stage of actualization in a full-fledged utterance, its social orientation acquires added complexity by focusing on the immediate social circumstances of discourse and, above all, upon actual addressees.

Our analysis casts a new light upon the problem of consciousness and ideology that we examined earlier.

Outside objectification, outside embodiment in some particular material (the material of gesture, inner word, outcry), *consciousness is a fic-*

tion. It is an improper ideological construct created by way of abstraction from the concrete facts of social expression. But consciousness as organized, material expression (in the ideological material of word, a sign, drawing, colors, musical sound, etc.)—consciousness, so conceived, is an objective fact and a tremendous social force. To be sure, this kind of consciousness is not a supraexistential phenomenon and cannot determine the constitution of existence. It itself is part of existence and one of its forces, and for that reason it possesses efficacy and plays a role in the arena of existence. Consciousness, while still inside a conscious person's head as inner-word embryo of expression, is as yet too tiny a piece of existence, and the scope of its activity is also as yet too small. But once it passes through all the stages of social objectification and enters into the power system of science, art, ethics, or law, it becomes a real force, capable even of exerting in turn an influence on the economic bases of social life. To be sure, this force of consciousness is incarnated in specific social organizations, geared into steadfast ideological modes of expression (science, art, and so on), but even in the original, vague form of glimmering thought and experience, it had already constituted a social event on a small scale and was not an inner act on the part of the individual.

From the very start experience is set toward fully actualized outward expression and, from the very start, tends in that direction. The expression of an experience may be realized or it may be held back, inhibited. In the latter case, the experience is inhibited expression (we shall not go into the extremely complex problem of the causes and conditions of inhibition). Realized expression, in its turn, exerts a powerful, reverse influence on experience: it begins to tie inner life together, giving it more definite and lasting expression.

This reverse influence by structured and stabilized expression on experience (i.e., inner expression) has tremendous importance and must always be taken into account. The claim can be made that it is a matter *not so much of expression accomodating itself to our inner world but rather of our inner world accomodating itself to the potentialities of our expression, its possible routes and directions.*

To distinguish it from the established systems of ideology—the systems of art, ethics, law, etc.—we shall use the term *behavioral ideology* for the whole aggregate of life experiences and the outward expressions directly connected with it. Behavioral ideology is that atmosphere of unsystematized and unfixed inner and outer speech which endows our every instance of behavior and action and our every "conscious" state with meaning. Considering the sociological nature of the structure of expression and experience, we may say that behavioral ideology in our conception corresponds basically to what is termed "social psychology" in Marxist literature. In the present context, we should prefer to avoid the word "psychology," since we are concerned exclusively with the content of the psyche and the consciousness. That content is ideological through and through, determined not by individual, organismic (biological or physiological) factors, but by factors of a purely sociological character. The individual, organismic factor is completely irrelevant to an understanding of the basic creative and living lineaments of the content of consciousness.

The established ideological systems of social ethics, science, art, and religion are crystallizations of behavioral ideology, and these crystallizations, in turn, exert a powerful influence back upon behavioral ideology, normally setting its tone. At the same time, however, these already formalized ideological products constantly maintain the most vital organic contact with behavioral ideology and draw sustenance from it; otherwise, without that contact, they would be dead, just as any literary work or cognitive idea is dead without living, evaluative perception of it. Now, this ideological perception, for which alone any ideological piece of work can and does exist, is carried out in the language of behavioral ideology. Behavioral ideology draws the work into some particular social situation. The work combines with the whole conte   of the consciousness of those who perceive it and derives its apperceptive values only in the context of that consciousness. It is interpreted in the spirit of the particular content of consciousness (the consciousness of the perceiver) and is illuminated by it anew. This is what constitutes the vitality of an ideological production. In each period of its historical existence, a work must enter into ated with it, and draw new sustenance from it. Only to the degree that a work can enter into that kind of integral, organic association with the behavioral ideology of a given period is it viable for that period (and of course, for a given social group). Outside its connection with behavioral ideology it ceases to exist, since it ceases to be experienced as something ideologically meaningful.

We must distinguish several different strata in behavioral ideology. These strata are defined by the social scale on which experience and expression are measured, or by the social forces with respect to which they must directly orient themselves.

The purview in which an experience or expression comes into being may, as we know, vary in scope. The world of an experience may be narrow and dim; its social orientation may be haphazard and ephemeral and characteristic only for some adventitious and loose coalition of a small number of persons. Of course, even these erratic experiences are ideological and sociological, but their position lies on the borders of the normal and the pathological. Such an experience will remain an isolated fact in the psychological life of the person exposed to it. It will not take firm root and will not receive differentiated and full-fledged expression; indeed, if it lacks a socially grounded and stable audience, where could it possibly find bases for its differentiation and finalization? Even less likely would such an adventitious experience be set down, in writing or even more so in print. Experiences of that kind, experiences born of a momentary and accidental state of affairs, have, of course, no chance of further social impact or efficacy.

The lowest, most fluid, and quickly changing stratum of behavioral ideology consists of experiences of that kind. To this stratum, consequently, belong all those vague and undeveloped experiences, thoughts, and idle, accidental words that flash across our minds. They are all of them cases of miscarriages of social orientations, novels without heroes, performances without audiences. They lack any sort of logic or unity. The sociological regulatedness in these ideological scraps is extremely difficult to detect. In this lowest stratum of behavioral ideology only statistical regularity is detectable; given a huge quantity of products of this sort, the outlines of socioeconomic regulatedness could be revealed. Needless to say, it would be a practical impossibility to descry in any one such accidental experience or expression its socioeconomic premises.

The upper strata of behavioral ideology, the ones directly linked with ideological systems, are more vital, more serious and bear a creative character. Compared to an established ideology, they are a great deal more mobile and sensitive: they convey changes in the socioeconomic basis more quickly and more vividly. Here, precisely, is where those creative energies build up through whose agency partial or radical restructuring of ideological systems comes about. Newly emerging social forces find ideological expression and take shape first in these upper strata of behavioral ideology before they can succeed in dominating the arena of some organized, official ideology. Of course, in the process of this struggle, in the process of their gradual infiltration into ideological organizations (the press, literature, and science), these new currents in behavioral ideology, no matter how revolutionary they may be, undergo the influence of the established ideological systems and, to some extent, incorporate forms, ideological practices, and approaches already in stock.

What usually is called "creative individuality" is nothing but the expression of a particular person's basic, firmly grounded, and consistent line of social orientation. This concerns primarily the uppermost, fully structured strata of inner speech (behavioral ideology), each of whose terms and intonations have gone through the stage of expression and have, so to speak, passed the test of expression. Thus what is involved here are words, intonations, and inner-word gestures that have undergone the experience of outward expression on a more or less ample social scale and have acquired, as it were, a high social polish and lustre by the effect of reactions and responses, resistance or support, on the part of the social audience.

In the lower strata of behavioral ideology, the biological-biographical factor does, of course, play a crucial role, but its importance constantly diminishes as the utterance penetrates more deeply into an ideological system. Consequently, while bio-biographical explanations are of some value in the lower strata of experience and expression (utterance), their role in the upper strata is extremely modest. Here the objective sociological method takes full command.

So, then, the theory of expression underlying individualistic subjectivism must be rejected. *The organizing center of any utterance, of any experience, is not within but outside—in the social milieu surrounding the individual being.* Only the inarticulate cry of an animal is really organized from inside the physiological apparatus of an individual creature. Such a cry lacks any positive ideological factor vis-à-vis the physiological reaction. Yet, even the most primitive human utterance produced by the individual organism is, from the point of view of its content, import, and meaning, organized outside the organism, in the extraorganismic conditions of the social milieu. Utterance as such is wholly a product of social interaction, both of the immediate sort as determined by the circumstances of the discourse, and of the more general kind, as determined by the whole aggregate of conditions under which any given community of speakers operates.

The individual utterance (*parole*), despite the contentions of abstract objectivism, is by no means an individual fact not susceptible to sociological analysis by virtue of its individuality. Indeed, if this were so, neither the sum total of these individual acts nor any abstract features common to all such individual acts (the "normatively identical forms") could possibly engender a social product.

Individualistic subjectivism is *correct* in that individual utterances *are* what constitute the actual, concrete reality of language, and in that they *do have* creative value in language.

But individualistic subjectivism is *wrong* in ignoring and failing to understand the social nature of the utterance and in attempting to derive the utterance from the speaker's inner world as an expression of that inner world. The structure of the utterance and of the very experience being expressed is a *social structure*. The stylistic shaping of an utterance is shaping of a social kind, and the very verbal stream of utterances, which is what the reality of language actually amounts to, is a social stream. Each drop of that stream is social and the entire dynamics of its generation are social.

Individualistic subjectivism is also completely *correct* in that linguistic form and its ideological impletion are *not* severable. Each and every word is ideological and each and every application of language involves ideological change. But individualistic subjectivism is *wrong* insofar as it also derives this ideological impletion of the word from the conditions of the individual psyche.

Individualistic subjectivism is *wrong* in taking the monologic utterance, just as abstract objectivism does, as its basic point of departure. Certain Vosslerites, it is true, have begun to consider the problem of dialogue and so to approach a more correct understanding of verbal interaction. Highly symptomatic in this regard is one of Leo Spitzer's books we have already cited—his *Italienische Umgangssprache*, a book that attempts to analyze the forms of Italian conversational language in close connection with the conditions of discourse and above all with the issue of the addressee.[4] However, Leo Spitzer utilizes a *descriptive psychological* method. He does not draw from his analysis the fundamentally sociological conclusions it suggests. For the Vosslerites, therefore, the monologic utterance still remains the basic reality.

The problem of verbal interaction has been posed clearly and distinctly by Otto Dietrich.[5] He proceeds by way of subjecting to criticism the theory of utterance as expression. For him, the basic function of language is not expression but *communication* (in the strict sense), and this leads him to consider the role of the addressee. The minimal condition for a linguistic manifestation is, according to Dietrich, *twofold* (speaker and listener). However, Dietrich shares assumptions of a general psychological type with individualistic subjectivism. Dietrich's investigations likewise lack any determinate sociological basis.

Now we are in a position to answer the question we posed at the end of the first chapter of this section of our study. *The actual reality of language-speech is not the abstract system of linguistic forms, not the isolated monologic utterance, and not the psychophysiological act of its implementation, but the social event of verbal interaction implemented in an utterance or utterances.*

Thus, verbal interaction is the basic reality of language.

Dialogue, in the narrow sense of the word, is, of course, only one of the forms—a very important form, to be sure—of verbal interaction. But dialogue can also be understood in a broader sense, meaning not only direct, face-to-face, vocalized verbal communication between persons, but also verbal communication of any type whatsoever. A book, i.e., a *verbal performance in print*, is also an element of verbal communication. It is something discussable in actual, real-life dialogue, but aside from that, it is calculated for active perception, involving attentive reading and inner responsiveness, and for organized, *printed* reaction in the various forms devised by the particular sphere of verbal communication in question (book reviews, critical surveys, defining influence on subsequent works, and so on). Moreover, a verbal performance of this kind also inevitably orients itself with respect to previous performances in the same sphere, both those by the same author and those by other authors. It inevitably takes its point of departure from some particular state of affairs involving a scientific problem or a literary style. Thus the printed verbal performance engages, as it were, in ideological colloquy of large scale: it

responds to something, objects to something, affirms something, anticipates possible responses and objections, seeks support, and so on.

Any utterance, no matter how weighty and complete in and of itself, *is
only a moment in the continuous process of verbal communication*. But
that continuous verbal communication is, in turn, itself only a moment in
the continuous, all-inclusive, generative process of a given social collective. An important problem arises in this regard: the study of the connection between concrete verbal interaction and the extraverbal situation—
both the immediate situation and, through it, the broader situation. The
forms this connection takes are different, and different factors in a situation may, in association with this or that form, take on different meanings (for instance, these connections differ with the different factors of
situation in literary or in scientific communication). *Verbal communication can never be understood and explained outside of this connection
with a concrete situation*. Verbal intercourse is inextricably interwoven
with communication of other types, all stemming from the common
ground of production communication. It goes without saying that word
cannot be divorced from this eternally generative, unified process of communication. In its concrete connection with a situation, verbal communication is always accompanied by social acts of a nonverbal character (the
performance of labor, the symbolic acts of a ritual, a ceremony, etc.), and
is often only an accessory to these acts, merely carrying out an auxiliary
role. *Language acquires life and historically evolves precisely here, in
concrete verbal communication, and not in the abstract linguistic system
of language forms, nor in the individual psyche of speakers.*

From what has been established, it follows that the methodologically
based order of study of language ought to be: (1) the forms and types of
verbal interaction in connection with their concrete conditions; (2) forms
of particular utterances, of particular speech performances, as elements
of a closely linked interaction—i.e., the genres of speech performance in
human behavior and ideological creativity as determined by verbal interaction; (3) a reexamination, on this new basis, of language forms in their
usual linguistic presentation.

This is the order that the actual generative process of language follows: *social intercourse is generated* (stemming from the basis); *in it verbal communication and interaction are generated; and in the latter, forms
of speech performances are generated; finally, this generative process is
reflected in the change of language forms.*

One thing that emerges from all that has been said is the extreme importance of the problem of the forms of an utterance *as a whole*. We have
already pointed out that contemporary linguistics lacks any approach to
the utterance itself. Its analysis goes no further than the elements that
constitute an utterance. Meanwhile, utterances are the real units that
make up the stream of language-speech. What is necessary in order to

study the forms of this real unit is precisely that it not be isolated from the historical stream of utterances. As a whole entity, the utterance is implemented only in a stream of verbal intercourse. The whole is, after all, defined by its boundaries, and these boundaries run along the line of contact between a given utterance and the extraverbal and verbal (i.e., made up of other utterances) milieu.

The first and last words, the beginning and end points of real-life utterance—that is what already constitutes the problem of the whole. The process of speech, broadly understood as the process of inner and outer verbal life, goes on continuously. It knows neither beginning nor end. The outwardly actualized utterance is an island rising from the boundless sea of inner speech; the dimensions and forms of this island are determined by the particular *situation* of the utterance and its *audience*. Situation and audience make inner speech undergo actualization into some kind of specific outer expression that is directly included into an unverbalized behavioral context and in that context is amplified by actions, behavior, or verbal responses of other participants of the utterance. The full-fledged question, exclamation, command, request—these are the most typical forms of wholes in behavioral utterances. All of them (especially the command and request) require an extraverbal complement and, indeed, an extraverbal commencement. The very type of structure these little behavioral *genres* will achieve is determined by the effect, upon a word, of its coming up against the extraverbal milieu and against another word (i.e., the words of other people). Thus, the form a command will take is determined by the obstacles it may encounter, the degree of submissiveness expected, and so on. The structure of the genre in these instances will be in accord with the accidental and unique features of behavioral situations. Only when social custom and circumstances have fixed and stabilized certain forms in behavioral interchange to some appreciable degree, can one speak of specific types of structure in genres of behavioral speech. So, for instance, an entirely special type of structure has been worked out for the genre of the light and casual causerie of the drawing room where everyone "feels at home" and where the basic differentiation within the gathering (the audience) is that between men and women. Here we find devised special forms of insinuation, half-sayings, allusions to little tales of an intentionally nonserious character, and so on. A different type of structure is worked out in the case of conversation between husband and wife, brother and sister, etc. In the case where a random assortment of people gathers—while waiting in a line or conducting some business— statements and exchanges of words will start and finish and be constructed in another, completely different way. Village sewing circles, urban carouses, workers' lunchtime chats, etc., will all have their own types. Each situation, fixed and sustained by social custom, commands a particular kind of organization of audience and, hence, a particular repertoire of little behavioral genres. The behavioral genre fits everywhere into the channel of social intercourse assigned to it and functions as an ideological reflection of its type, structure, goal, and social composition. The behavioral genre is a fact of the social milieu: of holiday, leisure time, and of social contact in the parlor, the workshop, etc. It meshes with that milieu and is delimited and defined by it in all its internal aspects.

The production processes of labor and the processes of commerce know different forms for constructing utterances.

As for the forms of ideological intercourse in the strict sense of the term—forms for political speeches, political acts, laws, regulations, manifestos, and so forth; and forms for poetic utterances, scientific treatises, etc.—these have been the object of special investigation in rhetoric and poetics, but, as we have seen, these investigations have been completely divorced from the problem of language on the one hand, and from the problem of social intercourse on the other.[6] Productive analysis of the forms of the whole of utterances as the real units in the stream of speech is possible only on a basis that regards the individual utterance as a purely sociological phenomenon. Marxist philosophy of language should and must stand squarely on the utterance as the real phenomenon of language-speech and as a socioideological structure.

Now that we have outlined the sociological structure of the utterance, let us return to the two trends in philosophical linguistic thought and make a final summing up.

R. Šor, a Moscow linguist and an adherent of the second trend of thought in philosophy of language, ends a brief sketch of the contemporary state of linguistics with the following words:

"Language is not an artifact (*ergon*) but a natural and congenital activity of mankind"—so claimed the romanticist linguistics of the 19th century. Theoretical linguistics of modern times claims otherwise: "Language is not individual activity (*energeia*) but a cultural-historical legacy of mankind (*ergon*).[7]

This conclusion is amazing in its bias and one-sidedness. On the factual side, it is completely untrue. Modern theoretical linguistics includes, after all, the Vossler school, one of Germany's most powerful movements in contemporary linguistic thought. It is impermissible to identify modern linguistics with only one of its trends.

From the theoretical point of view, both the thesis and the antithesis made up by Šor must equally be rejected, since they are equally inadequate to the real nature of language.

Let us conclude the argument with an attempt to formulate our own point of view in the following set of propositions:

1. *Language as a stable system of normatively identical forms is merely a scientific abstraction,* productive only in connection with certain particu-

⌇ lar practical and theoretical goals. This abstraction is not adequate to the concrete reality of language.

2. *Language is a continuous generative process implemented in the social-verbal interaction of speakers.*

3. *The laws of the generative process of language are not at all the laws of individual psychology, but neither can they be divorced from the activity of speakers.* The laws of language generation are *sociological* laws.

⌇4. *Linguistic creativity does not coincide with artistic creativity nor with any other type of specialized ideological creativity. But, at the same time, linguistic creativity cannot be understood apart from the ideological meanings and values that fill it.* The generative process of language, as is true of any historical generative process, can be perceived as blind mechanical necessity, but it can also become "free necessity" once it has reached the position of a conscious and desired necessity.

5. *The structure of the utterance is a purely sociological structure.* The utterance, as such, obtains between speakers. The individual speech act (in the strict sense of the word "individual") is *contradictio in adjecto*.

NOTES

1. "Spoken thought is a lie" (Tjutčev); "Oh, if one could speak from the soul without words" (Fet). These statements are extremely typical of idealistic romanticism.

2. On the possibility of a set of human sexual experiences falling out of social context with concomitant loss of verbal cognizance, see our [Vološinov's] book, *Frejdizm* [Freudianism] (1927), pp. 135–136. [*Freudianism* is the title of the English translation; see recommendations for further reading at the end of the introduction to this selection.]

3. Interesting material about expressions of hunger can be found in Leo Spitzer's books, *Italienische Kriegsgefangenenbriefe* and *Die Umschreibungen des Begriffes Hunger*. The basic concern in these studies is the adaptability of work and image to the conditions of an exceptional situation. The author does not, however, operate with a genuine sociological approach.

4. In this respect, the very organization of the book is symptomatic. The book divides into four main chapters. Their titles are as follows: I. *Eröffnungsformen des Gesprächs*. II. *Sprecher und Hörer: A. Höflichkeit (Rücksicht auf den Partner)*; B. *Sparsamkeit und Verschwendung im Ausdruck*; C. *In einandergreifen von Rede und Gegenrede*. III. *Sprecher und Situation*. IV. *Der Abschluss des Gesprächs*. Spitzer's predecessor in the study of conversational language under conditions of real-life discourse was Hermann Wunderlich. See his book, *Unsere Umgangssprache* (1894).

5. See *Die Probleme der Sprachpsychologie* (1914).

6. On the topic of disjuncture of a literary work of art with conditions of artistic communication and the resulting inertness of the work, see our [Vološinov's] study, "Slovo v žizni i slovo v poèzii" [Word in Life and Word in Poetry], *Zvezda*, 5 (1926). [Translated as "Discourse in Life and Discourse in Art," in *Freudianism.*—R. E. I.]

7. R. Sor, "Krizis sovremennoj lingvistiki" [The Crisis in Contemporary Linguistics], *Jafetičeskij sbornik*, V (1927), p. 71.

KARL BÜHLER

Bühler's text expands upon and adds important modifications to the definition of language as a system of signs. This definition depends upon Saussure, to whom Bühler, nevertheless, has a rather ambivalent attitude, for he subjects certain parts of Saussure's language theory to a nuanced and pointed critique. It was a keystone of Bühler's language theory—dealt with at length in his massive and still untranslated *Sprachtheorie* (*Language Theory*), described by Jakobson (in 1970) as "still for linguists probably the most inspiring among all the contributions to the psychology of language" (*Main Trends in the Science of Language*, New York: Harper and Row, 1974, p. 41)—that a purely physical (or external, non-mentalistic) approach to sign theory and to language theory is impossible, since the essential nature of a sign resides not in its "physical" reality but in its capacity to "stand for" something else, that is, in its relational reality. Following Husserl and Cassirer, as well as the Scholastic tradition, Bühler points out that what makes possible this "standing for" is the ability of the sign-user to take up a particular "set" (*Einstellung*) vis-à-vis the physical reality of the sign, regarded as a material entity, and by means of this set to endow the material entity with sense, in effect, to "besoul" it. This thesis has also been vigorously defended, outside the framework of semiotics as such, by Karl Popper, who was Bühler's student in Vienna during the 1920s. (See Popper's famous essay "Language and the Mind-Body Problem," in *Conjectures and Refutations*, New York: Harper and Row, 1968). This set results from a particular *abstractive* act, upon which Peirce also focused (the two positions being worthy of explicit confrontation) that regards as semiotically—or representationally—relevant only a part of the material reality of the sign. Bühler labeled this the "principle of abstractive relevance."

The main support of Bühler's position here is the fundamental distinction—foreseen by Saussure, definitively established by Trubetzkoy, exploited extensively by Jakobson and others—between phonetics and phonology. Manifesting the radical difference between a materially oriented and a formally oriented science, this distinction, nevertheless, looks rather different in Schapiro's discussion of "field" and "vehicle" in image signs. For Bühler, the insights of phonology and the principles on which it is based point to the primacy of abstractive procedures not just in the apprehension of signs but in perceptual and cognitive procedures quite generally, as in concept formation and metaphor. In a comment bearing on the semiotic structure of perception, for example, Bühler contended that "the theory of perception in psychology cannot be brought to anything without considering the sign-functions of the sense-data found in it" (see the selections from Peirce, Saussure, Barthes, Thom, and Morris). Bühler had detailed in his *Sprachtheorie* and in his "Axiomatization of the Language Sciences" the systematic relations between *signals*, which are addressed to the behavior of the addressee, *indexes*, which reveal the interiority of the speaker or sign-giver, and *symbols*, which are bearers of "representational" content. This trichotomy gives rise to the appellative (conative), expressive, and representational functions of language. Bühler's guiding question in this selection is to determine how it is possible for signs to come to "represent" something at all. Now, in another work, *Die Krise der Psychologie*, which deals with the semiotic foundations of psychology, Bühler had contended, with reference to the three sign-functions (*Sinnfunktionen*) represented by signals, indexes, and symbols, that they enabled us to master theoretically "the whole domain of perceptions." Signals steer pragmatic action (see the selection from Morris), indexes reveal properties of objects, and symbols formulate "ideal" senses or structures embedded in experience. Each type of sign generates a particular type of "sense." Here Bühler's work intersects directly with that of Peirce, Thom, and Morris. Moreover, as Jakobson attests in his famous essay "Linguistics and Poetics," the Bühlerian trichotomy became the source of the first three functions upon which he built his own sixfold functional matrix.

Bühler clearly shows how the concept of "representation," which lies at the heart of his language theory, makes no sense apart from specific abstractive procedures, the ability to make, through coding and stipulation, a material mark mediate a content to the partners in the exchange of signs, "semiotic exchange." Bühler's approach to the sign-character of language was shared by Ernst Cassirer and Heinrich Gomperz and pointed the way to a doctrine of synthesis or of mediational *acts* of conferring sense, although Bühler, by reason of his general anti-Cartesianism, constantly focused on the primacy of the social matrix in the genesis of sense and by no means allowed the essential determinant of sense or meaning to be confided to a private mental act. Wittgenstein's later work on these themes may have been influenced by Bühler, with whom he was associated for a time in the Austrian School Reform Movement. Bühler insisted on the primacy of social and hence publicly observable data for laying the foundations of language theory, combating in this way Husserl's tendency to explain all differences in meaning by differences in acts of meaning, themselves accessible to some form of introspective procedures.

Throughout all Bühler's work, the central and ever-recurring thesis, upheld also with great vigor by Vološinov, is the irreducible social matrix of meaning in both the human and nonhuman spheres. Bühler argued, in a way analogous to the work of Mead and Morris, that the origin of meaning and of the conditions of sense is to be found not in the individual but in society or social life as lived (*Gemeinschaft*) and that, as a matter of fact, there is an intrinsic reference to meaning (as embodied in objective structures)—a constitutive semantic factor—in all animal or human social life. Social life is characterized first and foremost by a mutual steering or guiding of its members, involving the "set" (*Einstellung*) of one individual or group of individuals toward another. This set issues into a covariance of movements, a mutual coordination of activities that can be externally observed and, in fact, read off from individuals' behaviors. Traffic on the busy street and its coordination, the way we navigate on a sidewalk or in a subway—these are clear examples of externally verifiable covariance. This mutual coordination of living systems, both individual and group, involves quite generally the giving and receiving of signs (a theme developed in closely related fashion in the work of Cassirer, von Uexküll, and now, comprehensively, by Thomas Sebeok). In this respect, Bühler insisted on an irreducible duality of sign-giver and sign-receiver as the key to social life and some commentators have remarked on the "cybernetic" orientation of his language theory, which is, it must be admitted, truly there, and which also runs through the work of Gregory Bateson.

An important theme in Bühler's text, which is echoed elsewhere in the materials collected in this book, is that social life takes place at the beginning chiefly in common perceptual—and hence "spatial" (see Morris and Thom)—situations, making up a shared "field," and that the direction of guidance or steering is also to be found in the common perceptual field. It is only when the crucial determinant of behavior or of change of behavior no longer lies in the perceptual field that a diacriticon is needed to signal the shift. Hence a sign is a "tool" or "organon" for performing a diacritical function of exchanging "information." Bühler, in fact, sees his "organon-theory" of language already prefigured in Plato's *Cratylus*. The diacriticon can be of almost any sort so long as it is perceptible. The contact of a higher order, however, which characterizes discursively formed institutions and societies, involves not mere signaling—deictic expressions, Peircean indexes—but an appeal to the representations and concepts in possession of the hearer. Bühler is concerned to specify essential conditions and implications for the genesis of representations, and in fact his *Sprachtheorie* is subtitled "The Representational Function of Language."

For Bühler, the anthropologically decisive step in the genesis of sense comes with the step from immediately intelligible gestures to symbolic gestures, a topic taken up, perhaps in deep opposition, by Bateson's essay and also in the first volume of Ernst Cassirer's *Philosophy of Symbolic Forms*, which is devoted to language. Even before the advent of speech, social life is replete with meaning that functions as a social bond. Bühler points out that "semantics in the animal domain lets us acknowledge analoga to human signals," though he insisted that the third function of a sign, the representational use constituted by words and sentences, is lacking, strictly speaking, in the animal realm and is proper to humans alone, a position about which there is, of course, considerable controversy. Here is a fertile point of confrontation with the reflections of Bateson and Sebeok as well with Thom's comments at the end of his essay on the differences between animal and human symbolic capacities.

Although an important figure in the history of twentieth century semiotics and language theory, little of Bühler's work, or work about him, exists in English. For a discussion of his language theory as a whole, principally as found in his *Sprachtheorie*, see Robert E. Innis, *Karl Bühler: Semiotic Foundations of Language Theory* (New York and London: Plenum, 1982), which also contains a translation of Bühler's "Axiomatization of the Language Sciences." See in addition Robert E. Innis, "Bühler and Gardiner: From Indication to Predication," in *Bühler-Studien*, edited by Achim Eschbach (Frankfurt: Suhrkamp, 1984), Robert E. Innis, "Perception, Abstraction, and Subjectivity in Bühler's Language Theory," in *Rassegna italiana di linguistica applicata*, January-April, 1984, and Robert E. Innis, "The Semiotic Relevance of Bühler's *Sprachtheorie*," in *Semiotics Unfolding*, edited by Tasso Borbé (Berlin and New York: Mouton, 1984), pp. 143–149. Thomas A. Sebeok has an essay on Bühler, rich in historical context and anecdote, in his *The Play of Musement* (Bloomington: Indiana University Press, 1981). The chapter on "Language" in Susanne K. Langer's *Philosophy in a New Key*, third edition (Cambridge: Harvard University Press, 1957), has many stimulating references to Bühler and the marvelous work by Sir Alan Gardiner, *The Theory of Speech and Language*, second edition (Oxford: Oxford University Press, 1951), also has many specific and acknowledged points of intersection with Bühler's language theory.

The Key Principle: The Sign-Character of Language

KARL BÜHLER

That every language is a system of signs, that the sounds of language are posited by the speaker as signs and received by the hearer as signs, that the phenomenon of language arises as the mediator between individuals in the exchange of signs—in this or some similar way we can begin to speak about language. In any case, the first thing needed logically in order to define it is a general term such as sign ($\sigma\hat{\eta}\mu\alpha$, *signum*, *seign*). What are signs?

1. In the domain of the Indo-Germanic languages and, within this group, especially in Greek, Latin, and German, as the languages in which Western thought grew, the roots of the two chief groups of words denoting signs point to the realm of what is visible. The two originally grasped moments are, then, 'brightness, visible' or 'to make bright and visible,' and, on the other hand, 'to place before the eyes'; the 'lighting up' directs attention to itself, that which has been 'put before the eyes' enters in this fashion into the field of perception. It is, to put it briefly, the [notions of] making present and disclosing things or [the] pointing to things that, as a rule, characterize the multistemmed [*Mehrstämmige*] kinship of the Indo-European words for signs.[1]

Basically, the same explanation of the sign function is arrived at if we go farther and, with the help of the comparative psychologist, investigate *the means of guidance in the social life* of animals and men. We can reduce to an extremely simple formula the multiform complex of facts that belong to it, a formula that I recommended in the *Crisis of Psychology* and justified in detail. It is apparent that the biological point of origin of the production of signs is universally to be found in the higher social life of animals only where a cooperation adapted to specific situations demands from individuals the widening of the common perceptual horizon. If *one* of the individuals participating in the cooperative life is in possession of more information relevant to the perception or remembering of important aspects of the situation, this constitutes the cognitional surplus that becomes the content of the communication.

If we imagine what must be described here using human words, which are only partially adequate, and if we imagine it in a primitive way for the simplest cases, especially of animal life, and in a sufficiently sophisticated way for the complicated cases of refined human social life, then the formula touches without remainder on everything that comparative psychology has found out about the sign-constituted means of communication possessed by animals. It also touches on, above all, the most conclusive cases for the question of origin, where we can observe newly appearing signs. For example, those who drive trucks on our bustling streets some years ago invented their well-known traffic signals and introduced them precisely for the situations that our formula describes, and only for them. The directing of the trucks in the busy traffic is successful without the aid of signs as long as and insofar as the indispensable attention that one person must pay to another can be *directly* determined from a personal perception of what is going on. If someone decides to stop suddenly or to veer off from the direction he is driving in, in each case, and only then, he has to give a sign. Why? Because the behavior of the traffic partners has to be determined before the event. What still lies in the bosom of the future—imperceptible to the partners, but known to the one acting—must be incorporated into something that can be commonly perceived. The sign offers a supplementary stimulus to the given perceptual data, which no longer suffice alone.

Or take an example from the animal realm: If an individual in a herd of animals, by reason of his position or heightened attentiveness, is the only one who detects an ominous smell or catches sight of a danger and reacts, in addition to fleeing, with a 'cry of fright' [*Schreckruf*], the behavior of his fellow members of the herd, which we can thereby observe, is the same as if they all themselves had had the same original impression of danger. It is 'as if' their own perceptual horizon had been widened. The supplementary stimulus of the cry of fright, which breaks into their field of perception, fulfills the function of a communication that is of significance to life itself. This is not the place to address other analyses of the 'as if' formula.

Only one point remains to be noted: The etymologies of the words for signs, which refer back to the indicating of 'things' or the steering of a fellow observer in the direction of 'things,' presuppose altogether something specifically human. The authentic finger gesture of man is frequently already characterized as beyond the animal realm; it appears conspicuously in the etymologies of the Indo-European words for signs, and only a single case is still disputed, namely, in the Greek word μηνύειν. However, it remains true that the factor of thing constancy in the field of application of signs, which is contained implicitly in the aforementioned etymologies, has not been able to be proved up to the present day for any of the animal means of communication.[2] So much for introduction.

A satisfactory *phenomenological* explanation and exact definition of the sign concept demand both more and something other than pointing to etymological and genetic facts. I will put off a discussion of the notable difficulties that confront such an attempt to the place in the total language theory where signs will be distinguished from other spiritual or mental structures. In Section D of our essay [not included in this selection], we will at least succeed in one thing: getting clear on the multiplicity of *linguistic* functions of signs. In the present context, it is sufficient to grasp a *genus proximum* of the sign concept, which the Scholastics found, and, with its help, to put in its proper light a single, but fundamental, property of language, a property that defines the whole activity of research and the results of the empirical sciences of language. What I have in mind is valid for all those things—whether they be persons or things or events—that we are accustomed to call *representatives* [*Stellvertretendes*]. Wherever there is a representation [*Stellvertretung*], a standing in for something or someone, there are, just as in every relation, two foundations, a thing [*ein etwas*] and then something that must distinguish our way of considering it. In order to characterize in a general way the relation in the case of representation, the Scholastics put it that *aliquid stat pro aliquo*, a formula that they found through a considera-tion of language.[3] Now, if *hic et nunc* a concrete thing is functioning as a representative, the question can constantly be raised by what *reason* or what *properties* it sustains and enters into the relation and brings it to fulfillment. A twofold determination of this *concretum* must be possible. The first of these abstracts from the function of the representative as representative in order to determine what it is or would be *for itself*.[4] The second way of considering it, however, looks for and finds in the *concretum* precisely those properties to which the relation of representation is bound. In the case of the being of the sign, it is always only abstract moments by reason of which and with which the *concretum* functions 'as' a sign. I have characterized this fundamental state of affairs of linguistic theory as the *principle of abstractive relevance* and explained it with the help of the distinction between phonetics and phonology.[5]

Before I illustrate and concretize what I have just said, let us touch on two more determinations that are, in our present context, in need of no closer specification. The "*stare pro*" belongs—whatever else it may be—in all the known examples drawn from life to the class of nonreversible relations. The ambassador is a representative of a state, but not vice versa; the advocate stands before the court for his client, but not vice versa. That is also the case for signs, and we can add that here, for specific reasons, the representative member of the structure (*id quod stat pro aliquo*) belongs constantly to the perceptual realm, while the same cannot be asserted of the other member. There is no need to waste words on this last point if we look on signs in general and from the start as intersubjective mediators (mediating structures in societies), because it is derived from its definition. The matter could be grasped in an even more general way; but we will place no value on that here because the assertion needs no proof, at any rate for the case of language. The distinction between a sense-perceptible element in linguistic phenomena (the sound) and the other element, which it stands for, is completely familiar here to all those competent in these matters.[6]

2. Now to the explanations. Two decades ago, Heinrich Gomperz had already taken up the fruitful *aliquid stat pro aliquo* of the Scholastics and developed it in his own way. What no one today could explain in a more flexible and at the same time conceptually sharper fashion than he did (with the help of an intentionally colorful flock of examples) is the two-fold way, everywhere realizable, of conceiving and determining the first member in the relational structure of representation. For example, if I consider the *actor* (so reasons Gomperz), the actor standing there before me on the stage, he is now Wallenstein and yet not Wallenstein himself *in persona*. Rather he is Mr. Bassermann, who is playing him. Now to be sure, that is a play and a spectacle. There are many ways of considering it and talking about it. But we are going to concentrate with Gomperz on the remarkable duality that appears in the words "he is something and yet he is not that." It makes good sense to use the following formula for it: The perceptible *accidents* of the actor Bassermann are ascribed as in-hering in a foreign *substance*, the Wallenstein of the writer. The spectator takes the costume and gestures, the words and deeds of Bassermann the individual as something that enables him to experience the Wallenstein created by the writer. Or, to define the issue from the other side, Basser-mann puts at the disposal of the Wallenstein of the writer the previously mentioned elements so that the figure created by the writer can come to appearance. The scholastic conceptual pair 'substance and accidents' is in the formulation of Gomperz separated from its ontological meaning and applied to give a convenient first description.

If we add a second and a third explanatory example taken from the collection of Gomperz, gradually the same abstractly grasped structure of representation will necessarily emerge even more clearly from these dif-ferent items. If a canvas covered with spots of color awakens in the viewer the charming appearance of a landscape, this state of affairs is, according to Gomperz, also describable with the aid of the same formula: the can-vas lends its accidents, so to speak, to the, in the present case, *imaginally* presented thing [*Etwas*]. And, once again, although it is in many points not the same but still essentially [*dem Kern der Sache nach*] comparable, the meaningful sound with its accidents stands *symbolically* for what it means. The precise wording of this conception with Gomperz runs as fol-lows: "When an object possesses such a structure that its accidents inhere not in the substance that normally belongs to it but rather in the sub-stance of another object, there exists between that first and this second object the relation of *meaning*, of *standing in the place of* or *represent-ing*" [*Bedeutens, Vertretens oder Repräsentierens*].[7]

Talking about accidents, which are borrowed for the purpose of representing another substance, is, it seems to me, a fitting and impressive description. It is also verified completely coherently for the case of pure
symbolic representation, such as is found in language. All that is missing
is the easily fulfilled demand that one count among the accidents rather
more than the so-called primary or elementary or founding sense data.
We will have something more exact to say about this when we treat the
question of phonemes. At that time, there will be no reason to alter,
through either deletion or addition, a single thing we have determined in
this first sketch. The psychological verification of the *aliquid stat pro aliquo* in the case of a painting can be carried through today in more detail
and with a much better empirical knowledge than Gomperz had at his
disposal in the year 1905.[8]

An incidental criticism, which can lead to the development of what
Gomperz began, can be brought against *one* point. The question is
whether we ought to regard it as terminologically apt, and thereby leave
as is, to define the three expressions *meaning, standing for,* and *representing* as synonyms. Synonyms are, it seems to me, an evil in scientific
language. We cannot avoid them everywhere, but we can do so here. In
respect to the equation "*Vertreten = Repräsentieren,*" we will put it to
the jurists and have to consider, with the aid of the best legal theorists,
whether what is specific to *juridical* representation has been touched on.
If not, then it is necessary to organize matters in such a way that the adjective *juridical* is added to standing-in-place-of [*Stellvertretung*] as a
genuine *differentia specifica*, and that standing-in-place-of [*Stellvertretung*] steps forth as the generic concept. Once this is settled, then we are
forced to conclude that precisely what was common to the three joint
cases of theatrical, imaginal, and symbolic 'representation' [*Repräsenta-
tion*] is not to be found in juridical representation. The advocate before
the tribunal does not behave as the representative of his client in the way
Bassermann is related to Wallenstein, nor as the colored canvas is related
to the landscape, nor as a linguistic symbol is related to what is symbolized, but the relation is essentially different. To put it crudely: the advocate as an actual Bassermann would be a ludicrous fool before the tribunal; the advocate as an actual image or symbol would be an unusable
strawman or a dressed doll, and therefore not exactly the ideal of a successful advocate. And from all of this, there is only one way out for logic:
to consider the concept of standing-in-place-of [*Stellvertretung*] as the
highest genus and to look around for the species of this genus. We have to
distinguish many things from the class to which the theatrical, imaginal,
and symbolic representation belongs: besides juridical representation,
also the representative function of *money*, for which the relations once
again, I believe (at least in certain points), are specifically different.

But enough of criticism. At the beginning, we are discussing not the species of representation but only the *aliquid stat pro aliquo*, which we have recognized as *a* useful *genus proximum* of the sign concept. Gomperz is generally right in his "he is something and yet he is not it really": – his substance-accidents formula, however, fits, it seems to me, to a useful extent, only the cases of representation in the narrower sense of the word.

There are many other noteworthy items in Gomperz's investigations of the two determinations which in the very nature of the case must result if, on the one hand, we treat the representative element as what it is in itself [*für sich*] and, on the other hand, we treat it only under the aspect of its representative function. We will discover that linguistics, too, has its share of theoretical mistakes and gratuitous discussions, which Gomperz uncovered there as such.

However, I first want to say something about the positive progress, aimed at since Gomperz, that language theory achieved thanks to 'phonology,' and about the *principle of abstractive relevance*. It is a principle valid for every sign and beyond. With its aid, however, the *differentia specifica* of the sign concept cannot be discovered because it also extends to other things.

3. A fictive agreement [*Verabredung*], found in my essay "Phonetics and Phonology" and adapted to a situation discussed by phonology, may serve as a point of departure: if we assume that two men want to make themselves understood and come to agreement by means of flag signals, we do not have to advert to the form and size of the signals, only to their color. It will be agreed (just as in the case of a determinate system of sounds) that we need three meaning-relevant levels of color saturation. *First*: The completely unsaturated nuances of the black-and-white series have uniformly the meaning A. Whether in the concrete case black, gray, or white is used is irrelevant. *Second*: The flags of a medium level of saturation have uniformly the meaning B. Whether in a concrete case sky blue, or pink, or tobacco brown is used makes no difference and is irrelevant to the meaning. *Thirdly*: The flags of the highest domains of saturation have uniformly the meaning C. Whether in a concrete case a saturated red, blue, green, or gold is used makes no meaning-relevant difference. I assume that we admit without discussion that an unhesitating functioning of such a mode of coming to agreement is possible. Naturally, each participant has to know the system, remember it, and, in concrete cases, be able to rightly order the precise nuances of the saturation levels that are used; then he can take part without error in the business of giving and receiving signals.

There is still a rather small but theoretically important modification that may be brought to bear on the imagined signal procedure. This makes easier an exact comparison with the relations that obtain for the single sounds in the association of the stream of sound in speech. In every concrete case of signaling, we can imagine lawfully milieu-defined the selection of nuances within the free dimension belonging to the level of saturation. Assume that an agreement is made between a secret bride and her secret bridegroom, for whom what is important is that the exchange of signals proceed as unobtrusively and in as milieu-adapted a way as possible. The woman signals, for example, simply by means of the color of her dress. Then she may—if there are available three dresses of unsaturated color, black, gray, and white—in any given case try on before the mirror whatever one agrees best today with her complexion, or she can let the weather and other concrete circumstances dictate whether she will put on the gray, white, or black one. Exactly the same relations here obtain in principle everywhere in the sound flow of speech with regard to the influences of the environment. They are there and follow one another in an irrelevant dimension of variations. In "Phonetics and Phonology," this contention is confirmed by means of well-accepted facts. There exists, for example, in the West Caucasian group of languages one (Adyghe) that at first sight exhibits a multiplicity of vowel lengths similar to German; among other nuances there also appear those between u-ü-i. But we see that in that language two words are never distinguished through the vowel differences u-i, as they are with us in words *Tusche* and *Tische*; the nuances u-ü-i have no diacritical value in that language. Just as little do o-ö-e or a-ä have diacritical value. To be sure, they all appear, indeed regularly appear, as milieu-conditioned, but they cannot become diacritically relevant. In order to grasp in exact concepts this central fact of phonology, I thought up the fiction of the signal flags. It makes clear the validity of the principle of abstractive relevance for the domain of the so-called single sounds of language.

Consequently, if we are on the right track, then there are two ways of considering the human speech sound, because one can make *first* its material properties purely in themselves the object of a scientific determination and *second* that component of the properties that is decisive for their task of functioning as signs. The fundamental knowledge that we need concerning the relationship between these two ways can be derived from the comparative model of the exchange of signals by means of flags. This model is intentionally chosen as being so simple that the principle of abstractive relevance can be clearly derived from it. Black, gray, and white are different colors; no one will haggle about that. But they can (just as in the imagined case of agreement) mean *the same thing*, be *identical in meaning*, because, for their task of serving as signs, the only thing that is determinative is that abstract moment consisting in the lowest level of saturation that is common to them.

This fact can be made clear to every child. And once this fact is established, then it is only the philosophers and the psychologists who can wonder about it and engage in further meaningful questioning. The philosopher will say reflectively: in the case of meaningful signs, things are such that the sensible thing [*Sinnending*], the perceptible something, *hic et nunc*, must enter into the semantic function without the total fullness of its concrete properties. Rather, only this or that abstract moment can become relevant for its task of functioning as a sign. Put in a simple form: that is the principle of abstractive relevance. *That this fundamental principle of abstractive relevance is valid in language right up to the realm of the single isolated sounds is the thesis, and the discovery, of phonology.* So much for citations from "Phonetics and Phonology." I am now of the opinion that the principle is valid for all *concreta* that are applied *as* signs, but in the interest of brevity, I will not at this point attempt to justify it sematologically, that is, by reference to our model [*modelleinsichtig*].

With reference to language signs, before my contact with phonology, I had arrived in my own work on the problems of language theory [*Sprachtheorie*] at the point where conclusions from many areas were converging to formulate the key proposition of the sign nature of language. But the whole block of sound theory [*Lautlehre*] did not appear to be in agreement with the position that the object of the empirical sciences of languages belongs without remainder in the same fashion to sematology as the object of physics belongs to mathematics. The *"ubi materia ibi geometria"* of Kepler governs and defines without remainder the procedure and results of physics; on the contrary, the sound theory of the linguists appeared to exhibit another character than that shown by the usual grammar. Philosophical (scientific-theoretic) amazement about it was shown to be fruitful and was removed when the monograph of N. Trubetzkoy, "On the General Theory of Phonological Sound Systems," came into my hands.[9] There, all of a sudden, was a well-grounded contribution to the study of sounds within the horizon of a new well-rounded scientific discipline for studying language, which did not have the character of a phonetics and, what is more, was just what I was looking for. It is possible, therefore, and necessary, to divide up the scientific treatment of the sounds of language in exactly the fashion that is demanded by the insights of logic. On the one hand, they can be considered what they are 'in themselves' [*für sich*] and, on the other hand, under the aspect of their task of functioning as signs; phonetics does one thing and phonology does another. The concept of 'sound elements,' under which one is accustomed to subsume the vowels and the consonants, is defined in a usable fashion only through the conception of a phonology, so that it is apparent that there is in every language only a limited multiplicity, a transparent system (vocalic, consonantal, and many others) of discrete *sound signs*. Their semantic function is, according to the terminological recommendation that I made to the phonologists, that of serving as *diacritica* of the complex phenomena that one calls *words*. Then phonemes are the natural 'marks' (tokens) by means of which in the sound flow of speech the semantically decisive units of this sound flow are recognized and distinguished from one another.

A reflection back on the history of the empirical sciences of language shows, then, as is the case with all great things, that the 'new' knowledge is new only in its exact formulation but otherwise is very old [*uralt*]. It is implicitly contained in the discovery of the alphabet and it governed axiomatically, although they did not know it, the procedures of all linguists who attempted to present the fund of sounds of a language as a system of discrete units. In any case, we see, to emphasize this once again, that even considered from the point of view of sounds, the proposition that language is through and through a system of signs is justified. Even in the existence of the word as a sound unit, the system of tonal marks is once again visible as an underlevel; their existence prepares the logician for a counterpart of the tonal characteristics, for characteristics found in the object, for the criterial properties of traditional logic. If I say "counterpart" [*Pendant*], the hasty reader must guard himself against misunderstanding that I am saying that the tonal characteristics of the word are element-for-element correlated with the distinguishing characteristics of the object. I am so far from saying such a thing that we must, on the contrary, start from the other pure case, where simply no such coordination in detail is to be found.

4. Perhaps it will be profitable and offer a new impulse to sematology, when in the course of its new forward progress it has achieved a certain rounding off, if a competent person writes the history of the discovery of the sign nature of language. He would find, regarding this task, important contributions in the case of Gomperz and Cassirer, to mention only two modern systematic attempts. We will have to refer here and there, as we proceed, to the specifically idealistic and functionally monistic (*funktionsmonistische*] tone [*Färbung*] of Cassirer's sematology; on the whole, the problem of the great project of his philosophy of symbolic forms lies outside the boundaries of our essay. It is enough to say that the axiom is central also for Cassirer and receives an epistemological justification. The person who aims at something else and keeps carefully in mind the stimulating interaction that must exist between language theory [*Sprachtheorie*] and individual linguistic researches will in the interest of both, in the present situation, also look into a pair of noteworthy propositions in F. de Saussure's *Course in General Linguistics*. I am citing them as a convenient springboard to an unavoidable criticism of the widespread devaluation—widespread, even today—of the axiom by the linguists and the psychologists. My critical comments, which are intended in a purely programmatic way, are meant to promote the theoretically purifying influence that the acceptance of the central idea of phonology will putatively exercise on the concept of linguistics. They should clarify the cur-

rent slogan of linguistic psychologism, the target of so much criticism, and assign to it a fixed meaning. In his *Course in General Linguistics* F. de Saussure writes:

> Language is a system of signs that express ideas and is therefore comparable to a system of writing, the alphabet of deaf-mutes, symbolic rites, polite formulas, military signs, etc. But it is the most important of all these systems.
>
> A science that studies the life of signs within society is conceivable; it would be a part of social psychology and consequently of general psychology; I shall call it *semiology* (from Greek σημεῖον, 'sign'). Semiology would show what constitutes signs, what laws govern them. Since the science does not yet exist, no one can say what it would be; but it has a right to exist, a place staked out in advance. Linguistics is only a part of the general science of semiology; the laws discovered by semiology will be applicable to linguistics, and the latter will circumscribe a well-defined area within the mass of anthropological facts.
>
> To determine the exact place of semiology is the task of the psychologist. The task of the linguist is to find out what makes language a special system within the mass of semiological data. (p. 16, *Course in General Linguistics*, trans. Wade Baskin. New York: McGraw-Hill, 1966.)

A word, first of all, about terminology: We recommend *sematology*, because the Greek work σῆμα makes possible a rich group of good-sounding derivates in modern form (for example, *sematological*, which one can use in contrast to *semantic* and as against *semeological*). The word *semasiology* has been used only by Gomperz as synonymous with *sematology*, but otherwise, as even the editors of the "Course" note, with another nuance of meaning. Bally and Sechehaye (the editors) define: *Semasiology* = the discipline that studies changes of meaning. That was in fact the idea behind the old study of meaning; from Reisig on, as far as I can tell. It is and remains, according to our criticism, a logically unobjectionable and determinate undertaking to think of all the phenomena of language as divided by a cut into sound and meaning. But as a result *semasiology* must then also be in the position to exhibit and define the realm that it is investigating as it is in itself, and to follow its historical transformation. It has to be in exactly the same position as the phonetician is in his own area if it wants to endure. The old-style *semasiology* can be nothing more than a materially oriented treatment. Only, it is not the sound materials, but—to have recourse to a social-psychological way of speaking—the world of representations (the world of ideas), the world of feeling, and so forth, of a human linguistic community that it takes as its subject. This world is understood insofar as it becomes manifest in language. In exactly the same fashion as the object of phonetics is determined through the fact that its assigned task is to investigate the sounds of language, so on the other hand the same situation obtains for the old-style semasiology. The world of ideas, and so forth, of a group of men is revealed by all their deeds, works, and institutions; the semasiologist seeks to determine what is revealed in language. He does not need to limit his object more, and what is specific to language, its sign character, he must strike from his framework in exactly the same way as the phonetician does.

Let us begin with a bow to de Saussure. We will acknowledge his demand for the construction of a general theory of signs as important to linguistics and will realize its importance, but we will correct the opinion that it does not yet exist. In placing his hope for its construction in *psychology* de Saussure speaks as a child of his times, as a Frenchman at the end of the nineteenth century influenced by the predominance of social psychology at that time; one thinks of the influence of Durkheim and his school. It is correct that all three sciences that have been brought together here (sociology, psychology, and linguistics) would have a vital interest in the insights resulting from sematology's having developed a wide range of application; it is scarcely possible to say which of them is of more interest than the others. Psychology finds signs everywhere in its own field of investigation, and far beyond the processes of human intercourse by means of language sounds; for example, the theory of perception in psychology cannot be brought to anything without considering the sign functions of the sense data found in it. Sematology may be inclined toward such a concern; nevertheless, it can never be derived from the three aforementioned sciences. For if it wants to be to the point, it has to be produced in correspondence to the subject matter, and the insights of sematology that offer support to the other sciences must be derived constructively by reliance on a model, just as the propositions of mathematics are. That goes for all the propositions, such as that of abstractive relevance, and there is a lot to be said about it. Every attempt to 'prove' it inductively with the means of special sciences would be just as contradictory as the physicist's wanting to prove inductively with his own means any mathematical proposition.

And now to the application of this developed conception to the analysis of the *concrete speech event*. The linguists and psychologists of the second half of the nineteenth century knew, if one heard them speak about it, only that kind of analytical treatment and description of the concrete speech event that is still found today in all those texts—linguistic as well as psychological—that deal with language. We assume—as de Saussure, for example, works it out in his chapter on the "speech circuit"—that two people, A and B, are conversing. What is going on there? The answer is that there is a chain of processes that begins in the experience and thereby in the brain of A, then finds its continuation, through purely physiological events, in the nerve-muscle apparatus of the speech organs; "then the sound waves travel from the mouth of A to the ear of B: a purely *physical* process" (p. 12). Now, the process once again marches on in the psychophysical system of B in reverse order (like a mirror image). Thereupon, B can bring himself to answer. The concrete speech event appeared in this way to be separated purely into its components, which then was handed over for close determination to the auxiliary sciences of linguistics (psychology, physiology, and physics).

One who has a little feel for thinking in visual terms, spicing thereby with some irony even a serious matter, sees the linguist standing before him with empty hands if the material is divided according to this recipe. Would not this man have to feel practically like that well-known tanner whose hides swam away from him? Indeed, it is understood that he will get back what has been handed over to other departments for pretreatment [*Vorbearbeitung*], but what remains for him to do with it? To fish out what is important for him and to paste it together? Actually, the professional linguist *never* derived his specific theme from the texts of anatomy, physiology, and psychology, but it was considered and induced in a way proper to it [*in seinem Aspekt*], or it was also derived from a sematological reflection. Was it a false path, then, if from the time of Steinthal on, one became 'exact' and listened to one's neighbor sciences? It is quite simple to avoid a new historical swing of the pendulum back to the other extreme situation—it does not have to be the reservations of the Hegelians to Steinthal—if one acknowledges and keeps apart two *ways of considering the matter* that are prescribed by the object itself: (1) the analysis of the raw material (*Stoffanalyse*) and (2) specifically linguistic research predefined by the fundamental principle of the sign character of language. But it would be completely mistaken to apply the division into compartments, which appears very clear, also to the matter at hand. Separation into aspects can never be accomplished in the concrete with a dismembering instrument such as the butcher's knife. Seen from afar, it looked like a butcher analysis, if time and again one emphasized—as for example even de Saussure did in his weak moments—that the specific object of linguistics (*la langue*) is localizable at that place in the process chain where the representation of sound appears to be associated with the representation of the thing. *La langue* is a piece cut out of 'discourse' [*Rede*], he says in his weak moments.

5. Certain opponents of the 'naturalistic' linguistics and psychology of the nineteenth century contend that the historical moral is that no one should be amazed at an experience that repeatedly appears and is constituted in human history, as a real wandering Jew in the most different dress. If spirit is extruded anywhere or if it has axiomatically had the door blocked to it, then it is no more to be found, not with the dissecting knife, as the physicians of the nineteenth century truly assured us, nor with a precision scale or a spectroscope. Indeed, in order to complete what they say, we add: also the violent means of a *salto mortale*, of a leap back and forth into and out of the two worlds of physics and of experi-

ence, does not accomplish nor fulfill what is needed. The Cartesian division has to be taken up for our purposes in a way different from that of Descartes. His 'extended' world may continue to endure, but the 'mental' sciences (human sciences) do not find their method and sufficiency in his second world; they do not find their method and its sufficiency in a domain that can be established by the *scio me scire*, by self-observation.

In order to prepare a better contrast, let us let, peacefully for once, the determined nominalists, both the old and the new ones, have their say in the matter of the concrete speech event. What does the speaker speak and send, and the hearer hear and receive? *Flatus vocis*, say the old nominalists; sound waves, say the modern; and no philosopher in the world is in a position to shake their position. There are certainly no *species*, whether sensible or intelligible, that could endure and fly along with the air current; these *wandering* species are, indeed, nothing other than the philosophically most sublime extract from the inventory of fictions belonging to magical thought; and magical thought is a disguised, matter-bound thought [*Stoffdenken*]. What is 'Spirit' then? I contend that for all who have not discovered God's plan in creating the world, the chance of finding the way into language research is so apparent that these unenlightened ones may avoid a conclusive answer to the question of the essence of spirit and, in spite of this, be in a position to protect their enterprise from the dangers of the estrangement from spirit that we have described. It is sufficient if we consider the full content of the protocol sentences of successful linguistic research and do not let ourselves be diverted—by any dictate of a historically famous but impertinently false analysis of what the data of observation can contain—from taking seriously everything to be found in good protocol sentences. Here is the way things stand, in outline, with the method of observation as used by the language researcher: there are life situations that contain the moments enumerated by Plato; namely, sounds are used as an *organum* for one person to communicate with another about things. The language researcher who has reached this point and looks over this situation at one time grasps and determines the sound phenomenon as it has to be determined 'taken in itself,' that is, as a happening in the world of the physicist with everything that belongs to it. Another time, however, or immediately with the other eye (to use a visual metaphor), he sees (it can also be the ear he attends with), perceives, and determines this sound phenomenon *sub specie* of its representative function, whether it be one or many. He understands it as a phenomenon mediating between the partners of the social situation, as a means of exchange in their exchange of signs.

Regarding the theory of observables and observations, it is important to answer preliminary questions. *First*, whether relations belong *in general* to the data of perception, and if so, whether, *second*, the order in which the *stare pro* obtains belongs to those data whose relations can be perceptually determined. The genial but unhappily erroneous idea of Hume and Mach denied that 'in general' and treated the manifold—simultaneously or successfully given—as something to which the principle, which Leibniz placed at the beginning of his monadology, is to be applied: "car le composé n'est autre chose qu'un amas ou aggregatum des simples" ('the complex is the result of addition [*ein Additive*], a summation of simples'). And only sense data are valid as simples. They are believed to be given and defined, in principle, with no reference to relations. Psychophysical research should be in a position to accomplish this task neatly. Now, the knowledge of the inadequacy of this assumption (more concretely the inadequacy of the Machian analysis of instants) belongs today to the common property and to the most fruitful possessions of psychology. Data having no reference to relations are simply not to be found. Even chickens and fish show through their behavior in aptly set-up experiments that, in principle, even their perceptual data accomplish and contain what one had wanted to deny to the human.[10] Concerning the second point, the Hering shadow experiment—explicitly discussed in my pictorial optics—shows very simply and clearly that and how a sense datum can undergo a change of determination through no more than a mere change of the order in which its *stare pro quo* proceeds. Summarily, it is true that all color data, which the (representing) painter prepares technically on his palette and then puts onto the picture surface, possess an 'image value' [*Bildwert*] for the one who considers it, a value that (not just according to the simpler rules governing relations of proximity, such as contrast and so forth) is determined by the *image or picture context as such*. It is therefore no exception, but rather the rule, that the data of perception are codetermined by that which they are perceived to be standing for. Normally, they contain relations of the kind with which we are concerned.

To make a long story short: if the linguist thinks he is indebted for his scientific knowledge of language to specific observations and protocol sentences in which theses appear concerning the sound phenomenon 'as' a representative, no epistemologist or logician may think, on the contrary, that this researcher is fundamentally mistaken about what can belong to the truly primary observational data and thereby to 'pure experience.' For no one's eye, or ear, has delivered up the data of 'pure experience.' What one called here and there the immediately given—that is, what was immediately evident as a fact and as such was perceived by the empirical researcher—does not exclude, but includes, relations. This has to be said to all element hunters and to all pointillists among the analyzers of perception.

I repeat that in our context my intention has not been to say anything regarding the final epistemological validation or even only regarding the concept of the 'immediately given.' Even the Kantian question, how much is to be ascribed to the 'senses' and how much to the 'understanding,' is not under discussion. But it is worth the trouble defending just this; the existence of something immediately given does not exclude a precise shift in the mode of apprehending; a shift, namely, of the same sort as when I stand as an observer before a picture and perceive at one time 'only' a canvas bearing spots of color and at another time perceive, on the contrary, a painting. In the relational complex, the data are grasped and 'interpreted' first one way and then another; but in each case there is a different relational whole. The phonetician defines the sound phenomena completely as a natural researcher, who values the axiom *ubi materia ibi geometria*; the phonologist and grammarian, however, define them as one who is inspired by the linguist's axiom of the sign nature of language. If the concrete speech situation is rich enough in *fundamenta* for relations and transparent enough for the observer, then the relations with which the speech researcher is concerned can be more-or-less exactly codetermined, partly by one observation, and partly in a series of them, just as is the case in every other inductive investigation.

The real concerns and doubts of linguistic observers who have given close thought to the reliability and extent of their protocol sentences are found elsewhere. We know that, as everywhere, only rather few characteristics of a concrete object can be grasped exactly enough all at once. We know that it is only through comparison that the invariants and covariants, with which linguistics is concerned, can be found. And the language researcher sees himself, wherever he works at the boundaries of his investigation, confronted with an individual theory enmeshed in a complex systematic context [*Systemgetragenheit*] that places the highest demands on his breadth of vision. In his observations what he *in vivo* has to take into consideration all at once is not comparable with what is accessible to the physicist under laboratory conditions and is to be paralleled most of all with biological observations and, of course, with forms of observations proper to other human sciences. Fortunately for him, a great part of what he establishes can be verified in language texts that have been fixed in writing, and that submit to repeated comparison. Then things become otherwise. In spite of this, the fullness of systematic relations—which, for example, de Saussure described in the best parts of his work (Chapters 4–6)—remains permanently the authentic, immanent difficulty of language research. That it is not an insurmountable difficulty is shown best by its success.

6. In a looser form, let us now add another pair of glosses on the axiom of the sign nature of language. Fundamental principles should, as one knows, not only define the right way but also guard against wrong paths and blind alleys. What does the axiom of language research guard against? Against symbol-blind matter-boundness [*Stoffentgleisung*] on the one

hand and against magical theories on the other. Take the case of an enlightened European who comes to an Indian tribe and discovers about an idol that is worshiped there that there is nothing to investigate other than that it is made completely of wood. A friend schooled in the methods of the human sciences may engage him in conversation about this by drawing (with chalk signs on a board) and asking what this and that 'are.' If the stubborn answer runs that it is chalk and nothing but chalk, even though the whole figure looks basically like this, I call this,

IDIOT

in basic agreement with Gomperz, a consistent matter-bound thinking. Compared with this, one is accustomed to characterize as manifestations of a magical mode of thought what the Indians and similar thinkers, at least in so far as we understand them, say about their idols and what they are accustomed to do with them. Indeed, it does not stand so terribly far in every respect from the thought of the radical apostle of enlightenment as one would presume at first sight; for also, every form of 'magical' thought, however it may function in individual cases, understands itself just as he does with the help of the axiom of the sign nature of the object functioning as a sign [*Zeichenhaftem*] and answers with causal considerations (in the widest sense of the word) at places where the word belongs by right to sematology or to a structural theory related to sematology. That is, I think, the most exact delineation of the magical spiritual attitude, so far as we understand it. It is an interesting and extremely important question of just what, from the domain of facts most pregnantly entitled *inner language form*, is revealed in the moments of such a magical spiritual attitude in the case of this or that given language (also the one that we speak). To be sure, that is something quite different from taking such a spiritual attitude right up into language theory itself. Besides, it seems to me that the weight of these characteristics in this or that human language—with regard to the nonmagical, which indeed is and can be just as little lacking where language was also the means of exchange in daily life outside of the magic circle—has been strongly overestimated. I will present in another place the arguments that I think I have found for this assertion.

To everything of a signlike character that exists in the world there belong in the nature of the case beings who take it to be and deal with it as a sign. Where the *concreta*, which fulfill the functions of signs, are produced or established [*hergerichtet*] by acting beings, where these *concreta* stand to those beings in the relation of a work to the creator or (merely to change the focus) in the relation of a deed to the doer—in those cases, one can call these beings sign givers. In the animal kingdom, there are signal givers and signal receivers in all those situations that we have delineated by means of the formula on page 70. That from that point human language was already seen to belong to the category of instruments—or to put it in Platonic terms, that it is an *organon*—means no more than to consider it in relation to those who deal with them and are their producers [*Täter*]. Language research, therefore, runs up against, in the axiom of the sign nature of language, the thought model of *homo faber*, or a maker and user of tools. We will keep this model in mind and step by step add to it new determinations derived from each new axiom.

NOTES

1. This is one of the results of a (still unpublished) study by Bruno Sonneck, "Sprachliche Untersuchungen zur Zeichentheorie," which is supported by J. Gonda, ΔΕΙΚΝΥΜΙ, Semantische Studie über den indogemannschen Wortel deik-(1929), as well as the pertinent article in the etymological dictionaries of Walde-Pokorny, Walde, Kluge, and Paul. However, in its results it does not depart essentially from the general positions reached by Gonda. It would appear to me to be essential to bring language theory into connection with etymological issues. As far as it is today possible, Mr. Sonneck may have accomplished this task in the circumscribed area.

2. Compare on this K. Bühler, *Die geistige Entwicklung des Kindes*, 1, ed. (1918), pp. 116ff.; 5 ed. (1929), pp. 224ff.; and the discussions concerning what distinguishes the signals of ants and bees from symbolic signs which are found in *Die Krise*, pp. 51ff.

3. William of Occam preferred to write *supponere* for this: "Occam uses *supponere pro aliquo*, as this, according to the evidence of Thurot, was customary from the year 1200, in the intransitive sense as equivalent to *stare pro aliquo*" (M. Baumgartner, *Ueberwegs Grundriss der Geschichte der Philosophie*, II[10], p. 602).

4. We do not write "in itself" but rather "for itself," that is, abstracting from the function of representing [*Vertretung*].

5. K. Bühler, "Phonetik und Phonologie," *Travaux du Cercle Linguistique de Prague* 4 (1931): 22–53.

6. The so-called externally unheard 'inner' speech does not contravene the rule. For also here, for the single person himself, there are given in perceptual fashion 'sounds' or a substitute for sounds in some form or other (acoustical, motoric, optical), therefore something that can be perceived; otherwise, there would not be a true speech event.

7. H. Gomperz, *Semasiologie* (n.d.), p. 278. Compare also the essay "Über einige philosophische Voraussetzungen der naturalistischen Kunst," *Beilage zur Allgemeinen Zeitung*, Nos. 160 and 161 of 14 and 15 July 1905.

8. Compare on this the section "Gemäldeoptik" in K. Bühler, *Die Erscheinungsweisen der Farben* (Jena, 1922).

9. *Travaux du Cercle de Prague* 1(1929), pp. 39–67.

10. Also, the analysis of observations in the structure of J. S. Mill's theory of induction and the theory of Stumpf were free from the error we are discussing. According to Mill, as well as according to Stumpf, relations can be 'observed'; in Mill's theory of observation, the extremely empiricist notion that even mathematics is based on experiences is explicitly bound up with the thesis we are discussing.

SUSANNE K. LANGER

What are the semiotically relevant philosophical foundations for the "grammar" of articulate forms? Langer attempts to answer this question by uncovering the ultimate syntactic and semantic bases for the distinction between symbolisms. In this endeavor her text parallels Peirce's especially. Langer's chief concern in the selection before us is to establish the "limits of articulation" and the legitimacy and proper place of a true "semantic" beyond the linguistic realm. This she does by establishing, beyond language, the syntactic and semantic conditions for understanding the "morphology of feeling," which appears in "presentational" forms. Her chief analytical category, which derives from a creative appropriation of Ludwig Wittgenstein's *Tractatus Logico-Philosophicus* and work in philosophical logic by Russell, Whitehead, and others, is the distinction between saying and showing. But whereas Wittgenstein concluded, in his *Tractatus* at least, with the claim that "what we cannot speak about we must pass over in silence," Langer goes on to detail how in art—verbal, plastic, musical, and so forth—we are able to produce a true symbol, a bearer of articulate content and meaning, with a "logical form," which is radically different from that of language, which is a "discursive" form.

It is through this "logical" opposition that Langer offers a challenge—similar to but differently motivated from Benveniste's, which should be read along with this selection—to all those who want to employ a linguistic model—appropriately generalized to be sure—to conceptualize works of art. Discursive forms, Langer points out, using arguments once again paralleling Benveniste's, are marked by linearity, individual and isolable signifying units, a syntax, and the possibility of translation. Presentational forms, however, are meant to be perceived as whole Gestalten. According to Langer, they are not composed of autonomous, relatively context-free signifying units. Their forms of combinations are predominantly either stylistically or perceptually conditioned, topics which are given a precise airing in Schapiro's essay. They are, as "showing things," beyond translatability, and their sense is inseparable from their embodiment in an articulate, perceptible form. Langer does not, in effect, pursue the great Saussurian analogy which has been used in the

Russian semiotics of "secondary modelling systems" which has looked for nonlinguistic analogues of properly linguistic units: phoneme, word, phrase, sentence, text, and so forth. She writes instead: "A work of art is a *single symbol*, not a system of significant elements which may be variously compounded. Its elements have no symbolic value in isolation. They take their expressive character from their functions in the perceptual whole" (*Mind: An Essay on Human Feeling*. Baltimore: The Johns Hopkins University Press, 1967, p. 84; my italics). Still, her concern is with a properly "semiotic" theory, since it focuses on the foundations of the theory of signs from within a highly differentiated philosophical matrix. Langer could also be looked upon as contributing to clarifying Peirce's distinction between icons and symbols.

Aesthetic forms for Langer grow out of the natural, intrinsic "pregnance" of perceptual forms, a theme dear to Thom. Langer derives some of her perceptual preconditions from a transformation of Gestalt psychology of perception and from her contention that perceptual forms are themselves "naturally significant," intrinsically metaphorical, and bearers of articulate, though immanent, meaning. The semantic character of perceptual forms, their possession of what Polanyi called "existential" or "physiognostic" meaning, is potentiated by the specifically constructed character of aesthetic forms in which the dynamics of affectivity and perception are differentiated and exploited. As Langer put it in her magnum opus dealing with aesthetics, *Feeling and Form* (New York: Scribner's, 1953): "What it [the work of art] does to us is to formulate our conceptions of feeling and our conceptions of visual, tactual, and audible reality together. It gives us *forms of imagination* and *forms of feeling*, inseparably; that is to say, it clarifies and organizes intuition itself" (397). In art, as a symbolic form, we experience a "tacit, personal, illuminating contact with symbols of feeling" (401).

Thus, rather than seeing art as derivative from a prior form of articulation and constructed according to its model—that is, after language—Langer sees art emerging out of the innate trajectories and possibilities of perception and then being raised to a higher power by the general procedures of symbolic transformation, whose internal powers contain the key to understanding human mentation, a theme continued in her trilogy, *Mind*. The "aesthetic," then, is defined by Langer in her own way in properly "semiotic" terms, independently of recourse to the "subjective" responses or "attitudes" of the perceiver.

Aesthetic forms in the presentational mode and linguistic forms in the discursive mode, then, are more dissimilar than similar, though both are the result of "articulation." Strictly speaking, there is no double articulation—of any significant sort and parallel to the linguistic realm—in artistic artifacts, a theme frequently touched upon by Lévi-Strauss (see the "Ouverture" to *The Raw and the Cooked*, "The Science of the Concrete," in *The Savage Mind*, and his "conversations" with Georges Charbonniers.) As she sees it, the elements out of which any art form is constructed have no antecedent systematic ordering or "coding," with relations of mutual opposition and complementarity such as we find in phonemic systems. "There is . . . no basic vocabulary of lines and colors, or elementary tonal structures, or poetic phrases, with conventional emotional meanings, from which complex expressive forms, i.e., works of art, can be composed by rules of manipulation" (*Mind* 90). Langer's position bears, in fact, remarkable similarities to that of Nelson Goodman, whose distinction between syntactically and semantically "dense" and "discrete" symbol systems and schemes Umberto Eco exploited very fruitfully in the section on "The Aesthetic Text as Invention" in his *A Theory of Semiotics*. For the sake of balance, however, I recommend looking at Galvano della Volpe's *Critique of Taste*, translated by Michael Caesar (New York: New Left Books, 1978), where a large set of analyses, based on Hjelmslev's "glossematics," are presented. Especially important is part III "Laocoon 1960," which takes up topics discussed at length in Lessing's famous book.

Langer's formulation and treatment of the issues leads us to reflect upon the unity of semiotics as a science that, with an integrated set of categories, can go beyond any one domain of sign-constituted objects to encompass them all. Thus, her reflections in the piece offered here can lead us to discuss not just substantial points of aesthetic theory in the semiotic key but to engage in methodological reflections upon the coherence of the semiotic project with an eye to a further determination of semiotics' self-consciousness.

In addition to the whole book from which this selection has been taken, see also Langer's *Feeling and Form* (New York: Scribner's, 1953), which contains Langer's mature aesthetic theory. For another approach to a semiotic theory of art, from within philosophy, see Nelson Goodman, *Languages of Art* (Indianapolis: Hackett Publishing Co., 1976; first published 1968). A comparison between their two aesthetic theories will be found in Robert E. Innis, "Art, Symbol, Consciousness," in *International Philosophical Quarterly* 17/4, 1977, 455–476. See also Samuel Bufford, "Langer Evaluated: Susanne Langer's Two Philosophies of Art," *The Journal of Aesthetics and Art Criticism*, Fall 1972, 9–20; reprinted in George Dickie and Richard J. Sclafani, *Aesthetics: A Critical Anthology* (New York: St. Martin's Press, 1977). We still need a comprehensive English language survey of the "semiotics" of art and aesthetic experience.

Discursive and Presentational Forms

SUSANNE K. LANGER

The logical theory on which this whole study of symbols is based is essentially that which was set forth by Wittgenstein, some twenty years ago, in his *Tractatus Logico-Philosophicus*:

"One name stands for one thing, and another for another thing, and they are connected together. And so the whole, like a living picture, presents the atomic fact. (4.0311)

"At the first glance the proposition—say as it stands printed on paper—does not seem to be a picture of the reality of which it treats. But neither does the musical score appear at first sight to be a picture of a musical piece; nor does our phonetic spelling (letters) seem to be a picture of our spoken language. . . . (4.015)

"In the fact that there is a general rule by which the musician is able to read the symphony out of the score, and that there is a rule by which one could reconstruct the symphony from the line on a phonograph record and from this again—by means of the first rule—construct the score, herein lies the internal similarity between the things which at first sight seem to be entirely different. And the rule is the law of projection which projects the symphony into the language of the musical score. It is the rule of translation of this language into the language of the gramophone record." (4.0141)

"Projection" is a good word, albeit a figurative one, for the process by which we draw purely *logical* analogies. Geometric projection is the best instance of a perfectly faithful representation which, without knowledge of some logical rule, appears to be a misrepresentation. A child looking at a map of the world in Mercator projection cannot help believing that Greenland is larger than Australia; he simply *finds* it larger. The projection employed is not the usual principle of copying which we use in all visual comparisons or translations, and his training in the usual rule makes him unable to "see" by the new one. It takes sophistication to "see" the relative sizes of Greenland and Australia on a Mercator map. Yet a mind educated to appreciate the projected image brings the eye's habit with it. After a while, we genuinely "see" the thing as we apprehend it.

Language, our most faithful and indispensable picture of human experience, of the world and its events, of thought and life and all the march of time, contains a law of projection of which philosophers are sometimes unaware, so that their reading of the presented "facts" is obvious and yet wrong, as a child's visual experience is obvious yet deceptive when his judgment is ensnared by the trick of the flattened map. The transformation which facts undergo when they are rendered as propositions is that the relations in them are turned into something like *objects*. Thus, "A killed B" tells of a *way* in which A and B were unfortunately combined; but our only means of expressing this way is to *name* it, and presto!—a new entity, "killing," seems to have added itself to the complex of A and B. The event which is "pictured" in the proposition undoubtedly involved a *succession* of acts by A and B, but not the succession which the proposition seems to exhibit—first A, then "killing," then B. Surely A and B were simultaneous with each other and with the killing. But words have a linear, discrete, successive order; they are strung one after another like beads on a rosary; beyond the very limited meanings of inflections, which can indeed be incorporated in the words themselves, we cannot talk in simultaneous bunches of names. We must name one thing and then another, and symbols that are not names must be stuck between or before or after, by convention. But these symbols, holding proud places in the chain of names, are apt to be mistaken for names, to the detriment of many a metaphysical theory. Lord Russell regrets that we cannot construct a language which would express all relations by analogous relations; then we would not be tempted to misconstrue language, as a person who knows the meaning of the Mercator map, but has not used one freely enough to "see" in its terms, misconstrues the relative sizes of its areas.

"Take, say, that lightning precedes thunder," he says. "To express this by a language closely reproducing the structure of the fact, we should have to say simply: 'lightning, thunder,' where the fact that the first word precedes the second means that what the first word means precedes what the second word means. But even if we adopted this method for temporal order, we should still need words for all other relations, because we could not without intolerable ambiguity symbolize them by the order of our words."[1]

It is a mistake, I think, to symbolize things by entities too much like themselves; to let words in temporal order represent things in temporal order. If relations such as temporal order are symbolized at all, let the symbols not be those same relations themselves. A structure cannot include as *part of a symbol* something that should properly be *part of the meaning*. But it is unfortunate that names and syntactical indicators look so much alike in language; that we cannot represent objects by words, and relations by pitch, loudness, or other characteristics of speech.[2]

As it is, however, all language has a form which requires us to string out our ideas even though their objects rest one within the other; as pieces of clothing that are actually worn one over the other have to be strung side by side on the clothesline. This property of verbal symbolism is known as *discursiveness*; by reason of it, only thoughts which can be arranged in this peculiar order can be spoken at all; any idea which does not lend itself to this "projection" is ineffable, incommunicable by means of words. That is why the laws of reasoning, our clearest formulation of exact expression, are sometimes known as the "laws of discursive thought."

There is no need of going further into the details of verbal symbolism and its poorer substitutes, hieroglyphs, the deaf-and-dumb language, Morse Code, or the highly developed drum-telegraphy of certain jungle tribes. The subject has been exhaustively treated by several able men, as the many quotations in this chapter indicate; I can only assent to their findings. The relation between word-structures and their meanings is, I believe, one of logical analogy, whereby, in Wittgenstein's phrase, "we make ourselves pictures of facts." This philosophy of language lends itself, indeed, to great technical development, such as Wittgenstein envisaged:

"In the language of everyday life it very often happens that the same word signifies in different ways—and therefore belongs to two different symbols—or that two words, which signify in different ways, are apparently applied in the same way in the proposition. (3.323)

"In order to avoid these errors, we must employ a symbolism which excludes them, by not applying the same sign in different symbols and by not applying signs in the same way which signify in different ways. A symbolism, that is to say, which obeys the rules of *logical* grammar—of logical syntax.

"(The logical symbolism of Frege and Russell is such a language, which, however, does still not exclude all errors.)" (3.325)[3]

Carnap's admirable book, *The Logical Syntax of Language*, carries out the philosophical program suggested by Wittgenstein. Here an actual, detailed technique is developed for determining the *capacity for expression* of any given linguistic system, a technique which predicts the limit of all combinations to be made in that system, shows the equivalence of certain forms and the differences among others which might be mistaken for equivalents, and exhibits the conventions to which any thought or experience must submit in order to become conveyable by the symbolism in question. The distinctions between scientific language and everyday speech, which most of us can feel rather than define, are clearly illumined by Carnap's analysis; and it is surprising to find how little of our ordinary communication measures up to the standard of "meaning" which a serious philosophy of language, and hence a logic of discursive thought, set before us.

In this truly remarkable work the somewhat diffuse apprehension of our intellectual age, that *symbolism* is the key to epistemology and "natural knowledge," finds precise and practical corroboration. The Kantian challenge: "What can I know?" is shown to be dependent on the prior question: "What can I ask?" And the answer, in Professor Carnap's formulation, is clear and direct. I can ask whatever language will express; I can know whatever experiment will answer. A proposition which could not, under any (perhaps ideal, impracticable) conditions, be verified or refuted, is a pseudo-proposition, it has no literal meaning. It does not belong to the framework of knowledge that we call logical conception; it is not true or false, but *unthinkable*, for it falls outside the order of symbolism.

Since an inordinate amount of our talk, and therefore (we hope) of our cerebration too, defies the canons of literal meaning, our philosophers of language—Russell, Wittgenstein, Carnap, and others of similar persuasions—are faced with the new question: What is the true function of those verbal combinations and other pseudo-symbolic structures that have no real significance, but are freely used as though they meant something?

According to our logicians, those structures are to be treated as "expressions" in a different sense, namely as "expressions" of emotions, feelings, desires. They are not symbols for thought, but symptoms of the inner life, like tears and laughter, crooning, or profanity.

"Many linguistic utterances," says Carnap, "are analogous to laughing in that they have only an expressive function, no representative function. Examples of this are cries like 'Oh, Oh,' or, on a higher level, lyrical verses. The aim of a lyrical poem in which occur the words 'sunshine' and 'clouds,' is not to inform us of certain meteorological facts, but to express certain feelings of the poet and to excite similar feelings in us. . . . Metaphysical propositions—like lyrical verses—have only an expressive function, but no representative function. Metaphysical propositions are neither true nor false, because they assert nothing. . . . But they are, like laughing, lyrics and music, expressive. They express not so much temporary feelings as permanent emotional and volitional dispositions."[4]

Lord Russell holds a very similar view of other people's metaphysics:

"I do not deny," he says, "the importance or value, within its own sphere, of the kind of philosophy which is inspired by ethical notions. The ethical work of Spinoza, for instance, appears to me of the very highest significance, but what is valuable in such a work is not any metaphysical theory as to the nature of the world to which it may give rise, nor indeed anything that can be proved or disproved by argument. What is valuable is the indication of some new way of feeling toward life and the world, some way of feeling by which our own existence can acquire more of the characteristics which we must deeply desire."[5]

And Wittgenstein:

"Most propositions and questions, that have been written about philosophical matters, are not false, but senseless. We cannot, therefore, answer questions of this kind at all, but only state their senselessness. Most questions and propositions of the philosophers result from the fact that we do not understand the logic of our language. (4.003)"

"A proposition presents the existence and non-existence of atomic facts. (4.1)

"The totality of true propositions is the total of natural science (or the totality of the natural sciences). (4.11)

"Everything that can be thought at all can be thought clearly. Everything that can be said can be said clearly." (4.116)[6]

In their criticism of metaphysical propositions, namely that such propositions are usually pseudo-answers to pseudo-questions, these logicians have my full assent; problems of "First Cause" and "Unity" and "Substance," and all the other time-honored topics, are insoluble, because they arise from the fact that we attribute to the world what really belongs to the "logical projection" in which we conceive it, and by misplacing our questions we jeopardize our answers. This source of bafflement has been uncovered by the philosophers of our day, through their interest in the functions and nature of symbolism. The discovery marks a great intellectual advance. But it does not condemn philosophical inquiry as such; it merely requires *every philosophical problem to be recast*, to be conceived in a different form. Many issues that seemed to concern the *sources* of knowledge, for instance, now appear to turn partly or wholly on the *forms* of knowledge, or even the forms of expression, of symbolism. The center of philosophical interest has shifted once more, as it has shifted several times in the past. That does not mean, however, that rational people should now renounce metaphysics. The recognition of the intimate relation between symbolism and experience, on which our whole criticism of traditional problems is based, is itself a metaphysical insight. For metaphysics is, like every philosophical pursuit, a study of *meanings*. From it spring the special sciences, which can develop their techniques and verify their propositions one by one, *as soon as their initial concepts are clear enough to allow systematic handling*, i.e. as soon as the philosophical work behind them is at least tentatively accomplished.[7] Metaphysics is not itself a science with fixed presuppositions, but progresses from problem to problem rather than from premise to consequence. To suppose that we have outgrown it is to suppose that all "the sciences" are finally established, that human language is complete, or at least soon to be completed, and additional facts are all we lack of the greatest knowledge ever possible to man; and though this knowledge may be small, it is all that we shall ever have.

This is, essentially, the attitude of those logicians who have investigated the limits of language. Nothing that is not "language" in the sense of their technical definition can possess the character of symbolic expressiveness (though it may be "expressive" in the symptomatic way). Consequently nothing that cannot be "projected" in discursive form is accessible to the human mind at all, and any attempt to understand anything but demonstrable fact is bootless ambition. The knowable is a clearly defined field, governed by the requirement of discursive projectability. Outside this domain is the inexpressible realm of feeling, of formless desires and satisfactions, immediate experience, forever incognito and incommunicado. A philosopher who looks in that direction is, or should be, a mystic; from the ineffable sphere nothing but nonsense can be conveyed, since language, our only possible semantic, will not clothe experiences that elude the discursive form.

But intelligence is a slippery customer; if one door is closed to it, it finds, or even breaks, another entrance to the world. If one symbolism is inadequate, it seizes another; there is no eternal decree over its means and methods. So I will go with the logisticians and linguists as far as they like, but do not promise to go no further. For there is an unexplored possibility of genuine semantic beyond the limits of discursive language.

This logical "beyond," which Wittgenstein calls the "unspeakable," both Russell and Carnap regard as the sphere of subjective experience, emotion, feeling, and wish, from which only *symptoms* come to us in the form of metaphysical and artistic fancies. The study of such products they relegate to psychology, not semantics. And here is the point of my radical divergence from them. Where Carnap speaks of "cries like 'Oh, Oh,' or, on a higher level, lyrical verses," I can see only a complete failure to apprehend a fundamental distinction. Why should we cry our feelings at such high levels that anyone would think we were *talking*?[8] Clearly, poetry means more than a cry; it has reason for being articulate; and metaphysics is more than the croon with which we might cuddle up to the world in a comfortable attitude. We are dealing with symbolisms here, and what they express is often highly intellectual. Only, the form and function of such symbolisms are not those investigated by logicians, under the heading of "language." The field of semantics is wider than that of language, as certain philosophers—Schopenhauer, Cassirer, Delacroix, Dewey, Whitehead, and some others—have discovered; but it is blocked for us by the two fundamental tenets of current epistemology, which we have just discussed.

These two basic assumptions go hand in hand: (1) That *language*[9] *is the only means of articulating thought*, and (2) That *everything which is not speakable thought, is feeling*. They are linked together because all genuine thinking *is* symbolic, and the limits of the expressive medium are, therefore, really the limits of our conceptual powers. Beyond these we can have only blind feeling, which records nothing and conveys nothing, but has to be discharged in action or self-expression, in deeds or cries or other impulsive demonstrations.

But if we consider how difficult it is to construct a meaningful language that shall meet neo-positivistic standards, it is quite incredible that people should ever *say* anything at all, or understand each other's propositions. At best, human thought is but a tiny, grammar-bound island, in the midst of a sea of feeling expressed by "Oh-oh" and sheer babble. The island has a periphery, perhaps, of mud—factual and hypothetical concepts broken down by the emotional tides into the "material mode," a mixture of meaning and nonsense. Most of us live the better part of our lives on this mudflat; but in artistic moods we take to the deep, where we flounder about with symptomatic cries that sound like propositions about life and death, good and evil, substance, beauty, and other nonexistent topics.

So long as we regard only scientific and "material" (semi-scientific) thought as really cognitive of the world, this peculiar picture of mental life must stand. And *so long as we admit only discursive symbolism as a bearer of ideas, "thought" in this restricted sense must be regarded as our only intellectual activity*. It begins and ends with language; without the elements, at least, of scientific grammar, conception must be impossible.

A theory which implies such peculiar consequences is itself a suspicious character. But the error which it harbors is not in its reasoning. It is in the very premise from which the doctrine proceeds, namely that all articulate symbolism is discursive. As Lord Russell, with his usual precision and directness, has stated the case, "it is clear that anything that can be said in an inflected language can be said in an uninflected language; therefore, anything that can be said in language can be said by means of a temporal series of uninflected words. This places a limitation upon what can be expressed in words. It may well be that there are facts which do not lend themselves to this very simple schema; if so, they cannot be expressed in language. Our confidence in language is due to the fact that it . . . shares the structure of the physical world, and therefore can express that structure. But if there be a world which is not physical, or not in space-time, it may have a structure which we can never hope to express or to know. . . . Perhaps that is why we know so much physics and so little of anything else." [10]

Now, I do not believe that "there is a world which is not physical, or not in space-time," but I do believe that in this physical, space-time world of our experience there are things which do not fit the grammatical scheme of expression. But they are not necessarily blind, inconceivable, mystical affairs; they are simply matters which require to be conceived through some symbolistic schema other than discursive language. And to demonstrate the possibility of such a non-discursive pattern one needs only to review the logical requirements for any symbolic structure whatever. Language is by no means our only articulate product.

Our merest sense-experience is a process of *formulation*. The world that actually meets our senses is not a world of "things," about which we are invited to discover facts as soon as we have codified the necessary logical language to do so; the world of pure sensation is so complex, so fluid and full, that sheer sensitivity to stimuli would only encounter what William James has called (in characteristic phrase) "a blooming, buzzing confusion." Out of this bedlam our sense-organs must select certain predominant forms, if they are to make report of *things* and not of mere dissolving sensa. The eye and the ear must have their logic—their "categories of understanding," if you like the Kantian idiom, or their "primary imagination," in Coleridge's version of the same concept.[11] An object is not a datum, but a form construed by the sensitive and intelligent organ, a form which is at once an experienced individual thing and a symbol for the concept of it, for *this sort of thing*.

A tendency to organize the sensory field into groups and patterns of sense-data, to perceive forms rather than a flux of light-impressions, seems to be inherent in our receptor apparatus just as much as in the higher nervous centers with which we do arithmetic and logic. But this unconscious appreciation of forms is the primitive root of all abstraction, which in turn is the keynote of rationality; so it appears that the conditions for rationality lie deep in our pure animal experience—in our power of perceiving, in the elementary functions of our eyes and ears and fingers. Mental life begins with our mere physiological constitution. A little reflection shows us that, since no experience occurs more than once, so-called "repeated" experiences are really *analogous* occurrences, all fitting a form that was abstracted on the first occasion. *Familiarity* is nothing but the quality of fitting very neatly into the form of a previous experience. I believe our ingrained habit of hypostatizing impressions, of seeing *things* and not sense-data, rests on the fact that we promptly and unconsciously abstract a form from each sensory experience, and use this form to *conceive* the experience as a whole, as a "thing."

No matter what heights the human mind may attain, it can work only with the organs it has and the functions peculiar to them. Eyes that did not see forms could never furnish it with *images*; ears that did not hear articulated sounds could never open it to *words*. Sense-data, in brief, would be useless to a mind whose activity is "through and through a symbolic process," were they not *par excellence* receptacles of meaning. But meaning, as previous considerations have shown, accrues essentially to forms. Unless the *Gestalt*-psychologists are right in their belief that *Gestaltung* is of the very nature of perception, I do not know how the hiatus between perception and conception, sense-organ and mind-organ, chaotic stimulus and logical response, is ever to be closed and welded. A mind that works primarily with meanings must have organs that supply it primarily with forms.

The nervous system is the organ of the mind; its center is the brain, its extremities the sense-organs; and any characteristic function it may possess must govern the work of all its parts. In other words, the activity of our senses is "mental" not only when it reaches the brain, but in its very inception, whenever the alien world outside impinges on the furthest and smallest receptor. All sensitivity bears the stamp for mentality. "Seeing," for instance, is not a passive process, by which meaningless impressions are stored up for the use of an organizing mind, which construes forms out of these amorphous data to suit its own purposes. "Seeing" is itself a process of formulation; our understanding of the visible world begins in the eye.[12]

This psychological insight, which we owe to the school of Wertheimer, Köhler, and Koffka, has far-reaching philosophical consequences, if we take it seriously; for it carries rationality into processes that are usually deemed pre-rational, and points to the existence of forms, i.e. of *possible symbolic material*, at a level where symbolic activity has certainly never been looked for by any epistemologist. The eye and the ear make their own abstractions, and consequently dictate their own peculiar forms of conception. But these forms are derived from exactly the same world that furnished the totally different forms known to physics. There is, in fact, no such thing as *the* form of the "real" world; physics is one pattern which may be found in it, and "appearance," or the pattern of *things* with their qualities and characters, is another. One construction may indeed preclude the other; but to maintain that the consistency and universality of the one brands the other as *false* is a mistake. The fact that physical analysis does not rest in a final establishment of irreducible "qualities" does not refute the belief that there are red, blue, and green things, wet or oily or dry substances, fragrant flowers, and shiny surfaces in the real world. These concepts of the "material mode" are not approximations to "physical" notions at all. Physical concepts owe their origin and development to the application of *mathematics* to the world of "things," and mathematics never—even in the beginning—dealt with qualities of objects. It measured their proportions, but never treated its concepts—triangularity, circularity, etc.—as qualities of which *so-and-so much* could become an ingredient of certain objects. Even though an elliptical race-track may approximate a circle, it is not to be improved by the addition of more circularity. On the other hand, wine which is not sweet enough requires more sweetening, paint which is not bright enough is given an ingredient of more white or more color. The world of physics is essentially the real world construed by mathematical abstractions, and the world of sense is the real world construed by the abstractions which the sense-organs immediately furnish. To suppose that the "material mode" is a primitive and groping attempt at physical conception is a fatal error in epistemology, because it cuts off all interest in the developments of which sensuous conception is capable, and the intellectual uses to which it might be put.

These intellectual uses lie in a field which usually harbors a slough of despond for the philosopher, who ventures into it because he is too honest to ignore it, though really he knows no path around its pitfalls. It is the field of "intuition," "deeper meaning," "artistic truth," "insight," and so forth. A dangerous-looking sector, indeed, for the advance of a rational spirit! To date, I think, every serious epistemology that has regarded mental life as greater than discursive reason, and has made concessions to "insight" or "intuition," has just so far capitulated to *unreason*, to mysticism and irrationalism. Every excursion beyond propositional thought has dispensed with thought altogether, and postulated some inmost soul of pure feeling in direct contact with a Reality unsymbolized, unfocused, and incommunicable (with the notable exception of the theory set forth by L. A. Reid in the last chapter of his *Knowledge and Truth*, which admits the facts of non-propositional conception in a way that invites rather than precludes logical analysis).

The abstractions made by the ear and the eye—the forms of direct perception—are our most primitive instruments of intelligence. They are genuine symbolic materials, media of understanding, by whose office we apprehend a world of *things*, and of events that are the histories of things. To furnish such conceptions is their prime mission. Our sense-organs make their habitual, unconscious abstractions, in the interest of this "*reifying*" function that underlies ordinary recognition of objects, knowledge of signals, words, tunes, places, and the possibility of classifying such things in the outer world according to their kind. We recognize the elements of this sensuous analysis in all sorts of combination; we can use them imaginatively, to conceive prospective changes in familiar scenes.

Visual forms—lines, colors, proportions, etc.—are just as capable of *articulation*, i.e. of complex combination, as words. But the laws that govern this sort of articulation are altogether different from the laws of syntax that govern language. The most radical difference is that *visual forms are not discursive*. They do not present their constituents successively, but simultaneously, so the relations determining a visual structure are grasped in one act of vision. Their complexity, consequently, is not limited, as the complexity of discourse is limited, by what the mind can retain from the beginning of an apperceptive act to the end of it. Of course such a restriction on discourse sets bounds to the complexity of speakable ideas. An idea that contains too many minute yet closely related parts, too many relations within relations, cannot be "projected" into discursive form; it is too subtle for speech. A language-bound theory of mind, therefore, rules it out of the domain of understanding and the sphere of knowledge.

But the symbolism furnished by our purely sensory appreciation of forms is a *non-discursive symbolism*, peculiarly well suited to the expression of ideas that defy linguistic "projection." Its primary function, that of conceptualizing the flux of sensations, and giving us concrete *things* in place of kaleidoscopic colors or noises, is itself an office that no language-born thought can replace. The understanding of space which we owe to sight and touch could never be developed, in all its detail and definiteness, by a discursive knowledge of geometry. Nature speaks to us, first of all, through our senses; the forms and qualities we distinguish, remember, imagine, or recognize are symbols of entities which exceed and outlive our momentary experience. Moreover, the same symbols—qualities, lines, rhythms—may occur in innumerable presentations; they are abstractable and combinatory. It is quite natural, therefore, that philosophers who have recognized the symbolical character of so-called "sense-data," especially in their highly developed uses, in science and art, often speak of a "language" of the senses, a "language" of musical tones, of colors, and so forth.

Yet this manner of speaking is very deceptive. Language is a special mode of expression, and not every sort of semantic can be brought under this rubric; by generalizing from linguistic symbolism to symbolism as such, we are easily led to misconceive all other types, and overlook their most interesting features. Perhaps it were well to consider, here, the salient characteristics of true language, or discourse.

In the first place, *every language has a vocabulary and a syntax*. Its elements are words with fixed meanings. Out of these one can construct, according to the rules of the syntax, composite symbols with resultant new meanings.

Secondly, in a language, some words are equivalent to whole combinations of other words, so that most meanings can be expressed in several different ways. This makes it possible *to define the meanings of the ultimate single words*, i.e., to construct a dictionary.

Thirdly, there may be alternative words for the same meaning. When two people systematically use different words for almost everything, they are said to speak different languages. But the two languages are roughly equivalent; with a little artifice, an occasional substitution of a phrase for a single word, etc., the propositions enunciated by one person, in his system, may be *translated* into the conventional system of the other.

Now consider the most familiar sort of non-discursive symbol, a picture. Like language, it is composed of elements that represent various respective constituents in the object; but these elements are not units with independent meanings. The areas of light and shade that constitute a portrait, a photograph for instance, have no significance by themselves. In isolation we would consider them simply blotches. Yet they are faithful representatives of visual elements composing the visual object. However, they do not represent, item for item, those elements which have *names*; there is not one blotch for the nose, one for the mouth, etc.; their shapes, in quite indescribable combinations, convey a total picture in which nameable features may be pointed out. The gradations of light and shade cannot be enumerated. They cannot be correlated, one by one, with parts or characteristics by means of which we might *describe* the person who posed for the portrait. The "elements" that the camera represents are not the "elements" that language represents. They are a thousand times more numerous. For this reason the correspondence between a word-picture and a visible object can never be as close as that between the object and its photograph. Given all at once to the intelligent eye, an incredible wealth and detail of information is conveyed by the portrait, where we do not have to stop to construe verbal meanings. That is why we use a photograph rather than a description on a passport or in the Rogues' Gallery.

Clearly, a symbolism with so many elements, such myriad relationships, cannot be broken up into basic units. It is impossible to find the smallest independent symbol, and recognize its identity when the same unit is met in other contexts. Photography, therefore, *has no vocabulary*. The same is obviously true of painting, drawing, etc. There is, of course, a technique of picturing objects, but the law governing this technique cannot properly be called a "syntax," since there are no items that might be called, metaphorically, the "words" of portraiture.

Since we have no words, there can be no dictionary of meanings for lines, shadings, or other elements of pictorial technique. We may well pick out some line, say a certain curve, in a picture, which serves to represent one nameable item; but in another place the same curve would have an entirely different meaning. It has no fixed meaning apart from its context. Also, there is no complex of other elements that is equivalent to it at all times, as "2 + 2" is equivalent to "4." Non-discursive symbols cannot be defined in terms of others, as discursive symbols can.

If there can be no defining dictionary, of course we have no translating dictionary, either. There are different media of graphic representation, but their respective elements cannot be brought into one-to-one correlation with each other, as in languages: *"chien"* = *"dog,"* *"moi"* = *"me,"* etc. There is no standard key for translating sculpture into painting, or drawing into ink-wash, because their equivalence rests on their common *total reference*, not on bit-for-bit equivalences of parts such as underlie a literal translation.

Furthermore, verbal symbolism, unlike the non-discursive kinds, has primarily a *general* reference. Only convention can assign a proper name—and then there is no way of preventing some other convention from assigning the same proper name to a different individual. We may name a child as oddly as we will, yet we cannot guarantee that no one else will ever bear that designation. A description may fit a scene ever so closely, but it takes some known proper name to refer it without possible doubt to one and only one place. Where the names of persons and places are withheld, we can never *prove* that a discourse refers—not merely applies—to a certain historic occasion. In the non-discursive mode that speaks directly to sense, however, there is no intrinsic generality. It is first and foremost a direct *presentation* of an individual object. A picture has to be schematized if it is to be capable of various meanings. In itself it represents just one object—real or imaginary, but still a unique object. The definition of a triangle fits triangles in general, but a drawing always presents a triangle of some specific kind and size. We have to abstract from the conveyed meaning in order to conceive triangularity in general. Without the help of words this generalization, if possible at all, is certainly incommunicable.

It appears, then, that although the different media of non-verbal representation are often referred to as distinct "languages," this is really a loose terminology. Language in the strict sense is essentially discursive; it has permanent units of meaning which are combinable into larger units; it has fixed equivalences that make definition and translation possible; its connotations are general, so that it requires non-verbal acts, like pointing, looking, or emphatic voice-inflections, to assign specific denotations to its terms. In all these salient characters it differs from wordless symbolism, which is non-discursive and untranslatable, does not allow of definitions within its own system, and cannot directly convey generalities. The meanings given through language are successively understood, and gathered into a whole by the process called discourse; the meanings of all other symbolic elements that compose a larger, articulate symbol are understood only through the meaning of the whole, through their relations within the total structure. Their very functioning as symbols depends on the fact that they are involved in a simultaneous, integral presentation. This kind of semantic may be called "presentational symbolism," to characterize its essential distinction from discursive symbolism, or "language" proper.[13]

The recognition of presentational symbolism as a normal and prevalent vehicle of meaning widens our conception of rationality far beyond the traditional boundaries, yet never breaks faith with logic in the strictest sense. Wherever a symbol operates, there is a meaning; and conversely, different classes of experience—say, reason, intuition, appreciation—correspond to different types of symbolic mediation. No symbol is exempt from the office of logical formulation, of *conceptualizing* what it conveys; however simple its import, or however great, this import is a *meaning*, and therefore an element for understanding. Such reflection invites one to tackle anew, and with entirely different expectations, the whole problem of the limits of reason, the much-disputed life of feeling, and the great controversial topics of fact and truth, knowledge and wisdom, science and art. It brings within the compass of reason much that has been traditionally relegated to "emotion," or to that crepuscular depth of the mind where "intuitions" are supposed to be born, without any midwifery of symbols, without due process of thought, to fill the gaps in the edifice of discursive, or "rational," judgment.

The symbolic materials given to our senses, the *Gestalten* or fundamental perceptual forms which invite us to construe the pandemonium of sheer impression into a world of things and occasions, belong to the "presentational" order. They furnish the elementary abstractions in terms of which ordinary sense-experience is understood.[14] This kind of understanding is directly reflected in the pattern of *physical reaction*, impulse and instinct. May not the order of perceptual forms, then, be a possible principle for symbolization, and hence the conception, expression, and apprehension, of impulsive, instinctive, and sentient life? May not a non-discursive symbolism of light and color, or of tone, be formulative of that life? And is it not possible that the sort of "intuitive" knowledge which Bergson extols above all rational knowledge because it is supposedly not mediated by any formulating (and hence deforming) symbol[15] is itself perfectly rational, but not to be conceived through language—a product of that presentational symbolism which the mind reads in a flash, and preserves in a disposition or an attitude?

This hypothesis, though unfamiliar and therefore somewhat difficult, seems to me well worth exploring. For, quite apart from all questions of the authenticity of intuitive, inherited, or inspired knowledge, about which I do not wish to cavil, the very idea of a *non-rational source* of any knowledge vitiates the concept of mind as an organ of understanding. "The power of reason is simply the power of the whole mind at its fullest stretch and compass," said Professor Creighton, in an essay that sought to stem the great wave of irrationalism and emotionalism following the World War.[16] This assumption appears to me to be a basic one in any study of mentality. Rationality is the essence of mind, and symbolic transformation its elementary process. It is a fundamental error, therefore, to recognize it only in the phenomenon of systematic, explicit reasoning. That is a mature and precarious product.

Rationality, however, is embodied in every mental act, not only when the mind is "at its fullest stretch and compass." It permeates the peripheral activities of the human nervous system, just as truly as the cortical functions.

"The facts of perception and memory maintain themselves only in so far as they are mediated, and thus given significance beyond their mere isolated existence. . . . What falls in any way within experience partakes of the rational form of the mind. As mental content, any part of experience is something more than a particular impression having only the attributes of existence. As already baptized into the life of the mind, it partakes of its logical nature and moves on the plane of universality. . . .

"No matter how strongly the unity and integrity of the mind is asserted, this unity is nothing more than verbal if the mind is not in principle the expression of reason. For it can be shown that all attempts to render comprehensible the unity of the mental life in terms of an alogical principle fail to attain their goal." [17]

The title of Professor Creighton's trenchant little article is "Reason and Feeling." Its central thesis is that if there is something in our mental life besides "reason," by which he means, of course, discursive thinking, then it cannot be an alogical factor, but must be in essence cognitive, too; and since the only alternative to this reason is feeling (the author does not question that axiom of epistemology), feeling itself must somehow participate in knowledge and understanding.

All this may be granted. The position is well taken. But the most crucial *problem* is barely broached: this problem is epitomized in the word "somehow." *Just how* can feelings be conceived as possible ingredients of rationality? We are not told, but we are given a generous hint, which in the light of a broader theory of symbolism points to explanation.

"In the development of mind," he says, "feeling does not remain a static element, constant in form and content at all levels, but . . . is transformed and disciplined through its interplay with other aspects of experience. . . . Indeed, the character of the feeling in any experience may be taken as an index of the mind's grasp of its object; at the lower levels of experience, where the mind is only partially or superficially involved, feeling appears as something isolated and opaque, as the passive accompaniment of mere bodily sensations. . . . In the higher experiences, the feelings assume an entirely different character, just as do the sensations and the other contents of mind." [18]

The significant observation voiced in this passage is that *feelings have definite forms, which become progressively articulated.* Their development is effected through their "interplay with the other aspects of experience"; but the nature of that interplay is not specified. Yet it is here, I think, that cogency for the whole thesis must be sought. *What* character of feeling is "an index of the mind's grasp of its object," and by what tokens is it so? If feeling has articulate forms, what are they like? For what these are *like* determines by what symbolism we might understand them. Everybody knows that language is a very poor medium for expressing our emotional nature. It merely names certain vaguely and crudely conceived states, but fails miserably in any attempt to convey the ever-moving patterns, the ambivalences and intricacies of inner experience, the interplay of feelings with thoughts and impressions, memories and echoes of memories, transient fantasy, or its mere runic traces, all turned into nameless, emotional stuff. If we say that we understand someone else's feeling in a certain matter, we mean that we understand why he should be sad or happy, excited or indifferent, in a general way; that we can see due cause for his attitude. We do not mean that we have insight into the actual flow and balance of his feelings, into that "character" which "may be taken as an index of the mind's grasp of its object." Language is quite inadequate to articulate such a conception. Probably we would not impart our actual, inmost feelings even if they could be spoken. We rarely speak in detail of entirely personal things.

There is, however, a kind of symbolism peculiarly adapted to the explication of "unspeakable" things, though it lacks the cardinal virtue of language, which is denotation. The most highly developed type of such purely connotational semantic is music. We are not talking nonsense when we say that a certain musical progression is significant, or that a given phrase lacks meaning, or a player's rendering fails to convey the import of a passage. Yet such statements make sense only to people with a natural understanding of the medium, whom we describe, therefore, as "musical." Musicality is often regarded as an essentially unintellectual, even a biologically sportive trait. Perhaps that is why musicians, who know that it is the prime source of their mental life and the medium of their clearest insight into humanity, so often feel called upon to despise the more obvious forms of understanding, that claim practical virtues under the names of reason, logic, etc. But in fact, musical understanding is not hampered by the possession of an active intellect, nor even by that love of pure reason which is known as rationalism or intellectualism; and *vice versa*, common-sense and scientific acumen need not defend themselves against any "emotionalism" that is supposed to be inherent in a respect for music. Speech and music have essentially different functions, despite their oft-remarked union in song. Their original relationship lies much deeper than any such union (of which more will be said in a subsequent chapter), and can be seen only when their respective natures are understood.

The problem of meaning deepens at every turn. The longer we delve into its difficulties, the more complex it appears. But in a central philosophical concept, this is a sign of health. Each question answered leads to another which previously could not be even entertained: the logic of symbolism, the possible types of representation, the fields proper to them, the actual functions of symbols according to their nature, their relationships to each other, and finally our main theme, their integration in human mentality.

Of course it is not possible to study every known phenomenon in the realm of symbolism. But neither is this necessary even in an intimate study. The logical structures underlying all semantic functions, which I have discussed in this chapter, suggest a general principle of division. Signs are logically distinct from symbols; discursive and presentational patterns show a formal difference. There are further natural divisions due to various ways of *using* symbols, no less important than the logical distinctions. Altogether, we may group meaning-situations around certain outstanding types, and make these several types the subjects of individual studies. Language, ritual, myth, and music, representing four respective modes, may serve as central topics for the study of actual symbolisms; and I trust that further problems of significance in art, in science or mathematics, in behavior or in fantasy and dream, may receive some light by analogy, and by that most powerful human gift, the adaptation of ideas.

NOTES

1. *Philosophy*, p. 264.

2. In the same chapter from which I have just quoted, Lord Russell attributes the power of language to represent *events* to the fact that, like events, it is a temporal series. I cannot agree with him in this matter. It is by virtue of *names for relations* that we can depict dynamic relations. We do not mention past events earlier in a sentence than present ones, but subject temporal order to the same "projection" as, for instance, attribution or classification; temporal order is usually rendered by the syntactical (nontemporal) device of *tense*.

3. *Tractatus*.

4. *Philosophy and Logical Syntax*, p. 28.

5. "Scientific Method in Philosophy," in *Mysticism and Logic* (1918), p. 109.

6. Op. cit.

7. I have presented a fuller discussion of philosophy as the "mother of sciences" in *The Practice of Philosophy* (1930), ch. ii.

8. Cf. Urban, *Language and Reality*, p. 164.

9. Including, of course, its refinements in mathematical and scientific symbolisms, and its approximations by gesture, hieroglyphics, or graphs.

10. *Philosophy*, p. 265.

11. An excellent discussion of Coleridge's philosophy may be found in D. G. James, *Skepticism and Poetry* (1937), a book well worth reading in connection with this chapter.

12. For a general account of the *Gestalt*-theory, see Wolfgang Köhler, *Gestalt Psychology* (1929), from which the following relevant passage is taken:

"It is precisely the original organization and segregation of circumscribed wholes which make it possible for the sensory world to appear so utterly imbued with meaning to the adult because, in its gradual entry into the sensory field, meaning follows the lines drawn by natural organization. It usually enters into segregated wholes. . . .

"Where 'form' *exists* originally, it acquires a meaning very easily. But here a whole with its form is given first and then a meaning 'creeps into it.' That meaning automatically produces a form where beforehand there is none, has not been shown experimentally in a single case, as far as I know" (p. 208).

See also Max Wertheimer, *Drei Abhandlungen zur Gestalttheorie* (1925), and Kurt Koffka, *Principles of Gestalt Psychology* (1935).

13. It is relevant here to note that "picture language," which uses *separate pictures in place of words*, is a discursive symbolism, though each "word" is a presentational symbol; and that all codes, e.g., the conventional gestures of deaf-mutes or the drum communications of African tribes, are discursive systems.

14. Kant thought that the *principles* of such formulation were supplied by a faculty of the mind, which he called *Verstand*; but his somewhat dogmatic delimitation of the field of knowledge open to *Verstand*, and the fact that he regarded the mind-engendered forms as *constitutive* of experience rather than *interpre-*

tative (as principles must be), prevented logicians from taking serious note of such forms as possible machinery of reason. They abode by the forms of *Vernunft*, which are, roughly speaking, the forms of discourse. Kant himself exalted *Vernunft* as the special gift and glory of man. When an epistemology of medium and meaning began to crowd out the older epistemology of percept and concept, his *Verstandesformen*, in their role of *conceptual ingredients* of phenomena, were lumped with his metaphysical doctrines, and eclipsed by "metalogical" interests.

15. See Henri Bergson, *La pensée et le mouvement* (1934), esp. essays ii ("De la position des problèmes") and iv ("L'intuition philosophique"): also his *Essai sur les données immédiates de la conscience* (1889), and *Introduction to Metaphysics* (1912).

16. J. E. Creighton, "Reason and Feeling," *Philosophical Review*, XXX (1921), 5: 465−481. See p. 469.

17. Ibid., pp. 470−472.

18. Ibid., pp. 478−479.

CLAUDE LÉVI-STRAUSS

Lévi-Strauss has made one of the main goals of his life's work to fuse the key points of the Saussurian structural linguistic framework into an analytical instrument and model for anthropological analysis. Following Mauss's statement that "sociology would certainly have progressed much further if it had everywhere followed the lead of the linguists," Lévi-Strauss has gone on to develop the grand structural analogy for the anthropological understanding of kinship, myth, and the structure of the "savage mind." In the present text we have one of his chief programmatic and methodologically oriented essays wherein his research program—which for the sake of detail must be supplemented from other writings—is laid out with especial clarity. Anthropology is to follow structural linguistics in shifting from the study of conscious linguistic phenomena to their unconscious infrastructure, from focusing on terms to focusing on relations, and in turning to the organizing system of these relations and their general laws. These themes permeate the mature and wide-ranging work of Lévi-Strauss.

The nature of this transformation of structural linguistics into an analytical instrument is illustrated, in the present text, by the example of kinship structures, though the same type of considerations, so argues Lévi-Strauss, would illuminate the underlying logic of mythological structures and of the "savage mind." Lévi-Strauss's key claim in this essay is that "although they belong to *another order of reality*, kinship phenomena are *of the same type* as linguistic phenomena." His guiding question, which has been the *leitmotiv* of all his subsequent work, is: "Can the anthropologist, using a method analogous *in form* (if not in content) to the method used in structural linguistics, achieve the same kind of progress in his own science as that which has taken place in linguistics?" This is the question the reader will have to put to Lévi-Strauss himself in light of his own criteria for a "truly scientific analysis" that must be "real, simplifying, and explanatory." While admitting the profound differences between the phonemic chart of a language and that of kinship terms of society, Lévi-Strauss nevertheless holds to the strong analogy between them and indeed, going beyond terms, extends the grand analogy to the *system of attitudes*, whose function—to "insure group cohesion and equilibrium"—is known, but whose underlying system is unknown. The task of anthropology is to thematize this system, and in the analyses given in the text Lévi-Strauss proceeds to show how it could be done, focusing on the problem of the avunculate.

The semiotic upshot of this type of analysis—which extends way beyond kinship—is that "a kinship system does not consist in the objective ties of descent or consanguinity between individuals. It exists only in human consciousness; it is an arbitrary system of representations, not the spontaneous development of a real situation." This stems from the fact that anthropological and linguistic research deals "strictly with symbolism," and the key to symbolism, once we bracket questions of origin, is the differential system of relationships which constitute their signifying units. Such a position has had rather startling implications in Lévi-Strauss's later contentious and highly disputed expansion of his methodologial imperative and sheds a peculiar light on the types of analyses found in the other contributions to this volume.

First, Lévi-Strauss foresees a science of social life as such that would be a study of all the various aspects of social life—economic, linguistic, and so forth—expressed as relationships. Seen in this way, "anthropology will become a general theory of relationships" (Postscript to Chapters III and IV of *Structural Anthropology, I*). This will make possible an analysis of societies "in terms of the differential features characteristic of the systems of relationships which define them," the grand project of structuralism, in all its variegated forms, and a continuation of the project Marx foresaw in his *Contribution to a Critique of Political Economy*. As Lévi-Strauss has written elsewhere: "I am persuaded that these systems do not exist in limitless numbers, and that human societies, like individuals . . . do not create in any absolute way, but are limited to a choice of certain combinations from an ideal repertory, which it should be possible to reconstruct" (as cited by Michael Lane in *Introduction to Structuralism*. New York: Basic Books, 1970, pp. 30–31).

Second, Lévi-Strauss accordingly foresees "an anthropology conceived in a broader way" which provides "a knowledge of man that incorporates all the different approaches which can be used" to decipher the way "our uninvited guest, the human mind, works." Lévi-Strauss hypothesized, and then tried to show in *The Savage Mind*, "that the same logical processes operate in myth as in science, and that man has always been thinking equally well; the improvement lies, not in an alleged progress of man's mind, but in the discovery of new areas to which it may apply its unchanged and unchanging powers." Writing in the "introduction" to *Structural Anthropology, I*, Lévi-Strauss argued:

If, as we believe to be the case, the unconscious activity of the mind consists in imposing forms upon content, and if these forms are fundamentally the same for all minds—ancient and modern, primitive and civilized (as the

study of the symbolic function, expressed in language, so strikingly indicates)—it is necessary and sufficient to grasp the unconscious structure underlying each institution and each custom, in order to obtain a principle of
interpretation valid for other institutions and other customs, provided of
course that the analysis is carried far enough (21–22).

Whether these methodological promissory notes—with their poten-
tiation of the linguistic model—can be cashed in remains a matter of
heated discussion, but it is clear that Lévi-Strauss has drawn the problem-
space in clear lines.

See the two volumes of *Structural Anthropology* (New York: Basic
Books, 1963 and 1976), which contain essays on a wide range of topics,
including Lévi-Strauss's inaugural lecture at the Collège de France, "The
Scope of Anthropology." The first chapter of *The Savage Mind* (Chicago:
University of Chicago Press, 1966), "The Science of the Concrete," com-
pares mythic and scientific forms of thought in an exciting and readable
fashion. A handy introduction to Lévi-Strauss's work is Edmund Leach,
Claude Lévi-Strauss (New York: The Viking Press, 1970; revised edition,
1974). Michael Lane has a clear discussion in his introduction to *Introduction to Structuralism* (see reading recommendations for Saussure).
Other materials are readily available from these two books.

Structural Analysis in Linguistics and in Anthropology

CLAUDE LÉVI-STRAUSS

Linguistics occupies a special place among the social sciences, to
whose ranks it unquestionably belongs. It is not merely a social science
like the others, but, rather, the one in which by far the greatest progress
has been made. It is probably the only one which can truly claim to be a
science and which has achieved both the formulation of an empirical
method and an understanding of the nature of the data submitted to its
analysis. This privileged position carries with it several obligations. The
linguist will often find scientists from related but different disciplines

drawing inspiration from his example and trying to follow his lead. *Noblesse oblige.* A linguistic journal like *Word* cannot confine itself to the illustration of strictly linguistic theories and points of view. It must also welcome psychologists, sociologists, and anthropologists eager to learn from modern linguistics the road which leads to the empirical knowledge of social phenomena. As Marcel Mauss wrote already forty years ago: "Sociology would certainly have progressed much further if it had everywhere followed the lead of the linguists. . . ."[1] The close methodological analogy which exists between the two disciplines imposes a special obligation of collaboration upon them.

Ever since the work of Schrader[2] it has been unnecessary to demonstrate the assistance which linguistics can render to the anthropologist in the study of kinship. It was a linguist and a philologist (Schrader and Rose)[3] who showed the improbability of the hypothesis of matrilineal survivals in the family in antiquity, to which so many anthropologists still clung at that time. The linguist provides the anthropologist with etymologies which permit him to establish between certain kinship terms relationships that were not immediately apparent. The anthropologist, on the other hand, can bring to the attention of the linguist customs, prescriptions, and prohibitions that help him to understand the persistence of certain features of language or the instability of terms or groups of terms. At a meeting of the Linguistic Circle of New York, Julien Bonfante once illustrated this point of view by reviewing the etymology of the word for uncle in several Romance languages. The Greek Θεῖος corresponds in Italian, Spanish, and Portuguese to *zio* and *tio*; and he added that in certain regions of Italy the uncle is called *barba*. The "beard," the "divine" uncle—what a wealth of suggestions for the anthropologist! The investigations of the late A. M. Hocart into the religious character of the avuncular relationship and the "theft of the sacrifice" by the maternal kinsmen immediately come to mind.[4] Whatever interpretation is given to the data collected by Hocart (and his own interpretation is not entirely satisfactory), there is no doubt that the linguist contributes to the solution of the problem by revealing the tenacious survival in contemporary vocabulary of relationships which have long since disappeared. At the same time, the anthropologist explains to the linguist the bases of etymology and confirms its validity. Paul K. Benedict, in examining, as a linguist, the kinship systems of Southeast Asia, was able to make an important contribution to the anthropology of the family in that area.[5]

But linguists and anthropologists follow their own paths independently. They halt, no doubt, from time to time to communicate to one another certain of their findings; these findings, however, derive from different operations, and no effort is made to enable one group to benefit from the technical and methodological advances of the other. This attitude might have been justified in the era when linguistic research leaned most heavily on historical analysis. In relation to the anthropological research conducted during the same period, the difference was one of degree rather than of kind. The linguists employed a more rigorous method, and their findings were established on more solid grounds; the sociologists could follow their example in "renouncing consideration of the spatial distribution of contemporary types as a basis for their classifications."[6] But, after all, anthropology and sociology were looking to linguistics only for insights; nothing foretold a revelation.[7]

The advent of structural linguistics completely changed this situation. Not only did it renew linguistic perspectives; a transformation of this magnitude is not limited to a single discipline. Structural linguistics will certainly play the same renovating role with respect to the social sciences that nuclear physics, for example, has played for the physical sciences. In what does this revolution consist, as we try to assess its broadest implications? N. Troubetzkoy, the illustrious founder of structural linguistics, himself furnished the answer to this question. In one programmatic statement,[8] he reduced the structural method to four basic operations. First, structural linguistics shifts from the study of *conscious* linguistic phenomena to study of their *unconscious* infrastructure; second, it does not treat *terms* as independent entities, taking instead as its basis of analysis the *relations* between terms; third, it introduces the concept of *system*: "Modern phonemics does not merely proclaim that phonemes are always part of a system; it *shows* concrete phonemic systems and elucidates their structure"[9]; finally, structural linguistics aims at discovering *general laws*, either by induction "or . . . by logical deduction, which would give them an absolute character."[10]

Thus, for the first time, a social science is able to formulate necessary relationships. This is the meaning of Troubetzkoy's last point, while the preceding rules show how linguistics must proceed in order to attain this end. It is not for us to show that Troubetzkoy's claims are justified. The vast majority of modern linguists seem sufficiently agreed on this point. But when an event of this importance takes place in one of the sciences of man, it is not only permissible for, but required of, representatives of related disciplines immediately to examine its consequences and its possible application to phenomena of another order.

New perspectives then open up. We are no longer dealing with an occasional collaboration where the linguist and the anthropologist, each working by himself, occasionally communicate those findings which each thinks may interest the other. In the study of kinship problems (and, no doubt, the study of other problems as well), the anthropologist finds himself in a situation which formally resembles that of the structural linguist. Like phonemes, kinship terms are elements of meaning; like phonemes, they acquire meaning only if they are integrated into systems. "Kinship systems," like "phonemic systems," are built by the mind on the level of unconscious thought. Finally, the recurrence of kinship patterns, marriage rules, similar prescribed attitudes between certain types of relatives, and so forth, in scattered regions of the globe and in fundamentally different societies, leads us to believe that, in the case of kinship as well as linguistics, the observable phenomena result from the action of laws which are general but implicit. The problem can therefore be formulated as follows: Although they belong to *another order of reality*, kinship phenomena are *of the same type* as linguistic phenomena. Can the anthropologist, using a method analogous *in form* (if not in content) to the method used in structural linguistics, achieve the same kind of progress in his own science as that which has taken place in linguistics?

We shall be even more strongly inclined to follow this path after an additional observation has been made. The study of kinship problems is today broached in the same terms and seems to be in the throes of the same difficulties as was linguistics on the eve of the structuralist revolution. There is a striking analogy between certain attempts by Rivers and the old linguistics, which sought its explanatory principles first of all in history. In both cases, it is solely (or almost solely) diachronic analysis which must account for synchronic phenomena. Troubetzkoy, comparing structural linguistics and the old linguistics, defines structural linguistics as a "systematic structuralism and universalism," which he contrasts with the individualism and "atomism" of former schools. And when he considers diachronic analysis, his perspective is a profoundly modified one: "The evolution of a phonemic system at any given moment is directed by the *tendency toward a goal.* . . . This evolution thus has a direction, an internal logic, which historical phonemics is called upon to elucidate."[11] The "individualistic" and "atomistic" interpretation, founded exclusively on historical contingency, which is criticized by Troubetzkoy and Jakobson, is actually the same as that which is generally applied to kinship problems.[12] Each detail of terminology and each special marriage rule is associated with a specific custom as either its consequence or its survival. We thus meet with a chaos of discontinuity. No one asks how kinship systems, regarded as synchronic wholes, could be the arbitrary product of a convergence of several heterogeneous institutions (most of which are hypothetical), yet nevertheless function with some sort of regularity and effectiveness.[13]

However, a preliminary difficulty impedes the transposition of the phonemic method to the anthropological study of primitive peoples. The superficial analogy between phonemic systems and kinship systems is so strong that it immediately sets us on the wrong track. It is incorrect to equate kinship terms and linguistic phonemes from the viewpoint of their formal treatment. We know that to obtain a structural law the linguist analyzes phonemes into "distinctive features," which he can then group into one or several "pairs of oppositions."[14] Following an analogous method, the anthropologist might be tempted to break down analytically the kinship terms of any given system into their components. In our own kinship system, for instance, the term *father* has positive connotations with respect to sex, relative age, and generation; but it has a zero value on the dimension of collaterality, and it cannot express an affinal relationship. Thus, for each system, one might ask what relationships are expressed and, for each term of the system, what connotation—positive or negative—it carries regarding each of the following relationships: generation, collaterality, sex, relative age, affinity, etc. It is at this "microsociological" level that one might hope to discover the most general structural laws, just as the linguist discovers his at the infra-phonemic level or the physicist at the infra-molecular or atomic level. One might interpret the interesting attempt of Davis and Warner in these terms.[15]

But a threefold objection immediately arises. A truly scientific analysis must be real, simplifying, and explanatory. Thus the distinctive features which are the product of phonemic analysis have an objective existence from three points of view: psychological, physiological, and even physical; they are fewer in number than the phonemes which result from their combination; and, finally, they allow us to understand and reconstruct the system. Nothing of the kind would emerge from the preceding hypothesis. The treatment of kinship terms which we have just sketched is analytical in appearance only; for, actually, the result is more abstract than the principle; instead of moving toward the concrete, one moves away from it, and the definitive system—if system there is—is only conceptual. Secondly, Davis and Warner's experiment proves that the system achieved through this procedure is infinitely more complex and more difficult to interpret than the empirical data.[16] Finally, the hypothesis has no explanatory value; that is, it does not lead to an understanding of the nature of the system and still less to a reconstruction of its origins.

What is the reason for this failure? A too literal adherence to linguistic method actually betrays its very essence. Kinship terms not only have a sociological existence; they are also elements of speech. In our haste to apply the methods of linguistic analysis, we must not forget that, as a part of vocabulary, kinship terms must be treated with linguistic methods in direct and not analogous fashion. Linguistics teaches us precisely that structural analysis cannot be applied to words directly, but only to words previously broken down into phonemes. *There are no necessary relationships at the vocabulary level.*[17] This applies to all vocabulary elements, including kinship terms. Since this applies to linguistics, it ought to apply *ipso facto* to the sociology of language. An attempt like the one whose possibility we are now discussing would thus consist in extending the method of structural linguistics while ignoring its basic requirements. Kroeber prophetically foresaw this difficulty in an article written many years ago.[18] And if, at that time, he concluded that a structural analysis of kinship terminology was impossible, we must remember that linguistics itself was then restricted to phonetic, psychological, and historical analysis. While it is true that the social sciences must share the limitations of linguistics, they can also benefit from its progress.

Nor should we overlook the profound differences between the phonemic chart of a language and the chart of kinship terms of a society. In the first instance there can be no question as to function; we all know that language serves as a means of communication. On the other hand, what the linguist did not know and what structural linguistics alone has allowed him to discover is the way in which language achieves this end. The function was obvious; the system remained unknown. In this respect, the anthropologist finds himself in the opposite situation. We know, since the work of Lewis H. Morgan, that kinship terms constitute systems; on the other hand, we still do not know their function. The misinterpretation of this initial situation reduces most structural analyses of kinship systems to pure tautologies. They demonstrate the obvious and neglect the unknown.

This does not mean that we must abandon hope of introducing order and discovering meaning in kinship nomenclature. But we should at least recognize the special problems raised by the sociology of vocabulary and the ambiguous character of the relations between its methods and those of linguistics. For this reason it would be preferable to limit the discussion to a case where the analogy can be clearly established. Fortunately, we have just such a case available.

What is generally called a "kinship system" comprises two quite different orders of reality. First, there are terms through which various kinds of family relationships are expressed. But kinship is not expressed solely through nomenclature. The individuals or classes of individuals who employ these terms feel (or do not feel, as the case may be) bound by prescribed behavior in their relations with one another, such as respect or familiarity, rights or obligations, and affection or hostility. Thus, along with what we propose to call the *system of terminology* (which, strictly speaking, constitutes the vocabulary system), there is another system, both psychological and social in nature, which we shall call the *system of attitudes*. Although it is true (as we have shown above) that the study of systems of terminology places us in a situation analogous, but opposite, to the situation in which we are dealing with phonemic systems, this difficulty is "inversed," as it were, when we examine systems of attitudes. We can guess at the role played by systems of attitudes, that is, to insure group cohesion and equilibrium, but we do not understand the nature of the interconnections between the various attitudes, nor do we perceive their necessity.[19] In other words, as in the case of language, we know their function, but the system is unknown.

Thus we find a profound difference between the *system of terminology* and the *system of attitudes*, and we have to disagree with A. R. Radcliffe-

Brown if he really believed, as has been said of him, that attitudes are nothing but the expression or transposition of terms on the affective level.[20] The last few years have provided numerous examples of groups whose chart of kinship terms does not accurately reflect family attitudes, and vice versa.[21] It would be incorrect to assume that the kinship system constitutes the principal means of regulating interpersonal relationships in all societies. Even in societies where the kinship system does function as such, it does not fulfill that role everywhere to the same extent. Furthermore, it is always necessary to distinguish between two types of attitudes: first, the diffuse, uncrystallized, and non-institutionalized attitudes, which we may consider as the reflection or transposition of the terminology on the psychological level; and second, along with, or in addition to, the preceding ones, those attitudes which are stylized, prescribed, and sanctioned by taboos or privileges and expressed through a fixed ritual. These attitudes, far from automatically reflecting the nomenclature, often appear as secondary elaborations, which serve to resolve the contradictions and overcome the deficiencies inherent in the terminological system. This synthetic character is strikingly apparent among the Wik Munkan of Australia. In this group, joking privileges sanction a contradiction between the kinship relations which link two unmarried men and the theoretical relationship which must be assumed to exist between them in order to account for their later marriages to two women who do not stand themselves in the corresponding relationship.[22] There is a contradiction between two possible systems of nomenclature, and the emphasis placed on attitudes represents an attempt to integrate or transcend this contradiction. We can easily agree with Radcliffe-Brown and assert the existence of "real relations of interdependence between the terminology and the rest of the system."[23] Some of his critics made the mistake of inferring, from the absence of a rigorous parallelism between attitudes and nomenclature, that the two systems were mutually independent. But this relationship of interdependence does not imply a one-to-one correlation. The system of attitudes constitutes, rather, a dynamic integration of the system of terminology.

Granted the hypothesis (to which we whole-heartedly subscribe) of a functional relationship between the two systems, we are nevertheless entitled, for methodological reasons, to treat independently the problems pertaining to each system. This is what we propose to do here for a problem which is rightly considered the point of departure for any theory of attitudes—that of the maternal uncle. We shall attempt to show how a formal transposition of the method of structural linguistics allows us to shed new light upon this problem. Because the relationship between nephew and maternal uncle appears to have been the focus of significant elaboration in a great many primitive societies, anthropologists have devoted special attention to it. It is not enough to note the frequency of this theme; we must also account for it.

Let us briefly review the principal stages in the development of this problem. During the entire nineteenth century and until the writings of Sydney Hartland,[24] the importance of the mother's brother was interpreted as a survival of matrilineal descent. This interpretation was based purely on speculation, and, indeed, it was highly improbable in the light of European examples. Furthermore, Rivers' attempt[25] to explain the importance of the mother's brother in southern India as a residue of cross-cousin marriage led to particularly deplorable results. Rivers himself was forced to recognize that this interpretation could not account for all aspects of the problem. He resigned himself to the hypothesis that *several* heterogeneous customs which have since disappeared (cross-cousin marriage being only one of them) were needed to explain the existence of a *single* institution.[26] Thus, atomism and mechanism triumphed. It was Lowie's crucial article on the matrilineal complex[27] which opened what we should like to call the "modern phase" of the problem of the avunculate. Lowie showed that the correlation drawn or postulated between the prominent position of the maternal uncle and matrilineal descent cannot withstand rigorous analysis. In fact, the avunculate is found associated with patrilineal, as well as matrilineal, descent. The role of the maternal uncle cannot be explained as either a consequence or a survival of matrilineal kinship; it is only a specific application "of a very general tendency to associate definite social relations with definite forms of kinship regardless of maternal or paternal side." In accordance with this principle, introduced for the first time by Lowie in 1919, there exists a general tendency to *qualify attitudes*, which constitutes the only empirical foundation for a theory of kinship systems. But, at the same time, Lowie left certain questions unanswered. What exactly do we call an avunculate? Do we not merge different customs and attitudes under this single term? And, if it is true that there is a tendency to qualify all attitudes, why are only certain attitudes associated with the avuncular relationship, rather than just any possible attitudes, depending upon the group considered?

A few further remarks here may underline the striking analogy between the development of this problem and certain stages in the evolution of linguistic theory. The variety of possible attitudes in the area of interpersonal relationships is almost unlimited; the same holds true for the variety of sounds which can be articulated by the vocal apparatus—and which are actually produced during the first months of human life. Each language, however, retains only a very small number among all the possible sounds, and in this respect linguistics raises two questions: Why are certain sounds selected? What relationships exist between one or several of the sounds chosen and all the others?[28] Our sketch of the historical development of the avuncular problem is at precisely the same stage. Like language, the social group has a great wealth of psychophysiological material at its disposal. Like language too, it retains only certain elements, at least some of which remain the same throughout the most varied cultures and are combined into structures which are always diversified. Thus we may wonder about the reason for this choice and the laws of combination.

For insight into the specific problem of the avunculate we should turn to Radcliffe-Brown. His well-known article on the maternal uncle in South Africa[29] was the first attempt to grasp and analyze the modalities of what we might call the "general principle of attitude qualification." We shall briefly review the fundamental ideas of that now-classic study.

According to Radcliffe-Brown, the term *avunculate* covers two antithetical systems of attitudes. In one case, the maternal uncle represents family authority; he is feared and obeyed, and possesses certain rights over his nephew. In the other case, the nephew holds privileges of familiarity in relation to his uncle and can treat him more or less as his victim. Second, there is a correlation between the boy's attitude toward his maternal uncle and his attitude toward his father. We find the two systems of attitudes in both cases, but they are inversely correlated. In groups where familiarity characterizes the relationship between father and son, the relationship between maternal uncle and nephew is one of respect; and where the father stands as the austere representative of family authority, it is the uncle who is treated with familiarity. Thus the two sets of attitudes constitute (as the structural linguist would say) two pairs of oppositions. Radcliffe-Brown concluded his article by proposing the following interpretation: In the final analysis, it is descent that determines the choice of oppositions. In patrilineal societies, where the father and the father's descent group represent traditional authority, the maternal uncle is considered a "male mother." He is generally treated in the same fashion, and sometimes even called by the same name, as the mother. In matrilineal societies, the opposite occurs. Here, authority is vested in the maternal uncle, while relationships of tenderness and familiarity revolve about the father and his descent group.

It would indeed be difficult to exaggerate the importance of Radcliffe-Brown's contribution, which was the first attempt at synthesis on an empirical basis following Lowie's authoritative and merciless criticism of evolutionist metaphysics. To say that this effort did not entirely succeed does not in any way diminish the homage due this great British anthropologist; but we should certainly recognize that Radcliffe-Brown's article leaves unanswered some fundamental questions. First, the avunculate does not occur in all matrilineal or all patrilineal systems, and we find it present in some systems which are neither matrilineal or patrilineal.[30] Further, the avuncular relationship is not limited to two terms, but presupposes four, namely, brother, sister, brother-in-law, and nephew. An interpretation such as Radcliffe-Brown's arbitrarily isolates particular elements of global structure which must be treated as a whole. A few simple examples will illustrate this twofold difficulty.

The social organization of the Trobriand Islanders of Melanesia is characterized by matrilineal descent, free and familiar relations between father and son, and a marked antagonism between maternal uncle and nephew.[31] On the other hand, the patrilineal Cherkess of the Caucasus place the hostility between father and son, while the maternal uncle assists his nephew and gives him a horse when he marries.[32] Up to this point we are still within the limits of Radcliffe-Brown's scheme. But let us consider the other family relationships involved. Malinowski showed that in the Trobriands husband and wife live in an atmosphere of tender intimacy and that their relationship is characterized by reciprocity. The relations between brother and sister, on the other hand, are dominated by an extremely rigid taboo. Let us now compare the situation in the Caucasus. There, it is the brother-sister relationship which is tender—to such an extent that among the Pschav an only daughter "adopts" a "brother" who will play the customary brother's role as her chaste bed companion.[33] But the relationship between spouses is entirely different. A Cherkess will not appear in public with his wife and visits her only in secret. According to Malinowski, there is no greater insult in the Trobriands than to tell a man that he resembles his sister. In the Caucasus there is an analogous prohibition: It is forbidden to ask a man about his wife's health.

When we consider societies of the Cherkess and Trobriand types it is not enough to study the correlation of attitudes between *father / son* and *uncle / sister's son*. This correlation is only one aspect of a global system containing four types of relationships which are organically linked, namely: *brother / sister, husband / wife, father / son,* and *mother's brother/ sister's son*. The two groups in our example illustrate a law which can be formulated as follows: In both groups, the relation between maternal uncle and nephew is to the relation between brother and sister as the relation between father and son is to that between husband and wife. Thus if we know one pair of relations, it is always possible to infer the other.

Let us now examine some other cases. On Tonga, in Polynesia, descent is patrilineal, as among the Cherkess. Relations between husband and wife appear to be public and harmonious. Domestic quarrels are rare, and although the wife is often of superior rank, the husband ". . . is nevertheless of higher authority in all domestic matters, and no woman entertains the least idea of rebelling against that authority."[34] At the same time there is great freedom between nephew and maternal uncle. The nephew is *fahu*, or above the law, in relation to his uncle, toward whom extreme familiarity is permitted. This freedom strongly contrasts with the father-son relationship. The father is *tapu*; the son cannot touch his father's head or hair; he cannot touch him while he eats, sleep in his bed or on his pillow, share his food or drink, or play with his possessions. However, the strongest *tapu* of all is the one between brother and sister, who must never be together under the same roof.

Although they are also patrilineal and patrilocal, the natives of Lake Kutubu in New Guinea offer an example of the opposite type of structure. F. E. Williams writes: "I have never seen such a close and apparently affectionate association between father and son. . . ."[35] Relations between husband and wife are characterized by the very low status ascribed to women and "the marked separation of masculine and feminine interests. . . ."[36] The women, according to Williams, "are expected to work hard for their masters . . . they occasionally protest, and protest may be met with a beating."[37] The wife can always call upon her brother for protection against her husband, and it is with him that she seeks refuge. As for the relationship between nephew and maternal uncle, it is ". . . best summed up in the word 'respect' . . . tinged with apprehensiveness,"[38] for the maternal uncle has the power to curse his nephew and inflict serious illness upon him (just as among the Kipsigi of Africa).

Although patrilineal, the society described by Williams is structurally of the same type as that of the Siuai of Bougainville, who have matrilineal descent. Between brother and sister there is ". . . friendly interaction and mutual generosity. . . ."[39] As regards the father-son relationship, Oliver writes, ". . . I could discover little evidence that the word 'father' evokes images of hostility or stern authority or awed respect."[40] But the relationship between the nephew and his mother's brother "appears to range between stern discipline and genial mutual dependence. . . ." However, ". . . most of the informants agreed that all boys stand in some awe of their mother's brothers, and are more likely to obey them than their own fathers. . . ."[41] Between husband and wife harmonious understanding is rare: ". . . there are few young wives who remain altogether faithful . . . most young husbands are continually suspicious and often give vent to jealous anger . . . marriages involve a number of adjustments, some of them apparently difficult. . . ."[42]

The same picture, but sharper still, characterizes the Dobuans, who are matrilineal and neighbors of the equally matrilineal Trobrianders, while their structure is very different. Dobuan marriages are unstable, adultery is widespread, and husband and wife constantly fear death induced by their spouse's witchcraft. Actually, Fortune's remark, "It is a most serious insult to refer to a woman's witchcraft so that her husband will hear of it"[43] appears to be a variant of the Trobriand and Caucasian taboos cited above.

In Dobu, the mother's brother is held to be the harshest of all the relatives. "The mother's brother may beat children long after their parents have ceased to do so," and they are forbidden to utter his name. There is a tender relationship with the "navel," the mother's sister's husband, who is the father's double, rather than with the father himself. Nevertheless, the father is considered "less harsh" than the mother's brother and will always seek, contrary to the laws of inheritance, to favor his son at the expense of his uterine nephew. And, finally, "the strongest of all social bonds" is the one between brother and sister.[44]

What can we conclude from these examples? The correlation between types of descent and forms of avunculate does not exhaust the problem. Different forms of avunculate can coexist with the same type of descent, whether patrilineal or matrilineal. But we constantly find the same fundamental relationship between the four pairs of oppositions required to construct the system. This will emerge more clearly from the diagrams which illustrate our examples. The sign + indicates free and familiar relations, and the sign − stands for relations characterized by hostility, antagonism, or reserve (Figure 1). This is an oversimplification, but we can tentatively make use of it. We shall describe some of the indispensable refinements farther on.

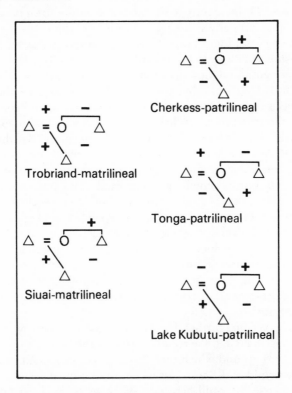

The synchronic law of correlation thus suggested may be validated diachronically. If we summarize, after Howard, the evolution of family relationships during the Middle Ages, we find approximately this pattern: The brother's authority over his sister wanes, and that of the prospective husband increases. Simultaneously, the bond between father and son is weakened and that between maternal uncle and nephew is reinforced.[45]

This evolution seems to be confirmed by the documents gathered by Léon Gautier, for in the "conservative" texts (Raoul de Cambrai, Geste des Loherains, etc.),[46] the positive relationship is established chiefly between father and son and is only gradually displaced toward the maternal uncle and nephew.[47]

Thus we see[48] that in order to understand the avunculate we must treat it as one relationship within a system, while the system itself must be considered as a whole in order to grasp its structure. This structure rests upon four terms (brother, sister, father, and son), which are linked by two pairs of correlative oppositions in such a way that in each of the two generations there is always a positive relationship and a negative one. Now, what is the nature of this structure, and what is its function? The answer is as follows: This structure is the most elementary form of kinship that can exist. It is, properly speaking, *the unit of kinship*.

One may give a logical argument to support this statement. In order for a kinship structure to exist, three types of family relations must always be present: a relation of consanguinity, a relation of affinity, and a relation of descent—in other words, a relation between siblings, a relation between spouses, and a relation between parent and child. It is evident that the structure given here satisfies this threefold requirement, in accordance with the scientific principle of parsimony. But these considerations are abstract, and we can present a more direct proof for our thesis.

The primitive and irreducible character of the basic unit of kinship, as we have defined it, is actually a direct result of the universal presence of an incest taboo. This is really saying that in human society a man must obtain a woman from another man who gives him a daughter or a sister. Thus we do not need to explain how the maternal uncle emerged in the kinship structure: He does not emerge—he is present initially. Indeed, the presence of the maternal uncle is a necessary precondition for the structure to exist. The error of traditional anthropology, like that of traditional linguistics, was to consider the terms, and not the relations between the terms.

Before proceeding further, let us briefly answer some objections which might be raised. First, if the relationship between "brothers-in-law" is the necessary axis around which the kinship structure is built, why need we bring in the child of the marriage when considering the elementary structure? Of course the child here may be either born or yet unborn. But, granting this, we must understand that the child is indispensable in validating the dynamic and teleological character of the initial step, which establishes kinship on the basis of and through marriage. Kinship is not a static phenomenon: it exists only in self-perpetuation. Here we are not thinking of the desire to perpetuate the race, but rather of the fact that in most kinship systems the initial disequilibrium produced in one generation between the group that gives the woman and the group that receives her can be stabilized only by counter-prestations in following generations. Thus, even the most elementary kinship structure exists both synchronically and diachronically.

Second, could we not conceive of a symmetrical structure, equally simple, where the sexes would be reversed? Such a structure would involve a sister, her brother, brother's wife, and brother's daughter. This is certainly a theoretical possibility. But it is immediately eliminated on empirical grounds. In human society, it is the men who exchange the women, and not vice versa. It remains for further research to determine whether certain cultures have not tended to create a kind of fictitious image of this symmetrical structure. Such cases would surely be uncommon.

We come now to a more serious objection. Possibly we have only inverted the problem. Traditional anthropologists painstakingly endeavored to explain the origin of the avunculate, and we have brushed aside that research by treating the mother's brother not as an extrinsic element, but as an immediate *given* of the simplest family structure. How is it then that we do not find the avunculate at all times and in all places? For although the avunculate has a wide distribution, it is by no means universal. It would be futile to explain the instances where it is present and then fail to explain its absence in other instances.

Let us point out, first, that the kinship system does not have the same importance in all cultures. For some cultures it provides the active principle regulating all or most of the social relationships. In other groups, as in our own society, this function is either absent altogether or greatly reduced. In still others, as in the societies of the Plains Indians, it is only partially fulfilled. The kinship system is a language; but it is not a universal language, and a society may prefer other modes of expression and action. From the viewpoint of the anthropologist this means that in dealing with a specific culture we must always ask a preliminary question: Is the system systematic? Such a question, which seems absurd at first, is absurd only in relation to language; for language is the semantic system par excellence; it cannot but signify, and exists only through signification. On the contrary, this question must be rigorously examined as we move from the study of language to the consideration of other systems which also claim to have semantic functions, but whose fulfillment remains partial, fragmentary, or subjective, like, for example, social organization, art, and so forth.

Furthermore, we have interpreted the avunculate as a characteristic trait of elementary structure. This elementary structure, which is the product of defined relations involving four terms, is, in our view, the true *atom of kinship*.[49] Nothing can be conceived or given beyond the fundamental requirements of its structure, and, in addition, it is the sole building block of more complex systems. For there are more complex systems;

or, more accurately speaking, all kinship systems are constructed on the basis of this elementary structure, expanded or developed through the integration of new elements. Thus we must entertain two hypotheses: first, one in which the kinship system under consideration operates through the simple juxtaposition of elementary structures, and where the avuncular relationship therefore remains constantly apparent; second, a hypothesis in which the building blocks of the system are already of a more complex order. In the latter case, the avuncular relationship, while present, may be submerged within a differentiated context. For instance, we can conceive of a system whose point of departure lies in the elementary structure but which adds, at the right of the maternal uncle, his wife, and, at the left of the father, first the father's sister and then her husband. We could easily demonstrate that a development of this order leads to a parallel splitting in the following generation. The child must then be distinguished according to sex—a boy or a girl, linked by a relation which is symmetrical and inverse to the terms occupying the other peripheral positions in the structure (for example, the dominant position of the father's sister in Polynesia, the South African *nhlampsa*, and inheritance by the mother's brother's wife). In this type of structure the avuncular relationship continues to prevail, but it is no longer the predominant one. In structures of still greater complexity, the avunculate may be obliterated or may merge with other relationships. But precisely because it is part of the elementary structure, the avuncular relationship re-emerges unmistakably and tends to become reinforced each time the system under consideration reaches a crisis—either because it is undergoing rapid transformation (as on the Northwest Coast), or because it is a focus of contact and conflict between radically different cultures (as in Fiji and southern India), or, finally, because it is in the throes of a mortal crisis (as was Europe in the Middle Ages).

We must also add that the positive and negative symbols which we have employed in the above diagrams represent an oversimplification, useful only as a part of the demonstration. Actually, the system of basic attitudes comprises at least four terms: an attitude of affection, tenderness, and spontaneity; an attitude which results from the reciprocal exchange of prestations and counter-prestations; and, in addition to these bilateral relationships, two unilateral relationships, one which corresponds to the attitude of the creditor, the other to that of the debtor. In other words there are: mutuality ($=$), reciprocity ($\pm$), rights ($+$), and obligations ($-$). These four fundamental attitudes are represented in their reciprocal relationships in Figure 2.

In many systems the relationship between two individuals is often expressed not by a single attitude, but by several attitudes which together form, as it were, a "bundle" of attitudes (as in the Trobriands, where we find both mutuality *and* reciprocity between husband and wife). This

is an additional reason behind the difficulty in uncovering the basic structure.

We have tried to show the extent to which the preceding analysis is indebted to outstanding contemporary exponents of the sociology of primitive peoples. We must stress, however, that in its most fundamental principle this analysis departs from their teachings. Let us cite as an example Radcliffe-Brown:

> The unit of structure from which a kinship is built up is the group which I call an "elementary family," consisting of a man and his wife and their child or children. . . . The existence of the elementary family creates three special kinds of social relationship, that between parent and child, that between children of the same parents (siblings), and that between husband and wife as parents of the same child or children. . . . The three relationships that exist within the elementary family constitute what I call the first order. Relationships of the second order are those which depend on the connection of two elementary families through a common member, and are such as father's father, mother's brother, wife's sister, and so on. In the third order are such as father's brother's son and mother's brother's wife. Thus we can trace, if we have genealogical information, relationships of the fourth, fifth or n^{th} order.[50]

The idea expressed in the above passage, that the biological family constitutes the point of departure from which all societies elaborate their kinship systems, has not been voiced solely by Radcliffe-Brown. There is scarcely an idea which would today elicit greater consensus. Nor is there one more dangerous, in our opinion. Of course, the biological family is ubiquitous in human society. But what confers upon kinship its socio-cultural character is not what it retains from nature, but, rather, the essential way in which it diverges from nature. A kinship system does not consist in the objective ties of descent or consanguinity between individuals. It exists only in human consciousness; it is an arbitrary system of representations, not the spontaneous development of a real situation. This certainly does not mean that the real situation is automatically contradicted, or that it is to be simply ignored. Radcliffe-Brown has shown, in studies that are now classic, that even systems which are apparently extremely rigid and artificial, such as the Australian systems of marriage-classes, take biological parenthood carefully into account. But while this observation is irrefutable, still the fact (in our view decisive) remains that, in human society, kinship is allowed to establish and perpetuate itself only through specific forms of marriage. In other words, the relationships which Radcliffe-Brown calls "relationships of the first order" are a function of, and depend upon, those which he considers secondary and derived. The essence of human kinship is to require the establishment of relations among what Radcliffe-Brown calls "elementary families." Thus, it is not the families (isolated terms) which are truly "elementary," but, rather, the relations between those terms. No other interpretation can account for the universality of the incest taboo; and the avuncular relationship, in its most general form, is nothing but a corollary, now covert, now explicit, of this taboo.

Because they are symbolic systems, kinship systems offer the anthropologist a rich field, where his efforts can almost (and we emphasize the "almost") converge with those of the most highly developed of the social sciences, namely, linguistics. But to achieve this convergence, from which it is hoped a better understanding of man will result, we must never lose sight of the fact that, in both anthropological and linguistic research, we are dealing strictly with symbolism. And although it may be legitimate or even inevitable to fall back upon a naturalistic interpretation in order to understand the emergence of symbolic thinking, once the latter is given, the nature of the explanation must change as radically as the newly appeared phenomenon differs from those which have preceded and prepared it. Hence, any concession to naturalism might jeopardize the immense progress already made in linguistics, which is also beginning to characterize the study of family structure, and might drive the sociology of the family toward a sterile empiricism, devoid of inspiration.

NOTES

1. Marcel Mauss, "Rapports réels et pratiques de la psychologie et de la sociologie," *Journal de Psychologie Normale et Pathologique* (1924); reprinted in *Sociologie et Anthropologie* (Paris: 1951), p. 299.

2. O. Schrader, *Prehistoric Antiquities of the Aryan Peoples*, trans. F. B. Jevons (London: 1890), Chapter XII, Part 4.

3. Ibid. See also H. J. Rose, "On the Alleged Evidence for Mother-Right in Early Greece," *Folklore*, XXII (1911), and the more recent studies by George Thomson, which support the hypothesis of matrilineal survivals.

4. A. M. Hocart, "Chieftainship and the Sister's Son in the Pacific," *American Anthropologist*, n.s., XVII (1915); "The Uterine Nephew," *Man*, XXIII, No. 4 (1923); "The Cousin in Vedic Ritual," *Indian Antiquary*, LIV (1925); etc.

5. Paul K. Benedict, "Tibetan and Chinese Kinship Terms," *Harvard Journal of Asiatic Studies*, VI (1942); "Studies in Thai Kinship Terminology," *Journal of the American Oriental Society*, LXIII (1943).

6. L. Brunschvicg, *Le Progrès de la conscience dans la philosophie occidentale* (Paris: 1927), II, p. 562.

7. Between 1900 and 1920 Ferdinand de Saussure and Antoine Meillet, the founders of modern linguistics, placed themselves determinedly under the wing of the anthropologists. Not until the 1920s did Marcel Mauss begin—to borrow a phrase from economics—to reverse this tendency.

8. N. Troubetzkoy, "La Phonologie actuelle," in *Psychologie du langage* (Paris: 1933).

9. Ibid., p. 243.

10. Loc. cit.

11. Ibid., p. 245; Roman Jakobson, "Principien der historischen Phonologie," *Travaux du Cercle linguistique de Prague*, IV (1931); and also Jakobson, "Remarques sur l'évolution phonologique du russe," ibid., II (1929).

12. W. H. R. Rivers, *The History of Melanesian Society* (London: 1914), *passim*; *Social Organization*, ed. W. J. Perry (London: 1924), Chapter IV.

13. In the same vein, see Sol Tax, "Some Problems of Social Organization," in Fred Eggan (ed.), *Social Anthropology of North American Tribes* (Chicago: 1937).

14. Roman Jakobson, "Observations sur le classement phonologique des consonnes," *Proceedings of the Third International Congress of Phonetic Sciences* (Ghent: 1938).

15. K. Davis and W. L. Warner, "Structural Analysis of Kinship," *American Anthropologist*, n.s., XXXVII (1935).

16. Thus at the end of the analysis carried out by these authors, the term *husband* is replaced by the formula:

$$C^{2a} /^{2d} /^0 S U^{1a \, 8}/ \text{Ego (Ibid.)}$$

There are now available two works which employ a much more refined logical apparatus and offer greater interest in terms both of method and of results. See F. G. Lounsbury, "A Semantic Analysis of the Pawnee Kinship Usage," *Language*, XXXII, No. 1 (1956), and W. H. Goodenough, "The Componential Analysis of Kinship," ibid.

17. As will be seen in Chapter V [not included in this selection], I have now refined this formulation.

18. A. L. Kroeber, "Classificatory Systems of Relationship," *Journal of the Royal Anthropological Institute*, XXXIX (1909).

19. We must except the remarkable work of W. L. Warner, "Morphology and Functions of the Australian Murngin Type of Kinship," *American Anthropologist*, n.s., XXXII–XXXIII (1930–1931), in which his analysis of the system of attitudes, although fundamentally debatable, nevertheless initiates a new phase in the study of problems of kinship.

20. A. R. Radcliffe-Brown, "Kinship Terminology in California," *American Anthropologist*, n.s., XXXVII (1935); "The Study of Kinship Systems," *Journal of the Royal Anthropological Institute*, LXXI (1941).

21. M. E. Opler, "Apache Data Concerning the Relationship of Kinship Terminology to Social Classification," *American Anthropologist*, n.s., XXXIX (1937); A. M. Halpern, "Yuma Kinship Terms," *American Anthropologist*, n.s., XLIV (1942).

22. D. F. Thomson, "The Joking Relationship and Organized Obscenity in North Queensland," *American Anthropologist*, n.s., XXXVII (1935).

23. Radcliffe-Brown, "The Study of Kinship Systems," p. 8. This later formulation seems to us more satisfactory than his 1935 statement that attitudes present "a fairly high degree of correlation with the terminological classification" (*American Anthropologist*, n.s., XXXVII [1935], p. 53).

24. Sydney Hartland, "Matrilineal Kinship and the Question of its Priority," *Memoirs of the American Anthropological Association*, No. 4 (1917).

25. W. H. R. Rivers, "The Marriage of Cousins in India," *Journal of the Royal Asiatic Society* (July, 1907).

26. Ibid., p. 624.

27. R. H. Lowie, "The Matrilineal Complex," *University of California Publications in American Archaeology and Ethnology*, XVI, No. 2 (1919).

28. Roman Jakobson, *Kindersprache, Aphasie und allgemeine Lautgesetze* (Uppsala: 1941).

29. A. R. Radcliffe-Brown, "The Mother's Brother in South Africa," *South African Journal of Science*, XXI (1924).

30. As among the Mundugomor of New Guinea, where the relationship between maternal uncle and nephew is always familiar, although descent is alternately patrilineal or matrilineal. See Margaret Mead, *Sex and Temperament in Three Primitive Societies* (New York: 1935), pp. 176–185.

31. B. Malinowski, *The Sexual Life of Savages in Northwestern Melanesia* (London: 1929), 2 vols.

32. Dubois de Monpereux (1839), cited in M. Kovalevski, "La Famille matriarcale au Caucase," *L'Anthropologie*, IV (1893).

33. Ibid.

34. E. W. Gifford, "Tonga Society," *Bernice P. Bishop Museum Bulletin*, No. 61 (Honolulu: 1929), pp. 16–22.

35. F. E. Williams, "Group Sentiment and Primitive Justice," *American Anthropologist*, n.s., XLIII, No. 4, Part 1 (1941), p. 523.

36. F. E. Williams, "Natives of Lake Kutubu, Papua," *Oceania*, XI (1940–1941), p. 266.

37. Ibid., p. 268.

38. Ibid., p. 280. See also *Oceania*, XII (1941–1942).

39. Douglas L. Oliver, *A Solomon Island Society: Kinship and Leadership among the Siuai of Bougainville* (Cambridge, Mass.: 1955), p. 255.

40. Ibid., p. 251.

41. Ibid., p. 257.

42. Ibid., pp. 168–9.

43. R. F. Fortune, *The Sorcerers of Dobu* (New York: 1932), p. 45.

44. Ibid., pp. 8, 10, 62–4.

45. G. E. Howard, *A History of Matrimonial Institutions*, 3 vols. (Chicago: 1904).

46. *Translator's note*: The "Chansons de Geste," which survive in manuscript versions of the twelfth to the fifteenth century, are considered to be remodelings of much earlier originals, dating back to the age of Charlemagne. These poems of heroic and often legendary exploits also constitute a source of information on the family life of that period.

47. Léon Gautier, *La Chevalerie* (Paris: 1890). See also: F. B. Gummere, "The Sister's Son," in *An English Miscellany Presented to Dr. Furnivall* (London: 1901); W. O. Farnsworth, *Uncle and Nephew in the Old French Chanson de Geste* (New York: 1913).

48. The preceding paragraphs were written in 1957 and substituted for the original text, in response to the judicious remark by my colleague Luc de Heusch of the Université Libre of Brussels that one of my examples was incorrect. I take this opportunity to thank him.

49. It is no doubt superfluous to emphasize that the atomism which we have criticized in Rivers refers to classical philosophy and has nothing to do with the structural conception of the atom developed in modern physics.

50. A. R. Radcliffe-Brown, "The Study of Kinship Systems," p. 2.

GREGORY BATESON

Bateson's analytical framework comes from a rather different tradition than the majority of texts presented in this volume. It is concerned with the "logic" of communication and the problem of levels in the exchange of messages. Bateson himself thinks of his project as being a part of a properly understood and extended cybernetics, and in fact his theory of knowledge and model of mind, which are his primary concerns, are based on cybernetic considerations.

The focal point of Bateson's essay here, which has enormous heuristic fertility and implications far beyond the often summary comments which Bateson was forced to restrict himself to, is the problem of determining the levels of abstraction in the exchange of messages, both on the nonverbal and verbal levels, and the relations of metalinguistic and metacommunicative messages to the straightforward processes of communication. The pivot of the process wherein metalinguistic and metacommunicative levels are differentiated is the movement from "automatic" responses to what Bateson calls "mood-signs" in semiotic exchange to the recognition of "signals" as signals "which can be trusted, distrusted, falsified, denied, amplified, corrected, and so forth." This process is of extraordinary complexity, and Bateson attempts in this essay to show its logical scaffolding and structuring under the rubric of the "paradoxes of communication."

These so-called paradoxes are illustrated by Bateson on the example of "play," a phenomenon which, as it turns out, is not by any means restricted to the human level. Play involves, in Bateson's reckoning, a process of "double denotation" in which the play-action, understood as a virtual utterance, is equivalent to the statement, "these actions in which we now engage do not denote what those actions *for which they stand* would denote." Although such a statement, expressed in a contextually structured set of actions, contravenes the theory of logical types, Bateson notes that "it would be bad natural history to expect the mental processes and communicative habits of mammals to conform to the logician's ideal," and in fact Bertrand Russell himself, the source of the theory of types which underlies Bateson's analysis, could not have formulated the theory without himself contradicting it. Now, central to the main thesis of Bateson's argument is the claim that "it appears . . . that the evolution of play may have been an important step in the evolution of communication," a theme treated with great perspicacity in his essay "Redundancy and Coding," in his *Steps to an Ecology of Mind*.

What makes play so important is that it is also intrinsically and logically connected with threat and histrionics in contributing to the "discrimination between map and territory," one of the key insights of the general semantics of Alfred Korzybski, to which Bateson is indeed indebted. The distinction between map and territory, and, further, the ability to differentiate the one from the other, is of crucial importance in the evolution of mentality, and it is formalized not in the straightforward intercourse with the world, which is marked by immediacy, but in the marking of a divide between the message, as direct semiotic exchange, and the framework in which it is to be taken. In this sense we can see both the peculiarities of play and its exemplary importance for understanding the embedded double logical structure of human communication: "the messages or signals exchanged in play are in a certain sense untrue or not meant" and "that which is denoted by these signals is nonexistent." Although the reverse, in terms of content, is generally the case with normal communication, the *logic* of the communication is the same, for it reveals the all-important role that frames and contexts play in human life.

An explication of these terms takes up a great deal of space in Bateson's essay, and they are illustrated through examples which have a marvelous generalizability. Although the original notion of a frame is psychological, it is able to be illustrated through recourse to set theory and to important considerations taken from the psychology of Gestalt perception and from the role of the picture frame in painting, a topic about which Meyer Schapiro has much to say in his essay, where it is clear that metasemiotic functions are also being performed in the visual domain (in Schapiro's case not just by the frame but by the material substance of the image-sign itself, which for the most part is not directed to *trompe l'oeil* artifacts). In this discussion Bateson is able to evoke the wider implications of his thesis—which deals with the logical structure of communication as such, independent, in fact, of domain and of medium, being a "pure" semiotic phenomenon—and it will be extremely important to work through and work out in detail his many examples. They raise questions of utter generality, such as does all experience have a "figure/ground" structure? Is this able to be translated into semiotic terms? What are the ultimate "grounds" for various forms of communicative exchange?

Bateson's essay intersects, then, with logical, evolutionary, biological, psychological, aesthetic, and semiotic problems. Each dimension is brought into proximity with every other and all are shown to comprise, when taken together, a comprehensive semiotically based framework for the analysis of an exceedingly wide range of phenomena. Although the immediate context for the development of the theory was its relevance for psychotherapy, which is treated in the last section of the essay, its scope extends to the totality of all communicative interchange between organisms, both individually and in groups, for which Bateson has constructed an heuristically fertile model. As Bateson puts it, "our central thesis may be summed up as a statement of the necessity of the paradoxes of abstraction. . . . The paradoxes of abstraction must make their appearance in all communication more complex than that of mood-signals, and . . . without these paradoxes the evolution of communication would be at an end. Life would then be an endless interchange of stylized messages, a game with rigid rules, unrelieved by change or humor." It is this dialectic between rule-following and rule-changing, which manifests the "logical" matrix of creativity, that Bateson has so successfully foregrounded.

Bateson is best approached directly and his two later books *Steps to an Ecology of Mind* (New York: Ballantine Books, 1972) and *Mind and Nature: A Necessary Unity* (New York: Bantam Books, 1980) are essential reading. For a kind of intellectual biography, with good bibliographic materials and photographs, see David Lipset, *Gregory Bateson: The Legacy of a Scientist* (Boston: Beacon Press, 1982). Anthony Wilden makes extensive use of Bateson in his *System and Structure*, second edition (London and New York: Tavistock, 1980; U.S. edition in association with Methuen).

A Theory of Play and Fantasy

GREGORY BATESON

This research was planned and started with an hypothesis to guide our investigations, the task of the investigators being to collect relevant observational data and, in the process, to amplify and modify the hypothesis.

The hypothesis will here be described as it has grown in our thinking.

Earlier fundamental work of Whitehead, Russell,[1] Wittgenstein,[2] Carnap,[3] Whorf,[4] and others, as well as my own attempt[5] to use this earlier thinking as an epistemological base for psychiatric theory, led to a series of generalizations:

This essay was read (by Jay Haley) at the A.P.A. Regional Research Conference in Mexico City, March 11, 1954. Reprinted from *A.P.A. Psychiatric Research Reports*, II, 1955, by permission of the American Psychiatric Association.

(1) That human verbal communication can operate and always does operate at many contrasting levels of abstraction. These range in two directions from the seemingly simple denotative level ("The cat is on the mat"). One range or set of these more abstract levels includes those explicit or implicit messages where the subject of discourse is the language. We will call these metalinguistic (for example, "The verbal sound 'cat' stands for any member of such and such class of objects," or "The word, 'cat,' has no fur and cannot scratch"). The other set of levels of abstraction we will call metacommunicative (e.g., "My telling you where to find the cat was friendly," or "This is play"). In these, the subject of discourse is the relationship between the speakers.

It will be noted that the vast majority of both metalinguistic and metacommunicative messages remain implicit; and also that, especially in the psychiatric interview, there occurs a further class of implicit messages about how metacommunicative messages of friendship and hostility are to be interpreted.

(2) If we speculate about the evolution of communication, it is evident that a very important stage in this evolution occurs when the organism gradually ceases to respond quite "automatically" to the mood-signs of another and becomes able to recognize the sign as a signal: that is, to recognize that the other individual's and its own signals are only signals, which can be trusted, distrusted, falsified, denied, amplified, corrected, and so forth.

Clearly this realization that signals are signals is by no means complete even among the human species. We all too often respond automatically to newspaper headlines as though these stimuli were direct object-indications of events in our environment instead of signals concocted and transmitted by creatures as complexly motivated as ourselves. The non-human mammal is automatically excited by the sexual odor of another; and rightly so, inasmuch as the secretion of that sign is an "involuntary" mood-sign; i.e., an outwardly perceptible event which is a part of the physiological process which we have called a mood. In the human species a more complex state of affairs begins to be the rule. Deodorants mask the involuntary olfactory signs, and in their place the cosmetic industry provides the individual with perfumes which are not involuntary signs but voluntary signals, recognizable as such. Many a man has been thrown off balance by a whiff of perfume, and if we are to believe the advertisers, it seems that these signals, voluntarily worn, have sometimes an automatic and autosuggestive effect even upon the voluntary wearer.

Be that as it may, this brief digression will serve to illustrate a stage of evolution—the drama precipitated when organisms, having eaten of the fruit of the Tree of Knowledge, discover that their signals are signals. Not only the characteristically human invention of language can then follow, but also all the complexities of empathy, identification, projection, and so on. And with these comes the possibility of communicating at the multiplicity of levels of abstraction mentioned above.

(3) The first definite step in the formulation of the hypothesis guiding this research occurred in January, 1952, when I went to the Fleishhacker Zoo in San Francisco to look for behavioral criteria which would indicate whether any given organism is or is not able to recognize that the signs emitted by itself and other members of the species are signals. In theory, I had thought out what such criteria might look like—that the occurrence of metacommunicative signs (or signals) in the stream of interaction between the animals would indicate that the animals have at least some awareness (conscious or unconscious) that the signs about which they metacommunicate are signals.

I knew, of course, that there was no likelihood of finding denotative messages among nonhuman mammals, but I was still not aware that the animal data would require an almost total revision of my thinking. What I encountered at the zoo was a phenomenon well known to everybody: I saw two young monkeys *playing*, i.e., engaged in an interactive sequence of which the unit actions or signals were similar to but not the same as those of combat. It was evident, even to the human observer, that the sequence as a whole was not combat, and evident to the human observer that to the participant monkeys this was "not combat."

Now, this phenomenon, play, could only occur if the participant organisms were capable of some degree of metacommunication, i.e., of exchanging signals which would carry the message "this is play."

(4) The next step was the examination of the message "This is play," and the realization that this message contains those elements which necessarily generate a paradox of the Russellian or Epimenides type—a negative statement containing an implicit negative metastatement. Expanded, the statement "This is play" looks something like this: "These actions in which we now engage do not denote what those actions *for which they stand* would denote."

We now ask about the italicized words, *"for which they stand."* We say the word "cat" stands for any member of a certain class. That is, the phrase "stands for" is a near synonym of "denotes." If we now substitute "which they denote" for the words "for which they stand" in the expanded definition of play, the result is: "These actions, in which we now engage, do not denote what would be denoted by those actions which these actions denote." The playful nip denotes the bite, but it does not denote what would be denoted by the bite.

According to the Theory of Logical Types such a message is of course inadmissible, because the word "denote" is being used in two degrees of abstraction, and these two uses are treated as synonymous. But all that we learn from such a criticism is that it would be bad natural history to expect the mental processes and communicative habits of mammals to

conform to the logician's ideal. Indeed, if human thought and communication always conformed to the ideal, Russell would not—in fact could
not—have formulated the ideal.

(5) A related problem in the evolution of communication concerns the
origin of what Korzybski[6] has called the map-territory relation: the fact
that a message, of whatever kind, does not consist of those objects which
it denotes ("The word 'cat' cannot scratch us"). Rather, language bears
to the objects which it denotes a relationship comparable to that which a
map bears to a territory. Denotative communication as it occurs at the
human level is only possible *after* the evolution of a complex set of metalinguistic (but not verbalized)[7] rules which govern how words and sentences shall be related to objects and events. It is therefore appropriate to
look for the evolution of such metalinguistic and/or metacommunicative
rules at a prehuman and preverbal level.

It appears from what is said above that play is a phenomenon in which
the actions of "play" are related to, or denote, other actions of "not
play." We therefore meet in play with an instance of signals standing for
other events, and it appears, therefore, that the evolution of play may
have been an important step in the evolution of communication.

(6) *Threat* is another phenomenon which resembles play in that actions denote, but are different from, other actions. The clenched fist of
threat is different from the punch, but it refers to a possible future (but at
present nonexistent) punch. And threat also is commonly recognizable
among nonhuman mammals. Indeed it has lately been argued that a great
part of what appears to be combat among members of a single species is
rather to be regarded as threat (Tinbergen,[8] Lorenz[9]).

(7) Histrionic behavior and deceit are other examples of the primitive
occurrence of map-territory differentiation. And there is evidence that
dramatization occurs among birds: a jackdaw may imitate her own mood-
signs (Lorenz[10]), and deceit has been observed among howler monkeys
(Carpenter[11]).

(8) We might expect threat, play, and histrionics to be three independent phenomena all contributing to the evolution of the discrimination
between map and territory. But it seems that this would be wrong, at least
so far as mammalian communication is concerned. Very brief analysis of
childhood behavior shows that such combinations as histrionic play,
bluff, playful threat, teasing play in response to threat, histrionic threat,
and so on form together a single total complex of phenomena. And such
adult phenomena as gambling and playing with risk have their roots in
the combination of threat and play. It is evident also that not only threat
but the reciprocal of threat—the behavior of the threatened individual—
are a part of this complex. It is probable that not only histrionics but also
spectatorship should be included within this field. It is also appropriate
to mention self-pity.

(9) A further extension of this thinking leads us to include ritual within this general field in which the discrimination is drawn, but not completely, between denotative action and that which is to be denoted. Anthropological studies of peace-making ceremonies, to cite only one example, support this conclusion.

In the Andaman Islands, peace is concluded after each side has been given ceremonial freedom to strike the other. This example, however, also illustrates the labile nature of the frame "This is play," or "This is ritual." The discrimination between map and territory is always liable to break down, and the ritual blows of peace-making are always liable to be mistaken for the "real" blows of combat. In this event, the peace-making ceremony becomes a battle (Radcliffe-Brown[12]).

(10) But this leads us to recognition of a more complex form of play; the game which is constructed not upon the premise "This is play" but rather around the question "Is this play?" And this type of interaction also has its ritual forms, e.g., in the hazing of initiation.

(11) Paradox is doubly present in the signals which are exchanged within the context of play, fantasy, threat, etc. Not only does the playful nip not denote what would be denoted by the bite for which it stands, but, in addition, the bite itself is fictional. Not only do the playing animals not quite mean what they are saying but, also, they are usually communicating about something which does not exist. At the human level, this leads to a vast variety of complications and inversions in the fields of play, fantasy, and art. Conjurers and painters of the *trompe l'oeil* school concentrate upon acquiring a virtuosity whose only reward is reached after the viewer detects that he has been deceived and is forced to smile or marvel at the skill of the deceiver. Hollywood film-makers spend millions of dollars to increase the realism of a shadow. Other artists, perhaps more realistically, insist that art be nonrepresentational; and poker players achieve a strange addictive realism by equating the chips for which they play with dollars. They still insist, however, that the loser accept his loss as part of the game.

Finally, in the dim region where art, magic, and religion meet and overlap, human beings have evolved the "metaphor that is meant," the flag which men will die to save, and the sacrament that is felt to be more than "an outward and visible sign, given unto us." Here we can recognize an attempt to deny the difference between map and territory, and to get back to the absolute innocence of communication by means of pure mood-signs.

(12) We face then two peculiarities of play: (*a*) that the messages or signals exchanged in play are in a certain sense untrue or not meant; and (*b*) that that which is denoted by these signals is nonexistent. These two peculiarities sometimes combine strangely to reverse a conclusion reached above. It was stated (4) that the playful nip denotes the bite, but

does not denote that which would be denoted by the bite. But there are other instances where an opposite phenomenon occurs. A man experiences the full intensity of subjective terror when a spear is flung at him out of the 3D screen or when he falls headlong from some peak created in his own mind in the intensity of nightmare. At the moment of terror there was no questioning of "reality," but still there was no spear in the movie house and no cliff in the bedroom. The images did not denote that which they seemed to denote, but these same images did really evoke that terror which would have been evoked by a real spear or a real precipice. By a similar trick of self-contradiction, the film-makers of Hollywood are free to offer to a puritanical public a vast range of pseudosexual fantasy which otherwise would not be tolerated. In *David and Bathsheba*, Bathsheba can be a Troilistic link between David and Uriah. And in *Hans Christian Andersen*, the hero starts out accompanied by a boy. He tries to get a woman, but when he is defeated in this attempt, he returns to the boy. In all of this, there is, of course, no homosexuality, but the choice of these symbolisms is associated in these fantasies with certain characteristic ideas, e.g., about the hopelessness of the heterosexual masculine position when faced with certain sorts of women or with certain sorts of male authority. In sum, the pseudohomosexuality of the fantasy does not stand for any real homosexuality, but does stand for and express attitudes which might accompany a real homosexuality or feed its etiological roots. The symbols do not denote homosexuality, but do denote ideas for which homosexuality is an appropriate symbol. Evidently it is necessary to re-examine the precise semantic validity of the interpretations which the psychiatrist offers to a patient, and, as preliminary to this analysis, it will be necessary to examine the nature of the frame in which these interpretations are offered.

(13) What has previously been said about play can be used as an introductory example for the discussion of frames and contexts. In sum, it is our hypothesis that the message "This is play" establishes a paradoxical frame comparable to Epimenides' paradox. This frame may be diagrammed thus:

All statements within this frame are untrue.
I love you.
I hate you.

The first statement within this frame is a self-contradictory proposition about itself. If this first statement is true, then it must be false. If it be false, then it must be true. But this first statement carries with it all the other statements in the frame. So, if the first statement be true, then all the others must be false; and vice versa, if the first statement be untrue then all the others must be true.

(14) The logically minded will notice a *non-sequitur*. It could be urged that even if the first statement is false, there remains a logical possibility that some of the other statements in the frame are untrue. It is, however, a characteristic of unconscious or "primary-process" thinking that the thinker is unable to discriminate between "some" and "all," and unable to discriminate between "not all" and "none." It seems that the achievement of these discriminations is performed by higher or more conscious mental processes which serve in the nonpsychotic individual to correct the black-and-white thinking of the lower levels. We assume, and this seems to be an orthodox assumption, that primary process is continually operating, and that the psychological validity of the paradoxical play frame depends upon this part of the mind.

(15) But, conversely, while it is necessary to invoke the primary process as an explanatory principle in order to delete the notion of "some" from between "all" and "none," this does not mean that play is simply a primary-process phenomenon. The discrimination between "play" and "nonplay," like the discrimination between fantasy and nonfantasy, is certainly a function of secondary process, or "ego." Within the dream the dreamer is usually unaware that he is dreaming, and within "play" he must often be reminded that "This is play."

Similarly, within dream or fantasy the dreamer does not operate with the concept "untrue." He operates with all sorts of statements but with a curious inability to achieve metastatements. He cannot, unless close to waking, dream a statement referring to (i.e., framing) his dream.

It therefore follows that the play frame as here used as an explanatory principle implies a special combination of primary and secondary processes. This, however, is related to what was said earlier, when it was argued that play marks a step forward in the evolution of communication—the crucial step in the discovery of map-territory relations. In primary process, map and territory are equated; in secondary process, they can be discriminated. In play, they are both equated and discriminated.

(16) Another logical anomaly in this system must be mentioned: that the relationship between two propositions which is commonly described by the word "premise" has become intransitive. In general, all asymmetrical relationships are transitive. The relationship "greater than" is typical in this respect; it is conventional to argue that if A is greater than B, and B is greater than C, then A is greater than C. But in psychological processes the transitivity of asymmetrical relations is not observed. The proposition P may be a premise for Q; Q may be a premise for R; and R may be a premise for P. Specifically, in the system which we are considering, the circle is still more contracted. The message, "All statements

within this frame are untrue" is itself to be taken as a premise in evaluating its own truth or untruth. (Cf. the intransivity of psychological preference discussed by McCulloch.[13] The paradigm for all paradoxes of this general type is Russell's[14] "class of classes which are not members of themselves." Here Russell demonstrates that paradox is generated by treating the relationship, "is a member of," as an intransitive.) With this caveat, that the "premise" relation in psychology is likely to be intransitive, we shall use the word "premise" to denote a dependency of one idea or message upon another comparable to the dependency of one proposition upon another which is referred to in logic by saying that the proposition P is a premise for Q.

(17) All this, however, leaves unclear what is meant by "frame" and the related notion of "context." To clarify these, it is necessary to insist first that these are psychological concepts. We use two sorts of analogy to discuss these notions: the physical analogy of the picture frame and the more abstract, but still not psychological, analogy of the mathematical set. In set theory the mathematicians have developed axioms and theorems to discuss with rigor the logical implications of membership in overlapping categories or "sets." The relationships between sets are commonly illustrated by diagrams in which the items or members of a larger universe are represented by dots, and the smaller sets are delimited by imaginary lines enclosing the members of each set. Such diagrams then illustrate a topological approach to the logic of classification. The first step in defining a psychological frame might be to say that it is (or delimits) a class or set of messages (or meaningful actions). The play of two individuals on a certain occasion would then be defined as the set of all messages exchanged by them within a limited period of time and modified by the paradoxical premise system which we have described. In a set-theoretical diagram these messages might be represented by dots, and the "set" enclosed by a line which would separate these from other dots representing nonplay messages. The mathematical analogy breaks down, however, because the psychological frame is not satisfactorily represented by an imaginary line. We assume that the psychological frame has some degree of real existence. In many instances, the frame is consciously recognized and even represented in vocabulary ("play," "movie," "interview," "job," "language," etc.). In other cases, there may be no explicit verbal reference to the frame, and the subject may have no consciousness of it. The analyst, however, finds that his own thinking is simplified if he uses the notion of an unconscious frame as an explanatory principle; usually he goes further than this and infers its existence in the subject's unconscious.

But while the analogy of the mathematical set is perhaps over abstract, the analogy of the picture frame is excessively concrete. The psychological concept which we are trying to define is neither physical nor logical. Rather, the actual physical frame is, we believe, added by human beings to physical pictures because these human beings operate more easily in a universe in which some of their psychological characteristics are externalized. It is these characteristics which we are trying to discuss, using the externalization as an illustrative device.

(18) The common functions and uses of psychological frames may now be listed and illustrated by reference to the analogies whose limitations have been indicated in the previous paragraph:

(*a*) Psychological frames are exclusive, i.e., by including certain messages (or meaningful actions) within a frame, certain other messages are excluded.

(*b*) Psychological frames are inclusive, i.e., by excluding certain messages certain others are included. From the point of view of set theory these two functions are synonymous, but from the point of view of psychology it is necessary to list them separately. The frame around a picture, if we consider this frame as a message intended to order or organize the perception of the viewer, says, "Attend to what is within and do not attend to what is outside." Figure and ground, as these terms are used by gestalt psychologists, are not symmetrically related as are the set and nonset of set theory. Perception of the ground must be positively inhibited and perception of the figure (in this case the picture) must be positively enhanced.

(*c*) Psychological frames are related to what we have called "premises." The picture frame tells the viewer that he is not to use the same sort of thinking in interpreting the picture that he might use in interpreting the wallpaper outside the frame. Or, in terms of the analogy from set theory, the messages enclosed within the imaginary line are defined as members of a class by virtue of their sharing common premises or mutual relevance. The frame itself thus becomes a part of the premise system. Either, as in the case of the play frame, the frame is involved in the evaluation of the messages which it contains, or the frame merely assists the mind in understanding the contained messages by reminding the thinker that these messages are mutually relevant and the messages outside the frame may be ignored.

(*d*) In the sense of the previous paragraph, a frame is metacommunicative. Any message, which either explicitly or implicitly defines a frame, *ipso facto* gives the receiver instructions or aids in his attempt to understand the messages included within the frame.

(*e*) The converse of (*d*) is also true. Every metacommunicative or metalinguistic message defines, either explicitly or implicitly, the set of messages about which it communicates, i.e., every metacommunicative message is or defines a psychological frame. This, for example, is very evident in regard to such small metacommunicative signals as punctuation marks in a printed message, but applies equally to such complex metacommunicative messages as the psychiatrist's definition of his own curative role in terms of which his contributions to the whole mass of messages in psychotherapy are to be understood.

(f) The relation between psychological frame and perceptual gestalt needs to be considered, and here the analogy of the picture frame is useful. In a painting by Rouault or Blake, the human figures and other objects represented are outlined. "Wise men see outlines and therefore they draw them." But outside these lines, which delimit the perceptual gestalt or "figure," there is a background or "ground" which in turn is limited by the picture frame. Similarly, in set-theoretical diagrams, the larger universe within which the smaller sets are drawn is itself enclosed in a frame. This double framing is, we believe, not merely a matter of "frames within frames" but an indication that mental processes resemble logic in *needing* an outer frame to delimit the ground against which the figures are to be perceived. This need is often unsatisfied, as when we see a piece of sculpture in a junk shop window, but this is uncomfortable. We suggest that the need for this outer limit to the ground is related to a preference for avoiding the paradoxes of abstraction. When a logical class or set of items is defined—for example, the class of matchboxes—it is necessary to delimit the set of items which are to be excluded, in this case, all those things which are not matchboxes. But the items to be included in the background set must be of the same degree of abstraction, i.e., of the same "logical type" as those within the set itself. Specifically, if paradox is to be avoided, the "class of matchboxes" and the "class of nonmatchboxes" (even though both these items are clearly not matchboxes) must not be regarded as members of the class of nonmatchboxes. No class can be a member of itself. The picture frame then, because it delimits a background, is here regarded as an external representation of a very special and important type of psychological frame—namely a frame whose function is to delimit a logical type. This, in fact, is what was indicated above when it was said that the picture frame is an instruction to the viewer that he should not extend the premises which obtain between the figures within the picture to the wallpaper behind it.

But, it is precisely this sort of frame that precipitates paradox. The rule for avoiding paradoxes insists that the items outside any enclosing line be of the same logical type as those within, but the picture frame, as analyzed above, is a line dividing items of one logical type from those of another. In passing, it is interesting to note that Russell's rule cannot be stated without breaking the rule. Russell insists that all items of inappropriate logical type be excluded (i.e., by an imaginary line) from the background of any class, i.e., he insists upon the drawing of an imaginary line of precisely the sort which he prohibits.

(19) This whole matter of frames and paradoxes may be illustrated in terms of animal behavior, where three types of message may be recognized or deduced: (a) Messages of the sort which we here call mood-

signs; (*b*) messages which simulate mood-signs (in play, threat, histrionics, etc.); and (*c*) messages which enable the receiver to discriminate between mood-signs and those other signs which resemble them. The message "This is play" is of this third type. It tells the receiver that certain nips and other meaningful actions are not messages of the first type.

The message "This is play" thus sets a frame of the sort which is likely to precipitate paradox: it is an attempt to discriminate between, or to draw a line between, categories of different logical types.

(20) This discussion of play and psychological frames establishes a type of triadic constellation (or system of relationships) between messages. One instance of this constellation is analyzed in paragraph 19, but it is evident that constellations of this sort occur not only at the non-human level but also in the much more complex communication of human beings. A fantasy or myth may simulate a denotative narrative, and, to discriminate between these types of discourse, people use messages of the frame-setting type, and so on.

(21) In conclusion, we arrive at the complex task of applying this theoretical approach to the particular phenomena of psychotherapy. Here the lines of·our thinking may most briefly be summarized by presenting and partially answering these questions:

(*a*) Is there any indication that certain forms of psychopathology are specifically characterized by abnormalities in the patient's handling of frames and paradoxes?

(*b*) Is there any indication that the techniques of psychotherapy necessarily depend upon the manipulation of frames and paradoxes?

(*c*) Is it possible to describe the process of a given psychotherapy in terms of the interaction between the patient's abnormal use of frames and the therapist's manipulation of them?

(22) In reply to the first question, it seems that the "word salad" of schizophrenia can be described in terms of the patient's failure to recognize the metaphoric nature of his fantasies. In what should be triadic constellations of messages, the frame-setting message (e.g., the phrase "as if") is omitted, and the metaphor or fantasy is narrated and acted upon in a manner which would be appropriate if the fantasy were a message of the more direct kind. The absence of metacommunicative framing which was noted in the case of dreams (15) is characteristic of the waking communications of the schizophrenic. With the loss of the ability to set metacommunicative frames, there is also a loss of ability to achieve the more primary or primitive message. The metaphor is treated directly as a message of the more primary type. (This matter is discussed at greater length in the paper given by Jay Haley at this Conference.)

(23) The dependence of psychotherapy upon the manipulation of frames follows from the fact that therapy is an attempt to change the patient's metacommunicative habits. Before therapy, the patient thinks and

operates in terms of a certain set of rules for the making and understanding of messages. After successful therapy, he operates in terms of a different set of such rules. (Rules of this sort are in general, unverbalized, and unconscious both before and after.) It follows that, in the process of therapy, there must have been communication at a level *meta* to these rules. There must have been communication about a *change* in rules.

But such a communication about change could not conceivably occur in messages of the type permitted by the patient's metacommunicative rules as they existed either before or after therapy.

It was suggested above that the paradoxes of play are characteristic of an evolutionary step. Here we suggest that similar paradoxes are a necessary ingredient in that process of change which we call psychotherapy.

The resemblance between the process of therapy and the phenomenon of play is, in fact, profound. Both occur within a delimited psychological frame, a spatial and temporal bounding of a set of interactive messages. In both play and therapy, the messages have a special and peculiar relationship to a more concrete or basic reality. Just as the pseudocombat of play is not real combat, so also the pseudolove and pseudohate of therapy are not real love and hate. The "transfer" is discriminated from real love and hate by signals invoking the psychological frame; and indeed it is this frame which permits the transfer to reach its full intensity and to be discussed between patient and therapist.

The formal characteristics of the therapeutic process may be illustrated by building up a model in stages. Imagine first two players who engage in a game of canasta according to a standard set of rules. So long as these rules govern and are unquestioned by both players, the game is unchanging, i.e., no therapeutic change will occur. (Indeed many attempts at psychotherapy fail for this reason.) We may imagine, however, that at a certain moment the two canasta players cease to play canasta and start a discussion of the rules. Their discourse is now of a different logical type from that of their play. At the end of this discussion, we can imagine that they return to playing but with modified rules.

This sequence of events is, however, still an imperfect model of therapeutic interaction, though it illustrates our contention that therapy necessarily involves a combination of discrepant logical types of discourse. Our imaginary players avoided paradox by separating their discussion of the rules from their play, and it is precisely this separation that is impossible in psychotherapy. As we see it, the process of psychotherapy is a framed interaction between two persons, in which the rules are implicit but subject to change. Such change can only be proposed by experimental action, but every such experimental action, in which a proposal to change the rules is implicit, is itself a part of the ongoing game. It is this combination of logical types within the single meaningful act that gives to therapy the character not of a rigid game like canasta but, instead, that of an evolving system of interaction. The play of kittens or otters has this character.

(24) In regard to the specific relationship between the way in which the patient handles frames and the way in which the therapist manipulates them, very little can at present be said. It is, however, suggestive to observe that the psychological frame of therapy is an analogue of the frame-setting message which the schizophrenic is unable to achieve. To talk in "word salad" within the psychological frame of therapy is, in a sense, not pathological. Indeed the neurotic is specifically encouraged to do precisely this, narrating his dreams and free associations so that patient and therapist may achieve an understanding of this material. By the process of interpretation, the neurotic is driven to insert an "as if" clause into the productions of his primary process thinking, which productions he had previously deprecated or repressed. He must learn that fantasy contains truth.

For the schizophrenic the problem is somewhat different. His error is in treating the metaphors of primary process with the full intensity of literal truth. Through the discovery of what these metaphors stand for he must discover that they are only metaphors.

(25) From the point of view of the project, however, psychotherapy constitutes only one of the many fields which we are attempting to investigate. Our central thesis may be summed up as a statement of the necessity of the paradoxes of abstraction. It is not merely bad natural history to suggest that people might or should obey the Theory of Logical Types in their communications; their failure to do this is not due to mere carelessness or ignorance. Rather, we believe that the paradoxes of abstraction must make their appearance in all communication more complex than that of mood-signals, and that without these paradoxes the evolution of communication would be at an end. Life would then be an endless interchange of stylized messages, a game with rigid rules, unrelieved by change or humor.

NOTES

1. A. N. Whitehead and B. Russell, *Principia Mathematica*, 3 vols., 2nd ed. (Cambridge, England: Cambridge University Press, 1910–1913).

2. L. Wittgenstein, *Tractatus Logico-Philosophicus* (London: Routledge and Kegan Paul, 1922).

3. R. Carnap, *The Logical Syntax of Language* (New York: Harcourt, Brace, 1937).

4. B. L. Whorf, "Science and Linguistics," *Technology Review* (1940), 44: 229–248.

5. J. Ruesch and G. Bateson, *Communication: The Social Matrix of Psychiatry* (New York: Norton, 1951).

6. A. Korzybski, *Science and Sanity* (New York: Science Press, 1941).

7. The verbalization of these metalinguistic rules is a much later achievement which can only occur after the evolution of a nonverbalized meta-metalinguistics.

8. N. Tinbergen, *Social Behavior in Animals with Special Reference to Verte-brates* (London: Methuen, 1953).

9. K. Z. Lorenz, *King Solomon's Ring* (New York: Crowell, 1952).

10. Ibid.

11. C. R. Carpenter, "A Field Study of the Behavior and Social Relations of Howling Monkeys," *Comp. Psychol. Monogr.* (1934), 10: 1–168.

12. A. R. Radcliffe-Brown, *The Andaman Islanders* (Cambridge, England: Cambridge University Press, 1922).

13. W. S. McCulloch, "A Heterarchy of Values, etc.," *Bulletin of Math. Bio-phys.* (1945), 7: 89–93.

14. Whitehead and Russell, *Principia Mathematica*.

ROMAN JAKOBSON

The goal of Roman Jakobson's famous essay, which has attained the status of a true semiotic "classic" and an indispensable starting point for later discussion of "poetics," is to construct a coherent sixfold functional matrix of language and then, within the framework of a general linguistic theory, to thematize the poetic function in particular. Poetics, as Jakobson conceives it, "deals primarily with the question, *What makes a verbal message a work of art?*" Just as the analysis of painting, which will be one of the concerns of the essay by Meyer Schapiro, deals with pictorial structure, "poetics deals with problems of verbal structure" and in fact is "an integral part of linguistics." The extreme heuristic fertility of Jakobson's essay is further indicated by his contention, which should be put to the test through the analysis of concrete instances, that "many poetic features belong not only to the science of language but to the whole theory of signs, that is, to general semiotics." Indeed, in light of the existence of what Jakobson calls "pansemiotic features," that is, features that some or perhaps all other systems of signs share with language, such as rhythm, good order, "pregnance," expressivity, the analysis he makes of strictly verbal art can be extended to other systems of expression, too. Thus, Jakobson also belongs in part, even if ambiguously, to that large current of perhaps essentially problematic thought which has taken the great linguistic analogy as its key to semiotic phenomena and which is further illustrated in the essays by Lévi-Strauss and Barthes and put into question by Benveniste and Langer. A substantial confrontation with Jakobson's work will then involve dialectical comparison with other positions and will attempt to apply the principles of his analysis, to the degree that they deal with pansemiotic features, to other art forms which in their own way instantiate the poetic function specifically as "aesthetic function," the great theme of the Russian and Prague Formalists.

The poetic "function" of language is only one among a group of functions which a "speech event" can implement in any act of verbal communication. These functions make up the "constitutive factors" of the act of speech, highlighting the predominant function that it is, on the occasion, implementing. Focusing on the addresser highlights the emotive or expressive function, on the addressee, the conative or appellative function, on the context, the referential function, on the message, the poetic function, on contact, the phatic function, on the code, the metalingual function. Now the peculiarity of the poetic function, which results from focusing on the message, is the promotion of "the palpability of signs" and the deepening of "the fundamental dichotomy of signs and objects," a comment which shows that the poetic function overspills the realm of poetry *quâ tale* and is extended to the "aesthetic" as such as "self-focusing" expression.

The proximate and acknowledged source of Jakobson's attempt to outline the structure and mutual relations of linguistic functions is Karl Bühler, whose *Sprachtheorie* had predominantly focused on the "representational" or "referential" function, while also specifying the emotive (the expressive) and the conative (the appellative) as essential and constitutive functions of a complete speech act. Bühler's account of the representational function is outlined very clearly in his essay. Jakobson potentiates Bühler's original schema, which was itself the result of systematizing materials handed on from the linguistic and philosophical tradition. He also exploited Saussure's thesis on the axes of language, although he did not follow Saussure's radical opposition of synchrony and diachrony, for in his work on the theory of the phoneme Jakobson showed that they were not mutually exclusive.

The Saussurian doctrine on the syntagmatic and paradigmatic axes became for Jakobson the axes of "selection" and "combination" which are "the two basic modes of arrangement used in verbal behavior." On the axis of selection, which is Saussure's paradigmatic axis, we find, in the words of Jakobson's and Halle's *Fundamentals of Language* (72), "a filing cabinet of *prefabricated* representations," all of them equivalent in a certain respect, embodied in the vocabulary of a language, while on the axis of combination we find "linguistic units of a higher degree of complexity," namely, speech chains ranging from sentences to texts of all sorts. Now Jakobson's central thesis is that "the poetic function projects the principle of equivalence from the axis of selection into the axis of combination" (Jakobson underlines the whole) and hence "equivalence is promoted to the constitutive device of the sequence." The production of a self-focusing "figure of sound" does not remain just on the sound level but involves, at its deepest level, the level of sense. Thus, Jakobson ascribes to Valéry's view of poetry as "hesitation between the sound and the sense." It is one of the chief merits of his essay to have shown by means of a wealth of examples just how the principle of equivalence functions in the poetic realm. It would be worthwhile to confront Jakobson's theses here, which are primarily illustrated in the realm of verbal art, with what Langer says about the so-called "morphology of feeling" which comes to expression in an aesthetic symbolic form, for the principle of equivalence becomes constitutive in the aesthetic realm quite generally, and it participates paradigmatically in that set of "pansemiotic features" noted earlier.

The clear exposition by Elmar Holenstein, *Roman Jakobson's Approach to Language: Phenomenological Structuralism*, translated by Catherine Schelbert and Tarcisius Schelbert (Bloomington and London: Indiana University Press, 1976) should be consulted first. It contains a useful bibliography. Then, on the basis of the information given in this book, turn to the seven volumes of Jakobson's *Selected Writings* (The Hague: Mouton). An extremely accessible introduction to Jakobson's key ideas is found in his two small books, *Fundamentals of Language*, written with Morris Halle (The Hague: Mouton, 1971) and *Six Lectures on Sound and Meaning*, translated by John Mepham with a preface by Claude Lévi-Strauss (Cambridge: MIT Press, 1978).

Closing Statement: Linguistics and Poetics

ROMAN JAKOBSON

Fortunately, scholarly and political conferences have nothing in common. The success of a political convention depends on the general agreement of the majority or totality of its participants. The use of votes and vetoes, however, is alien to scholarly discussion where disagreement generally proves to be more productive than agreement. Disagreement discloses antinomies and tensions within the field discussed and calls for novel exploration. Not political conferences but rather exploratory activities in Antarctica present an analogy to scholarly meetings: international experts in various disciplines attempt to map an unknown region and find out where the greatest obstacles for the explorer are, the insurmountable peaks and precipices. Such a mapping seems to have been the chief task of our conference, and in this respect its work has been quite successful. Have we not realized what problems are the most crucial and the most controversial? Have we not also learned how to switch our codes, what terms to expound or even to avoid in order to prevent misunderstandings with people using different departmental jargon? Such questions, I believe, for most of the members of this conference, if not for all of them, are somewhat clearer today than they were three days ago.

I have been asked for summary remarks about poetics in its relation to linguistics. Poetics deals primarily with the question, *What makes a verbal message a work of art?* Because the main subject of poetics is the *differentia specifica* of verbal art in relation to other arts and in relation to other kinds of verbal behavior, poetics is entitled to the leading place in literary studies.

Poetics deals with problems of verbal structure, just as the analysis of painting is concerned with pictorial structure. Since linguistics is the global science of verbal structure, poetics may be regarded as an integral part of linguistics.

Arguments against such a claim must be thoroughly discussed. It is evident that many devices studied by poetics are not confined to verbal art. We can refer to the possibility of transposing *Wuthering Heights* into a motion picture, medieval legends into frescoes and miniatures, or *L'après-midi d'un faune* into music, ballet, and graphic art. However ludicrous may appear the idea of the *Iliad* and *Odyssey* in comics, certain structural features of their plot are preserved despite the disappearance of their verbal shape. The question whether Blake's illustrations to the *Divina Commedia* are or are not adequate is a proof that different arts are comparable. The problems of baroque or any other historical style transgress the frame of a single art. When handling the surrealistic metaphor, we could hardly pass by Max Ernst's pictures or Luis Buñuel's films, *The Andalusian Dog* and *The Golden Age*. In short, many poetic features belong not only to the science of language but to the whole theory of signs, that is, to general semiotics. This statement, however, is valid not only for verbal art but also for all varieties of language since language shares many properties with some other systems of signs or even with all of them (pansemiotic features).

Likewise a second objection contains nothing that would be specific for literature: the question of relations between the word and the world concerns not only verbal art but actually all kinds of discourse. Linguistics is likely to explore all possible problems of relation between discourse and the "universe of discourse": what of this universe is verbalized by a given discourse and how is it verbalized. The truth values, however, as far as they are—to say with the logicians—"extralinguistic entities," obviously exceed the bounds of poetics and of linguistics in general.

Sometimes we hear that poetics, in contradistinction to linguistics, is concerned with evaluation. This separation of the two fields from each other is based on a current but erroneous interpretation of the contrast between the structure of poetry and other types of verbal structure: the latter are said to be opposed by their "casual," designless nature to the "noncasual," purposeful character of poetic language. In point of fact, any verbal behavior is goal-directed, but the aims are different and the conformity of the means used to the effect aimed at is a problem that evermore preoccupies inquirers into the diverse kinds of verbal communication. There is a close correspondence, much closer than critics believe, between the question of linguistic phenomena expanding in space and time and the spatial and temporal spread of literary models. Even such discontinuous expansion as the resurrection of neglected or forgotten poets—for instance, the posthumous discovery and subsequent canonization of Gerard Manley Hopkins (d. 1889), the tardy fame of Lautréamont (d. 1870) among surrealist poets, and the salient influence of the hitherto ignored Cyprian Norwid (d. 1883) on Polish modern poetry—find a parallel in the history of standard languages which are prone to revive outdated models, sometimes long forgotten, as was the case in literary Czech which toward the beginning of the nineteenth century leaned to sixteenth-century models.

Unfortunately the terminological confusion of "literary studies" with "criticism" tempts the student of literature to replace the description of the intrinsic values of a literary work by a subjective, censorious verdict. The label "literary critic" applied to an investigator of literature is as erroneous as "grammatical (or lexical) critic" would be applied to a linguist. Syntactic and morphologic research cannot be supplanted by a normative grammar, and likewise no manifesto, foisting a critic's own tastes and opinions on creative literature, may act as substitute for an objective scholarly analysis of verbal art. This statement is not to be mistaken for the quietist principle of *laissez faire*; any verbal culture involves programmatic, planning, normative endeavors. Yet why is a clear-cut discrimination made between pure and applied linguistics or between phonetics and orthoëpy but not between literary studies and criticism?

Literary studies, with poetics as their focal portion, consist like linguistics of two sets of problems: synchrony and diachrony. The synchronic description envisages not only the literary production of any given stage but also that part of the literary tradition which for the stage in question has remained vital or has been revived. Thus, for instance, Shakespeare on the one hand and Donne, Marvell, Keats, and Emily Dickinson on the other are experienced by the present English poetic world, whereas the works of James Thomson and Longfellow, for the time being, do not belong to viable artistic values. The selection of classics and their reinterpretation by a novel trend is a substantial problem of synchronic literary studies. Synchronic poetics, like synchronic linguistics, is not to be confused with statics; any stage discriminates between more conservative and more innovatory forms. Any contemporary stage is experienced in its temporal dynamics, and, on the other hand, the historical approach both in poetics and in linguistics is concerned not only with changes but also with continuous, enduring, static factors. A thoroughly comprehensive historical poetics or history of language is a superstructure to be built on a series of successive synchronic descriptions.

Insistence on keeping poetics apart from linguistics is warranted only when the field of linguistics appears to be illicitly restricted, for example, when the sentence is viewed by some linguists as the highest analyzable construction or when the scope of linguistics is confined to grammar alone or uniquely to nonsemantic questions of external form or to the inventory of denotative devices with no reference to free variations. Voegelin has clearly pointed out the two most important and related problems which face structural linguistics, namely, a revision of "the monolithic hypothesis of language" and a concern with "the interdependence of diverse structures within one language." No doubt, for any speech community, for any speaker, there exists a unity of language, but this over-all code represents a system of interconnected subcodes; each language encompasses several concurrent patterns which are each characterized by a different function.

Obviously we must agree with Sapir that, on the whole, "ideation reigns supreme in language . . ." (40), but this supremacy does not authorize linguistics to disregard the "secondary factors." The emotive elements of speech which, as Joos is prone to believe, cannot be described "with a finite number of absolute categories," are classified by him "as nonlinguistic elements of the real world." Hence, "for us they remain vague, protean, fluctuating phenomena," he concludes, "which we refuse to tolerate in our science" (19). Joos is indeed a brilliant expert in reduction experiments, and his emphatic requirement for an "expulsion" of the emotive elements "from linguistic science" is a radical experiment in reduction—*reductio ad absurdum*.

Language must be investigated in all the variety of its functions. Before discussing the poetic function we must define its place among the other functions of language. An outline of these functions demands a concise survey of the constitutive factors in any speech event, in any act of verbal communication. The ADDRESSER sends a MESSAGE to the ADDRESSEE. To be operative the message requires a CONTEXT referred to ("referent" in another, somewhat ambiguous, nomenclature), seizable by the addressee, and either verbal or capable of being verbalized; a CODE fully, or at least partially, common to the addresser and addressee (or in other words, to the encoder and decoder of the message); and, finally, a CONTACT, a physical channel and psychological connection between the addresser and the addressee, enabling both of them to enter and stay in communication. All these factors inalienably involved in verbal communication may be schematized as follows:

CONTEXT

ADDRESSER . . . . . . MESSAGE . . . . . . ADDRESSEE
CONTACT

CODE

Each of these six factors determines a different function of language. Although we distinguish six basic aspects of language, we could, however, hardly find verbal messages that would fulfill only one function. The diversity lies not in a monopoly of some one of these several functions but in a different hierarchical order of functions. The verbal structure of a message depends primarily on the predominant function. But even though a set (*Einstellung*) toward the referent, an orientation toward the CON-TEXT—briefly the so-called REFERENTIAL, "denotative," "cognitive" function—is the leading task of numerous messages, the accessory participation of the other functions in such messages must be taken into account by the observant linguist.

The so-called EMOTIVE or "expressive" function, focused on the AD-DRESSER, aims a direct expression of the speaker's attitude toward what he is speaking about. It tends to produce an impression of a certain emotion whether true or feigned; therefore, the term "emotive" launched and advocated by Marty (30) has proved to be preferable to "emotional." The purely emotive stratum in language is presented by the interjections. They differ from the means of referential language both by their sound pattern (peculiar sound sequences or even sounds elsewhere unusual) and by their syntactic role (they are not components but equivalents of sentences). "*Tut! Tut!* said McGinty": the complete utterance of Conan Doyle's character consists of two suction clicks. The emotive function, laid bare in the interjections, flavors to some extent all our utterances, on their phonic, grammatical, and lexical level. If we analyze language from the standpoint of the information it carries, we cannot restrict the notion of information to the cognitive aspect of language. A man, using expressive features to indicate his angry or ironic attitude, conveys ostensible information, and evidently this verbal behavior cannot be likened to such nonsemiotic, nutritive activities as "eating grapefruit" (despite Chatman's bold simile). The difference between [big] and the emphatic prolongation of the vowel [bi:g] is a conventional, coded linguistic feature like the difference between the short and long vowel in such Czech pairs as [vi] 'you' and [vi:] 'knows,' but in the latter pair the differential information is phonemic and in the former emotive. As long as we are interested in phonemic invariants, the English /i/ and /i:/ appear to be mere variants of one and the same phoneme, but if we are concerned with emotive units, the relation between the invariant and variants is reversed: length and shortness are invariants implemented by variable phonemes. Saporta's surmise that emotive difference is a nonlinguistic feature, "attributable to the delivery of the message and not to the message," arbitrarily reduces the informational capacity of messages.

A former actor of Stanislavskij's Moscow Theater told me how at his audition he was asked by the famous director to make forty different messages from the phrase *Segodnja večerom* 'This evening,' by diversifying its expressive tint. He made a list of some forty emotional situations, then emitted the given phrase in accordance with each of these situations, which his audience had to recognize only from the changes in the sound shape of the same two words. For our research work in the description and analysis of contemporary Standard Russian (under the auspices of the Rockefeller Foundation) this actor was asked to repeat Stanislavskij's test. He wrote down some fifty situations framing the same elliptic sentence and made of it fifty corresponding messages for a tape record. Most of the messages were correctly and circumstantially decoded by Muscovite listeners. May I add that all such emotive cues easily undergo linguistic analysis.

Orientation toward the ADDRESSEE, the CONATIVE function, finds its purest grammatical expression in the vocative and imperative, which syntactically, morphologically, and often even phonemically deviate from other nominal and verbal categories. The imperative sentences cardinally differ from declarative sentences: the latter are and the former are not liable to a truth test. When in O'Neill's play *The Fountain*, Nano, "(in a fierce tone of command)," says "Drink!"—the imperative cannot be challenged by the question "is it true or not?" which may be, however, perfectly well asked after such sentences as "one drank," "one will drink," "one would drink." In contradistinction to the imperative sentences, the declarative sentences are convertible into interrogative sentences: "did one drink?" "will one drink?" "would one drink?"

The traditional model of language as elucidated particularly by Bühler (4) was confined to these three functions—emotive, conative, and referential—and the three apexes of this model—the first person of the addresser, the second person of the addressee, and the "third person," properly—someone or something spoken of. Certain additional verbal functions can be easily inferred from this triadic model. Thus the magic, incantatory function is chiefly some kind of conversion of an absent or inanimate "third person" into an addressee of a conative message. "May this sty dry up, *tfu, tfu, tfu, tfu*" (Lithuanian spell: 28, p. 69). "Water, queen river, daybreak! Send grief beyond the blue sea, to the sea-bottom, like a grey stone never to rise from the sea-bottom, may grief never come to burden the light heart of God's servant, may grief be removed and sink away." (North Russian incantation: 39, pp. 217f.). "Sun, stand thou still upon Gibeon; and thou, Moon, in the valley of Aj-a-lon. And the sun stood still, and the moon stayed . . ." (Josh. 10.12). We observe, however, three further constitutive factors of verbal communication and three corresponding functions of language.

There are messages primarily serving to establish, to prolong, or to discontinue communication, to check whether the channel works ("Hello, do you hear me?"), to attract the attention of the interlocutor or to confirm his continued attention ("Are you listening?" or in Shakespearean diction, "Lend me your ears!"—and on the other end of the wire "Um-hum!"). This set for CONTACT, or in Malinowski's terms PHATIC function (26), may be displayed by a profuse exchange of ritualized formulas, by entire dialogues with the mere purport of prolonging communication. Dorothy Parker caught eloquent examples: "'Well!' the young man said.

'Well!' she said. 'Well, here we are,' he said. 'Here we are,' she said, 'Aren't we?' 'I should say we were,' he said, 'Eeyop! Here we are.' 'Well!' she said. 'Well!' he said, 'well.'" The endeavor to start and sustain communication is typical of talking birds; thus the phatic function of language is the only one they share with human beings. It is also the first verbal function acquired by infants; they are prone to communicate before being able to send or receive informative communication.

A distinction has been made in modern logic between two levels of language, "object language" speaking of objects and "metalanguage" speaking of language. But metalanguage is not only a necessary scientific tool utilized by logicians and linguists; it plays also an important role in our everyday language. Like Molière's Jourdain who used prose without knowing it, we practice metalanguage without realizing the metalingual character of our operations. Whenever the addresser and/or the addressee need to check up whether they use the same code, speech is focused on the CODE: it performs a METALINGUAL (i.e., glossing) function. "I don't follow you—what do you mean?" asks the addressee, or in Shakespearean diction, "What is't thou say'st?" And the addresser in anticipation of such recapturing questions inquires: "Do you know what I mean?" Imagine such an exasperating dialogue: "The sophomore was plucked." "But what is *plucked*?" "*Plucked* means the same as *flunked*." "And *flunked*?" "*To be flunked* is *to fail in an exam*." "And what is *sophomore*?" persists the interrogator innocent of school vocabulary. "*A sophomore* is (or means) a *second-year student*." All these equational sentences convey information merely about the lexical code of English; their function is strictly metalingual. Any process of language learning, in particular child acquisition of the mother tongue, makes wide use of such metalingual operations; and aphasia may often be defined as a loss of ability for metalingual operations.

We have brought up all the six factors involved in verbal communication except the message itself. The set (*Einstellung*) toward the MESSAGE as such, focus on the message for its own sake, is the POETIC function of language. This function cannot be productively studied out of touch with the general problems of language, and, on the other hand, the scrutiny of language requires a thorough consideration of its poetic function. Any attempt to reduce the sphere of poetic function to poetry or to confine poetry to poetic function would be a delusive oversimplification. Poetic function is not the sole function of verbal art but only its dominant, determining function, whereas in all other verbal activities it acts as a subsidiary, accessory constituent. This function, by promoting the palpability of signs, deepens the fundamental dichotomy of signs and objects. Hence, when dealing with poetic function, linguistics cannot limit itself to the field of poetry.

"Why do you always say *Joan and Margery*, yet never *Margery and Joan*? Do you prefer Joan to her twin sister?" "Not at all, it just sounds smoother." In a sequence of two coordinate names, as far as no rank problems interfere, the precedence of the shorter name suits the speaker, unaccountably for him, as a well-ordered shape of the message.

A girl used to talk about "the horrible Harry." "Why horrible?" "Because I hate him." "But why not *dreadful, terrible, frightful, disgusting?*" "I don't know why, but *horrible* fits him better." Without realizing it, she clung to the poetic device of paronomasia.

The political slogan "I like Ike" /ay layk ayk/, succinctly structured, consists of three monosyllables and counts three diphthongs /ay/, each of them symmetrically followed by one consonantal phoneme, /..l..k..k/. The make-up of the three words presents a variation: no consonantal phonemes in the first word, two around the diphthong in the second, and one final consonant in the third. A similar dominant nucleus /ay/ was noticed by Hymes in some of the sonnets of Keats. Both cola of the trisyllabic formula "I like/Ike" rhyme with each other, and the second of the two rhyming words is fully included in the first one (echo rhyme), /layk/—/ayk/, a paronomastic image of a feeling which totally envelops its object. Both cola alliterate with each other, and the first of the two alliterating words is included in the second: /ay/—/ayk/, a paronomastic image of the loving subject enveloped by the beloved object. The secondary, poetic function of this electional catch phrase reinforces its impressiveness and efficacy.

As we said, the linguistic study of the poetic function must overstep the limits of poetry, and, on the other hand, the linguistic scrutiny of poetry cannot limit itself to the poetic function. The particularities of diverse poetic genres imply a differently ranked participation of the other verbal functions along with the dominant poetic function. Epic poetry, focused on the third person, strongly involves the referential function of language; the lyric, oriented toward the first person, is intimately linked with the emotive function; poetry of the second person is imbued with the conative function and is either supplicatory or exhortative, depending on whether the first person is subordinated to the second one or the second to the first.

Now that our cursory description of the six basic functions of verbal communication is more or less complete, we may complement our scheme of the fundamental factors by a corresponding scheme of the functions:

REFERENTIAL

EMOTIVE   POETIC   CONATIVE
                      PHATIC

METALINGUAL

What is the empirical linguistic criterion of the poetic function? In particular, what is the indispensable feature inherent in any piece of poetry? To answer this question we must recall the two basic modes of arrangement used in verbal behavior, *selection* and *combination*. If "child" is the topic of the message, the speaker selects one among the extant, more or less similar, nouns like child, kid, youngster, tot, all of them equivalent in a certain respect, and then, to comment on this topic, he may select one of the semantically cognate verbs—sleeps, dozes, nods, naps. Both chosen words combine in the speech chain. The selection is produced on the base of equivalence, similarity and dissimilarity, synonymity and antonymity, while the combination, the build up of the sequence, is based on contiguity. *The poetic function projects the principle of equivalence from the axis of selection into the axis of combination.* Equivalence is promoted to the constitutive device of the sequence. In poetry one syllable is equalized with any other syllable of the same sequence: word stress is assumed to equal word stress, as unstress equals unstress; prosodic long is matched with long, and short with short; word boundary equals word boundary, no boundary equals no boundary; syntactic pause equals syntactic pause, no pause equals no pause. Syllables are converted into units of measure, and so are morae or stresses.

It may be objected that metalanguage also makes a sequential use of equivalent units when combining synonymic expressions into an equational sentence: $A = A$ ("*Mare* is *the female of the horse*"). Poetry and metalanguage, however, are in diametrical opposition to each other: in metalanguage the sequence is used to build an equation, whereas in poetry the equation is used to build a sequence.

In poetry, and to a certain extent in latent manifestations of poetic function, sequences delimited by word boundaries become commensurable whether they are sensed as isochronic or graded. "Joan and Margery" showed us the poetic principle of syllable gradation, the same principle which in the closes of Serbian folk epics has been raised to a compulsory law (cf. 29). Without its two dactylic words the combination "*innocent* by*stander*" would hardly have become a hackneyed phrase. The symmetry of three disyllabic verbs with an identical initial consonant and identical final vowel added splendor to the laconic victory message of Caesar: "*Veni, vidi, vici.*"

Measure of sequences is a device which, outside of poetic function, finds no application in language. Only in poetry with its regular reiteration of equivalent units is the time of the speech flow experienced, as it is—to cite another semiotic pattern—with musical time. Gerard Manley Hopkins, an outstanding searcher in the science of poetic language, defined verse as "speech wholly or partially repeating the same figure of sound" (12). Hopkins' subsequent question, "but is all verse poetry?" can be definitely answered as soon as poetic function ceases to be arbitrarily confined to the domain of poetry. Mnemonic lines cited by Hopkins (like "Thirty days hath September"), modern advertising jingles, and versified medieval laws, mentioned by Lotz, or finally Sanscrit scientific treatises in verse which in Indic tradition are strictly distinguished from true poetry (*kāvya*)—all these metrical texts make use of poetic function without, however, assigning to this function the coercing, determining role it carries in poetry. Thus verse actually exceeds the limits of poetry, but at the same time verse always implies poetic function. And apparently no human culture ignores versemaking, whereas there are many cultural patterns without "applied" verse; and even in such cultures which possess both pure and applied verses, the latter appear to be a secondary, unquestionably derived phenomenon. The adaptation of poetic means for some heterogeneous purpose does not conceal their primary essence, just as elements of emotive language, when utilized in poetry, still maintain their emotive tinge. A filibusterer may recite *Hiawatha* because it is long, yet poeticalness still remains the primary intent of this text itself. Self-evidently, the existence of versified, musical, and pictorial commercials does not separate the questions of verse or of musical and pictorial form from the study of poetry, music, and fine arts.

To sum up, the analysis of verse is entirely within the competence of poetics, and the latter may be defined as that part of linguistics which treats the poetic function in its relationship to the other functions of language. Poetics in the wider sense of the word deals with the poetic function not only in poetry, where this function is superimposed upon the other functions of language, but also outside of poetry, when some other function is superimposed upon the poetic function.

The reiterative "figure of sound," which Hopkins saw to be the constitutive principle of verse, can be further specified. Such a figure always utilizes at least one (or more than one) binary contrast of a relatively high and relatively low prominence effected by the different sections of the phonemic sequence.

Within a syllable the more prominent, nuclear, syllabic part, constituting the peak of the syllable, is opposed to the less prominent, marginal, nonsyllabic phonemes. Any syllable contains a syllabic phoneme, and the interval between two successive syllables is in some languages always and in others overwhelmingly carried out by marginal, nonsyllabic phonemes. In the so-called syllabic versification the number of syllabics in a metrically delimited chain (time series) is a constant, whereas the presence of a nonsyllabic phoneme or cluster between every two syllables of a metrical chain is a constant only in languages with an indispensable occurrence of nonsyllabics between syllabics and, furthermore, in those verse systems where hiatus is prohibited. Another manifestation of a tendency toward a uniform syllabic model is the avoidance of closed syllables at the end of the line, observable, for instance, in Serbian epic songs. The Italian syllabic verse shows a tendency to treat a sequence of vowels unseparated by consonantal phonemes as one single metrical syllable (cf. 21, secs. VIII–IX).

In some patterns of versification the syllable is the only constant unit of verse measure, and a grammatical limit is the only constant line of demarcation between measured sequences, whereas in other patterns syllables in turn are dichotomized into more and less prominent, and/or two levels of grammatical limits are distinguished in their metrical function, word boundaries and syntactic pauses.

Except the varieties of the so-called vers libre that are based on conjugate intonations and pauses only, any meter uses the syllable as a unit of measure at least in certain sections of the verse. Thus in the purely accentual verse ("sprung rhythm" in Hopkins' vocabulary), the number of syllables in the upbeat (called "slack" by Hopkins) may vary, but the downbeat (ictus) constantly contains one single syllable.

In any accentual verse the contrast between higher and lower prominence is achieved by syllables under stress versus unstressed syllables. Most accentual patterns operate primarily with the contrast of syllables with and without word stress, but some varieties of accentual verse deal with syntactic, phrasal stresses, those which Wimsatt and Beardsley cite as "the major stresses of the major words" and which are opposed as prominent to syllables without such major, syntactic stress.

In the quantitative ("chronemic") verse, long and short syllables are mutually opposed as more and less prominent. This contrast is usually carried out by syllable nuclei, phonemically long and short. But in metrical patterns like Ancient Greek and Arabic, which equalize length "by position" with length "by nature," the minimal syllables consisting of a consonantal phoneme and one mora vowel are opposed to syllables with a surplus (a second mora or a closing consonant) as simpler and less prominent syllables opposed to those that are more complex and prominent.

The question still remains open whether, besides the accentual and the chronemic verse, there exists a "tonemic" type of versification in languages where differences of syllabic intonations are used to distinguish word meanings (15). In classical Chinese poetry (3), syllables with modulations (in Chinese *tsê*, 'deflected tones") are opposed to the nonmodulated syllables (*p'ing*, 'level tones'), but apparently a chronemic principle underlies this opposition, as was suspected by Polivanov (34) and keenly interpreted by Wang Li (46); in the Chinese metrical tradition the level tones prove to be opposed to the deflected tones as long tonal peaks of syllables to short ones, so that verse is based on the opposition of length and shortness.

Joseph Greenberg brought to my attention another variety of tonemic versification—the verse of Efik riddles based on the level feature. In the sample cited by Simmons (42, p. 228), the query and the response form two octosyllables with an alike distribution of *h*(igh)- and *l*(ow)-tone syllabics; in each hemistich, moreover, the last three of the four syllables present an identical tonemic pattern: *lhhl/hhhl//lhhl/hhhl//*. Whereas Chinese versification appears as a peculiar variety of the quantitative verse, the verse of the Efik riddles is linked with the usual accentual verse by an opposition of two degrees of prominence (strength or height) of the vocal tone. Thus a metrical system of versification can be based only on the opposition of syllabic peaks and slopes (syllabic verse), on the relative level of the peaks (accentual verse), and on the relative length of the syllabic peaks or entire syllables (quantitative verse).

In textbooks of literature we sometimes encounter a superstitious contraposition of syllabism as a mere mechanical count of syllables to the lively pulsation of accentual verse. If we examine, however, the binary meters of the strictly syllabic and at the same time, accentual versification, we observe two homogeneous successions of wavelike peaks and valleys. Of these two undulatory curves, the syllabic one carries nuclear phonemes in the crest and usually marginal phonemes in the bottom. As a rule the accentual curve superposed upon the syllabic curve alternates stressed and unstressed syllables in the crests and bottoms respectively.

For comparison with the English meters which we have lengthily discussed, I bring to your attention the similar Russian binary verse forms which for the last fifty years have verily undergone an exhaustive investigation (see particularly 44). The structure of the verse can be very thoroughly described and interpreted in terms of enchained probabilities. Besides the compulsory word boundary between the lines, which is an invariant throughout all Russian meters, in the classic pattern of Russian syllabic accentual verse ("syllabo-tonic" in native nomenclature) we observe the following constants: (1) the number of syllables in the line from its beginning to the last downbeat is stable; (2) this very last downbeat always carries a word stress; (3) a stressed syllable cannot fall on the upbeat if a downbeat is fulfilled by an unstressed syllable of the same word unit (so that a word stress can coincide with an upbeat only as far as it belongs to a monosyllabic word unit).

Along with these characteristics compulsory for any line composed in a given meter, there are features that show a high probability of occurrence without being constantly present. Besides signals certain to occur ("probability one"), signals likely to occur ("probabilities less than one") enter into the notion of meter. Using Cherry's description of human communication (5), we could say that the reader of poetry obviously "may be unable to attach numerical frequencies" to the constituents of the meter, but as far as he conceives the verse shape, he unwittingly gets an inkling of their "rank order."

In the Russian binary meters all odd syllables counting back from the last downbeat—briefly, all the upbeats—are usually fulfilled by unstressed syllables, except some very low percentage of stressed monosyllables. All even syllables, again counting back from the last downbeat, show a sizable preference for syllables under word stress, but the probabilities of their occurrence are unequally distributed among the successive down-beats of the line. The higher the relative frequency of word stresses in a given downbeat, the lower the ratio shown by the preceding downbeat. Since the last downbeat is constantly stressed, the next to last gives the lowest percentage of word stresses; in the preceding downbeat their amount is again higher, without attaining the maximum, displayed by the final downbeat; one downbeat further toward the beginning of the line, the amount of the stresses sinks once more, without reaching the minimum of the next-to-last downbeat; and so on. Thus the distribution of word stresses among the downbeats within the line, the split into strong and weak downbeats, creates a *regressive undulatory curve* super-posed upon the wavy alternation of downbeats and upbeats. Incidentally, there is a captivating question of the relationship between the strong downbeats and phrasal stresses.

The Russian binary meters reveal a stratified arrangement of three un-dulatory curves: (I) alternation of syllabic nuclei and margins; (II) divi-sion of syllabic nuclei into alternating downbeats and upbeats; and (III) alternation of strong and weak downbeats. For example, Russian mas-culine iambic tetrameter of the nineteenth and present centuries may be represented by Figure 1, and a similar triadic pattern appears in the cor-responding English forms.

Three of five downbeats are deprived of word stress in Shelley's iambic line "Laugh with an inextinguishable laughter." Seven of sixteen down-beats are stressless in the following quatrain from Pasternak's recent iam-bic tetrameter *Zemlja* ("Earth"):

> I úlica za panibráta
> S okónnicej podslepovátoj,
> I béloj nóči i zakátu
> Ne razminút'sja u reki.

Since the overwhelming majority of downbeats concur with word stresses, the listener or reader of Russian verses is prepared with a high degree of probability to meet a word stress in any even syllable of iambic lines, but at the very beginning of Pasternak's quatrain the fourth and, one foot fur-ther, the sixth syllable, both in the first and in the following line, present him with a *frustrated expectation*. The degree of such a "frustration" is higher when the stress is lacking in a strong downbeat and becomes par-ticularly outstanding when two successive downbeats are carrying un-stressed syllables. The stresslessness of two adjacent downbeats is the less probable and the most striking when it embraces a whole hemistich as in a later line of the same poem: "Čtoby za gorodskjóu grán' ju" [stəbyzəgə-rackóju grán'ju]. The expectation depends on the treatment of a given downbeat in the poem and more generally in the whole extant metrical tradition. In the last downbeat but one, unstress may, however, outweigh the stress. Thus in this poem only 17 of 41 lines have a word stress on their sixth syllable. Yet in such a case the inertia of the stressed even syllables alternating with the unstressed odd syllables prompts some expectancy of stress also for the sixth syllable of the iambic tetrameter.

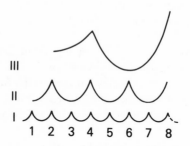

Quite naturally it was Edgar Allan Poe, the poet and theoretician of defeated anticipation, who metrically and psychologically appraised the human sense of gratification for the unexpected arising from expectedness, both of them unthinkable without the opposite, "as evil cannot exist without good" (33). Here we could easily apply Robert Frost's formula from "The Figure A Poem Makes": "The figure is the same as for love" (8).

The so-called shifts of word stress in polysyllabic words from the downbeat to the upbeat ("reversed feet"), which are unknown to the standard forms of Russian verse, appear quite usually in English poetry after a metrical and/or syntactic pause. A noticeable example is the rhythmical variation of the same adjective in Milton's "Infinite wrath and infinite despair." In the line "Nearer, my God, to Thee, nearer to Thee," the stressed syllable of one and the same word occurs twice in the upbeat, first at the beginning of the line and a second time at the beginning of a phrase. This license, discussed by Jespersen (18) and current in many languages, is entirely explainable by the particular import of the relation between an upbeat and the immediately preceding downbeat. Where such an immediate precedence is impeded by an inserted pause, the upbeat becomes a kind of *syllaba anceps*.

Besides the rules which underlie the compulsory features of verse, the rules governing its optional traits also pertain to meter. We are inclined to designate such phenomena as unstress in the downbeats and stress in upbeats as deviations, but it must be remembered that these are allowed oscillations, departures within the limits of the law. In British parliamentary terms, it is not an opposition to its majesty the meter but an opposition of its majesty. As to the actual infringements of metrical laws, the discussion of such violations recalls Osip Brik, perhaps the keenest of Russian formalists, who used to say that political conspirators are tried and condemned only for unsuccessful attempts at a forcible upheaval, because in the case of a successful coup it is the conspirators who assume the role of judges and prosecutors. If the violences against the meter take root, they themselves become metrical rules.

Far from being an abstract, theoretical scheme, meter—or in more explicit terms, *verse design*—underlies the structure of any single line—or, in logical terminology, any single *verse instance*. Design and instance are correlative concepts. The verse design determines the invariant features of the verse instances and sets up the limits of variations. A Serbian peasant reciter of epic poetry memorizes, performs, and, to a high extent, improvises thousands, sometimes tens of thousands of lines, and their meter is alive in his mind. Unable to abstract its rules, he nonetheless notices and repudiates even the slightest infringement of these rules. Any line of Serbian epics contains precisely ten syllables and is followed by a syntactic pause. There is furthermore a compulsory word boundary before the fifth syllable and a compulsory absence of word boundary before the fourth and tenth syllable. The verse has, moreover, significant quantitative and accentual characteristics (cf. 16, 17).

This Serbian epic break, along with many similar examples presented by comparative metrics, is a persuasive warning against the erroneous identification of a break with a syntactic pause. The obligatory word boundary must not be combined with pause and is not even meant to be perceptible by the ear. The analysis of Serbian epic songs phonographically recorded proves that there are no compulsory audible clues to the break, and yet any attempt to abolish the word boundary before the fifth syllable by a mere insignificant change in word order is immediately condemned by the narrator. The grammatical fact that the fourth and fifth syllables pertain to two different word units is sufficient for the appraisal of the break. Thus verse design goes far beyond the questions of sheer sound shape; it is a much wider linguistic phenomenon, and it yields to no isolating phonetic treatment.

I say "linguistic phenomenon" even though Chatman states that "the meter exists as a system outside the language." Yes, meter appears also in other arts dealing with time sequence. There are many linguistic problems—for instance, syntax—which likewise overstep the limit of language and are common to different semiotic systems. We may speak even about the grammar of traffic signals. There exists a signal code, where a yellow light when combined with green warns that free passage is close to being stopped and when combined with red announces the approaching cessation of the stoppage; such a yellow signal offers a close analogue to the verbal completive aspect. Poetic meter, however, has so many intrinsically linguistic particularities that it is most convenient to describe it from a purely linguistic point of view.

Let us add that no linguistic property of the verse design should be disregarded. Thus, for example, it would be an unfortunate mistake to deny the constitutive value of intonation in English meters. Not even speaking about its fundamental role in the meters of such a master of English free verse as Whitman, it is impossible to ignore the metrical significance of pausal intonation ("final juncture"), whether "cadence" or "anticadence" (20), in poems like "The Rape of The Lock" with its intentional avoidance of enjambments. Yet even a vehement accumulation of enjambments never hides their digressive, variational status; they always set off the normal coincidence of syntactic pause and pausal intonation with the metrical limit. Whatever is the reciter's way of reading, the intonational constraint of the poem remains valid. The intonational contour inherent to a poem, to a poet, to a poetic school is one of the most notable topics brought to discussion by the Russian formalists (6, 49).

The verse design is embodied in verse instances. Usually the free variation of these instances is denoted by the somewhat equivocal label "rhythm." A variation of *verse instances* within a given poem must be strictly distinguished from the variable *delivery instances*. The intention "to describe the verse line as it is actually performed" is of lesser use for the synchronic and historical analysis of poetry than it is for the study of its recitation in the present and the past. Meanwhile the truth is simple and clear: "There are many performances of the same poem—differing among themselves in many ways. A performance is an event, but the poem itself, if there *is* any poem, must be some kind of enduring object." This sage memento of Wimsatt and Beardsley belongs indeed to the essentials of modern metrics.

In Shakespeare's verses the second, stressed syllable of the word "absurd" usually falls on the downbeat, but once in the third act of *Hamlet* it falls on the upbeat: "No, let the candied tongue lick absurd pomp." The reciter may scan the word "absurd" in this line with an initial stress on the first syllable or observe the final word stress in accordance with the standard accentuation. He may also subordinate the word stress of the adjective in favor of the strong syntactic stress of the following head word, as suggested by Hill: "Nó, lèt thĕ cándĭed tóngue lìck ăbsùrd pómp" (11), as in Hopkins' conception of English antispasts—"regrét néver" (12). There is finally a possibility of emphatic modifications either through a "fluctuating accentuation" (*schwebende Betonung*) embracing both syllables or through an exclamational reinforcement of the first syllable [àb-súrd]. But whatever solution the reciter chooses, the shift of the word stress from the downbeat to the upbeat with no antecedent pause is still arresting, and the moment of frustrated expectation stays viable. Wherever the reciter put the accent, the discrepancy between the English word stress on the second syllable of "absurd" and the downbeat attached to the first syllable persists as a constitutive feature of the verse instance. The tension between the ictus and the usual word stress is inherent in this line independently of its different implementations by various actors and readers. As Gerard Manley Hopkins observes, in the preface to his poems, "two rhythms are in some manner running at once" (13). His description of such a contrapuntal run can be reinterpreted. The superinducing of an equivalence principle upon the word sequence or, in other terms, the *mounting* of the metrical form upon the usual speech form, necessarily gives the experience of a double, ambiguous shape to anyone who is familiar with the given language and with verse. Both the convergences and the divergences between the two forms, both the warranted and the frustrated expectations, supply this experience.

How the given verse-instance is implemented in the given delivery instance depends on the *delivery design* of the reciter; he may cling to a scanning style or tend toward prose-like prosody or freely oscillate between these two poles. We must be on guard against simplistic binarism which reduces two couples into one single opposition either by suppressing the cardinal distinction between verse design and verse instance (as well as between delivery design and delivery instance) or by an erroneous identification of delivery instance and delivery design with the verse instance and verse design.

> "But tell me, child, your choice; what shall I buy
> You?"—"Father, what you buy me I like best."

These two lines from "The Handsome Heart" by Hopkins contain a heavy enjambment which puts a verse boundary before the concluding monosyllable of a phrase, of a sentence, of an utterance. The recitation of these pentameters may be strictly metrical with a manifest pause between "buy" and "you" and a suppressed pause after the pronoun. Or, on the contrary, there may be displayed a prose-oriented manner without any separation of the words "buy you" and with a marked pausal intonation at the end of the question. None of these ways of recitation may, however, hide the intentional discrepancy between the metrical and syntactic division. The verse shape of a poem remains completely independent of its variable delivery, whereby I do not intend to nullify the alluring question of *Autorenleser* and *Selbstleser* launched by Sievers (41).

No doubt, verse is primarily a recurrent "figure of sound." Primarily, always, but never uniquely. Any attempts to confine such poetic conventions as meter, alliteration, or rhyme to the sound level are speculative reasonings without any empirical justification. The projection of the equational principle into the sequence has a much deeper and wider significance. Valéry's view of poetry as "hesitation between the sound and the sense" (cf. 45) is much more realistic and scientific than any bias of phonetic isolationism.

Although rhyme by definition is based on a regular recurrence of equivalent phonemes or phonemic groups, it would be an unsound over-simplification to treat rhyme merely from the standpoint of sound. Rhyme necessarily involves the semantic relationship between rhyming units ("rhyme-fellows" in Hopkins' nomenclature). In the scrutiny of a rhyme we are faced with the question of whether or not it is a homoeoteleuton, which confronts similar derivational and/or inflexional suffixes (congratulations-decorations), or whether the rhyming words belong to the same or to different grammatical categories. Thus, for example, Hopkins' four-fold rhyme is an agreement of two nouns—"kind" and "mind"—both contrasting with the adjective "blind" and with the verb "find." Is there a semantic propinquity, a sort of simile between rhyming lexical units, as in dove-love, light-bright, place-space, name-fame? Do the rhyming members carry the same syntactic function? The difference between the morphological class and the syntactic application may be pointed out in rhyme. Thus in Poe's lines, "While I nodded, nearly *napping*, suddenly there came a *tapping*, As of someone gently *rapping*," the three rhyming words, morphologically alike, are all three syntactically different. Are totally or partly homonymic rhymes prohibited, tolerated, or favored? Such full homonyms as son-sun, I-eye, eve-eave, and on the other hand, echo rhymes like December-ember, infinite-night, swarm-warm, smiles-miles? What about compound rhymes (such as Hopkins' "enjoyment—toy meant" or "began some—ransom"), where a word unit accords with a word group?

A poet or poetic school may be oriented toward or against grammatical rhyme; rhymes must be either grammatical or antigrammatical; an agrammatical rhyme, indifferent to the relation between sound and grammatical structure, would, like any agrammatism, belong to verbal pathology. If a poet tends to avoid grammatical rhymes, for him, as Hopkins said, "There are two elements in the beauty rhyme has to the mind, the likeness or sameness of sound and the unlikeness or difference of meaning" (12). Whatever the relation between sound and meaning in different rhyme techniques, both spheres are necessarily involved. After Wimsatt's illuminating observations about the meaningfulness of rhyme (48) and the shrewd modern studies of Slavic rhyme patterns, a student in poetics can hardly maintain that rhymes signify merely in a very vague way.

Rhyme is only a particular, condensed case of a much more general, we may even say the fundamental, problem of poetry, namely *parallelism*. Here again Hopkins, in his student papers of 1865, displayed a prodigious insight into the structure of poetry:

> The artificial part of poetry, perhaps we shall be right to say all artifice, reduces itself to the principle of parallelism. The structure of poetry is that of continuous parallelism, ranging from the technical so-called Parallelisms of Hebrew poetry and the antiphons of Church music up to the intricacy of

Greek or Italian or English verse. But parallelism is of two kinds necessarily—where the opposition is clearly marked, and where it is transitional
rather or chromatic. Only the first kind, that of marked parallelism, is concerned with the structure of verse—in rhythm, the recurrence of a certain sequence of syllables, in metre, the recurrence of a certain sequence of rhythm,
in alliteration, in assonance and in rhyme. Now the force of this recurrence is
to beget a recurrence or parallelism answering to it in the words or thought
and, speaking roughly and rather for the tendency than the invariable result, the more marked parallelism in structure whether of elaboration or of
emphasis begets more marked parallelism in the words and sense. . . . To
the marked or abrupt kind of parallelism belong metaphor, simile, parable,
and so on, where the effect is sought in likeness of things, and antithesis,
contrast, and so on, where it is sought in unlikeness (12).

Briefly, equivalence in sound, projected into the sequence as its constitutive principle, inevitably involves semantic equivalence, and on any linguistic level any constituent of such a sequence prompts one of the two
correlative experiences which Hopkins neatly defines as "comparison for
likeness' sake" and "comparison for unlikeness' sake."

Folklore offers the most clear-cut and stereotyped forms of poetry, particularly suitable for structural scrutiny (as Sebeok illustrated with Che-
remis samples). Those oral traditions that use grammatical parallelism to
connect consecutive lines, for example, Finno-Ugric patterns of verse (see
2, 43) and to a high degree also Russian folk poetry, can be fruitfully analyzed on all linguistic levels—phonological, morphological, syntactic,
and lexical: we learn what elements are conceived as equivalent and how
likeness on certain levels is tempered with conspicuous difference on
other ones. Such forms enable us to verify Ransom's wise suggestion that
"the meter-and-meaning process is the organic act of poetry, and involves
all its important characters" (37). These clear-cut traditional structures
may dispel Wimsatt's doubts about the possibility of writing a grammar
of the meter's interaction with the sense, as well as a grammar of the arrangement of metaphors. As soon as parallelism is promoted to canon,
the interaction between meter and meaning and the arrangement of tropes
cease to be "the free and individual and unpredictable parts of the poetry."

Let us translate a few typical lines from Russian wedding songs about
the apparition of the bridegroom:

> A brave fellow was going to the porch,
> Vasilij was walking to the manor.

The translation is literal; the verbs, however, take the final position in
both Russian clauses (Dobroj mólodec k sénička privoráčival, // Vasílij
k téremu prixážival). The lines wholly correspond to each other syntactically and morphologically. Both predicative verbs have the same pre-

fixes and suffixes and the same vocalic alternant in the stem; they are alike in aspect, tense, number, and gender; and, moreover, they are synonymic. Both subjects, the common noun and the proper name, refer to the same person and form an appositional group. The two modifiers of place are expressed by identical prepositional constructions, and the first one stands to the second in synecdochic relation.

These verses may occur preceded by another line of similar grammatical (syntactic and morphologic) make-up: "Not a bright falcon was flying beyond the hills" or "Not a fierce horse was coming at gallop to the court." The "bright falcon" and the "fierce horse" of these variants are put in metaphorical relation with "brave fellow." This is traditional Slavic negative parallelism—the refutation of the metaphorical state in favor of the factual state. The negation *ne* may, however, be omitted: "Jasjón sokol zá gory zaljótyval" (A bright falcon was flying beyond the hills) or "Retiv kon' kó dvoru priskákival" (A fierce horse was coming at a gallop to the court). In the first of the two examples the *metaphorical* relation is maintained: a brave fellow appeared at the porch, like a bright falcon from behind the hills. In the other instance, however, the semantic connection becomes ambiguous. A comparison between the appearing bridegroom and the galloping horse suggests itself, but at the same time the halt of the horse at the court actually anticipates the approach of the hero to the house. Thus before introducing the rider and the manor of his fiancee, the song evokes the contiguous, *metonymical* images of the horse and of the courtyard: possession instead of possessor, and outdoors instead of inside. The exposition of the groom may be broken up into two consecutive moments even without substituting the horse for the horseman: "A brave fellow was coming at a gallop to the court, // Vasilij was walking to the porch." Thus the "fierce horse," emerging in the preceding line at a similar metrical and syntactic place as the "brave fellow," figures simultaneously as a likeness to and as a representative possession of this fellow, properly speaking—*pars pro toto* for the horseman. The horse image is on a border line between metonymy and synecdoche. From these suggestive connotations of the "fierce horse" there ensues a metaphorical synecdoche: in the wedding songs and other varieties of Russian erotic lore, the masculine *retiv kon* becomes a latent or even patent phallic symbol.

As early as the 1880's, Potebnja, a remarkable inquirer into Slavic poetics, pointed out that in folk poetry a symbol appears to be materialized (*oveščestvlen*), converted into an accessory of the ambiance. "Still a symbol, it is put, however, in a connection with the action. Thus a simile is presented under the shape of a temporal sequence" (35). In Potebnja's examples from Slavic folklore, the willow, under which a girl passes, serves at the same time as her image; the tree and the girl are both copresent in the same verbal simulacrum of the willow. Quite similarly the horse of the love songs remains a virility symbol not only when the maid is asked by the lad to feed his steed but even when being saddled or put into the stable or attached to a tree.

In poetry not only the phonological sequence but in the same way any sequence of semantic units strives to build an equation. Similarity superimposed on contiguity imparts to poetry its thoroughgoing symbolic, multiplex, polysemantic essence which is beautifully suggested by Goethe's "Alles Vergängliche ist nur ein Gleichnis" (Anything transient is but a likeness). Said more technically, anything sequent is a simile. In poetry where similarity is superinduced upon contiguity, any metonymy is slightly metaphorical and any metaphor has a metonymical tint.

Ambiguity is an intrinsic, inalienable character of any self-focused message, briefly a corollary feature of poetry. Let us repeat with Empson: "The machinations of ambiguity are among the very roots of poetry" (7). Not only the message itself but also its addresser and addressee become ambiguous. Besides the author and the reader, there is the "I" of the lyrical hero or of the fictitious storyteller and the "you" or "thou" of the alleged addressee of dramatic monologues, supplications, and epistles. For instance the poem "Wrestling Jacob" is addressed by its title hero to the Saviour and simultaneously acts as a subjective message of the poet Charles Wesley to his readers. Virtually any poetic message is a quasiquoted discourse with all those peculiar, intricate problems which "speech within speech" offers to the linguist.

The supremacy of poetic function over referential function does not obliterate the reference but makes it ambiguous. The double-sensed message finds correspondence in a split addresser, in a split addressee, and besides in a split reference, as it is cogently exposed in the preambles to fairy tales of various peoples, for instance, in the usual exordium of the Majorca storytellers: "Aixo era y no era" (It was and it was not) (9). The repetitiveness effected by imparting the equivalence principle to the sequence makes reiterable not only the constituent sequences of the poetic message but the whole message as well. This capacity for reiteration whether immediate or delayed, this reification of a poetic message and its constituents, this conversion of a message into an enduring thing, indeed all this represents an inherent and effective property of poetry.

In a sequence, where similarity is superimposed on contiguity, two similar phonemic sequences near to each other are prone to assume a paronomastic function. Words similar in sound are drawn together in meaning. It is true that the first line of the final stanza in Poe's "Raven" makes wide use of repetitive alliterations, as noted by Valéry (45), but "the overwhelming effect" of this line and of the whole stanza is due primarily to the sway of poetic etymology.

And the Raven, never flitting, still is sitting, *still* is sitting
On the pallid bust of Pallas just above my chamber door;
And his eyes have all the seeming of a demon's that is dreaming,
And the lamp-light o'er him streaming throws his shadow on the floor;
And my soul from out that shadow that lies floating on the floor
Shall be lifted—nevermore.

The perch of the raven, "the pallid bust of Pallas," is merged through the "sonorous" paronomasia /pǽləd/—/pǽləs/ into one organic whole (similar to Shelley's molded line "Sculptured on alabaster obelisk" /sk.lp/—/l.b.st/—/b.l.sk/). Both confronted words were blended earlier in another epithet of the same bust—*placid* /plǽsɪd/—a poetic portmanteau, and the bond between the sitter and the seat was in turn fastened by a paronomasia: "*b*ird or *bea*st upon the . . . *bust*." The bird "is sitting // On the pallid bust of Pallas just above my chamber door," and the raven on his perch, despite the lover's imperative "take thy form from off my door," is nailed to the place by the words /ʒʌst əbʌ́v/, both of them blended in /bʌst/.

The never-ending stay of the grim guest is expressed by a chain of ingenious paronomasias, partly inversive, as we would expect from such a deliberate experimenter in anticipatory, regressive *modus operandi*, such a master in "writing backwards" as Edgar Allan Poe. In the introductory line of this concluding stanza, "raven," contiguous to the bleak refrain word "never," appears once more as an embodied mirror image of this "never:" /n.v.r/—/r.v.n/. Salient paronomasias interconnect both emblems of the everlasting despair, first "the Raven, never flitting," at the beginning of the very last stanza, and second, in its very last lines the "shadow that lies floating on the floor" and "shall be lifted—nevermore": /névər flítíŋ/—/flótíŋ/ . . . /flór/ . . . /líftəd névər/. The alliterations which struck Valéry build a paronomastic string: /stí . . . /—/sít . . . /—/stí . . . /—/sít . . . /. The invariance of the group is particularly stressed by the variation in its order. The two luminous effects in the chiaroscuro—the "fiery eyes" of the black fowl and the lamplight throwing "his shadow on the floor"—are evoked to add to the gloom of the whole picture and are again bound by the "vivid effect" of paronomasias: /ʃlðə símɪŋ/ . . . /dímənz/ . . . /ɪz drímɪŋ/—/ɔrɪm strímɪŋ/. "That shadow that lies /láyz/" pairs with the Raven's "eyes" /áyz/ in an impressively misplaced echo rhyme.

In poetry, any conspicuous similarity in sound is evaluated in respect to similarity and/or dissimilarity in meaning. But Pope's alliterative precept to poets—"the sound must seem an Echo of the sense"—has a wider application. In referential language the connection between *signans* and *signatum* is overwhelmingly based on their codified contiguity, which is often confusingly labeled "arbitrariness of the verbal sign." The relevance of the sound-meaning nexus is a simple corollary of the superposition of similarity upon contiguity. Sound symbolism is an undeniably objective relation founded on a phenomenal connection between different sensory modes, in particular between the visual and auditory experience. If the results of research in this area have sometimes been vague or controversial, it is primarily due to an insufficient care for the methods of psychological and/or linguistic inquiry. Particularly from the linguistic point of view the picture has often been distorted by lack of attention to the phonological aspect of speech sounds or by inevitably vain operations with complex phonemic units instead of with their ultimate components. But when, on testing, for example, such phonemic oppositions as grave versus acute we ask whether /i/ or /u/ is darker, some of the subjects may respond that this question makes no sense to them, but hardly one will state that /i/ is the darkest of the two.

Poetry is not the only area where sound symbolism makes itself felt, but it is a province where the internal nexus between sound and meaning changes from latent to patent and manifests itself most palpably and intensely, as it has been noted in Hymes's stimulating paper. The super-average accumulation of a certain class of phonemes or a contrastive assemblage of two opposite classes in the sound texture of a line, of a stanza, of a poem acts like an "undercurrent of meaning," to use Poe's picturesque expression. In two polar words phonemic relationship may be in agreement with semantic opposition, as in Russian /d,en,/ 'day' and /noč/ 'night' with the acute vowel and sharped consonants in the diurnal name and the corresponding grave vowel in the nocturnal name. A reinforcement of this contrast by surrounding the first word with acute and sharped phonemes, in contradistinction to a grave phonemic neighborhood of the second word, makes the sound into a thorough echo of the sense. But in the French *jour* 'day' and *nuit* 'night' the distribution of grave and acute vowels is inverted, so that Mallarmé's *Divagations* accuse his mother tongue of a deceiving perversity for assigning to day a dark timbre and to night a light one (27). Whorf states that when in its sound shape "a word has an acoustic similarity to its own meaning, we can notice it. . . . But, when the opposite occurs, nobody notices it." Poetic language, however, and particularly French poetry in the collision between sound and meaning detected by Mallarmé, either seeks a phonological alternation of such a discrepancy and drowns the "converse" distribution of vocalic features by surrounding *nuit* with grave and *jour* with acute phonemes, or it resorts to a semantic shift and its imagery of day and night replaces the imagery of light and dark by other synesthetic correlates of the phonemic opposition grave/acute and, for instance, puts the heavy, warm day in contrast to the airy, cool night; because "human subjects seem to associate the experiences of bright, sharp, hard, high, light (in weight), quick, high-pitched, narrow, and so on in a long series, with each other; and conversely the experiences of dark, warm, yielding, soft, blunt, low, heavy, slow, low-pitched, wide, etc., in another long series" (47, p. 267f).

However effective is the emphasis on repetition in poetry, the sound texture is still far from being confined to numerical contrivances, and a phoneme that appears only once, but in a key word, in a pertinent position, against a contrastive background, may acquire a striking significance. As painters used to say, "Un kilo de vert n'est pas plus vert qu'un demi kilo."

Any analysis of poetic sound texture must consistently take into account the phonological structure of the given language and, beside the over-all code, also the hierarchy of phonological distinctions in the given poetic convention. Thus the approximate rhymes used by Slavic peoples in oral and in some stages of written tradition admit unlike consonants in the rhyming members (i.e. Czech *boty, boky, stopy, kosy, sochy*) but, as Nitch noticed, no mutual correspondence between voiced and voiceless consonants is allowed (31), so that the quoted Czech words cannot rhyme with *body, doby, kozy, rohy*. In the songs of some American Indian peoples such as Pima-Papago and Tepecano, according to Herzog's observations—only partly communicated in print (10)—the phonemic distinction between voiced and voiceless plosives and between them and nasals is replaced by a free variation, whereas the distinction between labials, dentals, velars, and palatals is rigorously maintained. Thus in the poetry of these languages consonants lose two of the four distinctive features, voiced/voiceless and nasal/oral, and preserve the other two, grave/acute and compact/diffuse. The selection and hierarchic stratification of valid categories is a factor of primary importance for poetics both on the phonological and on the grammatical level.

Old Indic and Medieval Latin literary theory keenly distinguished two poles of verbal art, labeled in Sanskrit *Pāñcālī* and *Vaidarbhī* and correspondingly in Latin *ornatus difficilis* and *ornatus facilis* (see 1), the latter style evidently being much more difficult to analyze linguistically because in such literary forms verbal devices are unostentatious and language seems a nearly transparent garment. But one must say with Charles Sanders Peirce: "This clothing never can be completely stripped off, it is only changed for something more diaphanous" (32, p. 171). "Verseless composition," as Hopkins calls the prosaic variety of verbal art—where parallelisms are not so strictly marked and strictly regular as "continuous parallelism" and where there is no dominant figure of sound—present more entangled problems for poetics, as does any transitional linguistic area. In this case the transition is between strictly poetic and strictly referential language. But Propp's pioneering monograph on the structure of the fairy tale (36) shows us how a consistently syntactic approach may be of paramount help even in classifying the traditional plots and in tracing the puzzling laws that underlie their composition and selection. The new studies of Lévi-Strauss (22, 23, 24) display a much deeper but essentially similar approach to the same constructional problem.

It is no mere chance that metonymic structures are less explored than the field of metaphor. May I repeat my old observation that the study of poetic tropes has been directed mainly toward metaphor, and the so-called realistic literature, intimately tied with the metonymic principle, still defies interpretation, although the same linguistic methodology, which poetics uses when analyzing the metaphorical style of romantic poetry, is entirely applicable to the metonymical texture of realistic prose (14).

Textbooks believe in the occurrence of poems devoid of imagery, but actually scarcity in lexical tropes is counterbalanced by gorgeous grammatical tropes and figures. The poetic resources concealed in the morphological and syntactic structure of language, briefly the poetry of grammar, and its literary product, the grammar of poetry, have been seldom known to critics and mostly disregarded by linguists but skillfully mastered by creative writers.

The main dramatic force of Antony's exordium to the funeral oration for Caesar is achieved by Shakespeare's playing on grammatical categories and constructions. Mark Antony lampoons Brutus's speech by changing the alleged reasons for Caesar's assassination into plain linguistic fictions. Brutus's accusation of Caesar, "as he was ambitious, I slew him," undergoes successive transformations. First Antony reduces it to a mere quotation which puts the responsibility for the statement on the speaker quoted: "The noble Brutus // Hath told you. . . ." When repeated, this reference to Brutus is put into opposition to Antony's own assertions by an adversative "but" and further degraded by a concessive "yet." The reference to the alleger's honor ceases to justify the allegation, when repeated with a substitution of the merely copulative "and" instead of the previous causal "for," and when finally put into question through the malicious insertion of a modal "sure":

> The noble Brutus
> Hath told you Cæsar was ambitious;
> For Brutus is an honourable man,
> But Brutus says he was ambitious,
> And Brutus is an honourable man.
> Yet Brutus says he was ambitious,
> And Brutus is an honourable man.
> Yet Brutus says he was ambitious,
> And, sure, he is an honourable man.

The following polyptoton—"I speak . . . Brutus spoke . . . I am to speak"—presents the repeated allegation as mere reported speech instead of reported facts. The effect lies, modal logic would say, in the oblique context of the arguments adduced which makes them into unprovable belief sentences:

> I speak not to disprove what Brutus spoke,
> But here I am to speak what I do know.

The most effective device of Antony's irony is the *modus obliquus* of Brutus's abstracts changed into a *modus rectus* to disclose that these reified attributes are nothing but linguistic fictions. To Brutus's saying "he was ambitious," Antony first replies by transferring the adjective from the agent to the action ("Did this in Caesar seem ambitious?"), then by eliciting the abstract noun "ambition" and converting it into a subject of a concrete passive construction "Ambition should be made of sterner stuff" and subsequently to a predicate noun of an interrogative sentence, "Was this ambition?"—Brutus's appeal "hear me for my cause" is answered by the same noun *in recto*, the hypostatized subject of an interrogative, active construction: "What cause witholds you. . . ?" While Brutus calls "awake your senses, that you may the better judge," the abstract substantive derived from "judge" becomes an apostrophized agent in Antony's report: "O judgment, thou art fled to brutish beasts . . ." Incidentally, this apostrophe with its murderous paronomasia Brutus—brutish is reminiscent of Caesar's parting exclamation "Et tu, Brute!" Properties and activities are exhibited *in recto*, whereas their carriers appear either *in obliquo* ("withholds you," "to brutish beasts," "back to me") or as subjects of negative actions ("men have lost," "I must pause"):

> You all did love him once, not without cause;
> What cause withholds you then to mourn for him?
> O judgment, thou art fled to brutish beasts,
> And men have lost their reason!

The last two lines of Antony's exordium display the ostensible independence of these grammatical metonymies. The stereotyped "I mourn for so-and-so" and the figurative but still stereotyped "so-and-so is in the coffin and my heart is with him" or "goes out to him" give place in Antony's speech to a daringly realized metonymy; the trope becomes a part of poetic reality:

> My heart is in the coffin there with Cæsar,
> And I must pause till it come back to me.

In poetry the internal form of a name, that is, the semantic load of its constituents, regains its pertinence. The "Cocktails" may resume their obliterated kinship with plumage. Their colors are vivified in Mac Hammond's lines "The ghost of a Bronx pink lady // With orange blossoms afloat in her hair," and the etymological metaphor attains its realization: "O, Bloody Mary, // The cocktails have crowed not the cocks!" ("At an Old Fashion Bar in Manhattan"). Wallace Stevens' poem "An Ordinary Evening in New Haven" revives the head word of the city name first through a discreet allusion to heaven and then through a direct pun-like confrontation similar to Hopkins' "Heaven-Haven."

> The dry eucalyptus *seeks god in the rainy cloud.*
> Professor Eucalyptus of New Haven *seeks him in New Haven* . . .
> The instinct *for heaven* had its counterpart:
> The instinct for earth, *for New Haven,* for his room . . .

The adjective "New" of the city name is laid bare through the concatenation of opposites:

> The oldest-newest day is the newest alone.
> The oldest-newest night does not creak by . . .

When in 1919 the Moscow Linguistic Circle discussed how to define and delimit the range of *epitheta ornantia*, the poet Majakovskij rebuked us by saying that for him any adjective while in poetry was thereby a poetic epithet, even "great" in the *Great Bear* or "big" and "little" in such names of Moscow streets as *Bol'shaja Presnja* and *Malaja Presnja*. In other words, poeticalness is not a supplementation of discourse with rhetorical adornment but a total re-evaluation of the discourse and of all its components whatsoever.

A missionary blamed his African flock for walking undressed. "And what about yourself?" they pointed to his visage, "are not you, too, somewhere naked?" "Well, but that is my face." "Yet in us," retorted the natives, "everywhere it is face." So in poetry any verbal element is converted into a figure of poetic speech.

My attempt to vindicate the right and duty of linguistics to direct the investigation of verbal art in all its compass and extent can come to a conclusion with the same burden which summarized my report to the 1953 conference here at Indiana University: "Linguista sum; linguistici nihil a me alienum puto" (25). If the poet Ransom is right (and he is right) that "poetry is a kind of language" (38), the linguist whose field is any kind of language may and must include poetry in his study. The present conference has clearly shown that the time when both linguists and literary historians eluded questions of poetic structure is now safely behind us. Indeed, as Hollander stated, "there seems to be no reason for trying to separate the literary from the overall linguistic." If there are some critics who still doubt the competence of linguistics to embrace the field of poetics, I privately believe that the poetic incompetence of some bigoted linguists has been mistaken for an inadequacy of the linguistic science itself. All of us here, however, definitely realize that a linguist deaf to the poetic function of language and a literary scholar indifferent to linguistic problems and unconversant with linguistic methods are equally flagrant anachronisms.

REFERENCES

1. Arbusow, L. *Colores rhetorici*. Göttingen, 1948.
2. Austerlitz, R. *Ob-Ugric Metrics; Folklore Fellows Communications*, 174 (1958).
3. Bishop, J. L. "Prosodic Elements in T'ang Poetry," *Indiana University Conference on Oriental-Western Literary Relations*. Chapel Hill, 1955.
4. Bühler, K. "Die Axiomatik der Sprachwissenschaften." *Kant-Studien*, 38, pp. 19–90 (Berlin, 1933).
5. Cherry, C. *On Human Communication*. New York, 1957.
6. Èjxenbaum, B. *Melodika stixa*. Leningrad, 1922.
7. Empson, W. *Seven Types of Ambiguity*. New York, 3rd ed., 1955.
8. Frost, R. *Collected Poems*. New York, 1939.
9. Giese, W. "Sind Märchen Lügen?" *Cahiers S. Puscariu*, 1, pp. 137ff. (1952).
10. Herzog, G. "Some Linguistic Aspects of American Indian Poetry." *Word*, 2, p. 82 (1946).
11. Hill, A. A. Review in *Language*, 29, pp. 549–561 (1953).
12. Hopkins, G. M. *The Journals and Papers*, H. House, ed. London, 1959.
13. ———. *Poems*, W. H. Gardner, ed. New York and London, 3rd ed., 1948.
14. Jakobson, R. "The Metaphoric and Metonymic Poles." In *Fundamentals of Language*, pp. 76–82. 's-Gravenhage and New York, 1956.
15. ———. *O češskom stixe preimuščestvenno v sopostavlenii s russkim* (= Sborniki po teorii poètičeskogo jazyka, 5). Berlin and Moscow, 1923.
16. ———. "Studies in Comparative Slavic Metrics." *Oxford Slavonic Papers*, 3, pp. 21–66 (1952).
17. ———. "Über den Versbau der serbokroatischen Volksepen." *Archives néerlandaises de phonétique expérimentale*, pp. 7–9, 44–53 (1933).
18. Jespersen, O. "Cause psychologique de quelques phénomènes de métrique germanique," *Psychologie du langage*. Paris, 1933.
19. Joos, M. "Description of language design." *Journal of the Acoustical Society of America*, 22, pp. 701–708 (1950).
20. Karcevskij, S. "Sur la phonologie de la phrase." *Travaux du cercle linguistique de Prague*, 4, pp. 188–223 (1931).
21. Levi, A. "Della versificazione italiana." *Archivum Romanicum*, 14, pp. 449–526 (1930).
22. Lévi-Strauss, C. "Analyse morphologique des contes russes." *International Journal of Slavic Linguistics and Poetics*, 3 (1960).
23. ———. *La geste d' Asdival*, École Pratique des Hautes Études, Paris, 1958.
24. ———. "The Structural Study of Myth." in T. A. Sebeok, ed., *Myth: a Symposium*, pp. 50–66. Philadelphia, 1955.
25. ———, R. Jakobson, C. F. Voegelin, and T. A. Sebeok. *Results of the Conference of Anthropologists and Linguists*. Baltimore, 1953.
26. Malinowski, B. "The Problem of Meaning in Primitive Languages." In C. K. Ogden and I. A. Richards, *The Meaning of Meaning*, pp. 296–336. New York and London, 9th ed., 1953.
27. Mallarmé, S. *Divagations*. Paris, 1899.
28. Mansikka, V. T. *Litauische Zaubersprüche, Folklore Fellows Communications*, 87 (1929).
29. Maretić, T. "Metrika narodnih naših pjesama." *Rad Yugoslavenske Akademije*, 168, 170 (Zagreb, 1907).
30. Marty, A. *Untersuchungen zur Grundlegung der allgemeinen Grammatik und Sprachphilosophie*, Vol. 1. Halle, 1908.

31. Nitsch, K. "Z historii polskich rymów." *Wybór pism polonistycznych*, 1, pp. 33–77 (Wrocław, 1954).

32. Peirce, C. S. *Collected papers*, Vol. 1. Cambridge, Mass., 1931.

33. Poe, E. A. "Marginalia." *The Works*, Vol. 3. New York, 1857.

34. Polivanov, E. D. "O metričeskom xaraktere kitajskogo stixosloženija." *Doklady Rossijskoj Akademii Nauk*, serija V, 156–58 (1924).

35. Potebnja, A. *Ob" jasnenija malorusskix i srodnyx narodnyx pesen.* Warsaw, 1 (1883); 2 (1887).

36. Propp, V. *Morphology of the Folktale.* Bloomington, 1958.

37. Ransom, J. C. *The New Criticism.* Norfolk, Conn., 1941.

38. ——. *The World's Body.* New York, 1938.

39. Rybnikov, P. N. *Pesni*, Vol. 3. Moscow, 1910.

40. Sapir, E. *Language.* New York, 1921.

41. Sievers, E. *Ziele und Wege der Schallanalyse.* Heidelberg, 1924.

42. Simmons, D. C. "Specimens of Efik folklore." *Folk-Lore*, 66, pp. 417–424 (1955).

43. Steinitz, W. *Der Parallelismus in der finnisch-karelischen Volksdichtung, Folklore Fellows Communications*, 115 (1934).

44. Taranovski, K. *Ruski dvodelni ritmovi.* Belgrade, 1955.

45. Valéry, P. *The Art of Poetry*, Bollingen series 45. New York, 1958.

46. Wang Li. *Han-yü shih-lü hsüeh* (= Versification in Chinese). Shanghai, 1958.

47. Whorf, B. L. *Language, Thought, and Reality*, J. B. Carroll, ed. New York, 1956.

48. Wimsatt, W. K., Jr. *The Verbal Icon.* Lexington, 1954.

49. Žirmunskij, V. *Voprosy teorii literatury.* Leningrad, 1928.

CHARLES MORRIS

Following Peirce rather closely, Morris presents semiosis as a "five-term relation—v, w, x, y, z—in which v sets up in w the disposition to react in a certain way, x, to a certain kind of object, y, (not then acting as a stimulus), under certain conditions, z. The v's, in the cases where this relation obtains, are signs, the w's are interpreters, the x's are interpretants, the y's are significations, and the z's are the contexts in which the signs occur." Now two things are peculiar to the position argued by Morris in this selection. First, the interpretant of a sign—a notion he shares (even if rather modified) with Peirce and which corresponds roughly, with important qualifications, to Saussure's "signified"—is not defined in "mental" or strictly "cognitive" or "epistemological" terms, something that characterizes both Peirce and Saussure in the last analysis, but as "a disposition to react in a certain way," a way which is "behavioral" and hence open to objective study. Second, Morris holds to a "tridimensional" division of signification, but rather than seeing the correlation as obtaining between sign and object, which is the root of Peirce's classification, he thinks them to be "explicable in terms of three phases or aspects of action." Distinguishing with George Herbert Mead perceptual, manipulatory, and consummatory phases of action, and adding the premise that act and object are correlative, Morris distinguishes distance properties of an object, manipulatory properties, and consummatory properties. Now, "a sign is *designative* insofar as it signifies observable properties of the environment or of the actor, it is *appraisive* insofar as it signifies the consummatory properties of some object or situation, and it is *prescriptive* insofar as it signifies how the object or situation is to be reacted to so as to satisfy the governing impulse." It is clear that this way of setting up a semiotic framework dovetails with Peirce's emphasis on action and habit as "ultimate interpretants" but brings more explicitly into focus than Peirce does the internal differentiation of acts as "conditions" and "determinants" of signifying domains.

Thus, in a clear and unforced way Morris is able to correlate action requirements, dimensions of signification, interpretants (defined in terms of dispositions to respond), and significations. One of the most remarkable aspects of Morris's position—evident also in the case of Peirce—is the neat symmetry that arises from his choice of a starting point. In Morris's eyes, too, there is the further possibility of concrete empirical investigations of each aspect of the semiotic web. To change the metaphor, we can supply the flesh to his semiotic skeleton through putting his categorial scheme to the test. Morris himself did just this in later sections of the book from which this selection is taken. There he showed that just as stages of action can be set into relation with dimensions of signifying, so there exist further relations between these two domains and the dimensions of value (detachment, dominance, and dependence) and the forms of inquiry (which turn out to be terminologically identical with the dimensions of signifying). In this way Morris makes clear in a relatively unforced manner the points of intersection between semiotics (which thematizes semiosis in all its aspects) and the theory of perception and between theory of values and the theory of knowledge (understood in the broadest sense up to and including logic).

It remains to be seen whether the post-Peircean neatness of Morris's correlations and schematizations is due strictly speaking to the subject matter itself or is a result of his starting point and analytical scheme. Would, for example, Morris's semiotically structured epistemology really dovetail with Peirce's or with René Thom's, which begins with a rather different set of considerations? Can the "senses" articulated in systems of signs really be accounted for in "sociobehavioral" terms? Can the distinction between types of properties be applied as structural types to account for social forms? In an important sense, Morris, by reason of his dependence on Mead, belongs to the "pragmatic" heritage and it is necessary to see his work, and Peirce's, too, as a variety of "semiotic pragmatism."

Morris's major contributions have been collected in *Writings on the General Theory of Signs* (The Hague: Mouton, 1971). Perhaps more accessible, however, are separate and affordable editions of his key works contained in the Mouton edition: *Foundations of the Theory of Signs* (Chicago and London: University of Chicago Press, 1938, available in paperback edition), *Signs, Language, and Behavior* (New York: Prentice-Hall, 1946; George Braziller, 1955), and *Signification and Significance*, from which the selection in this volume is taken. For secondary literature on Morris, see the essay by Thomas A. Sebeok, "The Image of Charles Morris," in his *The Play of Musement* (Bloomington: Indiana University Press, 1981) and two essays by Ferruccio Rossi-Landi, "Signs about a Master of Signs," *Semiotica* 13/2, 1975, pp. 155–197 and "On Some Post-Morrisian Problems," *Ars semeiotica* 3, 1978, pp. 3–31. The extensive bibliographies in these last two essays will lead one to the other relevant materials.

Signs and the Act

CHARLES MORRIS

1. *The Scope of Semiotic*

Semiotic has for its goal a general theory of signs in all their forms and manifestations, whether in animals or men, whether normal or pathological, whether linguistic or nonlinguistic, whether personal or social. Semiotic is thus an interdisciplinary enterprise.

Part of the widespread interest in this area is motivated by the belief that higher-level sign processes (often called symbols) are of central importance in understanding man and his works. Ernst Cassirer called man "the symbolic animal" ("*animal symbolicum*"), instead of "the rational animal" ("*animal rationale*"), and much contemporary work has shown the aptness of this conception.

The term 'semiotic' was adapted by John Locke from the Greek Stoics, who in turn were influenced by the Greek medical tradition that interpreted diagnosis and prognosis as sign processes. Charles S. Peirce (1839–1914), who followed John Locke's usage, is responsible for the present widespread employment of the term 'semiotic'. The terms 'significs' and 'semantics' are also in use, though the tendency now is to use 'semantics' for only one branch of semiotic.

Philosophers and linguists made the main historical contributions to the general theory of signs, but today extensive work in this area is also being done by psychologists, psychiatrists, aestheticians, sociologists, and anthropologists.

2. *The Basic Terms of Semiotic*

For present purposes the basic terms of semiotic can be introduced as follows: Semiosis (or sign process) is regarded as a five-term relation—v, w, x, y, z—in which v sets up in w the disposition to react in a certain kind of way, x, to a certain kind of object, y (not then acting as a stimulus), under certain conditions, z. The v's, in the cases where this relation obtains, are *signs*, the w's are *interpreters*, the x's are *interpretants*, the y's are *significations*, and the z's are the *contexts* in which the signs occur.

Karl von Frisch[1] has shown that a bee which finds nectar is able, on

Reprinted from *Signification and Significance*, by Charles Morris, Cambridge, Mass.: The MIT Press. Copyright © 1964. Reprinted by permission of the publisher.

returning to the hive, to "dance" in such a way as to direct other bees to the food source. In this case the dance is the sign; the other bees affected by the dance are interpreters; the disposition to react in a certain kind of way by these bees, because of the dance,[2] is the interpretant; the kind of object toward which the bees are prepared to act in this way is the signification of the sign; and the position of the hive is part of the context.

Concerning this formulation of semiosis (or sign process, or sign behavior) several comments are in order.

First, the formulation is not proposed as a definition of 'sign', for there may be things we shall want to call signs that do not meet the requirements of this formulation—I prefer to leave this an open question. The formulation simply gives the conditions for recognizing certain events as signs.

Second, to say that what is signified is not at the moment a stimulus is not to deny that we may signify objects present in immediate experience—as in pointing to the desk upon which I am writing and saying "That is a desk." For 'desk' signifies an object with a rear, an underside, drawers that can be pulled out, etc.—none of which are at the present moment available to my observation. Only some aspects of the desk are directly observed.

Third, while this formulation is behavioral, and such sign behavior is open to objective study, an organism may experience and, in the case of human beings at least, may report on its own sign behavior. Nevertheless, a behavioral formulation is more basic than a self-observational formulation, since semiotic must deal with sign processes in animals, in children prior to the acquisition of language, and in personality disturbances where self-observational reports are absent or unreliable. Self-observational reports on sign processes are, however, not ruled out by a behavioral semiotic, since they are themselves a kind of sign behavior.

Fourth, I see no objection to introducing "significations" in this way. They are not "entities" in any objectionable sense, but certain describable aspects of complex behavioral processes in the natural world. As such they can be talked about without being "reified." That the bees are disposed by the dance to seek food objects in a certain context can be observed, just as in other contexts the dance serves to send the bees to explore certain locations as possible sites for a new hive. There is nothing "mythical" about significations when so interpreted.[3]

Fifth, the context in which something functions as a sign may include other signs, but need not do so.

Sixth, the interpretant, as a disposition to react in a certain way because of the sign (food-seeking behavior or site-probing behavior in the case of bees), has no necessarily "subjective" connotation. Such a disposition can, if one wishes, be interpreted in probabilistic terms, as the probability of reacting in a certain way under certain conditions because of the appearance of the sign. Or, as we shall see later, it can be interpreted as an intervening variable, postulated for theoretical purposes, and controllable by indirect empirical evidence.

3. Dimensions of Signification

It is widely recognized that signs which are commonly (but not universally) admitted to have signification differ greatly in the kind of signification they have. 'Black', 'good', and 'ought' are obvious examples. There are, however, many ways in which such differences are accounted for.

My suggestion is that signification is tridimensional, and that these three dimensions are explicable in terms of three phases or aspects of action. I shall follow George H. Mead's analysis of an act.[4]

According to Mead, if an impulse (as a disposition to a certain kind of action) is given, the resulting action has three phases: the perceptual, the manipulatory, and the consummatory. The organism must perceive the relevant features of the environment in which it is to act; it must behave toward these objects in a way relevant to the satisfaction of its impulse; and if all goes well, it then attains the phase of activity which is the consummation of the act. Since act and object are correlative in his account, Mead also speaks of the distance properties of the object, its manipulatory properties, and its consummatory properties.

Now, if signs are treated behaviorally, it may be that their significations are related to these three aspects of action and so exhibit tridimensionality. It is proposed that every sign be regarded as having three dimensions, though some signs will be strongest on certain dimensions, and in some cases they will have a null weighting on certain dimensions.

A sign is *designative* insofar as it signifies *observable*[5] properties of the environment or of the actor, it is *appraisive* insofar as it signifies the consummatory properties of some object or situation, and it is *prescriptive* insofar as it signifies how the object or situation is to be reacted to so as to satisfy the governing impulse. In these terms, usually 'black' is primarily designative, 'good' is primarily appraisive, and 'ought' is primarily prescriptive. It should of course be recognized that context is always relevant, so that in some contexts 'black' may be primarily appraisive or prescriptive, 'good' primarily designative or prescriptive, and 'ought' primarily designative or appraisive. One cannot tell from the mere inspection of an uttered or written word its strength on the three dimensions. This requires the study of specific action in a specific situation.

Nevertheless, there is some evidence that certain terms do have signification on the three dimensions,[6] and that there is some agreement as to their relative strengths on these dimensions. In three of my seminars, students were given the form 'X is ——', and were told that X was a man. They were then told successively that X was humble, proud, hard, wet, wise, severe, objective, kind, serious, cowardly, and old, and were asked to assign a percentage to each sentence indicating to what extent it was designative, appraisive, and prescriptive. In general, there was considerable agreement in the three groups as to whether a given sentence was, in this context, predominantly designative, appraisive, or prescriptive. Thus all groups thought of 'cowardly' as having considerable strength on all three dimensions, but most strength on the appraisive dimension; and they all thought of 'old' as primarily designative. These results are not scientifically impressive, but at any rate they indicate that experimental studies in this area are possible.

In relation to Mead's analysis of the act, the expectation would be for designative signs to be predominant in the perceptual stage of the act, for here the actor is seeking to obtain information concerning the situation in which he is acting. In the manipulatory stage of action it seems plausible that the signs involved would be primarily prescriptive, signifying how the object or situation is to be reacted to. In the consummatory phase of action, the signs involved would be primarily appraisive, signifying the consummatory properties of the object or situation.

4. Interpretants

Since on the present model all signs have interpretants, different kinds of interpretants would occur for the three dimensions of signification. The interpretant of a sign is a disposition to react in a certain kind of way because of the sign. Corresponding to the designative dimension of signification, the interpretant would be a disposition to react to the designated object as if it had certain observable properties. Thus if one is told that there is a black object in an adjoining room, one is set for certain visual experiences on entering the room.

In the case of appraisive signs, the interpretant would be a disposition to act toward a designated object as if it would be satisfying or unsatisfying. Thus if a mother tries to get her child to swallow a teaspoonful of castor oil by saying "nummy num," the child is set for something that he will favor. Since he does not like it when he tastes it, and if the mother continues to talk like this in a variety of situations, the term 'nummy num' will change from a positive appraisive sign to a negative appraisive sign—or the child will come to regard his mother as a liar.

In the case of primarily prescriptive signs the interpretant would be a disposition to act in a certain kind of way to the designated object or situation. If a person trying unsuccessfully to open a door is told that he ought to press down on the knob, he is disposed to perform that kind of action and in most cases to expect that in so performing it he will be able to get out of the room.

It is especially notable that any given sign may in varying degrees operate in all the dimensions of signification, and hence have all the corresponding interpretant dimensions. The sentence "He is a coward" may illustrate this.[7] Terms like 'black', 'good', and 'ought' are simply cases where certain dimensions of signification and certain kinds of interpretant are predominant. More will be said of such terms later.

5. Summary of the Analysis

For the moment let us shift the focus of our attention from the phases of action in Mead's sense to certain general requirements of action. Three requirements will be discussed.

The actor must obtain information concerning the situation in which he is to act, he must select among objects that he will favor or accord positive preferential behavior, and he must act on the selected object by some specific course of behavior. Thus if he is thirsty and finds that tea and coffee are available, he must act preferentially to one of these—say tea—and he must decide whether to drink the tea quickly or slowly, alone or with a companion, and so forth.

These three requirements of action are common to all action, non-human and human, and may take place without signs, or with signs at the prelinguistic level, or with linguistic signs in a complex process of inquiry. The behavior of an amoeba may be at the first level, the warning cry of a duck to her ducklings at the second level, and considerable human behavior at the third level. Inquiry will be considered at some length later. Here it need only be noted that appraisive signs operative in inquiry are signs of possible consummatory objects, while appraisive signs at the consummatory phase of the act report on the direct experience of consummation or frustration. The tea appraised in inquiry as nummy-num may or may not be called nummy-num when tasted.

Some of the results of the preceding analysis, in somewhat different terms, are presented in Table 1. The terminology of the interpretant column perhaps needs no elaboration. A possible hypothesis is that the interpretant of primarily designative signs strongly involves (among other things) the sensory nervous system including the sensory projection areas of the cortex, that primarily appraisive signs strongly involve the autonomic nervous system including the memory sections and pleasure centers, and that primarily prescriptive signs strongly involve the somatic (or motor) nervous system including the effector system of the brain. This suggestion of course does not deny that in all cases other aspects of the organism are operative, and since most signs actually have weights on all three dimensions of signification, it does not imply that the interpretant of a sign is limited to one aspect of nervous activity and its related organic accompaniments. But it does suggest that the tridimensionality of signification is reflected in a tridimensionality of interpretants.

The terminology in the significations column is borrowed from psychology, and it needs some explication. 'Stimulus property' is used here in a wide sense. It includes not merely the characteristics of the object

Table 1.   Signs and Action Requirements

Action Requirements	Dimensions of Signification	Interpretant (Disposition to Respond by):	Significations
1. Obtaining information	Designative	Sense organs	Stimulus properties of object
2. Selection of objects for preferential behavior	Appraisive	Object preferences	Reinforcing properties of object
3. Action on object by specific behavior	Prescriptive	Behavior preferences	Act as instrumental

which activate a sense organ but those which might do so under certain conditions (such as on the other side of the moon), and even those properties which though not themselves observable can affect an instrument which is observable (such as the temperature at the surface of the sun). Thus the range of designation is much wider than what can be directly observed.

By 'reinforcing property of an object' is meant the capacity of an object to increase the probability of the performance of a response made to it. Thus when certain kinds of food are tasted by a dog, he will eat them; but when others are tasted, they are spurned. The first kind of food is said to have a reinforcing property, and the second kind of food not to have it. Although such properties are not additional stimulus properties, I see no objection to speaking of them as properties of an object. It is true that they are properties of an object only in relation to an organism, so that an object which has reinforcing properties for the behavior of a dog may not have such properties for the behavior of a cat. But this is a common situation: we do not hesitate to say that some objects are edible and some are not, though the classification is relative to various kinds of digestive systems. Such properties may be said to be "objectively relative."

To call an act "instrumental" signifies that its performance permits the performance of some other act which an organism is disposed to perform. Thus a hungry animal may get food in an experimental situation if and only if it presses a lever. The act of pressing a lever is then instrumental. The act of pressing down on the doorknob in our earlier example is instrumental to the disposition to get out of the room.

6. The Terms 'Meaning' and 'Express'

The terms 'meaning' and 'express' have not been introduced as basic terms for semiotic, since they have such a variety of significations and are used in such a variety of ways that it is best not to employ them as basic terms for discussions in this area. But it is of course possible, if one wishes, to introduce them in terms of more basic semiotical terms. Thus it might be said that the "meaning" of a sign is *both* its signification and its interpretant, and neither alone.

In that case merely to say that a certain object has reinforcing properties is not to make an appraisive utterance (i.e., to say something which has appraisive "meaning"). The term 'good', for instance, would therefore have appraisive meaning only if it not merely signified an object as having reinforcing properties but also aroused in its interpreters a disposition to positive preferential behavior toward the object signified. A dietitian may say to his patient (perhaps a diabetic) that diet *A* is good and diet *B* is bad without inducing in himself a disposition to eat in manner *A* rather than in manner *B*—the term 'good' is for him then primarily designative, while for his patient, insofar as it disposes him to give preference to diet *A*, the term is appraisive as well (i.e., has appraisive "meaning").[8]

Similarly for the term 'ought', in some contexts it is purely designative, and in others it has an appraisive component. It has prescriptive meaning only if it signifies to its interpreter that the act which is prescribed is instrumental and in addition actually disposes its interpreter to perform the act in question. Here, too, the "meaning" of an ought-statement may be different for the utterer and for the person addressed.

In the case of designative "meaning," a sign has such meaning to the degree that the interpreter is disposed to sense-organ activity[9] of a certain kind to a certain kind of object. Many signs have all kinds of "meaning" in various degrees.

As for the term 'express', it could be introduced in the present scheme in at least two ways. One might say that every sign expresses its interpretant, without signifying it. Or one might say that a sign is expressive to the degree that its *production* is itself taken as a sign by an interpreter of some state of its producer.[10] In this case not every sign is actually "expressive" though it is potentially so. Of course, certain signs (such as a cry of alarm) are much more frequently interpreted as expressive in this sense than are other signs, and these are the signs which some persons perhaps intend by their use of 'expressive'. But all signs may be interpreted as expressive in this second sense of the term, and what is expressed is by no means limited to emotions or attitudes. Hence, the identification of 'expressive' with 'emotive' engenders many confusions which the present analysis avoids.

It might be maintained that the analysis of the act followed here is too simple—that it stresses what the actor does in relation to the object and neglects what the object does to the actor.[11] The hungry person not only scans his environment for food objects, manipulates them, and chews them, but the object in turn initiates a very complex set of processes in the organism. It seems suggestive to say that this more passive, more "undergoing" aspect of behavior has its own kind of sign functioning, and that such signs are primarily "expressive." This area certainly demands extensive exploration and may throw considerable light on mythic, aesthetic, and religious symbolism.

When the person eats an apple, he does become passive in a sense, and the apple "acts on him." But to signify what occurs seems to be describable in terms of the designative, appraisive, and prescriptive dimensions of signification. The person may designate what happens to him, he may appraise this, and he may then formulate prescriptions as to his future eating behavior. These signs may have "meaning" and be "expressive" in the sense of the previous discussion. But the question is whether such important analysis will also require the introduction of a new dimension of signification.

7. Formal Signs

So far, no account has been given of what are often called "logical" or "grammatical" or "structural" signs, to which are attributed logical or grammatical or structural signification (or "meaning"). Examples are terms like 'or', parentheses, and the '-ly' in 'He came quickly.'

In *Signs, Language, and Behavior* such items were called "formators," and an attempt was made to give them a fourth dimension of signification—"formative signification." Thus 'or', in some of its occurrences, was said to signify that an otherwise signified situation had the property of alternativity. Of the statement "The apple is on the first or second shelf of the ice box" one might say that it designates no observable property of apple and icebox, and neither appraises them nor prescribes action with respect to them. Hence, if we mean by 'lexical' those terms which designate, appraise, or prescribe, then 'or' in this occurrence would be nonlexical. Since it does seem to signify something about the signified situation, it might be said to have another type (or dimension) of signification, "formative" signification.[12]

It now seems worthwhile to explore the possibility of maintaining a tridimensional analysis. One of the reasons for introducing a formative dimension of signification is undoubtedly to have a way of explaining the status of formal logic, mathematics, and grammar. Thus if no fourth formative dimension is introduced, there remains the task within a tridimensional analysis of accounting for these statuses.

One possibility, sometimes held, is to regard formators as simply "auxiliary devices" which themselves have no signification but which influence in determinate ways the signification of the sign combinations in which they appear. They might then be called "synsigns." Thus the word order of '*X* hit *Y*', as contrasted to the word order of '*Y* hit *X*', might be regarded as a synsign in this sense, as determining different significations for the two expressions but without having a signification of its own.

Such an analysis may be sufficient to account for some (and perhaps all) of the vague class of items called formators. But there is another possibility, namely of regarding formators as a rather special class of lexical signs, and hence as being analyzable in terms of designative, appraisive, and prescriptive signification. One version of this possibility would be to regard them as metalinguistic signs signifying the signs they accompany. Thus 'or' in '*P* or *Q*' could be interpreted as signifying (in this case designating) the set of pairs of sentences such that at least one of the sentences in a given pair is true. Parentheses would be regarded as designating the expressions around which they occur and prescribing that these expressions are to be treated in a certain way. It is important to realize that there are relations of signification within the field of signs, and not merely to situations outside this field.

I believe that this approach can be carried quite far. Nevertheless, another version of this possibility is to consider (at least some) formators not as metalinguistic (in the sense that they explicitly signify other signs) but as being at a higher level than the signs they accompany (i.e., they presuppose these signs without actually signifying them). Thus in the case of 'or' mentioned above, it might be said that 'or' signifies something about the situation signified by the other signs of the combination in which it occurs; it would be a situation of alternativity and would be responded to in such and such a way ("If you don't find the apple on the first shelf, look for it on the second," etc.). This differs from the analysis first suggested in introducing the notion of *levels in the object language*, and by keeping the signification of formators lexical, it does not introduce a fourth dimension of signification.

8. Formative Discourse

Though a dimension of formative signification is not regarded as necessary, it is still necessary in semiotic to account for such formative discourse as is exemplified by mathematics and formal logic. Thus '$2+2=4$' differs from '2 quarts of alcohol added to 2 quarts of water give 4 quarts of liquid'. The first sentence is formative (and analytic); the second is lexical (and synthetic). The first is formally true; the second is empirically false. The negatives of these sentences are, respectively, formally false and empirically true.

It is not my concern here to discuss comprehensively the problems of formative discourse. A suggestion, however, may indicate a direction of possible analysis.

The relation of *analytic implicates* between two signs (or sets of signs) can be introduced as follows: Where the signification of S_1 is contained in or is identical with the signification of S_2, then S_2 is an analytic implicate of S_1. Thus in 'Men are animals', 'animals' is an analytic implicate of 'men'. If something is a man, then by the signification of the term 'man' that something is an animal. Similar examples would be found in 'A is A' and 'Black berries are black'. 'Blackberries are black' is not an example of such a formative sentence. It is an empirical sentence, and at an early stage of the growth of blackberries it is in fact false.

The relation of *contradictory implicates* can be introduced as follows: Where the signification of S_1 is the absence of the conditions which constitute the signification of S_2, S_1 and S_2 are said to be contradictory implicates of each other. 'Men are not-men', 'A is not-A', 'Black berries are not-black' are examples of sentences built upon contradictory implicates. By the signification of the signs it is known that if one of the signs applies to something, the other does not; and if one sign does not apply to something, the other one does.

Insofar as discourse is based on analytic implicates, it is analytic formative discourse; and insofar as it is based on contradictory implicates, it is contradictory formative discourse. Mathematical discourse often (or always) is of the former sort, and mystical discourse is often (or always) of the second sort.[13]

It is thus possible within the present framework of semiotic to admit a type of formative (as opposed to lexical) discourse, and yet not to introduce a fourth (formative) dimension of signification over and above the designative, appraisive, and prescriptive dimensions. Hence, we need not complicate the analysis of stages of the act to account for formative discourse.

9. The Uses of Signs

Contemporary analyses of signs stress strongly the many uses of signs, especially linguistic signs. But the terms 'signification', 'use', and 'usage', and their relations are conceived very diversely. Some persons identify the signification of a word with how it is used, and some with its usage. 'Use' and 'usage' are at times distinguished, and at times not.

If pragmatics is concerned with the origin, uses, and effects of signs, then to speak of the "use" of a sign presupposes that it already has a signification. Hence, in this framework 'signification' and 'use' are distinguished. 'Usage of a sign', however, if distinguished from 'use', does not suggest to me anything above and beyond the operation of something as a sign within a sign process (or sign behavior). As such, it adds nothing to the account which has been given.

In *Signs, Language, and Behavior* four main uses of signs were discussed. They were then called the informative, valuative, incitive, and systemic uses of signs. Signs may be used to inform someone of the properties of objects or situations, or to induce in someone preferential behavior toward some objects or situations, or to incite a specific course of action, or to organize the dispositions to behavior produced by other signs. There is no necessary selection of such uses in terms of the kinds of signification which signs have. But, in general, designative signs are used informatively, appraisive signs are used valuatively, prescriptive signs are used incitively, and formative signs are used systemically.

The distinguishing feature of work in semiotic in recent years has been the extension of interest into the diversity of dimensions of signification and into the variety of uses which signs perform. Earlier in the century, philosophers were concerned mainly with the designative and formative dimensions of signification as they occurred in science and mathematics.[14] This concern remains, but it has been supplemented by a growing interest in the place that signs have in the manipulatory and consummatory phases of action. Thus attention has been increasingly directed to rituals, myths, morality, art, law, politics, religion, and philosophy. Since these topics involve values, I shall turn now to the theory of value (axiology), the relation of signs and values, and the place of values in human action.[15]

NOTES

1. Karl von Frisch, *Bees, Their Vision, Chemical Senses, and Language* (Ithaca, New York: Cornell University Press, 1950).

2. Note the qualification, since not all dispositions occur in sign processes. Independent of signs, there are many dispositions to respond in certain ways to certain things.

3. My earlier formulations led to certain objections on this score. See my review of B. F. Skinner's *Verbal Behavior*, under the title "Words Without Meaning," in *Contemporary Psychology* 3 (1958), pp. 212–214.

4. George Herbert Mead, *The Philosophy of the Act*, Charles W. Morris, ed., with the collaboration of John M. Brewster, Albert M. Dunham, and David L. Miller (Chicago: University of Chicago Press, 1938).

5. The term "observable" is here employed in a fairly narrow sense: "observable directly by sense organs or indirectly by the observation of events which have been observed to act as evidence for events not observable directly by sense organs." The term "observation" has a wide range of application in the everyday language, and some thinkers will want to dispense with the term in this context, so that semiotic will not seem to set arbitrary limits to the range of signification of signs. Major philosophical views hang upon what are taken to be the limits of signification. These views cannot be discussed in this preliminary formulation. Attention may be called to the analysis of the phases of the referential function of language, in Willard Van Orman Quine's *Word and Object* (Cambridge, Mass.: The Technology Press of the Massachusetts Institute of Technology; New York: John Wiley & Sons, 1960), pp. 108–110.

6. Some readers will object to the use of the term "dimension" in this connection, and they may prefer such terms as "factor" and "respect." The semiotic "dimensions" are not dimensions in the strictest mathematical sense (as are the

value dimensions of Chapter 2 [of Morris's book]). But the values of the variables are partly independent, and while no scale is known which is common to all of them, the values of each dimension are to some extent quantifiable.

7. See John Dewey's analysis of "cowardly" and "friendly," in *Experience and Nature* (Chicago: Open Court Publishing Co., 1925), pp. 292–293.

8. The term "good" may even here have an appraisive component for the dietitian: If he becomes diabetic, he may then be disposed to diet *A* rather than diet *B* because of what he had previously said to his patient.

9. This must be qualified in terms of the earlier comments made upon the term "observation."

10. Of course, in some cases the interpreter of the sign may also be the producer. Abraham Kaplan calls the sign in this case *self-expressive*. It may be noted that not all signs expressive in the first sense of this term are expressive (or self-expressive) in the second sense of the term. In my *Signs, Language, and Behavior* (New York: Prentice-Hall, 1946; New York: George Braziller, 1955), I proposed to use "expressive" in the second sense, and I still favor this proposal.

11. Howard Parsons called this to my attention. He is at present working out what is involved here.

12. Most contemporary linguists still speak of "structural meaning," "grammatical meaning," "formal meaning," "linguistic meaning," or the like. The assumption of such meaning has been called in question by Noam Chomsky, in *Syntactic Structures* (The Hague: Mouton & Co., 1957).

13. See my paper, "Mysticism and Its Language," *Language: An Enquiry into Its Meaning and Function*, Ruth Nanda Anshen, ed. (New York: Harper & Brothers, 1957), pp. 179–187. The paper (in a slightly shorter form) originally appeared in *Etc. A Review of General Semantics* 9 (1951), pp. 3–8.

14. Of course this was not true of thinkers such as Ernst Cassirer, who was concerned with all the major forms of human symbolic activity.

15. Some readers may be interested in how the account [given here] differs from that of *Signs, Language, and Behavior*. There is here a different formulation of sign behavior, an attempt to do away with the formative dimension of signification, and in general a greater stress on the dimensions of signification (earlier called "modes of signifying").

ROLAND BARTHES

Roland Barthes's "spectral analysis" of the messages contained in the image breaks new ground in the extension of semiotic theory to nonverbal communication systems. The present essay gives us a semiotic epistemology of the image and reflects upon the fundamental novelty that the photographic image has introduced into social and conscious life, its implementation of new forms of perception. In a formula that puts him at odds with Langer's deepest thesis, Barthes's goal in the essay is to deal with "the most important problem facing the semiology of images: Can analogical representation (the 'copy') produce true systems of signs and not merely simple agglutinations of symbols? Is it possible to conceive of an analogical 'code' (as opposed to a digital one)?"

Although Barthes focuses upon an advertising image—because it is frank and emphatic, or "full"—what he says goes way beyond the immediate context of his analysis. In the image we have a fusion of perceptual knowledge—"an almost anthropological knowledge"—and cultural knowledge. Barthes proceeds to apply a highly differentiated, even if idiosyncratic, semiotic framework to the analysis of his chosen example, a "Panzani" ad for Italian food products, an analysis that has great heuristic fertility and generalizability.

Barthes's procedure is to sort out the semiotic structure of the messages contained in such an image and to show how several signifying systems come together and intersect. We encounter here "a veritable ontology of the process of signification"—the goal being to explain "the role of the image in society"—and another illustration of semiotics' ability to offer new insights through the application of a novel interpretative grid. Admitting that "all images are polysemous" Barthes is concerned to uncover the internal "grammar" of this polysemousness.

Barthes's analytical framework, which he himself worked out in his *Elements of Semiology*, fuses categories from Saussure and from the Danish linguist Louis Hjelmslev, author of *Prolegomena to a Theory of Language*. Barthes's guiding questions are the following. What is the relation between literal messages and symbolic messages in the image? How is a linguistic message, which often surrounds the iconic message, related to the image, and is this relationship always constant? What about images without a linguistic matrix? Is the image strictly speaking parasitic on language? How does language relate to images which are connected and not "free-standing"? Just how are images coded? What aspects of images are coded? Are they coded in the way language is coded or are other constraints and other conditions operative here? How does a drawing differ from a photograph? Just what is the unprecedented nature of the photographic image, which represents an "anthropological revolution" in human history? What is the exact nature and extent of the "pure spectatorial consciousness" attendant upon this revolution, which involves "a decisive mutation of informational economies" and which is itself connected with the permeation of image life by technologies (a phenomenon also discerned by Walter Benjamin in his famous essay, "The Work of Art in the Age of Mechanical Reproducibility")? What is the "architecture of signs drawn from a variable depth of lexicons" which make up the connotation of the sign? What are we to make of Barthes's claim, so often expressed in the strands of French structuralism (from Lévi-Strauss to Jacques Lacan) that "the image is penetrated through and through by the system of meaning, in exactly the same way as man is articulated to the very depths of his being in distinct languages," since "the *psyche* itself is articulated like a language"? Anthony Wilden has taken up this question on a number of occasions, especially in his brilliant book of essays, *System and Structure*, second edition (London and New York: Tavistock, 1980; U.S. edition in association with Methuen).

Barthes further wants to show us the principles for carrying out "a massive inventory of the systems of connotation" which images bear and in which they are embedded. Semiology, as Barthes conceived it—a semiology that "can only be conceived in a so to speak total framework"—then becomes identical with the study of ideology and with the study of the various "myths" of modern life which were subjected to close scrutiny in his *Mythologies*. The "rhetoric" of the image appears as "the signifying aspect of ideology" and the system of *connotators* make up the vast field making ideological forms possible, indeed, possibly instantiating, in their various instances, "a single rhetorical *form*, common . . . to dream, literature and image," a set of "figures" which are "never more than formal relations of elements." Hence, once again, the close connection to Lévi-Strauss's own project.

Only a close reading—and rereading—of Barthes's essay and various exercises on the vast array of images and messages which can be analyzed by means of his categorial apparatus will show, or not show, the power of such a semiotic approach to images. But the main lines of the grand linguistic analogy furnish the interpretative grid of Barthes's essay from the very beginning: denotation and connotation, signifier and signified, coded and noncoded, literal and symbolic, linguistic and iconic, lexia and lexicons, paradigmatic and syntagmatic (cf. Jakobson once again on the axes of language), ideology, and so forth. These are the main speculative instruments, so argues Barthes, for dealing with the "semiology" of images.

Barthes focused in many of his essays on "mythologies," which is also the title of an important collection of his analyses, which also contains his fundamental "Myth Today," translated by Annette Lavers (New York: Hill and Wang, 1972). Although he described himself as never having been in linguistics "anything but an amateur," it is still important to read his *Elements of Semiology*, translated by Annette Lavers and Colin Smith (Boston: Beacon Press, 1968). Consult the discussion of Barthes as well as the bibliography in Terence Hawkes, *Structuralism and Semiotics* (Berkeley and Los Angeles: University of California Press, 1977). For a "non-academic" discussion see "Writing Itself: On Roland Barthes," by Susan Sontag, in *The New Yorker* (April 26, 1982), pp. 122–141.

Rhetoric of the Image

ROLAND BARTHES

According to an ancient etymology, the word *image* should be linked to the root *imitari*. Thus we find ourselves immediately at the heart of the most important problem facing the semiology of images: can analogical representation (the 'copy') produce true systems of signs and not merely simple agglutinations of symbols? Is it possible to conceive of an analogical 'code' (as opposed to a digital one)? We know that linguists refuse the status of language to all communication by analogy—from the 'language' of bees to the 'language' of gesture—the moment such communications are not doubly articulated, are not founded on a combinatory system of digital units as phonemes are. Nor are linguists the only ones to be suspicious as to the linguistic nature of the image; general opinion too has a vague conception of the image as an area of resistance to meaning—this in the name of a certain mythical idea of Life: the image is representation, which is to say ultimately resurrection, and, as we know, the intelligible is reputed antipathetic to lived experience. Thus from both sides the image is felt to be weak in respect of meaning: there are those who think that the image is an extremely rudimentary system in comparison with language and those who think that signification cannot exhaust the image's ineffable richness. Now even—and above all if—the image is in a certain manner the *limit* of meaning, it permits the consideration of a veritable ontology of the process of signification. How does meaning get into the image? Where does it end? And if it ends, what is there *beyond*? Such are the questions that I wish to raise by submitting the image to a spectral analysis of the messages it may contain. We will start by making it considerably easier for ourselves: we will only study the advertising image. Why? Because in advertising the signification of the image is undoubtedly intentional; the signifieds of the advertising message are formed *a priori* by certain attributes of the product and these signifieds have to be transmitted as clearly as possible. If the image contains signs, we can be sure that in advertising these signs are full, formed with a view to the optimum reading: the advertising image is *frank*, or at least emphatic.

The three messages

Here we have a Panzani advertisement: some packets of pasta, a tin, a sachet, some tomatoes, onions, peppers, a mushroom, all emerging from a half-open string bag, in yellows and greens on a red background.[1] Let us try to 'skim off' the different messages it contains.

The image immediately yields a first message whose substance is linguistic; its supports are the caption, which is marginal, and the labels, these being inserted into the natural disposition of the scene, '*en abyme*'. The code from which this message has been taken is none other than that of the French language; the only knowledge required to decipher it is a knowledge of writing and French. In fact, this message can itself be further broken down, for the sign *Panzani* gives not simply the name of the firm but also, by its assonance, an additional signified, that of 'Italianicity'. The linguistic message is thus twofold (at least in this particular image): denotational and connotational. Since, however, we have here only a single typical sign,[2] namely that of articulated (written) language, it will be counted as one message.

Putting aside the linguistic message, we are left with the pure image (even if the labels are part of it, anecdotally). This image straightaway provides a series of discontinuous signs. First (the order is unimportant as these signs are not linear), the idea that what we have in the scene represented is a return from the market. A signified which itself implies two euphoric values: that of the freshness of the products and that of the essentially domestic preparation for which they are destined. Its signifier is

the half-open bag which lets the provisions spill out over the table, 'un-
packed'. To read this first sign requires only a knowledge which is in
some sort implanted as part of the habits of a very widespread culture
where 'shopping around for oneself' is opposed to the hasty stocking up
(preserves, refrigerators) of a more 'mechanical' civilization. A second
sign is more or less equally evident; its signifier is the bringing together of
the tomato, the pepper and the tricoloured hues (yellow, green, red) of
the poster; its signified is Italy or rather *Italianicity*. This sign stands in a
relation of redundancy with the connoted sign of the linguistic message
(the Italian assonance of the name *Panzani*) and the knowledge it draws
upon is already more particular; it is a specifically 'French' knowledge
(an Italian would barely perceive the connotation of the name, no more
probably than he would the Italianicity of tomato and pepper), based on
a familiarity with certain tourist stereotypes. Continuing to explore the
image (which is not to say that it is not entirely clear at the first glance),
there is no difficulty in discovering at least two other signs: in the first, the
serried collection of different objects transmits the idea of a total culinary
service, on the one hand as though Panzani furnished everything neces-

sary for a carefully balanced dish and on the other as though the concentrate in the tin were equivalent to the natural produce surrounding it; in the other sign, the composition of the image, evoking the memory of innumerable alimentary paintings, sends us to an aesthetic signified: the '*nature morte*' or, as it is better expressed in other languages, the 'still life'[3]; the knowledge on which this sign depends is heavily cultural. It might be suggested that, in addition to these four signs, there is a further information pointer, that which tells us that this is an advertisement and which arises both from the place of the image in the magazine and from the emphasis of the labels (not to mention the caption). This last information, however, is co-extensive with the scene; it eludes signification insofar as the advertising nature of the image is essentially functional: to utter something is not necessarily to declare *I am speaking*, except in a deliberately reflexive system such as literature.

Thus there are four signs for this image and we will assume that they form a coherent whole (for they are all discontinuous), require a generally cultural knowledge, and refer back to signifieds each of which is global (for example, *Italianicity*), imbued with euphoric values. After the linguistic message, then, we can see a second, iconic message. Is that the end? If all these signs are removed from the image, we are still left with a certain informational matter; deprived of all knowledge, I continue to 'read' the image, to 'understand' that it assembles in a common space a number of identifiable (nameable) objects, not merely shapes and colours. The signifieds of this third message are constituted by the real objects in the scene, the signifiers by these same objects photographed, for, given that the relation between thing signified and image signifying in analogical representation is not 'arbitrary' (as it is in language), it is no longer necessary to dose the relay with a third term in the guise of the psychic image of the object. What defines the third message is precisely that the relation between signified and signifier is quasi-tautological; no doubt the photograph involves a certain arrangement of the scene (framing, reduction, flattening) but this transition is not a *transformation* (in the way a coding can be); we have here a loss of the equivalence characteristic of true sign systems and a statement of quasi-identity. In other words, the sign of this message is not drawn from an institutional stock, is not coded, and we are brought up against the paradox (to which we will return) of a *message without a code*.[4] This peculiarity can be seen again at the level of the knowledge invested in the reading of the message; in order to 'read' this last (or first) level of the image, all that is needed is the knowledge bound up with our perception. That knowledge is not nil, for we need to know what an image is (children only learn this at about the age of four) and what a tomato, a string-bag, a packet of pasta are, but it is a matter of an almost anthropological knowledge. This message corresponds, as it were, to the letter of the image and we can agree to call it the literal message, as opposed to the previous symbolic message.

If our reading is satisfactory, the photograph analysed offers us three messages: a linguistic message, a coded iconic message, and a non-coded iconic message. The linguistic message can be readily separated from the other two, but since the latter share the same (iconic) substance, to what extent have we the right to separate them? It is certain that the distinction between the two iconic messages is not made spontaneously in ordinary reading: the viewer of the image receives *at one and the same time* the perceptual message and the cultural message, and it will be seen later that this confusion in reading corresponds to the function of the mass image (our concern here). The distinction, however, has an operational validity, analogous to that which allows the distinction in the linguistic sign of a signifier and a signified (even though in reality no one is able to separate the 'word' from its meaning except by recourse to the meta-language of a definition). If the distinction permits us to describe the structure of the image in a simple and coherent fashion and if this description paves the way for an explanation of the role of the image in society, we will take it to be justified. The task now is thus to reconsider each type of message so as to explore it in its generality, without losing sight of our aim of understanding the overall structure of the image, the final inter-relationship of the three messages. Given that what is in question is not a 'naive' analysis but a structural description,[5] the order of the messages will be modified a little by the inversion of the cultural message and the literal message; of the two iconic messages, the first is in some sort imprinted on the second: the literal message appears as the *support* of the 'symbolic' message. Hence, knowing that a system which takes over the signs of another system in order to make them its signifiers is a system of connotation,[6] we may say immediately that the literal image is *denoted* and the symbolic image *connoted*. Successively, then, we shall look at the linguistic message, the denoted image, and the connoted image.

The linguistic message

Is the linguistic message constant? Is there always textual matter in, under, or around the image? In order to find images given without words, it is doubtless necessary to go back to partially illiterate societies, to a sort of pictographic state of the image. From the moment of the appearance of the book, the linking of text and image is frequent, though it seems to have been little studied from a structural point of view. What is the signifying structure of 'illustration'? Does the image duplicate certain of the informations given in the text by a phenomenon of redundancy or does the text add a fresh information to the image? The problem could be posed historically as regards the classical period with its passion for books with pictures (it was inconceivable in the eighteenth century that editions of La Fontaine's *Fables* should not be illustrated) and its authors such as Menestrier who concerned themselves with the relations between figure and discourse.[7] Today, at the level of mass communications, it appears that the linguistic message is indeed present in every image: as title, caption, accompanying press article, film dialogue, comic strip balloon. Which shows that it is not very accurate to talk of a civilization of the image—we are still, and more than ever, a civilization of writing,[8] writing and speech continuing to be the full terms of the informational structure. In fact, it is simply the presence of the linguistic message that counts, for neither its position nor its length seem to be pertinent (a long text may only comprise a single global signified, thanks to connotation, and it is this signified which is put in relation with the image). What are the functions of the linguistic message with regard to the (twofold) iconic message? There appear to be two: *anchorage* and *relay*.

As will be seen more clearly in a moment, all images are polysemous; they imply, underlying their signifiers, a 'floating chain' of signifieds, the reader able to choose some and ignore others. Polysemy poses a question of meaning and this question always comes through as a dysfunction, even if this dysfunction is recuperated by society as a tragic (silent, God provides no possibility of choosing between signs) or a poetic (the panic 'shudder of meaning' of the Ancient Greeks) game; in the cinema itself, traumatic images are bound up with an uncertainty (an anxiety) concerning the meaning of objects or attitudes. Hence in every society various techniques are developed intended to *fix* the floating chain of signifieds in such a way as to counter the terror of uncertain signs; the linguistic message is one of these techniques. At the level of the literal message, the text replies—in a more or less direct, more or less partial manner—to the question: *what is it?* The text helps to identify purely and simply the elements of the scene and the scene itself; it is a matter of a denoted description of the image (a description which is often incomplete) or, in Hjelmslev's terminology, of an *operation* (as opposed to connotation).[9] The denominative function corresponds exactly to an *anchorage* of all the possible (denoted) meanings of the object by recourse to a nomenclature. Shown a plateful of something (in an *Amieux* advertisement), I may hesitate in identifying the forms and masses; the caption ('*rice and tuna fish with mushrooms*') helps me to choose *the correct level of perception*, permits me to focus not simply my gaze but also my understanding. When it comes to the 'symbolic message', the linguistic message no longer guides identification but interpretation, constituting a kind of vice which holds the connoted meanings from proliferating, whether towards excessively individual regions (it limits, that is to say, the projective power of the image) or towards dysphoric values. An advertisement (for *d'Arcy* preserves) shows a few fruits scattered around a ladder; the caption ('*as if from your own garden*') banishes one possible signified (parsimony, the paucity of the harvest) because of its unpleasantness and orientates the reading towards a more flattering signified (the natural and personal character of fruit from a private garden); it acts here as a counter-taboo, combatting the disagreeable myth of the artificial usually associated with preserves. Of course, elsewhere than in advertising, the anchorage may be ideological and indeed this is its principal function; the text *directs* the reader through the signifieds of the image, causing him to avoid some and receive others; by means of an often subtle *dispatching*, it remote-controls him towards a meaning chosen in advance. In all these cases of anchorage, language clearly has a function of elucidation, but this elucidation is selective, a metalanguage applied not to the totality of the iconic message but only to certain of its signs. The text is indeed the creator's (and hence society's) right of inspection over the image; anchorage is a control, bearing a responsibility—in the face of the projective power of pictures—for the use of the message. With respect to the liberty of the signifieds of the image, the text has thus a *repressive* value[10] and we can see that it is at this level that the morality and ideology of a society are above all invested.

Anchorage is the most frequent function of the linguistic message and is commonly found in press photographs and advertisements. The function of relay is less common (at least as far as the fixed image is concerned); it can be seen particularly in cartoons and comic strips. Here text (most often a snatch of dialogue) and image stand in a complementary relationship; the words, in the same way as the images, are fragments of a more general syntagm and the unity of the message is realized at a higher level, that of the story, the anecdote, the diegesis (which is ample confirmation that the diegesis must be treated as an autonomous system[11]). While rare in the fixed image, this relay-text becomes very important in film, where dialogue functions not simply as elucidation but really does advance the action by setting out, in the sequence of messages, meanings that are not to be found in the image itself. Obviously, the two functions of the linguistic message can co-exist in the one iconic whole, but the dominance of the one or the other is of consequence for the general economy of a work. When the text has the diegetic value of relay, the information is more costly, requiring as it does the learning of a digital code (the system of language); when it has a substitute value (anchorage, control), it is the image which detains the informational charge and, the image being analogical, the information is then 'lazier': in certain comic strips intended for 'quick' reading the diegesis is confided above all to the text, the image gathering the attributive informations of a paradigmatic order (the stereotyped status of the characters); the costly message and the discursive message are made to coincide so that the hurried reader may be spared the boredom of verbal 'descriptions', which are entrusted to the image, that is to say to a less 'laborious' system.

The denoted image

We have seen that in the image properly speaking, the distinction between the literal message and the symbolic message is operational; we never encounter (at least in advertising) a literal image in a pure state. Even if a totally 'naive' image were to be achieved, it would immediately join the sign of naivety and be completed by a third—symbolic—message. Thus the characteristics of the literal message cannot be substantial but only relational. It is first of all, so to speak, a message by eviction, constituted by what is left in the image when the signs of connotation are mentally deleted (it would not be possible actually to remove them for they can impregnate the whole of the image, as in the case of the 'still life composition'). This evictive state naturally corresponds to a plenitude of virtualities: it is an absence of meaning full of all the meanings. Then again (and there is no contradiction with what has just been said), it is a sufficient message, since it has at least one meaning at the level of the identification of the scene represented; the letter of the image corresponds in short to the first degree of intelligibility (below which the reader would perceive only lines, forms, and colours), but this intelligibility remains virtual by reason of its very poverty, for everyone from a real society always disposes of a knowledge superior to the merely anthropological and perceives more than just the letter. Since it is both evictive and sufficient, it will be understood that from an aesthetic point of view the denoted image can appear as a kind of Edenic state of the image; cleared utopianically of its connotations, the image would become radically objective, or, in the last analysis, innocent.

This utopian character of denotation is considerably reinforced by the paradox already mentioned, that the photograph (in its literal state), by virtue of its absolutely analogical nature, seems to constitute a message without a code. Here, however, structural analysis must differentiate, for of all the kinds of image only the photograph is able to transmit the (literal) information without forming it by means of discontinuous signs and rules of transformation. The photograph, message without a code, must thus be opposed to the drawing which, even when denoted, is a coded message. The coded nature of the drawing can be seen at three levels. Firstly, to reproduce an object or a scene in a drawing requires a set of *rule-governed* transpositions; there is no essential nature of the pictorial copy and the codes of transposition are historical (notably those concerning perspective). Secondly, the operation of the drawing (the coding) immediately necessitates a certain division between the significant and the insignificant: the drawing does not reproduce *everything* (often it reproduces very little), without its ceasing, however, to be a strong message; whereas the photograph, although it can choose its subject, its point of view and its angle, cannot intervene *within* the object (except by trick effects). In other words, the denotation of the drawing is less pure than that of the photograph, for there is no drawing without style. Finally, like all codes, the drawing demands an apprenticeship (Saussure attributed a great importance to this semiological fact). Does the coding of the denoted message have consequences for the connoted message? It is certain that the coding of the literal prepares and facilitates connotation since it at once establishes a certain discontinuity in the image: the 'execution' of a drawing itself constitutes a connotation. But at the same time, insofar as the drawing displays its coding, the relationship between the two messages is profoundly modified: it is no longer the relationship between a nature and a culture (as with the photograph) but that between two cultures; the 'ethic' of the drawing is not the same as that of the photograph.

In the photograph—at least at the level of the literal message—the relationship of signifieds to signifiers is not one of 'transformation' but of 'recording', and the absence of a code clearly reinforces the myth of photographic 'naturalness': the scene *is there*, captured mechanically, not humanly (the mechanical is here a guarantee of objectivity). Man's interventions in the photograph (framing, distance, lighting, focus, speed) all effectively belong to the plane of connotation; it is as though in the beginning (even if utopian) there were a brute photograph (frontal and clear) on which man would then lay out, with the aid of various techniques, the signs drawn from a cultural code. Only the opposition of the cultural code and the natural non-code can, it seems, account for the specific character of the photograph and allow the assessment of the anthropological revolution it represents in man's history. The type of consciousness the photograph involves is indeed truly unprecedented, since it establishes not a consciousness of the *being-there* of the thing (which any copy could provoke) but an awareness of its *having-been-there*. What we have is a new space-time category: spatial immediacy and temporal anteriority, the photograph being an illogical conjunction between the *here-now* and the *there-then*. It is thus at the level of this denoted message or message without code that the *real unreality* of the photograph can be fully understood: its unreality is that of the *here-now*, for the photograph is never experienced as illusion, is in no way a *presence* (claims as to the magical character of the photographic image must be deflated); its reality that of the *having-been-there*, for in every photograph there is the always stupefying evidence of *this is how it was*, giving us, by a precious miracle, a reality from which we are sheltered. This kind of temporal equilibrium (*having-been-there*) probably diminishes the projective power of the image (very few psychological tests resort to photographs while many use drawings): the *this was so* easily defeats the *it's me*. If these remarks are at all correct the photograph must be related to a pure spectatorial consciousness and not to the more projective, more 'magical' fictional consciousness on which film by and large depends. This would lend authority to the view that the distinction between film and photograph is not a simple difference of degree but a radical opposition. Film can no longer be seen as animated photographs: the *having-been-there* gives way before a *being-there* of the thing; which omission would explain how there can be a history of the cinema, without any real break with the previous arts of fiction, whereas the photograph can in some sense elude history (despite the evolution of the techniques and ambitions of the photographic art) and represent a 'flat' anthropological fact, at once absolutely new and definitively unsurpassable, humanity encountering for the first time in its history *messages without a code*. Hence the photograph is not the last (improved) term of the great family of images; it corresponds to a decisive mutation of informational economies.

At all events, the denoted image, to the extent to which it does not imply any code (the case with the advertising photograph), plays a special role in the general structure of the iconic message which we can begin to define (returning to this question after discussion of the third message): the denoted image naturalizes the symbolic message, it innocents the semantic artifice of connotation, which is extremely dense, especially in advertising. Although the *Panzani* poster is full of 'symbols', there nonetheless remains in the photograph, insofar as the literal message is sufficient, a kind of natural *being-there* of objects: nature seems spontaneously to produce the scene represented. A pseudo-truth is surreptitiously substituted for the simple validity of openly semantic systems; the absence of code disintellectualizes the message because it seems to found in nature the signs of culture. This is without doubt an important historical paradox: the more technology develops the diffusion of information (and notably of images), the more it provides the means of masking the constructed meaning under the appearance of the given meaning.

Rhetoric of the image

It was seen that the signs of the third message (the 'symbolic' message, cultural or connoted) were discontinuous. Even when the signifier seems to extend over the whole image, it is nonetheless a sign separated from the others: the 'composition' carries an aesthetic signified, in much the same way as intonation although suprasegmental is a separate signifier in language. Thus we are here dealing with a normal system whose signs are drawn from a cultural code (even if the linking together of the elements of the sign appears more or less analogical). What gives this system its originality is that the number of readings of the same lexical unit or *lexia* (of the same image) varies according to individuals. In the *Panzani* advertisement analysed, four connotative signs have been identified; probably there are others (the net bag, for example, can signify the miraculous draught of fishes, plenty, etc.). The variation in readings is not, however, anarchic; it depends on the different kinds of knowledge—practical, na-

tional, cultural, aesthetic—invested in the image and these can be classified, brought into a typology. It is as though the image presented itself to
the reading of several different people who can perfectly well co-exist in a
single individual: *the one lexia mobilizes different lexicons*. What is a
lexicon? A portion of the symbolic plane (of language) which corresponds to a body of practices and techniques.[12] This is the case for the
different readings of the image: each sign corresponds to a body of 'attitudes'—tourism, housekeeping, knowledge of art—certain of which may
obviously be lacking in this or that individual. There is a plurality and a
co-existence of lexicons in one and the same person, the number and
identity of these lexicons forming in some sort a person's *idiolect*.[13] The
image, in its connotation, is thus constituted by an architecture of signs
drawn from a variable depth of lexicons (of idiolects); each lexicon, no
matter how 'deep', still being coded, if, as is thought today, the *psyche*
itself is articulated like a language; indeed, the further one 'descends' into
the psychic depths of an individual, the more rarefied and the more classi-
fiable the signs become—what could be more systematic than the readings of Rorschach tests? The variability of readings, therefore, is no threat
to the 'language' of the image if it be admitted that that language is composed of idiolects, lexicons and sub-codes. The image is penetrated
through and through by the system of meaning, in exactly the same way
as man is articulated to the very depths of his being in distinct languages.
The language of the image is not merely the totality of utterances emitted
(for example at the level of the combiner of the signs or creator of the
message), it is also the totality of utterances received[14]: the language must
include the 'surprises' of meaning.

Another difficulty in analysing connotation is that there is no particular analytical language corresponding to the particularity of its signifieds—how are the signifieds of connotation to be named? For one of
them we ventured the term *Italianicity*, but the others can only be designated by words from ordinary language (*culinary preparation, still life,
plenty*); the metalanguage which has to take charge of them at the moment of the analysis is not specialized. This is a difficulty, for these signifieds have a particular semantic nature; as a seme of connotation,
'plenty' does not exactly cover 'plenty' in the denoted sense; the signifier
of connotation (here the profusion and the condensation of the produce)
is like the essential cipher of all possible plenties, of the purest idea of
plenty. The denoted word never refers to an essence for it is always caught
up in a contingent utterance, a continuous syntagm (that of verbal discourse), oriented towards a certain practical transitivity of language; the
seme 'plenty', on the contrary, is a concept in a pure state, cut off from
any syntagm, deprived of any context and corresponding to a sort of
theatrical state of meaning, or, better (since it is a question of a sign without a syntagm), to an *exposed* meaning. To express these semes of connotation would therefore require a special metalanguage and we are left

with barbarisms of the *Italianicity* kind as best being able to account for the signifieds of connotation, the suffix *-icity* deriving an abstract noun from the adjective: *Italianicity* is not Italy, it is the condensed essence of everything that could be Italian, from spaghetti to painting. By accepting to regulate artificially—and if needs be barbarously—the naming of the semes of connotation, the analysis of their form will be rendered easier.[15] These semes are organized in associative fields, in paradigmatic articulations, even perhaps in oppositions, according to certain defined paths or, as A. J. Greimas puts it, according to certain semic axes[16]: *Italianicity* belongs to a certain axis of nationalities, alongside Frenchicity, Germanicity or Spanishicity. The reconstitution of such axes—which may eventually be in opposition to one another—will clearly only be possible once a massive inventory of the systems of connotation has been carried out, an inventory not merely of the connotative system of the image but also of those of other substances, for if connotation has typical signifiers dependent on the different substances utilized (image, language, objects, modes of behavior) it holds all its signifieds in common: the same signifieds are to be found in the written press, the image or the actor's gestures (which is why semiology can only be conceived in a so to speak total framework). This common domain of the signifieds of connotation is that of *ideology*, which cannot but be single for a given society and history, no matter what signifiers of connotation it may use.

To the general ideology, that is, correspond signifiers of connotation which are specified according to the chosen substance. These signifiers will be called *connotators* and the set of connotators a *rhetoric*, rhetoric thus appearing as the signifying aspect of ideology. Rhetorics inevitably vary by their substance (here articulated sound, there image, gesture or whatever) but not necessarily by their form; it is even probable that there exists a single rhetorical *form*, common for instance to dream, literature and image.[17] Thus the rhetoric of the image (that is to say, the classification of its connotators) is specific to the extent that it is subject to the physical constraints of vision (different, for example, from phonatory constraints) but general to the extent that the 'figures' are never more than formal relations of elements. This rhetoric could only be established on the basis of a quite considerable inventory, but it is possible now to foresee that one will find in it some of the figures formerly identified by the Ancients and the Classics;[18] the tomato, for example, signifies *Italianicity* by metonymy and in another advertisement the sequence of three scenes (coffee in beans, coffee in powder, coffee sipped in the cup) releases a certain logical relationship in the same way as an asyndeton. It is probable indeed that among the metabolas (or figures of the substitution of one signifier for another[19]), it is metonymy which furnishes the image with the greatest number of its connotators, and that among the parataxes (or syntagmatic figures), it is asyndeton which predominates.

The most important thing, however, at least for the moment, is not to inventorize the connotators but to understand that in the total image they constitute *discontinuous* or better still *scattered traits*. The connotators do not fill the whole of the lexia, reading them does not exhaust it. In other words (and this would be a valid proposition for semiology in general), not all the elements of the lexia can be transformed into connotators; there always remaining in the discourse a certain denotation without which, precisely, the discourse would not be possible. Which brings us back to the second message or denoted image. In the *Panzani* advertisement, the Mediterranean vegetables, the colour, the composition, the very profusion rise up as so many scattered blocks, at once isolated and mounted in a general scene which has its own space and, as was seen, its 'meaning': they are 'set' in a syntagm *which is not theirs and which is that of the denotation*. This last proposition is important for it permits us to found (retroactively) the structural distinction between the second or literal message and the third or symbolic message and to give a more exact description of the naturalizing function of the denotation with respect to the connotation. We can now understand that *it is precisely the syntagm of the denoted message which 'naturalizes' the system of the connoted message*. Or again: connotation is only system, can only be defined in paradigmatic terms; iconic denotation is only syntagm, associates elements without any system: the discontinuous connotators are connected, actualized, 'spoken' through the syntagm of the denotation, the discontinuous world of symbols plunges into the story of the denoted scene as though into a lustral bath of innocence.

It can thus be seen that in the total system of the image the structural functions are polarized: on the one hand there is a sort of paradigmatic condensation at the level of the connotators (that is, broadly speaking, of the symbols), which are strong signs, scattered, 'reified'; on the other a syntagmatic 'flow' at the level of the denotation—it will not be forgotten that the syntagm is always very close to speech, and it is indeed the iconic 'discourse' which naturalizes its symbols. Without wishing to infer too quickly from the image to semiology in general, one can nevertheless venture that the world of total meaning is torn internally (structurally) between the system as culture and the syntagm as nature: the works of mass communications all combine, through diverse and diversely successful dialectics, the fascination of a nature, that of story, diegesis, syntagm, and the intelligibility of a culture, withdrawn into a few discontinuous symbols which men 'decline' in the shelter of their living speech.

NOTES

1. The *description* of the photograph is given here with prudence, for it already constitutes a metalanguage. The reader is asked to refer to the reproduction.

2. By *typical sign* is meant the sign of a system insofar as it is adequately defined by its substance: the verbal sign, the iconic sign, the gestural sign are so many typical signs.

3. In French, the expression *nature morte* refers to the original presence of funereal objects, such as a skull, in certain pictures.

4. Cf. "The photographic message," in *Image-Music-Text*, pp. 15–31.

5. 'Naive' analysis is an enumeration of elements, structural description aims to grasp the relation of these elements by virtue of the principle of the solidarity holding between the terms of a structure: if one term changes, so also do the others.

6. Cf. R. Barthes, *Eléments de sémiologie, Communications* 4, 1964, p. 130 [trans. *Elements of Semiology*, London 1967 & New York 1968, pp. 89–92].

7. Menestrier, *L'Art des emblèmes*, 1684.

8. Images without words can certainly be found in certain cartoons, but by way of a paradox; the absence of words always covers an enigmatic intention.

9. *Eléments de sémiologie*, pp. 131–132 [trans. pp. 90–94].

10. This can be seen clearly in the paradoxical case where the image is constructed according to the text and where, consequently, the control would seem to be needless. An advertisement which wants to communicate that in such and such a coffee the aroma is 'locked in' the product in powder form and that it will thus be wholly there when the coffee is used depicts, above this proposition, a tin of coffee with a chain and padlock round it. Here, the linguistic metaphor ('locked in') is taken literally (a well-known poetic device); in fact, however, it is the image which is read first and the text from which the image is constructed becomes in the end the simple choice of one signified among others. The repression is present again in the circular movement as a banalization of the message.

11. Cf. Claude Bremond, "Le message narratif," *Communications* 4, 1964.

12. Cf. A. J. Greimas, "Les problèmes de la description mécanographique," *Cahiers de Lexicologie*, 1, 1959, p. 63.

13. Cf. *Eléments de sémiologie*, p. 96 [trans. pp. 21–22].

14. In the Saussurian perspective, speech (utterances) is above all that which is emitted, drawn from the language-system (and constituting it in return). It is necessary today to enlarge the notion of language [*langue*], especially from the semantic point of view: language is the 'totalizing abstraction' of the messages emitted *and received*.

15. *Form* in the precise sense given it by Hjelmslev (cf. *Eléments de sémiologie*, p. 105 [trans. pp. 39–41]), as the functional organization of the signifieds among themselves.

16. A. J. Greimas, *Cours de Sémantique*, 1964 (notes roneotyped by the École Normale Supérieure de Saint-Cloud).

17. Cf. Émile Benveniste, "Remarques sur la fonction du langage dans la découverte freudienne," *La Psychanalyse* 1, 1956, pp. 3–16 [reprinted in E. Benveniste, *Problèmes de linguistique générale*, Paris 1966, Chapter 7; translated as *Problems of General Linguistics*, Coral Gables, Florida 1971].

18. Classical rhetoric needs to be rethought in structural terms (this is the object of a work in progress); it will then perhaps be possible to establish a general rhetoric or linguistics of the signifiers of connotation, valid for articulated sound, image, gesture, etc. See "L'ancienne Rhétorique (Aide-mémoire)," *Communications* 16, 1970.

19. We prefer here to evade Jakobson's opposition between metaphor and metonymy for if metonymy by its origin is a figure of contiguity, it nevertheless functions finally as a substitute of the signifier, that is as a metaphor.

MEYER SCHAPIRO

Schapiro's intention in his systematic and historically rich essay is to delineate "the non-mimetic—that is, non-representational or non-iconic—elements of the image-sign and their role in constituting the sign." These non-mimetic elements are subsumed under the rubric of "field" and "vehicle," and Schapiro invokes a rather different set of categories than Barthes, in accord with his rather different intent. He is concerned, in fact, with the visual analogues of that process of constituting the "palpability" of signs that Jakobson ascribed to the poetic function.

With regard to the image field Schapiro's problem or question space is the following. What, first of all, is the significance of the rectangular field within which images are found, a field which now is well-nigh taken for granted and even considered "natural"? This particular type of field has not always been present as the indispensable (back)ground for images, although it is clear that there has to be some sort of ground for images to appear at all. When did it appear and what variations on the limitation of ground, with respect to the placing of images on it, have obtained? What, more generally, is the significance of the prepared ground as such in the history of image production, since there have been wide variations in the condition of the ground from culture to culture and from period to period? How many different kinds of local properties of the picture field (left, right, upper, lower, directional orientation, sequence, symmetry and asymmetry, commutativity and disjunctivity, size, and so forth) are there and how do they "affect our sense of the signs" found on it? How many of these properties are "natural" and how many are "conventional"? Schapiro gives a stimulating and dense discussion of these and similar questions, with numerous examples and allusions, paralleling in the semiotic key what, for example, Rudolf Arnheim has done through a generalization of Gestalt-theoretical considerations.

After discussing the non-mimetic elements pertaining to the field or ground against which an image is seen or constructed, Schapiro turns to its "sign-bearing matter, the image-substance of inked or painted lines and spots." The starting point of Schapiro's discussion here is that "with respect to denotation by resemblance, which is specific to pictures as signs, these elements have properties different from the objects they represent," an observation bearing directly upon that thorny nest of problems concerning iconism, and which has been given an extensive treatment by Umberto Eco, Ernst Gombrich, and many others. The material picture-sign itself is both aesthetically relevant and, from one point of view, semantically—that is, representationally—irrelevant. Nevertheless, "distinctive for the picture-sign . . . is the pervasiveness of the semantic function, even with the arbitrariness of the qualities of the image-substance," such as "the firm black outline of the primitives and the Egyptians" or "the visibly discrete strokes of paint and the relief of crusty pigment which violate both the continuity and texture of the represented surfaces," as in the system of representation developed by Impressionism. Indeed, Schapiro notes, in one of the comments which stand out from practically every page, "if the elements of vehicle and their properties are roots of the aesthetic of the work, of its intimate formal structure and expression, they owe their development and variety in great part to their service in representation," a thesis which bears the closest scrutiny.

Visual forms, then, are material objects, playing a specific role in perception, which they do precisely through their material qualities. Eco remarks in his *A Theory of Semiotics* that "in the aesthetic text the matter of *the sign-vehicle becomes an aspect of the expression-form*" (266). He also refers to the work of art's "semiotic redemption of its basic matter" (268) and of the "culturalization of matter" (269), as well as of the problem of so-called "hyposemiotic stuff" (267–268), with which, it could be said, Schapiro's essay is concerned. Note further the bearing of Schapiro's analyses upon Eco's claim, denied by Langer, which reflects much current opinion in one form or another, that "a work of art has the same structural characteristics as does a *langue*. So that it cannot be mere 'presence'; there must be an underlying system of mutual correlations, and thus a semiotic design which cunningly gives the impression of non-semiosis" (271). In what sense are the elements singled out by Schapiro embedded in a system? What kind of system—semiotic or perceptual—is it in the last analysis? Or is such a distinction, in light of the principle of semiotic closure, illegitimate?

These are only some of the key points and questions in this exceedingly fertile and allusive essay. Other issues which it raises, and which can be profitably and thematically discussed from a semiotic point of view, are the nature of the various kinds of perspective, the relation between representational and non-representational or abstract painting, and so forth. It can also be fruitfully confronted with Barthes's discussion of the photographic image as paradigmatic modern form, and one might even want to try to translate Schapiro's conclusions into Barthesian terms and vice versa, even, in fact, bringing in Peirce's and Thom's discussion of the icon and Langer's characterization of a "presentational form." But these are exercises best left to the reader.

The greatest part of Schapiro's work has been devoted to historical studies of art, though we are still awaiting the appearance of the fourth volume of his selected papers which will deal with the theory and philosophy of art. An illustration of a semiotic analysis will be found in his *Words and Pictures* (The Hague: Mouton, 1973), which deals with medieval illustrated manuscripts. See also the works cited in the essay by Benveniste which bear upon these themes, especially those by Panofsky and Wallis. The bibliography in Eco's *A Theory of Semiotics* (Bloomington: Indiana University Press, 1976) and the references to the section on 'The Aesthetic Text as Invention' will lead one to other materials. Besides work in philosophical and semiotic aesthetics the seminal writings of Rudolf Arnheim, *Art and Visual Perception* (Berkeley and Los Angeles: University of California Press, 1954 (revised edition 1974) and *Visual Thinking* (Berkeley and Los Angeles: University of California Press, 1969) are indispensable both for their analyses and for their matrices of references. See also the important essay by Siegfried Giedion, "Space Conception in Prehistoric Art," in *Explorations in Communication*, edited by Edmund Carpenter and Marshall McLuhan (Boston: Beacon Press, 1960).

On Some Problems in the Semiotics of Visual Art:
Field and Vehicle in Image-Signs

MEYER SCHAPIRO

My theme is the non-mimetic elements of the image-sign and their role in constituting the sign. It is not clear to what extent these elements are arbitrary and to what extent they inhere in the organic conditions of imaging and perception. Certain of them, like the frame, are historically developed, highly variable forms; yet though obviously conventional,

This paper was originally presented at the Second International Colloquium on Semiotics, Kazimierz, Poland, September 1966; it is reprinted from *Semiotica*, 1/3 (1969): 223–242, by permission of Mouton Publishers.

they do not have to be learned for the image to be understood; they may even acquire a semantic value.

We take for granted today as indispensable means the rectangular form of the sheet of paper and its clearly defined smooth surface on which one draws and writes. But such a field corresponds to nothing in nature or mental imagery where the phantoms of visual memory come up in a vague unbounded void. The student of prehistoric art knows that the regular field is an advanced artifact presupposing a long development of art. The cave paintings of the Old Stone Age are on an unprepared ground, the rough wall of a cave; the irregularities of earth and rock show through the image. The artist worked then on a field with no set boundaries and thought so little of the surface as a distinct ground that he often painted his animal figure over a previously painted image without erasing the latter, as if it were invisible to the viewer. Or if he thought of his own work, perhaps, as occupying on the wall a place reserved for successive paintings because of a special rite or custom, as one makes fires year after year on the same hearth over past embers, he did not regard this place as a field in the same sense in which later artists saw their figures as standing out from a suitably contrasting ground.

The smooth prepared field is an invention of a later stage of humanity. It accompanies the development of polished tools in the Neolithic and Bronze Ages and the creation of pottery and an architecture with regular courses of jointed masonry. It might have come about through the use of these artifacts as sign-bearing objects. The inventive imagination recognized their value as grounds, and in time gave to pictures and writing on smoothed and symmetrical supports a corresponding regularity of direction, spacing and grouping, in harmony with the form of the object like the associated ornament of the neighboring parts. Through the closure and smoothness of the prepared picture surface, often with a distinct color of the reserved background, the image acquired a definite space of its own, in contrast to the prehistoric wall paintings and reliefs; these had to compete with the noise-like accidents and irregularities of a ground which was no less articulated than the sign and could intrude upon it. The new smoothness and closure made possible the later transparency of the picture-plane without which the representation of three-dimensional space would not have been successful.[1]

With this new conception of the ground, the art of representation constructs, I have said, a field with a distinct plane (or regular curvature) of the surface and a definite boundary that may be the smoothed edges of an artifact. The horizontals of this boundary are at first supporting ground lines which connect the figures with each other and also divide the surface into parallel bands, establishing more firmly the axes of the field as coordinates of stability and movement in the image.

We do not know just when this organization of the image field was introduced; students have given little attention to this fundamental change in art which is basic for our own imagery, even for the photograph, the film and the television screen. In scrutinizing the drawings of children for the most primitive processes of image-making, one forgets that these drawings, made on rectangular sheets of smoothed paper, often with a variety of colors, inherit the results of a long culture, just as their simple speech, after the phase of lallation, shows elements of an already developed phonetic system and syntax. Their forms are soon adapted to the artificial rectangular field in important respects; their solid filling of the background reflects the pictures they have seen; and their choice of colors presupposes an adult's palette, a system of tones acquired through a long experience of representation. The remarkable expressions of the monkey-painters in our zoos should also be considered from this point of view. It is we who elicit those fascinating results by putting paper and colors in the monkey's hands, just as we get monkeys in the circus to ride a bicycle and to perform other feats with devices that belong to civilization. No doubt that the monkey's activity as an artist displays impulses and reactions that are latent in his nature; but like his self-balancing adjustment on wheels the concrete result on paper, however spontaneous it appears, is a product of domestication, which means, of course, the influence of a culture. It is an experiment that a civilized society makes with the animal as it experiments, in a sense, with the child in eliciting from him the speech and other habits of his community.

The character of the oldest image-fields that we know—untreated and unbounded—is not just an archaic phenomenon of the past. If it seems to us natural to create a smooth delimited ground for the image as a necessity of clear perception, we must recognize, too, the continued use of the more primitive ground in later cultures including our own. The wall-paintings of Hierakonpolis in Egypt (ca. 3500 B.C.) recall in their scattered unbounded groups the cave and rock images of the Old Stone Age; and many primitive peoples continue to draw and incise their pictures on untreated, unenclosed surfaces. The spontaneous graffiti on the walls of ancient Roman buildings are, in this respect, not different from those drawn today; like the modern ones they disregard the field they have usurped, even defacing an existing picture. But the field of the image is not always inviolate even in a work preserved with reverence as a precious object. In China where painting was a noble art the owner did not hesitate to write a comment in verse or prose on the unpainted background of a sublime landscape and to stamp his seal prominently on the picture surface. The ground of the image was hardly felt to be part of the sign itself; figure and ground did not compose for the eye an inseparable unity. A connoisseur in looking at an admired work could regard the empty ground and margins as not truly parts of the painting, as the reader of a book might see the margins and interspaces of the text as open to annotation. It is clear that the sense of the whole depends on habits of seeing which may vary. A Chinese artist, sensitive to the smallest inflection of a brushstroke and its place in the picture, is not disturbed by the writing and seals affixed to the original work. He no more sees them as parts of the picture than we see a painter's signature in the lower part of a landscape painting as an object in the foreground of the represented space. In Assyrian art, too, which already possessed a prepared and enclosed ground, the represented bodies of kings and gods were sometimes incised with writing that crossed the outlines of the figures.

In a reverse order and from other motives artists in our own time preserve on the paper or canvas the earlier lines and touches of color which have been applied successively in the process of painting. They admit at least some of the preparatory and often tentative forms as a permanently visible and integrated part of the image; these are valued as signs of the maker's action in producing the work. We understand this as another aim than the overlay of image on image in prehistoric art; but it is worth noting as the source of a similar visual effect reached from an altogether different point of view. I have no doubt that the modern practice disposes us to see the prehistoric works as a beautiful collective palimpsest.

Modern art, since the Renaissance, while aiming at a stricter unity of a picture—a unity that includes the interplay of the figure and the reserved shapes of the ground—offers also examples of the deliberately made fragment or sketch as well as incomplete work that is prized for qualities of the unfinished state, and even the painting of a small part of the field without regard to the voids around it.

It is possible that the unprepared ground had a positive meaning for the prehistoric painter, but this idea must remain hypothetical. One can suppose that the artist identified with the rock or cave through the primordial roughness of the ground of his picture. A modern artist, Joan Miró, who probably knows the old rock paintings of his native and cherished Catalonia, has felt the attraction of the irregular surface of the enduring rock and used it as a ground on which to paint his directly conceived sign-like abstract forms. Others have painted on pebbles and on found fragments of natural and artificial objects, exploiting the irregularities of the ground and the physiognomy of the object as part of the charm of the whole. But I incline to think that the prehistoric surface was neutral, a still indeterminate bearer of the image.

Besides the prepared ground we tend to take for granted the regular margin and frame as essential features of the image. It is not commonly realized how late an invention is the frame. It was preceded by the rectangular field divided into bands; the horizontals as ground lines or strips connecting and supporting the figures were more pronounced visually than the separate vertical edges of the field. Apparently it was late in the second millennium B.C. (if even then) before one thought of a continuous isolating frame around an image, a homogeneous enclosure like a city wall. When salient and when enclosing pictures with perspective views, the frame sets the picture surface back into depth and helps to deepen the view; it is like a window frame through which is seen a space behind the glass. The frame belongs then to the space of the observer rather than of the illusory, three-dimensional world disclosed within and behind. It is a finding and focusing device placed between the observer and the image. But the frame may enter also into the shaping of that image; and not only through the contrasts and correspondences incited by its strong form, especially in architectural sculpture, but also, as in modern styles, in the practice of cutting the foreground objects oddly at the frame so that they appear to be close to the observer and seen from the side through an opening. By intercepting these objects the frame seems to cross a represented field that extends behind it at the sides. Degas and Toulouse-Lautrec were ingenious masters of this kind of imagery.

A related modern practice: The cropped rectangular picture, without frame or margin, helps us to see more clearly another role of the frame. Such cropping, now common in photographic illustrations in books and magazines, brings out the partial, the fragmentary and contingent in the image, even where the main object is centered. The picture seems to be arbitrarily isolated from a larger whole and brought abruptly into the observer's field of vision. The cropped picture exists as if for his momentary glance rather than for a set view. In comparison with this type, the framed picture appears to be more formally presented and complete and to exist in a world of its own.

More recently paintings have been hung altogether unframed. The frameless modern picture explains in a sense the functions of the frame in older art. The frame was dispensable when painting ceased to represent deep space and became more concerned with the expressive and formal qualities of the non-mimetic marks than with their elaboration into signs. If the painting once receded within the framed space, the canvas now stands out from the wall as an object in its own right, with a tangibly painted surface whether of abstract themes or with a representation which is predominantly flat and shows the activity of the artist in the pronounced lines and strokes or the high arbitrariness of the selected forms and colors. Although it is in keeping with this aspect of modern painting, the unframed canvas has not become universal even for new art. But the strips of wood or metal that now frame many paintings are no longer the salient and richly ornamented enclosures that once helped to accent the depth of simulated space in the picture and conveyed the idea of the preciousness of the work of art through its gilded mount. They are thin discreet borders often flush with the plane of the canvas, and in their simplicity they assert also the respect for frankness and integrity in the practice of the art. Without a frame, the painting appears more com-

pletely and modestly the artist's work. A parallel to the frameless painting is the modern sculpture without a pedestal; it is either suspended or
placed directly on the ground.

Our conception of the frame as a regular enclosure isolating the field of
representation from the surrounding surfaces does not apply to all frames.
There are pictures and reliefs in which elements of the image cross the
frame, as if the frame were only a part of the background and existed in a
simulated space behind the figure. Such crossing of the frame is often an
expressive device; a figure represented as moving appears more active in
crossing the frame, as if unbounded in his motion. The frame belongs
then more to the virtual space of the image than to the material surface;
the convention is naturalized as an element of the picture space rather
than of the observer's space or the space of the vehicle. In medieval art
this violation of the frame is common, but there are examples already in
classical art. The frame appears then not as an enclosure but as a pictorial milieu of the image. And since it may serve to enhance the movement of the figure, we can understand an opposite device: the frame that
bends and turns inward into the field of the picture to compress or en-
tangle the figures (the trumeau of Souillac, the Imago Hominis in the
Echternach Gospels, Paris, Bibl. nat. ms. lat. 9389).

Besides these variants of the frame-field relation in art I must mention
another that is equally interesting: The frame is sometimes an irregular
form that follows the outlines of the object. It is no longer a pre-existing
feature of the image-vehicle or ground but an added one that depends on
the contents of the image. The image comes first and the frame is traced
around it. Here the frame accents the forms of the signs rather than en-
closes a field on which the signs are set. As in the examples where the
figure bursts through the frame, the independence and energy of the sign
are asserted in the detours forced upon the frame by the image (Vézelay).

We learn from these works that although the strictly enclosing rectangular frame seems natural and satisfies a need for clarity in isolating
the image for the eye, it is only one possible use of the frame. The form
can be varied to produce quite opposite effects, which also satisfy some
need or concept. All these types are intelligible as devices of ordering and
expression, but no one of them is necessary or universal. They show the
freedom of artists in arbitrarily constructing effective deviations from
what might appear at first to be inherent and immutable *a priori* conditions of representation.

Let us return to the properties of the ground as a field. Although I have
used the word "neutral" to describe the untreated surface, it must be said
that the unpainted empty field around a figure is not entirely devoid of
expressive effect even in the most casual unbounded representations.
Imagine a drawn figure on the narrow space of a piece of field stone that
confines him between edges close to the body; and imagine the same figure on a broader though still irregular surface. In the first he will appear

more elongated and cramped, in the second he stands in a space that allows him more freedom of movement and suggests the potential activity of the body. The space around it is inevitably seen not only as ground in the sense of *Gestalt* psychology, but also as belonging to the body and contributing to its qualities. For the aesthetic eye the body, and indeed any object, seems to incorporate the empty space around it as a field of existence. The participation of the surrounding void in the image-sign of the body is still more evident where several figures are presented; then the intervals between them produce a rhythm of body and void and determine effects of intimacy, encroachment and isolation, like the intervals of space in an actual human group.

The same properties of the field as a space with a latent expressiveness are exploited in printed and painted verbal signs. In the hierarchy of words on the title page of a book or on a poster the more potent words are not only enlarged but often isolated on a ground which is more open at the sides.

It is clear that the picture field has located properties that affect our sense of the signs. These are most obvious in the differences of expressive quality between broad and narrow, upper and lower, left and right, central and peripheral, the corners and the rest of the space. Where there is no boundary of the field, as in cave paintings and unframed images on rocks or large walls, we center the image in our view; in the bounded field the center is predetermined by the boundaries or frame and the isolated figure is characterized in part by its place in the field. When stationed in the middle it has another quality for us than when set at the side, even if balanced then by a small detail that adds a weight to the larger void. A visual tension remains, and the figure appears anomalous, displaced, even spiritually strained; yet this appearance may be a deliberately sought expression as in a portrait by Munch in which the introverted subject stands a little to the side in an empty space. The effect is all the stronger since the self-constrained posture and other elements of the image work to reinforce an expression of the brooding and withdrawn. The tendency to favor an off-center position has been noticed in the drawings of emotionally disturbed children.

The qualities of upper and lower are probably connected with our posture and relation to gravity and perhaps reinforced by our visual experience of earth and sky. The difference can be illustrated by the uninvertibility of a whole with superposed elements of unequal size (Fig. 1).

Figure 1

Though formed of the same parts the rectangle with small A over large B is expressively not the same as the one with the same B over A. The composition is non-commutative, as architects recognize in designing a façade. The same effect holds for single elements; the cubist painter, Juan Gris, remarked that a patch of yellow has a different visual weight in the upper and lower parts of the same field. Nevertheless, in judging their work, artists often invert the painting in order to see the relationships of forms or colors, their balance and harmony, without reference to the objects represented. But this is only an experimental abstraction of one aspect; the unity is finally judged in a scrutiny of the work in its proper mimetic (or non-mimetic) orientation. However, abstract painters today discover new possibilities through that inversion, even a preferred form. The late Fernand Léger conceived as a goal of figurative painting an image equally valid in all positions of the rotated canvas; this idea inspired his paintings of divers and swimmers, seen from above, and has an obvious application in a floor mosaic.

The representation of movement calls into fuller play a cryptesthesia with respect to qualities of the different axes and directions in a field. We live more in the horizontal dimension than the vertical and we are not surprised to learn that the same line looks shorter when horizontal than when vertical. The felt space of everyday experience is anisotropic though we learn to use the metric properties of an objective uniform space in accommodating physical objects to each other.

Where representation is of figures in movement and of successive episodes, the image may be extended in broad and superposed bands which have to be read like a written text. There is then a prevailing direction in certain pictures, even if they are given to the eye as a simultaneous whole.

Directedness as such is not conventional; it arises from the transitive nature of the objects represented and the task of expressing an order of time in an order of space. The requirement of directedness in successive contiguous scenes admits a choice of direction. Though it becomes a convention, it is not an arbitrary choice, for we sometimes recognize in the direction chosen a good solution of a technical or artistic problem. The varying orders of left-to-right or right-to-left and even of downward vertical alignment in pictorial art, as in writing, were probably determined by special conditions of the field, the technique, and the dominant content of the art at an early stage. There are examples in which leftward and rightward directions coexist in the same work of narrative imagery; they accommodate the scenes to an architectural symmetry or a liturgical focus, as in the mosaics on the two nave walls of S. Apollinare Nuovo in Ravenna with processional figures advancing to the East end, while the Gospel scenes above them proceed from East to West. Within each series left-to-right and right-to-left have an identical goal and connotation.

One can find also representations in boustrophedon order, beginning left-to-right and returning in a second register from right to left (Vienna Genesis).

Less a matter of convention is the sequence from top to bottom in series of extended horizontal scenes. The same order governs the downward vertical sequence of horizontal writing, which must be distinguished from the vertical order of the signs in Chinese and Japanese writing and of the single letters in certain Greek and Latin inscriptions on pictures after the 6th century A.D. The priority of the upper part of a field with superposed representations is not a strict rule, however. One can point to medieval sculptures on doorways of churches with a narrative sequence proceeding from the lower panels upwards (Moissac, Verona). In some works this order is motivated by the content; where the climactic scene in a vertical series is the final one, as in images of the life of Christ, it will be placed at the top. One may note, too, that we see a vertical line or a column as moving upwards.

The problem of direction may arise also for the single isolated figure, particularly if it is presented in profile whether at rest or in action. A familiar example is the Egyptian striding figure in relief and painting. When represented in the round such a figure always stands with the left leg advanced; the rigidity of this rule suggests that the posture has a conventional meaning. Whether the choice of the left leg depends on a superstition concerning the first step in marching or on some natural disposition, I cannot say. However, when transposed to the field of painting or relief, the choice of leg to advance is determined by the direction of the profiled body; if it faces right, the left leg is brought forward; if it faces left, it is the right leg that is advanced. In both cases, the farther leg, from the observer's point of view, is the one chosen to represent movement. This principle may be reconciled with the strict rule governing the figure in the round by our assuming that the latter was conceived from his right side; he faces and moves rightward and hence his left leg, as the farther leg, is advanced.[2]

In the stationary isolated figure, unconditioned by a controlling context, the predominance of the left profile has been explained by a physiological fact. The leftward profile of the head, it is supposed, owes its greater frequency to the easier movement (pronation) of the artist's right hand and wrist inward, i.e., to the left, as appears also in the freehand drawing of circles: right-handed persons most often trace the circle counter-clockwise and left-handed, clockwise. (See the work of Zazzo on children's drawings.)

But often an internal context determines one or the other direction in profile portraits; a peculiarity of one side of the face of the portrait subject is enough to limit the choice. Where the artist is free to choose any position of the face, the particular profile is selected because of some valued quality found in this view.

These observations on the conventional, the natural, the freely chosen and the arbitrary in the use of left and right in the image field brings us to a larger problem: whether the left and right sides of a perceptual field have inherently different qualities. A literature has grown up on the subject, some authors affirming that the unlike qualities and irreversibility of the two sides are biologically innate and arise from the asymmetry of the organism and especially its handedness; others connect them with cultural habit in reading and writing and a customary orientation in space. A particular dominant content may also influence the feeling for left and right in images. We still lack a comparative experimental study of the reactions to reversal of pictures in different cultures and especially in those with different directions in writing.

Pertinent to semiotics is the fact that left and right are already distinguished sharply in the signified objects themselves. Everyone is aware of the vital importance of left and right in ritual and magic, which has influenced the meaning of these two words, their metaphorical extensions in everyday speech as terms for good and evil, correct and awkward, proper and deviant. The significance of the deity's or ruler's right side in pictures and ceremony as the commonly, though not universally, more favored side, determines, however, a representation in which, from the observer's viewpoint, the left part of the picture surface is the carrier of the preferred values. This reversal in the field, which is also that of the self-image in the mirror, is a good example of the conflict that may arise between the qualitative structure of the field, whether inherent or acquired, and that of the represented objects. In the Middle Ages one debated the significance of the variable positions of Peter and Paul at the left and right of Christ in old mosaics in Rome (Peter Damian). Where there is no dominant central figure to which left and right must be referred, the viewer's left and right determine by direct translation, rather than by reflection, the left and right of the field, just as in actual life. In both cases the parts of the field are potential signs; but the field is open to reversal in submitting to an order of values in the context of the represented objects or in the carrier of the image.

The lateral asymmetry of the field may be illustrated by another peculiarity of pictures and of buildings. If we pair two forms, one tall, the other short (as in Fig. 2), reversal alters their appearance noticeably.

Figure 2

Like the vertically joined unequal rectangles considered earlier, the lateral grouping is non-commutative. The *and* in "A and B", where the two elements differ decidedly in size or form or color, is adjunctive, not conjunctive; and the position in the field expresses this relation, just as the pair *Father and Son* has a quality lacking in *Son and Father*. If we grant this difference, the problem is whether the dominance of one side in the visual field is inherent or contingent. In asymmetrical compositions of figures or landscapes the choice of one or the other side for the more active or denser part of the picture affects the expression; the reversal gives a strange aspect to the whole, which may be more than the shock of reversal of a familiar or habitual form. Yet it must be said that some good artists in our time, like the early engravers of wood blocks, have been indifferent to the reversal of an asymmetrical composition in the printing of an etched plate, and have not bothered to anticipate it by first reversing the drawing on the plate. Picasso has often disregarded even the reversal of his signature in the print. It is an assertion of spontaneity, made all the more readily as the value of a drawing or print has come to be lodged in its energy and freedom and in the surprise of its forms rather than in the refinement of detail and subtlety of balance. One can doubt that the artist would accept the reversal of a carefully composed painting.

(I may note here as evidence of the sophisticated and acquired in the perception of the different visual quality of the leftward and rightward directions in asymmetrical wholes, the frequent reversal of capital N and S in the writing of children and unpracticed adults. These same two letters are also often reversed in early medieval Latin inscriptions. Apparently the difference in quality of the two diagonal directions is not enough to fix the correct one firmly in mind without continued motor practice.)

How shall we interpret the artist's tolerance of reversal if left and right are indeed different in quality? In certain contexts the choice of the supposedly anomalous side may be deliberate for a particular effect which is reinforced by the content of the representation. If the diagonal from lower left to upper right has come to possess an ascending quality, while the reversed counterpart has a descending effect, an artist who represents figures ascending a slope drawn from the upper left to the lower right gives thereby a more strained, effortful quality to the ascent. Reversal of the composition will disturb or weaken this effect. Yet in the reversal of a picture new qualities emerge that may be attractive to the artist and many viewers.

Besides these characteristics of the field—the prepared surface, the boundaries, the positions and directions—we must consider as an expressive factor the format of the image-sign.

By format I mean the shape of the field, its proportions and dominant axis, as well as its size. I shall pass over the role of proportions and shape of the field, which is a vast problem, and consider size.

The size of a representation may be motivated in different ways: by an external physical requirement, or by the qualities of the object represented. Colossal statues, painted figures larger than life, signify the greatness of their subjects; and the tiny format may express the intimate, the delicate and precious. But size may also be a means of making a sign visible at a distance, apart from the value of the content, as on the film screen and in the gigantic signs in modern publicity. Or a sign may be exceedingly small to satisfy a requirement of economy or ease of handling. (These different functions of size may be compared roughly with the functions of volume and length in speech.) It is obvious that they are not unconnected; a colossal statue serves both functions. We distinguish, at any rate, two sets of conditions in the size of visual signs: on the one hand, size as a function of value and as a function of visibility; on the other hand, the size of the field and the size of different components of the image relative to real objects which they signify and relative to each other. A work may be large like a lengthy picture scroll because it represents so many objects all of average height; or it may be small like a miniature painting and utilize the limited space to express differences of value in the figures by differences of size.

In many styles of art, where objects of quite different size in reality are represented in the same work, they are shown as of equal height. The buildings, trees and mountains in archaic arts look no larger than the human figures and sometimes smaller, and are thereby subordinated to them. Here value or importance is more decisive for virtual size than the real physical magnitude of the objects represented. I am not sure that this is a convention, for the dominance of the human figure over the environment appears independently in the art of many cultures and among our own children in representing objects. One does not suppose that the artist is unaware of the real differences in size between man and these objects of his environment. The sizes of things in a picture express a conception that requires no knowledge of a rule for its understanding. The association of size and a scale of value is already given in language: the words for superlatives of a human quality are often terms of size—greatest, highest, etc., even when applied to such intangibles as wisdom or love.

Size as an expressive factor is not an independent variable. Its effect changes with the function and context of the sign and with the scale and density of the image, i.e., with the natural size of the objects, their number and range of types; it varies also with the signified qualities. An interesting evidence of the qualitative non-linear relation of the size of the sign to the size of the signified object is given in an experiment: children who were asked to draw a very little man and a big man together, first on a small and then on a large sheet of paper, enlarged the big man but redrew the small man as before on the large sheet.

In Western medieval art (and probably in Asiatic too) the apportioning of space among various figures is often subject to a scale of significance in which size is correlated with position in the field and with posture and spiritual rank. In an image of Christ in Majesty with the evangelists, their symbols, and the prophets of the Old Testament (the Bible of Charles the Bald, Paris, Bibl. nat. ms. lat. 1), Christ is the largest figure, the evangelists are second in size, the prophets smaller, the symbols are the smallest of all. Christ sits frontally in the center within a mandorla framed by a lozenge; the evangelists in profile or three-quarters view fill the quadrants of the four corners; and the prophets are busts in the incompletely framed medallions that open at the four angles of the lozenge between the evangelists. Of the four symbols which are distributed in the narrow space between the prophets and Christ, the eagle of John is at the top, in accord with the higher theological rank of this evangelist; it is also distinguished from the other symbols by carrying a roll, while they hold books.

Here it is evident that size, employed systematically, is an expressive coefficient of the parts of the field as places of the graded figures. In certain systems of representation—which depend on systems of content— the distinctive values of the different places of the field and the different magnitudes reinforce each other. The fact that the use of these properties of the sign-space is conventional, appearing especially in religious art, does not mean that the significance of the various parts of the field and the various magnitudes is arbitrary. It is built on an intuitive sense of the vital values of space, as experienced in the real world. For a content that is articulated hierarchically, these qualities of the field become relevant to expression and are employed and developed accordingly. A corresponding content today would elicit from artists a similar disposition of the space of a sign-field. Given the task of mounting separate photographs of members of a political hierarchy in a common rectangular field, I have no doubt that some designers would hit on the medieval arrangement in which the founder is in the middle, his chief disciples at his sides, and lesser figures would be placed in the remaining spaces, above or below according to their relative importance. And it would seem to us natural that the photographs are of a diminishing order of size from the center to the periphery.

The relation of the size of the sign to the size of the represented object changes with the introduction of perspective—the change is the same whether the perspective is empirical as in Northern Europe or regulated by a strict rule of geometrical projection as in Italy. In pictures after the 15th century the size of a painted object, human or natural, relative to its real size, depends on its distance from the picture plane. In contrast to the medieval practice, perspective imposed a uniform scale on the natural magnitudes as projected on the picture surface. This was no devaluation of the human, as one might suppose; indeed, it corresponded to a further humanization of the religious image and its supernatural figures. Greatness, social or spiritual importance, were expressed then through other means such as insignia, costume, posture, illumination, and place in the field. In the perspective system the virtually largest figure may be an accessory one in the foreground and the noblest personages may appear quite small. This is a reversal of the normal etiquette of picture space in which the powerful individual is often represented as a large figure elevated above the smaller figures around him.

It is a common opinion that the two systems, the hierarchical and the geometric-optical, are equally arbitrary perspectives since both are governed by conventions. To call both kinds of pictures perspectives is to miss the fact that only the second presents in its scale of magnitudes a perspective in the visual sense. The first is a perspective only metaphorically. It ignores the variations of both the apparent and the constant sizes of objects in reality and replaces them by a conventional order of magnitudes that signify their power or spiritual rank. The correspondence of the sizes of the objects in the second system to their apparent size in real three-dimensional space at a given distance from the observer is not arbitrary; it is readily understood by the untrained spectator since it rests on the same cues that he responds to in dealing with his everyday visual world. The correspondence of the sizes of the figures in the hierarchical kind of picture to the roles of the figures is indeed conventional in a sense; but the convention rests on a natural association of a scale of qualities with a scale of magnitudes. To speak of Alexander as the Great and to represent him as larger than his soldiers may be a convention; but to the imagination it is natural and self-evident.

I turn now to the non-mimetic elements of the picture that may be called its sign-bearing matter, the image-substance of inked or painted lines and spots. (In sculpture the distinction between the modeled or carved material and the same substance as a field raises special problems that I shall ignore here.)

With respect to denotation by resemblance, which is specific to pictures as signs, these elements have properties different from the objects they represent. Consider as examples the drawn line of the pencil or brush or the incised line produced by a sharp tool in representing the same object. While from the viewpoint that fixes on the drawing as a sign every part of this line corresponds to a part of the object represented—unlike the parts of a word for that object—from the aesthetic point of view the line is an artificial mark with properties of its own. The artist and the sensitive viewer of the work of art are characterized by their ability to shift attention freely from one aspect to the other, but above all, to discriminate and judge the qualities of the picture substance in itself.

The blackness and thickness of the outline of a represented face need not correspond to particular attributes of that face. The same face can be represented in many different ways and with quite varied patterns of the lines or spots that denote the features. They may be thick or thin, continuous or broken, without our seeing these qualities as peculiarities of a real or imagined face. The picture will always be recognized as an image of that face in different portraits, regardless of the style, the medium or the technique, if the representation offers the minimal cues by which we recognize the designated face through all its variations of position and lighting in actual life. The thick black outline is an artificial equivalent of the apparent form of a face and has the same relation to the face that the color and thickness of the outline of a land mass in a map has to the character of the coast. It would still denote the same face for us, if the image-sign were outlined in white on a black ground, just as a written word is the same in different colored inks.

Distinctive for the picture-sign, however, is the pervasiveness of the semantic function, even with the arbitrariness of the qualities of the image-substance. The picture-sign seems to be through and through mimetic, and this is the source of many mis-readings of old works of art. Taken out of the image, the parts of the line will be seen as small material components: dashes, curves, dots which, like the cubes of a mosaic, have no mimetic meaning in themselves. All these assume a value as distinct signs once they enter into certain combinations, and their qualities as marks contribute something to the appearance of the represented objects. According to the context of adjoining or neighboring marks, the dot may be a nail-head, a button, or the pupil of an eye; and a semi-circle may be a hill, a cap, an eyebrow, the handle of a pot, or an arch. There are, it is true, on a represented object in a drawing or print many lines which are not viewed as signs of the real object and its parts in a morphological sense. The fine hatching of the grey tones and shadows in an engraving corresponds to no such network on the object. Yet when seen at a proper distance, it renders degrees of light and dark, the subtle gradations and strong contrasts that bring out the volume, modeling and illumination of the object. Produced by different techniques, the signs for these qualities may vary greatly in their small and large structure and still form a whole that corresponds sufficiently to the recognizable natural appearance. One discovers through such elements of execution another aspect of size in the image-signs, the variable scale of correspondence. Just as the small map shows nothing of the irregularities of terrain below a certain size, so in a picture the technical-artistic means of suggesting modeling and illumination affect the scale of correspondence. There is in the hatched lines a small unit that does not represent anything by itself through its form, yet when repeated in great numbers in the proper context vividly evokes a particular quality of the object. On the other hand, in Impressionist paintings fairly large elements have acquired a non-mimetic aspect. An extensive object-space, a landscape, is represented on a small field, with a consequent increase in the relative size of the units, i.e., relative to the whole complex sign of which they are a part. In the picture the parts of the painted tree are flecks without clear resemblance in shape or color to the parts of the real tree. Here the painting seems to approach a feature of verbal signs. The tree-sign as a whole is recognized as a tree, often through its context; but the parts are hardly like leaves and branches. Yet no basic change has taken place here in the semantic relation of image to object. The Impressionist has chosen to represent a particular appearance of the real tree in which the anatomical parts look indistinct as if fused with each other and with neighboring objects. They have been experienced in nature as distant things veiled by the atmosphere and as variations of light and color rather than as shapes. Perspective vision discerns such objects through the broad silhouette, the tone and context, without discriminating details. Though they do not clearly resemble objects, certain spots of color in the image correspond to sensations, and some of these are not of the local colors of objects but are induced contrast colors and effects of illumination.

It is this shift of interest to another aspect or content of reality that led painters to criticize the arbitrariness of the outline as a distinct entity, although every inflection of the line represents a known and recognizable part of its object. In asserting with the support of scientists that there are no lines in nature and that we see only colors, they undertook to represent the visible world more truly by juxtaposing patches of color without defining outlines. But if their system was defended as truer to the semblance of things and if it introduced into picture-making new signs for aspects of nature such as light and atmosphere and the interactions of colors that could not be represented in the older styles, it required a picture-substance too, and one that in several features is as arbitrary as the archaic black outline,—I mean the visibly discrete strokes of paint and the relief of crusty pigment which violate both the continuity and texture of the represented surfaces. These are material-technical components of the image no less arbitrary than the firm black outline of the primitives and the Egyptians.

The qualities of the image-substance, as every artist knows, are not altogether separate from the qualities of the represented objects. A thicker outline makes the figure look more massive; a thin line can add to its delicacy and grace; a broken line opens the form to the play of light and shadow with all their expressive implications for the concept of things. In a corresponding way the visible patching of pigment in an Impressionist work contributes to the general effect of luminosity and air. Both poles of substance, the ancient and the modern, enter into the visual manifestation of the whole and convey peculiarities of outlook and feeling as well as subtle meanings of the signs.

These variations of the "medium" constitute the poetry of the image, its musical rather than mimetic aspect. But a great modern painter, Georges Braque, having in mind the figurative in poetic language, has spoken paradoxically of the represented objects in the still life picture as the poetry of painting. We can understand this remark through his own work. We are often charmed by his inventiveness in making the strongly-marked structures of painted lines, spots and colors assume the aspect of objects in unexpected ways; and conversely his objects appear as the surprising carriers or sources of original patterns of form.

If the elements of the vehicle and their properties are roots of the aesthetic of the work, of its intimate formal structure and expression, they owe their development and variety in great part to their service in representation. In abstract painting the system of marks, strokes and spots and certain ways of combining and distributing them on the field have become available for arbitrary use without the requirement of correspondence as signs. The forms that result are not simplified abstracted forms of objects; yet the elements applied in a non-mimetic, uninterpreted whole retain many of the qualities and formal relationships of the preceding mimetic art. This important connection is overlooked by those who regard abstract painting as a kind of ornament or as regression to a primitive state of art. Impressionist painting, in which the parts have been freed from the rule of detailed correspondence to the parts of an object, is already a step toward modern abstract painting, though the following generation of artists found Impressionism too realistic.

I have noted several ways in which the ground and frame, conceived as a non-mimetic field for the elements of imagery, affect their meaning and in particular their expressive sense.

I wish, in conclusion, to indicate briefly the far-reaching conversion of these non-mimetic elements into positive representations. Their functions in representation in turn lead to new functions of expression and constructive order in a later non-mimetic art.

The ground line, thickened into a band and colored separately, becomes an element of landscape or architectural space. Its upper edge may be drawn as an irregular line that suggests a horizon, a terrain of rocks and hills.

The uniform background surface, through ornament or a color that sets it off sharply from the ground band, will appear as a represented wall or enclosure of space.

Finally, by the introduction of perspective, the intervals of the picture surface between the figures become signs of a continuous three-dimensional space in which the components owe their virtual size, their foreshortened shapes, their tonal values, to their distance from the transparent picture plane and the eye of an implied observer.

The boundary, too, is transformed into an element of representation, as I have already remarked. It may cut figures, especially at the sides but also above and below, in such a way as to represent the real boundaries of a proximate spectator's vision of the original scene. The boundary then is like a window frame through which one glimpses only a part of the space behind it. In older art this allusion to an actual bounded field of a spectator was most often made by representing within the picture-field itself the stable enclosing parts of an architecture—doorways and window ledges—that defined a real and permanent frame of vision in the field of the signata.

The conception of the picture-field as corresponding in its entirety to a segment of space excerpted from a larger whole is preserved in abstract painting. While no longer representing objects, Mondrian constructed a grid of vertical and horizontal lines of unequal thickness, forming rectangles of which some are incomplete, being intercepted by the edge of the field, as Degas's figures are cut by the frame. In these regular, though not obviously commensurable, forms we seem to behold only a small part of an infinitely extended structure; the pattern of the rest is not deducible from the fragmentary sample which is an odd and in some respects ambiguous segment and yet possesses a striking balance and coherence. In this construction one can see not only the artist's ideal of color and scrupulous precision, but also a model of one aspect of contemporary thought: the conception of the world as law-bound in the relation of simple, elementary components, yet open, unbounded and contingent as a whole.

NOTES

1. Certain of these observations, presented in my courses at Columbia University thirty years ago, will be found in the doctor's thesis of my pupil, Miriam S. Bunim, "Space in Medieval Painting and the Forerunners of Perspective" (New York, 1940).

2. See Heinrich Schäfer, *Grundlagen der ägyptischen Rundbildnerei und ihre Verwandschaft mit denen der Flachbildnerei* (Leipzig, 1923), p. 27.

ÉMILE BENVENISTE

Speaking of Peirce and Saussure as "antithetical geniuses," neither of which answered adequately the question, "What is the place of language among the systems of signs?," Benveniste lays out the essentials of the Saussurian framework, all the while subjecting it to certain (justified or unjustified?) criticisms of ambiguity, vagueness, imprecision. Although Saussure called language the "most important" of semiological systems, he did not clearly formulate just why and how it is this. "Semiology, as a science of signs, remains latent in Saussure's work as a prospect which in its most precise features models itself on linguistics," examples of which are found in the texts of Lévi-Strauss and Barthes especially. Just how far, however, can other sign systems, which exist in vast array and with amazing complexity, model themselves on language? This theme has been taken up by Russian semiotics under the rubric of "secondary modeling systems," an important issue in contemporary semiotics, but whose ultimate import has not yet been determined. The interested reader can turn to the texts collected in Daniel P. Lucid's *Soviet Semiotics*, which will lead him elsewhere. Benveniste, for his part, sketches the characteristics of a semiological system according to (1) mode of expression, (2) domain of its validity, (3) nature and number of its signs, (4) type of operation, and then proceeds to play the various sign and expression systems off against one another. In this way the various "orders of semiotic relationships" can be delineated and situated.

Concretely, Benveniste proceeds to study the (in his opinion) primarily binary system of traffic lights, music, and the plastic arts. He sets out the formal principles of sign systems, on the model of language, to be sure, and then asks for the possibility of mutual interchangeability between the various systems. In an enumeration that bears remarkable resemblance to Langer's, which has a very different point of derivation, Benveniste states the minimal conditions for comparison between systems of different orders are: "Every semiotic system based on signs must necessarily include (1) a finite repertory of *signs*, (2) and rules of order governing its *figures*, (3) existing independently of the nature and number of the *discourses* that the system allows to be produced." While the various systems are seen to have certain points in common, some of which are obvious and others not so, the upshot of Benveniste's careful, clear, and nuanced analysis is that language is the "interpreting" system par excellence and is *sui generis*. "Language provides us with the only model of a system that is at the same time semiotic in its formal structure and in its functioning. . . . It explains the function of a sign, and it alone offers an exemplary formula of the sign." "The nature of language, its representative function, its dynamic power, and its relational role make of it the great semiotic matrix, the modeling structure from which other structures reproduce its features and its mode of action." "It is the prerogative of language to comprise simultaneously the meaning of signs and the meaning of enunciation."

It is this overwhelming power of language that both sets the limits to other "signifying systems" and gives us the further clues to developing, to the degree that it is possible, a general semiotics. Benveniste's distinction between semiotic and semantic dimensions—"semiotic" referring to the intrasystematic domain, the relation of signs to one another, and "semantic" to the "referential" or enunciatory domain—allows us both to transcend the Saussurian-restricted focusing on the *sign* as minimal unit toward viewing the larger domain of discourse and hence to develop a "metasemantics" founded on the semantics of enunciation. "The instruments and methodology of this 'second generation' semiology shall in turn contribute to the development of other branches of general semiology," all of which—whether concerned with music, visual art, film, dance, or whatever—are occupied, in their own methodological reflections and concrete analyses, with "the intersemiotic validity of the notion of 'sign.'"

Benveniste's work may most easily be followed up in his *Problems of General Linguistics*, translated by Mary Elizabeth Meek (Coral Gables, Florida: University of Miami Press, 1971), which contains many stimulating and interesting essays. See especially, in the context of the topics treated in this reader, the essays "Saussure after Half a Century," "The Nature of the Linguistic Sign," "Remarks on the Function of Language in Freudian Theory," although all the essays are well worth the time and effort needed to appropriate them. Benveniste's own notes to his essay in this book give further indications of where one is to read further. The extension of semiotic analyses to non-linguistic domains such as film, painting, music, and so forth can be followed up by consulting the works of Metz, cited by Benveniste (which now exist in English), Peter Wollen, *Signs and Meaning in the Cinema* (Bloomington and London: Indiana University Press, 1972), Jean-Jacques Nattiez, "The Contribution of Musical Semiotics to the Semiotic Discussion in General," in *A Perfusion of Signs*, edited by Thomas A. Sebeok (Bloomington and London: Indiana

University Press, 1977), with an extensive bibliography. This volume also contains essays on semiotics and medical inquiry, semiotics and architecture, semiotics and culture, and so forth. The bibliographies there will lead one to other cross-semiotic studies.

The Semiology of Language

ÉMILE BENVENISTE

> *Semiology will have much to accomplish if it does nothing else but discover its own boundaries.*
> *Ferdinand de Saussure*[1]

Since the time when those two antithetical geniuses, Peirce and Saussure, almost simultaneously,[2] in total ignorance of one another, conceived of the possibility of a science of signs and worked at establishing it, an important problem has arisen which has not as yet found a precise formulation. In the midst of the confusion that reigns in this field, this problem has not even been clearly stated. What is the place of language among the systems of signs?

Peirce devoted his entire life to the further elaboration of concepts based on the term *semiotic*, returning to the designation Σημειωτική, which John Locke had applied to a science of signs and significations derived from logic, which was itself conceived of as a science of language. The enormous quantity of his notes bears witness to an obstinate effort to analyze logical, mathematical, physical, and even psychological and religious notions within the framework of semiotics. This study, pursued throughout his life, involved an increasingly complex apparatus of definitions aimed at distributing all of reality, the conceptual, and the experiential into various categories of signs. In order to construct this 'universal algebra of relations',[3] Peirce proposed a tripartite division of signs into *icons*, *indices*, and *symbols*: today this is nearly all we retain of the immense logical superstructure underlying this division.

As for language, Peirce made no precise or specific formulations. For

This article first appeared in *Semiotica* 1 (1969), 1–12 and 127–135; it was subsequently included in *Problèmes de linguistique générale*. The translation by Genette Ashby and Adelaide Russo is reprinted from *Semiotica*, special supplement (1981): 5–23, by permission of Mouton Publishers.

him, language was both everywhere and nowhere at all. He was never concerned with the way language functioned, if he even paid attention to it. Language for him was reduced to its components, words, which are certainly signs. Yet, they are not derived from a distinct category, or even from a constant type. Words belong, for the most part, to the category of 'symbols': certain ones, for example, demonstrative pronouns, are 'indices', and therefore are classified with their corresponding gestures, the gesture of pointing, for example. Consequently, Peirce did not recognize the fact that such a gesture is universally understood, whereas the demonstrative is part of a special system of oral signs, language, and of a particular linguistic system, the idiom. Moreover, in Peirce's terms the same word can appear as several varieties of "signs," such as the *qualisign*, the *sinsign*, or the *legisign*.[4] We do not see, therefore, the operative utility of similar distinctions, nor to what extent they would help the linguist construct a semiology of language as a system. The difficulty that prevents any specific application of Peirce's concepts (except for the well-known but much too general tripartite framework) is that the sign is definitively posited as the base of the entire universe, and functions simultaneously as the principle of definition for each element and as the principle of explanation for the entire ensemble, be it abstract or concrete. Man himself is a sign; his thought is a sign;[5] his every emotion is a 'sign.'[6] But finally, since these signs are all signs for each other, for what could they be a sign that is not a sign itself? Where could we find a fixed point to anchor the first signifying relationship? The semiotic edifice that Peirce constructs is not self-inclusive in its own definition. In order to keep the notion of sign from disappearing completely amidst this proliferation *ad infinitum*, we must recognize a difference, somewhere in this universe, between sign and signified. Therefore, each sign must be included and articulated within a system of signs. Therein lies the condition for *significance*. It then follows, to counter Peirce, that all signs cannot function identically, nor belong to one system alone. We have to establish several systems of signs, and among these systems, make explicit the relationships of difference and analogy.

It is here that Saussure presents himself directly as the exact opposite of Peirce, in methodology as well as in practice. In Saussure's work, reflection proceeds from language and adopts language as its exclusive object. Language is considered in itself. Linguistics has a threefold task: (1) to describe all known languages synchronically and diachronically; (2) to extract the general laws at work in languages; and (3) to delimit and define itself (1966: 6).

Under its external rational appearance, the peculiarity that this program conceals passes unnoticed; yet, this peculiarity is precisely its force and audacity. Hence, the third aim of linguistics: to define itself by itself. This task, if we are willing to understand it fully, absorbs the two others, and in a sense eliminates them. How will linguistics be able to set its own boundaries and define itself by itself, if not by delimiting and defining its very own object, language? But in such a case, can it accomplish the first two tasks that it must undertake, i.e., the description and history of language? How would linguistics be able "to determine the forces that are permanently and universally at work in all languages, and to deduce the general laws to which all specific historical phenomena can be deduced" (1966: 6), if we have not begun by defining the powers and resources of linguistics (that is to say, the hold it has on language, and consequently, the nature and characteristics peculiar to this entity called language)? Everything is dependent upon this requirement, and the linguist cannot deem any one of these tasks distinct from the others, nor fulfill any one of them, if he is not first aware of the singular nature of language with respect to all other objects of science. This insight contains the basic condition preliminary to all other active and cognitive linguistic proceedings. Far from being located on the same plane as the other two tasks, and thus implying their completion, this third task, "to delimit and define itself" (1966: 6), forces linguistics to postpone the fulfillment of the other two until it has discovered its own limits and definition as a science. Herein lies the great innovation of Saussure's program. Reference to his *Course* readily confirms that for Saussure a linguistic science is possible only on the condition that it ultimately find itself through the discovery of its own object.

Everything then proceeds from the question: "What is both the integral and concrete object of linguistics?" (1966: 7). Saussure's first step aims at destroying all previous responses to this question. "From whatever direction we approach the question, nowhere do we find the integral object of linguistics" (1966: 9). The field thus cleared, Saussure posits his first methodological requirement: language (*la langue*) must be separated from human speech (*le langage*). The essential concepts furtively slip into the following few lines:

> Taken as a whole, speech is many-sided and heterogeneous: straddling several areas simultaneously—physical, physiological, and psychological—it belongs both to the individual and to society; we cannot put it into any category of human facts, for we cannot discover its unity.
>
> Language, on the contrary, is a self-contained whole and a principle of classification. As soon as we give language first place among the facts of speech, we introduce a natural order into a mass that lends itself to no other classification. (1966: 9)

Saussure's chief concern is the discovery of the principle of unity dominating the multiplicity of forms under which languages appear. This principle alone allows us to classify linguistic facts among human activities. The reduction of human speech to language satisfies this double condition: it allows us to propose language as a unifying principle, and in the same stroke, establishes a place for language among human activities. In formulating the principle of unity and the principle of classification Saussure presents the two concepts which, in turn, introduce semiology.

Both principles are necessary to establish linguistics as a science. We could not conceive of a science uncertain of its object, undefined in terms of its relevance. This goes well beyond a concern for rigor; it proceeds from the very rules specific to the totality of human acts.

Here again, no one has sufficiently emphasized the originality of Saussure's procedure. It is not a question of deciding whether or not linguistics is closer to psychology or sociology, not of finding a place for it in the midst of existing disciplines. The problem is presented on another level, and in terms that create their own concepts. Linguistics is part of a science that does not yet exist, a science that has as its subject other systems of the same order in the totality of human activities: *semiology*, Saussure states and situates this relationship thusly:

> Language is a system of signs that expresses ideas, and is therefore comparable to a system of writing, the alphabet of deaf-mutes, symbolic rites, polite formulas, military signals, etc. But it is the most important of these systems.
>
> A *science that studies the life of signs within society* is conceivable; it would be a part of social psychology and consequently of general psychology; I shall call it *semiology* (from Greek sēmeîon 'sign'). Semiology would show what constitutes signs, what laws govern them. Since the science does not yet exist, no one can say what it would be; but it has a right to existence, a place staked out in advance. Linguistics is only a part of the general science of semiology; the laws discovered by semiology will be applicable to linguistics, and the latter will circumscribe a well-defined area within the mass of anthropological facts.
>
> To determine the exact place of semiology is the task of the psychologist.[7] The task of the linguist is to find out what makes language a special system within the mass of semiological data. This issue will be taken up later, here I wish merely to call attention to one thing: if I have succeeded in assigning linguistics a place among the sciences, it is because I have related it to semiology. (1966: 16)

The basics of the long commentary that this page demands are included in the discussion that we broach further on. In order to emphasize them, we shall consider only the primordial characteristics of semiology as Saussure perceives it, and furthermore, as he recognized it long before alluding to it in his teachings.[8]

Language, in all its aspects, appears as a duality: a social institution, set to work by the individual; continuous discourse, composed of fixed units. Language is independent of the phonoacoustic mechanism of speech: it consists of a "system of signs in which the only essential thing is the union of meanings and sound images, and in which both parts of the sign are psychological" (1966: 15). Where is language to find its unity and its functional principle? In its semiotic character. In that way it defines its own nature, and also integrates itself into a set of systems, all having the same characteristics.

For Saussure, in contrast to Peirce, the sign is a linguistic concept which extends more widely to certain orders of anthropological and social data. Thereby its domain is circumscribed. But besides language, this domain includes systems homologous to it. Saussure refers to several. The latter all have the characteristic of being systems of *signs*. Language "is the most important of these systems" (1966: 16). The most important in relation to what? Is it simply because language has more importance in social life than any other system? There is nothing which allows us to determine this.

Saussure's thought, most affirmative about the relationship of language to systems of signs, is less clear on the relationship of linguistics to semiology, the science of the systems of signs. The future of linguistics will be in its incorporation into semiology, which in turn will form "a part of social psychology and consequently of general psychology" (1966: 16). But we must wait for the establishment of semiology, "*a science that studies the life of signs within society,*" in order to learn "what constitutes signs, what laws govern them" (1966: 16). Saussure, therefore, defers the task of defining the sign itself to this future science. Nevertheless, he elaborates, for linguistics, the instrument of its own semiology, the linguistic sign: "To me, the language problem is mainly semiological, and all developments derive their significance from that important fact" (1966: 17).

This principle, that the linguistic sign is 'arbitrary' placed at the center of linguistics, connects linguistics to semiology. In a general manner, the principal object of semiology will be "the whole group of systems grounded on the arbitrariness of the sign" (1966: 68). Consequently, in the totality of systems of expression, preeminence belongs to language.

> Signs that are wholly arbitrary realize better than the others the ideal of the semiological process; this is why language, the most complex and universal of all systems of expression, is also the most characteristic; in this sense linguistics could become the master-pattern for all branches of semiology although language is only one particular semiological system (1966: 68).

In this way, while clearly formulating the idea that linguistics has a necessary relationship to semiology, Saussure refrains from defining the nature of that relationship, except by means of the principle of the "arbitrary nature of the sign," which would govern the totality of systems of expression, and above all, language. Semiology, as a science of signs, remains latent in Saussure's work as a prospect which in its most precise features models itself on linguistics.

Saussure limits himself to rapidly citing several systems which, along with language, are included under semiology; he far from exhausts the list, since he puts forth no delimiting criteria: "a system of writing, the alphabet of deaf-mutes, symbolic rites, polite formulas, military signals, etc." (1966: 16). Elsewhere he speaks of considering rites, customs, etc., as signs (1966: 17).

Taking up this important problem at the point where Saussure left off, we would like to insist first upon the necessity of establishing a preliminary classification if we are to advance the analysis and consolidate the bases of semiology at all.

We will say nothing about writing here, saving this difficult problem for special examination. Are symbolic rites and rules of etiquette autonomous systems? Can we really put them on the same level as language? They only occur in a semiological relationship through the intermediary of a discourse: the "myth," which accompanies the "rite"; the "protocol" which governs the rules of etiquette. These signs, if they are to be established as a system, presuppose the existence of language, which produces and interprets them. They are therefore of a distinct order in a hierarchy yet to be defined. We already suspect that, no less than the systems of signs, the *relationships* between these systems will constitute the subject of semiology.

It is finally time to forsake generalities and tackle the central problem of semiology, the status of language among the systems of signs. We cannot guarantee anything in this theory as long as we lack a clear idea of the sign's concept and worth within those groups where it is already accessible to study. We believe this examination should begin with nonlinguistic systems.

The role of the sign is to represent, to take the place of something else while alluding to it by virtue of a substitute. A more precise definition, one which would distinguish several varieties of signs specifically, presupposes a reflection upon the principle of a science of signs, of a semiology, and an effort to elaborate it. The smallest attention to our behavior, to the conditions of intellectual and social life, of our dealings with others, of the relationship between production and exchange, shows us that we are utilizing several systems of signs concurrently at every moment: first, the signs of language, which are those that we acquire the earliest, with the beginning of conscious life; graphic signs; the signs of politeness, of gratitude, and of persuasion in all their varieties and hierarchies; the signs regulating vehicular movement; the "external signs" indicating social conditions; "monetary signs," values and indices of economic life; cult signs, rites, and beliefs, and the signs of art in all its varieties (music, images, figurative reproductions). In short and without going beyond empiric verification, it is clear that our whole life is caught up in networks of signs that condition us to the point where we do not know how to omit a single one without endangering the equilibrium between society and individual. These signs seem to engender themselves and multiply by virtue of some internal necessity, apparently responding as well to a necessity within our mental organization. What principle can be introduced into the numerous and diverse ways in which signs arrange themselves in configurations that will order these relationships and delimit their sets?

The common characteristic of all these systems and the criterion for their inclusion in semiology is their signifying property, or *meaning*, and their composition into units of meaning, or *signs*. We have come to the point where we must describe their distinctive characteristics.

A semiological system is characterized by: (1) its mode of operation; (2) the domain of its validity; (3) the nature and number of its signs; and (4) its type of operation.

Each one of these features entails a certain number of variations.

The *mode of operation* is the manner in which the system acts, more particularly the sense (sight, hearing, etc.) to which it is directed.

The *domain of validity* is that area in which the system imposes itself and must be recognized or obeyed.

The *nature* and *number of signs* are a function of the aforesaid conditions.

The *type of operation* is the relationship that unites the signs and confers their distinguishing function upon them.

Let us put this definition to the test against an elementary system, the system of traffic signal lights: Its mode of operation is visual, generally diurnal, on a clear day; its domain of validity is vehicular traffic on highways; its signs are constituted by the chromatic opposition green/red (sometimes with an intermediary phase of simple transition, yellow), i.e., it is a binary system; its type of operation is a relationship of alternation (never of simultaneity), green/red signifying road open/road closed, or under its prescriptive form, stop/go.

This system is capable of expansion or transference, but only under one of its four conditions, the domain of validity. We can apply it to fluvial navigation, to channel buoy markers, or to aviation runways, provided that we keep the same chromatic opposition, with the same signification. The nature of the signs can only be modified temporarily, and for reasons of expediency.[9]

The traits subsumed under this definition form two groups: the first two, relative to the mode of operation and to the domain of validity, provide the external empirical conditions of the system; the last two, relative to signs and to their type of operation, indicate their internal semiotic conditions. The first two allow certain variations or accommodations;

the other two do not. This structure delineates a canonical model for the binary system, which we recognize, for example, in voting customs—using a black or white ball, standing or being seated, etc.—and in all the circumstances where the alternative could be (but is not) stated in linguistic terms such as: yes/no.

From now on, we are able to extract two principles which pertain to the relationships between semiotic systems.

The first principle can be stated as the *principle of nonredundancy* between systems. Semiotic systems are not "synonymous"; we are not able to say "the same thing" with spoken words that we can with music, as they are systems with different bases.

In other words, two semiotic systems of different types cannot be mutually interchangeable. In the example cited, speech and music have as a common trait the production of sounds and the fact that they appeal to hearing; but this relationship does not prevail, in view of the difference in nature between their respective units and their types of operation, as we shall show further on.

Nonredundancy in the universe of sign systems occurs as a result of the nonconvertibility of systems with different bases. Man does not have several distinct systems at his disposal for the *same* signifying relationship.

On the other hand, the written alphabet and the Braille alphabet, or Morse code, or the deaf-mute alphabet are mutually interchangeable, all being systems based on the alphabetic principle: one letter, one sound.

A second principle follows from and completes the preceding one.

Two systems can have the same sign in common without being, as a result, synonymous or redundant; that is to say, the functional difference of a sign alone matters, not its substantial identity. The red in the binary system of highway traffic signals has nothing in common with the red of the French tricolor flag, nor does the white of that flag have anything to do with the white worn for mourning in China. The value of a sign is defined only in the system which incorporates it. There is no sign that bridges several systems, that is transsystemic.

Are these systems, then, just so many closed worlds, having nothing between them except a relationship of coexistence, itself perhaps fortuitous? We have to draw up new methodological requirements. The relationship laid down between semiotic systems must itself be semiotic in nature. It is determined first of all by the same cultural background which in some way produces and nurtures all systems in its particular group. Therein, again, lies an external link which does not necessarily imply a coherent relationship between individual systems. There is a second condition: Can it be determined whether a given semiotic system can interpret itself by itself, or must it receive its interpretation from another system? The semiotic relationship between systems is expressed, then, as the relationship between *interpreting system* and *interpreted system*. It is this relationship that we shall propose on a grand scale between the signs of language and those of society. The signs of society can be interpreted integrally by those of language, but the reverse is not so. Language is therefore the interpreting system of society.[10] On a small scale, we shall consider the written alphabet as the interpreting system of Morse code or of Braille because of the larger extension of its domain of validity, and in spite of the fact that they are all mutually interchangeable.

We can already infer from this that the semiotic subsystems internal to society are logically interpreted by language, since society contains them, and society is interpreted by language. We already perceive a fundamental asymmetry in this relationship, and therefore, should return to the primary cause of this nonreversibility: Language occupies a special position in the universe of sign systems. If we decide to designate the totality of these systems with the letter S, and language with the letter L, the transformation always occurs in the direction of S to L (S → L), never in the reverse order. Herein we have a general principle of hierarchy suitable as an introduction for the classification of semiotic systems functioning as the basis for any semiological theory.

In order to highlight the difference between the orders of semiotic relationships, we now propose, in the same perspective, a totally different system: that of music. The differences appear essentially in the nature of the 'signs' and in their mode of operation.

Music is made up of sounds which have a musical status when they are designated and classified as *notes*. There are no other units in music directly comparable to the "signs" of language. These notes have an organizing framework, the *scale*, in which they are employed by virtue of being discrete units, discontinuous from one another, of a fixed number, each one characterized by a constant number of vibrations in a given time. The scales include the same notes at different pitches, defined by a number of vibrations in a geometric progression, while the intervals remain constant.

Musical sounds can occur in monophony or in polyphony; they function in an isolated state or simultaneously (chords), whatever the intervals separating them into their respective scales. There is no limit to the multiplicity of sounds produced simultaneously by a group of instruments, nor to the order, to the frequency, or to the scope of combinations. The composer freely organizes the sounds in a discourse that is never subjected to any 'grammatical' convention, but that obeys its own "syntax."

We see, therefore, in what respect the musical system can or cannot be considered semiotic. It is organized from an ensemble constituted by a scale that is itself formed of notes. The notes have no differential value except within the scale; and the scale itself is a recurrent whole at several (different) pitches, specified by the tone which indicates the key.

The basic unit will therefore be the note, a discrete and contrasting unit of sound; but it only assumes this value within the scale, which fixes the paradigm of notes. Is this a semiotic unit? We can discern that it is in its own order, since it determines the oppositions. But then it has no relationship with the semiotics of the linguistic sign, and, in fact, it is not convertible into units of language, at whatever level this may occur.

The following analogy, at the same time, discloses a profound difference. Music is a system which functions on two axes: a simultaneous and a sequential axis. We might think of a homology with the function of language along its paradigmatic and syntagmatic axes. However, the axis of simultaneity in music contradicts the very principle of the paradigm in language, which is the principle of selection, excluding all intrasegmental simultaneity; and the sequential axis in music does not coincide with the syntagmatic axis of language either, since the musical sequence is compatible with the simultaneity of sounds, and is not subjected to any restriction of liaison (syncopation) or of exclusion with regard to any sound or group of sounds.

In this way it can be seen that the musical combination derived from harmony and counterpoint has no equivalent in language, where paradigms as often as syntagms are subjected to specific arrangements: rules of consistency, of selectivity, of recurrence, etc., upon which depend frequency and statistical predictability on the one hand, and the possibility of constructing intelligible statements on the other. This difference does not depend on a special musical system or on a chosen sound scale: the twelve-tone serial scale is as rigorously bound here as the diatonic scale.

We can say, on the whole, if music is considered as a language, it has syntactic features, but not semiotic features. This difference delineates in advance a positive necessary feature of linguistic semiology that we should keep in mind.

Let us now go on to another field, that of the so-called plastic arts, an enormous area, where we will limit ourselves to pursuing some similarity or opposition capable of elucidating the semiology of language. Here from the very first we run up against a difficulty in principle: is there something common at the base of all these arts, aside from the vague notion of the 'plastic'? Can we find in each or in only one of them a formal entity which we may call the *unit* of the system under consideration? But what can be the unit in painting or drawing? Is it shape, line, color? Formulated in this fashion, is the question still meaningful?

At this point we can state the minimal conditions for comparison between systems of different orders. Every semiotic system based on signs must necessarily include (1) a finite repertory of *signs*, (2) and rules of order governing its *figures*, (3) existing independently of the nature and number of the *discourses* that the system allows to be produced. None of the plastic arts considered in its totality seems to reproduce such a model. At the most, we might be able to find some approximation of it in the work of a particular artist. However, it would no longer be a matter of constant general conditions, but of individual characteristics, and this again would lead us astray from language.

The notion of unit is central to the problems which concern us,[11] and no serious theory can be formulated without considering the question, since every signifying system must be defined by its mode of signification. Consequently, such a system must designate the units it brings into play in order to produce meaning and to specify the nature of the meaning produced.

Two questions then emerge: (1) Can we reduce all semiotic systems to units? (2) In the systems in which they exist, are these units signs?

The unit and the sign remain as distinct features. The sign is necessarily a unit, but the unit may not be a sign. We are assured of at least one thing: language is composed of units, and these units are signs. What about other semiological systems?

First we shall consider the functioning of the so-called artistic systems, those of image and sound, while deliberately ignoring their aesthetic function. Musical language is composed of diversely articulated sound combinations and sequences; the elementary unit, the sound, is not a sign; each sound is identifiable in the scalar structure upon which it depends; none is endowed with meaning in itself. This is a typical example of units which are not signs, which do not designate, because they are merely the degrees of a scale whose range has been arbitrarily set. We have here a principle of selection: The systems based upon units are divided between systems of signifying units and systems of nonsignifying units. Language is in the first category, and music in the second.[12]

In the figurative arts (painting, design, and sculpture), which have fixed or mobile images, it is the existence of units which comes under discussion. What would their nature be? If it is a matter of colors, we recognize that they can be divided into a scale whose principal degrees are identifiable by name. They are designated, they do not designate; they neither refer to anything, nor suggest anything in an univocal way. The artist chooses them, blends them, and arranges them on the canvas according to his taste; finally, it is in composition alone that, technically speaking, they assume a "signification" through selection and arrangement. Thus the artist creates his own semiotics; he sets up his own oppositions in features which he renders significant in their order. Therefore, he does not acquire a repertory of signs, recognized as such, nor does he establish one. Color, the material, comprises an unlimited variety of gradations in shade, of which none is equivalent to the linguistic sign.

With regard to the figurative arts, they are already derived from another level, that of representation, where feature, color, and movement combine to form a whole governed by its own necessities. In this case, they are separate systems of great complexity, in which the definition of the sign can only be precisely stated after the development of this still vague study of semiology.

The signifying relationships of any artistic language are to be found within the compositions that make us aware of it. Art is nothing more than a specific work of art in which the artist freely sets up contrasts and values over which he assumes supreme authority. He answers to no one, nor must he eliminate contradictions. He must merely express a vision, to which the entire composition bears witness, and of which it becomes a manifestation, according to conscious or unconscious criteria.

We can thus distinguish the systems in which meaning is imparted by the author to the composition from those in which meaning is expressed by the initial elements in an isolated state, independently of the inter-relationships which they may undergo. In the former, meaning emerges from the relationships forming a closed world; in the latter it is inherent in the signs themselves. Therefore, the meaning of art may never be reduced to a convention accepted by two partners.[13] New terms must always be found, since they are unlimited in number and unpredictable in nature; thus they must be redevised for each work and, in short, prove unsuitable as an institution. On the other hand, the meaning of language is meaning itself, establishing the possibility of all exchange and of all communication, and thus of all culture.

It is still permissible, taking into account certain metaphors, to compare the execution of a musical composition to the production of a linguistic statement; we can speak about a musical "discourse," analyzed into phrases separated by "pauses," or by "silences," set off by recognizable "motifs." We might also look for morphological and syntactical principles in the figurative arts.[14] One thing at least is certain: no semiology of sound, color, or image can be formulated or expressed in sounds, colors, or images. Every semiology of a nonlinguistic system must use language as an intermediary, and thus can only exist in and through the semiology of language. Whether language serves here as an instrument rather than as an object of analysis does not alter this situation which governs all semiotic relationships; language is the interpreting system of all other systems, linguistic and nonlinguistic.

At this point we must specify the nature and the feasibility of relationships among semiotic systems. We propose three kinds of relationships.

(1) One system can generate another system. Ordinary language generates logical and mathematical formalization; ordinary writing generates stenographic writing; the normal alphabet generates the Braille alphabet. This *generative relationship* is useful between two distinct, contemporaneous sytems, of the same kind, where the second one is constructed from the first one and fulfills a specific function. We should carefully distinguish this generative relationship from the derivative relationship, which supposes evolution and historical transition. Between

hieroglyphic writing and demotic writing there is derivation, not generation. The history of writing systems provides many examples of derivation.

(2) The second kind of relationship is the *relationship of homology*,
which establishes a correlation between the parts of two semiotic systems. In contrast to the preceding relationship, it is not explicitly stated,
but is set up by virtue of the connections we find or establish between two
distinct systems. The kind of homology may vary: intuitive or rational,
substantial or structural, conceptual or poetic. "Les parfums, les cou-
leurs, les sons se répondent." ["Fragrances, colors, and sounds mutually
respond."] These "correspondances" are unique to Baudelaire; they
organize his poetic universe and the imagery which reflects it. Of a more
intellectual nature is the homology that Panofsky sees between Gothic architecture and scholastic thought.[15] The homology between writing and
ritual gesture in China has also been pointed out. Two linguistic structures of different makeup can reveal partial or extended homologies. All
depends upon the way in which we lay down the two systems, the parame-
ters which we use, and the fields in which we perform. According to the
situation, the homology established will serve as a unifying principle between two fields and will be limited to this functional role, or it will
create new kinds of semiotic values. Nothing assures the validity of this
relationship in advance, nothing limits the extent of it.

(3) We will term the third relationship between semiotic systems a *relationship of interpretance*. We designate the relationship established between an interpreting system and an interpreted system in this way. From
the standpoint of language it is the fundamental relationship, the one
which divides the systems into articulate systems, because they exhibit
their own semiotics, and articulated systems, whose semiotics appears
only through the grid of another mode of expression. Thus we can introduce and justify the principle that language is in the interpreting system
(interpretant) of all other semiotic systems. No other system has at its disposal a "language" by which it can categorize and interpret itself according to its semiotic distinctions, while language can, in principle, categorize and interpret everything, including itself.

We see here how the semiological relationship is distinguished from
every other, especially from the sociological. If, for example, we question
ourselves on the respective status of language and of society—a topic of
interminable debate—and also on their mode of mutual dependency, the
sociologist and probably anyone else who perceives the question in di-
mensional terms will notice that language functions within the society
that encompasses it; from thence, it is relatively easy to determine that
society is the whole, and language, one of its parts. However, consideration from a semiological perspective reverses this relationship, because
language alone permits society to exist. Language forms that which holds
men together, the basis of all relationships, which in turn establish so-

ciety. We could say, then, that it is language which contains society.[16] In this way the *interpretance* relationship, which is semiotic, moves in an opposite direction to that of inclusion, a nesting relationship, which is sociological. While the former relationship makes language and society mutually dependent according to their capacity of semiotization, the latter, if we objectify the external dependencies, reifies language and society in a similar manner.

Thereupon we may verify a criterion we indicated above, when, in order to determine the relationships between semiotic systems, we proposed that these relationships ought to be themselves semiotic in nature. The irreversible relationship of *interpretance*, which includes other systems in language, satisfies this condition.

Language provides us with the only model of a system that is at the same time semiotic in its formal structure and in its functioning:

(1) it manifests itself by a statement making reference to a given situation; to speak is always to speak about;

(2) it consists formally of distinct units, each of which is a sign;

(3) it is produced and accepted with the same values of reference by all members of a community;

(4) it is the only actualization of intersubjective communication.

For these reasons, language is the preeminent semiotic organization. It explains the function of a sign, and it alone offers an exemplary formula of the sign. Thus language alone can—and, in fact, does—confer on other groups the rank of signifying system by acquainting them with the relationship of the sign. There is then a *semiotic modeling* which language practices and whose principle we cannot expect to find anywhere else than in language. The nature of language, its representative function, its dynamic power, and its relational role make of it the great semiotic matrix, the modeling structure from which other structures reproduce its features and its mode of action.

To what may we attribute this property? Can we discern why language is the interpreting system of every signifying system? Is it simply because language is the most common system, the one which has the largest field, the greatest frequency of use and—in practice—the greatest effectiveness? On the contrary, this privileged position of language in the pragmatic order of things is a consequence, not a cause, of its preeminence as a signifying system, and only a semiological principle can explain this preeminence. We will discover it by becoming aware of the fact that language signifies in a specific way which belongs to it alone, in a way that no other system copies. It is invested with *double meaning*. In this aspect it is appropriately a model without parallel. Language combines two distinct modes of meaning, which we designate on the one hand as the *semiotic* mode, and on the other, the *semantic* mode.[17]

Semiotics designates the mode of signification proper to the linguistic *sign* that establishes it as a unit. We can, for purposes of analysis, consider separately the two surfaces of the sign, but with respect to its signification, it is a unit; it remains a unit. The only question to which a sign gives rise, if it is to be recognized as such, is that of its existence, and the latter is answered by yes or no: *tree—song—to wash—nerve—yellow—on*, and not **tro—*rong—*dawsh—*lerve—*sellow—*ton*. Further, we compare the sign in order to define it, either to signifiers which are partially alike: saber:sober, or saber:sable, or saber:taber; or to neighboring things signified: saber:gun, or saber:epee. All semiotic research, in the strictest sense, consists of the identification of units, the description of characteristic features, and the discovery of the increasingly fine criteria of their distinctiveness. In this way each sign asserts its own meaning still more clearly in the midst of a constellation or among an ensemble of signs. Taken in itself, the sign is pure identity itself, totally foreign to all other signs, the signifying foundation of language, the material necessity for statement. It exists when it is recognized as signifier by all members of a linguistic community, and when it calls forth for each individual roughly the same associations and oppositions. Such is the province and the criterion of semiotics.

With the semantic, we enter into the specific mode of meaning which is generated by *discourse*. The problems raised here are a function of language as producer of messages. However, the message is not reduced to a series of separately identifiable units; it is not the sum of many signs that produces meaning; on the contrary, it is meaning (*l'intenté*), globally conceived, that is actualized and divided into specific signs, the *words*. In the second place, semantics takes over the majority of referents, while semiotics is in principle cut off and independent of all reference. Semantic order becomes identified with the world of enunciation and with the universe of discourse.

Whether or not it is a question of two distinct orders of ideas and of two conceptual universes, we can still demonstrate this distinction through the difference in criteria of validity required by each. Semiotics (the sign) must be *recognized*; semantics (the discourse) must be *understood*. The difference between recognition and comprehension refers to two distinct faculties of the mind: that of discerning the identity between the previous and the present, and that of discerning, on the other hand, the meaning of a new enunciation. In the pathological forms of language, these two powers are frequently dissociated.

Language is the only system whose meaning is articulated this way in two dimensions. The other systems have a unidimensional meaning; either semiotics (gestures of politeness, *mudras*) without semantics; or semantics (artistic expressions) without semiotics. It is the prerogative of language to comprise simultaneously the meaning of signs and the meaning of enunciation. Therein originates its major strength, that of creating a second level of enunciation, where it becomes possible to retain meaningful remarks about meaning. Through this metalinguistic faculty we discover the origin of the interpreting relationship through which language embraces all other systems.

When Saussure defined language as a system of signs, he laid the foundation for linguistic semiology. But we now see that if the sign corresponds well to the signifying units of language, we cannot set it up as a unique principle of language in its discursive operation. Saussure was not unaware of the sentence, but obviously it created a serious obstacle for him and it was relegated to 'speech' (cf. Saussure [1966: 106, 124–128] and Godel [1966: 490 ff.]), solving nothing; we must know precisely if and how we can proceed from the sign to 'speech'. In reality the world of the sign is closed. From the sign to the sentence there is no transition, either by syntagmatization or otherwise. A hiatus separates them. Consequently, we must admit that language comprises two separate domains, each of which requires its own conceptual apparatus. For the one which we call semiotics, Saussure's theory of the linguistic sign will serve as a basis for research. The semantic domain, on the other hand, should be recognized as separate. It will require a new conceptual and definitional apparatus.

The semiology of language has been obstructed, paradoxically, by the same instrument which created it, the sign. We cannot brush aside the idea of the linguistic sign without omitting the most important characteristic of language; nor can we extend it to discourse as a whole without contradicting its definition as a minimal unit.

In conclusion, we must go beyond Saussure's concern for the sign as a unique principle, on which depend both the structure and the function of language.

This transcendence is achieved through two channels: in intralinguistic analysis, through the opening of a new dimension of meaning, that of discourse (which we call semantic), henceforth distinct from that which is connected to the sign (which we call semiotic); and in the translinguistic analysis of texts and other manifestations through the elaboration of a metasemantics founded on the semantics of enunciation.

The instruments and methodology of this "second generation" semiology shall in turn contribute to the development of other branches of general semiology.

NOTES

1. Handwritten note (Saussure 1957: 19).
2. Charles Sanders Peirce (1839–1914); Ferdinand de Saussure (1857–1913).
3. "My universal algebra of relations, with the subjacent indices ε and π, is susceptible of being enlarged so as to comprise everything and so, still bet-

ter, though not to ideal perfection, is the system of existential graphs" (Peirce 1958: 389).

4. "As it is in itself, a sign is either of the nature of an appearance, when I call it a QUALISIGN; or secondly, it is an individual object or event, when I call it a SINSIGN (the syllable *sin* being the first syllable of *semel, simul, singular*, etc.); or thirdly, it is of the nature of a general type, when I call it a LEGISIGN. As we use the term 'word' in most cases, saying that 'the' is one 'word' and 'an' is a second 'word,' a 'word' is a legisign. But when we say of a page in a book that it has 250 'words' upon it, of which twenty are 'the's,' the 'word' is a sinsign. A sinsign so embodying a legisign, I term a 'replica' of the legisign" (1958: 391).

5. ". . . the word or sign which man uses is man himself. For, as the fact that every thought is a sign, taken in conjunction with the fact that life is a train of thought, proves that man is a sign; so that every thought is an EXTERNAL sign that proves that man is an external sign" (Peirce 1958: 71).

6. "Everything in which we take the least interest creates in us its particular emotion, however slight this emotion may be. This emotion is a sign and a predicate of the thing" (Peirce 1958: 67).

7. Here Saussure refers to Naville (1888: 104).

8. This idea and the term are already found in a handwritten note in Saussure's 1846 manuscript, published in Godel (1957: 46 and cf. 37).

9. Material impediments (fog) can require additional methods, auditory signals instead of visual ones, for example, but these temporary expedients do not change the normal conditions.

10. This point will be developed elsewhere.

11. Personally speaking, it seems hardly useful or even possible to burden these pages with a discussion of previous theories. The informed reader will see, in particular, what separates us from Louis Hjelmslev on an essential point. He defines *semiotics* as "a hierarchy, any of whose components admits of a further analysis into classes defined by mutual relations, so that any of these classes admits of an analysis into derivates defined by mutual mutation" (1963: 106). Such a definition will only be admissible if we totally adhere to the principles of glossematics. The considerations of the same author (1963: 109) on the place of language in semiotic structures, on the limits between the semiotic and the non-semiotic, reflect a completely temporary and still imprecise position. We can only approve the invitation to study the diverse semiotic disciplines from a similar point of view:

> it seems fruitful and necessary to establish a common point of view for a large number of disciplines, from the study of literature, art, and music, and general history, all the way to logistics and mathematics, so that from this common point of view these sciences are concentrated around a linguistically defined setting of problems (1963: 108).

However, this vast program remains a mere wish so long as we have not elaborated the theoretical bases for a comparison among the systems. That is what we are attempting to do here. More recently, Charles Morris (1964: 62) restricts himself to noting that for a number of linguists whose names he cites, linguistics is a part of semiotics, but he does not define the situation of language in this relationship.

12. Roland Harweg (1968: 273) verifies that "the sign theoretic approach is inadequate for the study of music, for the only thing it can provide with regard to it are negative statements—'negative' taken in a logical, not in an evaluative sense. All it can state may be comprised in the statement that music is NOT a

significational-representational institution as is language." This verification, however, lacks the support of theoretical formulation. The problem which we are discussing is precisely that of the intersemiotic validity of the notion of "sign."

13. Mieczyslaw Wallis (1964, 1966) makes useful observations on iconic signs, especially in medieval art, where he discerns a "vocabulary," and rules of "syntax." Surely, we can recognize in medieval sculpture a certain iconic repertory which corresponds to certain religious themes, to certain theological or moral teachings. But these are conventional messages, produced in an equally conventional topology where figures occupy symbolic places consistent with familiar representations. In addition, the figurative scenes are the iconic transposition of narratives or of parables; they reproduce an initial verbalization. The real semiological problem, which to our knowledge has not yet been formulated, would be to investigate *how* this transposition of a verbal statement into an iconic representation is carried out, what are the possible correspondences from one system to another and in what measure this confrontation could be pursued up to the ascertainment of the correspondences between distinct *signs*.

14. The possibility of extending semiological categories to pictorial techniques, and particularly to films, is discussed in an instructive manner by Christian Metz (1968). J. L. Scheffer (1969) inaugurates a semiological "reading" of painting and proposes an analysis of it similar to that of a "text." This research already shows an awakening of an original reflection on the fields and categories of nonlinguistic semiology.

15. Cf. Panofsky (1957: 104 ff.). In his translation of Erwin Panofsky's *Gothic Architecture and Scholasticism*, Pierre Bourdieu cites the homologies indicated by R. Marichal between writing and Gothic architecture (Panofsky 1967: 152).

16. We treat this relationship in more detail elsewhere (see Benveniste 1974: 91–102).

17. This distinction was proposed for the first time at the inaugural session of the 13th Congress of Societies for the Investigation of the Philosophy of the French Language, held in Geneva, 3 September 1966. The fruit of this analysis appears as "The levels of linguistic analysis" (Benveniste 1971: 85–100). In order to better emphasize the distinction, we would have preferred to choose terms less alike than *semiotics* and *semantics*, since both assume a technical meaning here. It was necessary, however, that both evoke the notion of *sema* to which both are effectively, although differently, connected. This terminological question should not inconvenience those who are willing to consider the entire perspective of our analysis.

REFERENCES

Benveniste, Émile. 1971. *Problems in General Linguistics*, translated by Mary Elizabeth Meek. Coral Gables, Fla.: University of Miami Press.
——. 1974. *Problèmes de linguistique générale*. Paris: Gallimard.
Godel, Robert. 1957. *Les Sources manuscrites du* Cours de linguistique générale *de F. de Saussure*. Geneva: Droz.
——. 1966. "Current trends in linguistics." *Theoretical Foundations*.
Harweg, Roland. 1968. "Language and music, an immanent sign theoretic approach." *Foundations of Language* 4.
Hjelmslev, Louis. 1963. *Prolegomena to a Theory of Language*, translated by Francis Whitfield. Madison: University of Wisconsin Press.
Metz, Christian. 1968. *Essais sur la signification au cinéma*. Paris: Klincksieck.

Morris, Charles. 1964. *Signification and Significance*. Cambridge, Mass.: MIT Press.

Naville, Adrien. 1888. *De la classification des sciences*. Geneva: H. Georg Bale.

Panofsky, Erwin. 1957. *Gothic Architecture and Scholasticism*. London: Meridian.

——. 1967. *Architecture gothique et pensée scolastique*, translated by Pierre Bourdieu. Paris: Minuit.

Peirce, Charles S. 1958. *Selected Writings*, edited by Philip Wiener. New York: Dover.

de Saussure, Ferdinand. 1966. *Course in General Linguistics*, translated by Wade Baskin. New York: McGraw-Hill.

——. 1957. *Les Cahiers F. De Saussure*, 15.

Sheffer, Jean Louis. 1969. *Scénographie d'un tableau*. Paris: Klincksieck.

Wallis, Mieczyslaw. 1964. "Medieval art as a language." *Actes du 5ᵉ Congrès International d'Esthétique*, Amsterdam.

——. 1966. "La Notion du champ sémantique et son application à la théorie de l'art." *Sciences de l'art*, special issue.

UMBERTO ECO

In its representational function, language as a system of symbols—
that is, conventional meaning-giving devices—gives rise to articulate
meanings through grasping significant units and relations in the field of
experience. Now the distinction between literal and "figured" discourse
or sense, which is the focus of Tzvetan Todorov's helpful manual on *Theories of the Symbol* (Ithaca, N.Y.: Cornell University Press, 1982), is one
of the most ancient and problematical of all distinctions and the paradigmatic example of figured discourse has always been metaphorical discourse. Umberto Eco's essay addresses—from an explicitly semiotic
point of view—this issue, which has been extensively and practically exhaustively discussed in an enormous literature. It not only deals with the
processes by which metaphorical senses are generated but also illustrates
the key principles of Eco's attempted synthesis of semiotic theory.

In a famous section of his *Fundamentals of Language* (written in collaboration with Morris Halle), Jakobson had made a fundamental distinction between metaphor, which is based on selection and similarity,
and metonymy, which is based on combination and contiguity. Ever since
Aristotle, metaphorical denomination has been thought to be based on
some grasp of resemblance or similarity between objects and events
which otherwise might differ profoundly but which, in the case at hand,
share a common "property." Metonymy, another form of denomination,
relied upon connections between units whether of a spatial, temporal, or
other nature. As Jakobson put it in *Fundamentals of Language* "a competition between both devices, metonymic and metaphoric, is manifest in
any symbolic process, be it intrapersonal or social" (94–95). In fact, the
bipolar structure of language or other semiotic systems for that matter—
that is, the opposition between similarity and contiguity—is labeled by
Jakobson a "dichotomy," and he claims that it "appears to be of primal
significance and consequence for all verbal behavior and for human behavior in general" (93).

Now the distinctive thesis of Eco's essay is that metaphor, by reason of
its being embedded in a global semantic field, one of the key notions of his
semiotic theory, is actually based on a subjacent chain of metonymies.

His goal is to uncover "the real linguistic mechanisms" in metaphor and to show how metaphor itself illustrates the process of unlimited semiosis, the continual generation of signs and senses that Peirce also made the touchstone of his semiotic theory. On this account any metaphor, which "institutes" a resemblance between the two or more semantic spaces that it is fusing, would be definable only through the metonymic chains of association in which it is embedded, in effect, an infinite chain of interpretants. The implication of such a position is that metaphorical expressions are already latent in the expressive possibilities of the global semantic field. "A metaphor can be invented because language, in its process of unlimited semiosis, constitutes a multidimensional network of metonymies, each of which is explained by a cultural convention rather than by an original resemblance" and thus a metaphor is supplied with a "subjacent network of arbitrarily stipulated contiguities." The contiguities can be between signifiers, between signifieds, in the code, in the co-text, and in the referent, each possibility being examined by Eco.

Eco's primary presupposition or premise (here and also in *A Theory of Semiotics*) is that metaphor must be founded on autonomously semiotic terms and not on any analogy or presumed resemblance between the referents, and thus his analysis focuses on the other types of contiguity. The seeming fusion of semantic spheres through an original creative act of grasping is really, so argues Eco, a "ratiocination that traverses the paths of the semantic labyrinth in a hurry and, in its haste, loses the sense of their rigid structure." This semantic labyrinth is the global semantic field, which Eco has constructed using as his model Ross M. Quillian's notion of a "semantic memory." Through a wide-ranging selection of examples, ranging from puns to poetry, Eco tries to establish the probability of his thesis.

Although Eco is concerned with metaphor quite generally and not with metaphor in its predominantly aesthetic sense, it may nevertheless be asked whether Eco's semiotic model of metaphor is the only possible semiotic model and whether indeed he has seen the very real connections between perception and metaphor. On Eco's reckoning, factual judgments operate "from the exterior of language" while metaphor "draws the idea of a possible connection *from the interior* of the circle of unlimited semiosis, even if the new connection restructures the circle itself in its structuring connections," that is, "in the current game of couplings." Karl Bühler, who saw quite clearly the intimate connections between perception and semiosis, though in a rather different way from Peirce (and even Eco), exploited rather the model of binocular vision where two images are fused into one perceived object. The resulting perceptual space is then the resultant of two component spaces. Bühler wanted to show that in metaphor the same thing occurs and that also in the linguistic realm we have to have recourse to real abstractive powers, powers of discrimination that are fundamentally akin to what are described in Gestalt theory of perception. It is true that there is always a clash—Beardsley's famous "metaphorical twist"—between the various semantic spaces that are fused in a metaphor, but Eco runs the risk of leaving the fusion groundless except for saying that it is latent in the code. This position borders on a version of nominalism and parallels that of Nelson Goodman who likewise, for different reasons, rejects the quest for grounds.

It is true that "metaphor is born from an internal disturbance of semiosis," but if, as Eco has himself insisted in his *A Theory of Semiotics*, semiosis comprises the whole of mental and conscious life, there seems no reason to exclude perception itself, with its grasp of structural similarities and resemblances, from functioning, along with the heuristic dynamism of the global semantic field, as one of the essential determinants of the metaphorical apprehension of the world. Metaphorical apprehension would demand the cooperation of both domains and the principle of semiotic closure would have to be appropriately modified to include perception itself as an interpretative and semiotic process. But these are matters to ponder and discuss when one reads Eco's profound and stimulating essay which not only limns essential contours of the metaphorical process but also outlines central features of semiotics' contributions to semantics in general.

Eco's mature position on semiotics is to be found in his *A Theory of Semiotics* (Bloomington: Indiana University Press, 1976). *The Role of the Reader: Explorations in the Semiotics of Texts* (Bloomington: Indiana University Press, 1979) offers another handy way into Eco's semiotic framework. To follow up the semiotic approach to metaphor the best places to begin are the many essays by Paul Ricoeur, which combine philosophical rigor with amazing synthetic power. See his *The Rule of Metaphor*, translated by Robert Czerny with Kathleen McLauglin and John Costello, S.J., and *Interpretation Theory: Discourse and the Surplus of Meaning* (Fort Worth, Texas: Texas Christian University Press, 1976). Nelson Goodman also develops a very provocative theory of metaphor in his *Languages of Art* (Indianapolis: Hackett, 1976 [first published 1968]). See also the important and helpful collection *Philosophical Perspectives on Metaphor*, edited by Mark Johnson (Minneapolis: University of Minnesota Press, 1981), which contains some of the most important materials of metaphor, especially Ricoeur's spectacular essay, "The Metaphorical Process as Cognition, Imagination, and Feeling." These materials, with their own bibliographies, will lead one right into the heart of the theory of metaphor.

The Semantics of Metaphor

UMBERTO ECO

1. *Foreword*

If a code allowed us only to generate semiotic judgments, all linguistic systems would serve to enunciate exclusively that which has already been determined by the system's conventions: each and every utterance (*énoncé*) would be—even though through a series of mediations—tautological. On the contrary, however, codes allow us to enunciate events that the code did not anticipate as well as *metasemiotic* judgments that call into question the legitimacy of the code itself.

If all codes were as simple and univocal as Morse code, there would be no problem. It is true that a great deal which the code cannot anticipate can be said with Morse code; it is equally true that one can transmit in Morse code instructions capable of modifying the code itself. This can occur because Morse code's signifiers take, as the signified, alphabetical signifiers which in turn refer us to that complex system of systems known as language—by language meaning, in this case, the total competence of a speaking subject and thus the system of semantic systems as well, that is, the total form of the content. Yet it is precisely this sort of competence, not entirely analyzable, which we have decided to call 'code' as well, not for the sake of simple analogy but in order to broaden the scope of the term.[1]

How can it be, then, that this code, which in principle ought to have structured the speaking subject's entire cultural system, is able to generate both factual messages which refer to original experiences and, above all, messages which place in doubt the very structure of the code itself?

The fact that the code, in referring to predictable cultural entities, nonetheless allows us to assign new semiotic marks to them, is singular to that feature of the code called 'rule-governed creativity'. That the code allows for factual judgments poses no difficulties either; the very nature of the code, which is arbitrary, explains how it can, by manipulating signifiers, refer to new signifieds produced in response to new experiences. It also explains why, once issued, factual judgments can be integrated into

"Semantica della metafora," in *Le forme del contenuto* (Milan: Bompiani, 1971). This chapter is a revised version of the Italian original, translated by John Snyder, and is reprinted from *The Role of the Reader* by Umberto Eco, Bloomington: Indiana University Press. Copyright ©1979 by Umberto Eco.

the code in such a way as to create new possibilities for semiotic judgment. How, though, does this 'rule-changing creativity' work?

Even prior to the specifically aesthetic usage of language, the first example of such creativity is provided in common speech by the use of different types of metaphors and thus of rhetorical figures. A series of problems that touch on rhetorical devices will allow us to respond to these questions. In the case under consideration we will at present deal with the problem of interaction between metaphoric mechanisms and metonymic mechanisms; to these one can probably ascribe the entire range of tropes, figures of speech, and figures of thought.[2]

The goal of this discussion is to show that each metaphor can be traced back to a subjacent chain of metonymic connections which constitute the framework of the code and upon which is based the constitution of any semantic field, whether partial or (in theory) global. This investigation takes as its point of origin a specific metaphoric substitution located in *Finnegans Wake* and explainable only through the exposure of a metonymic chain beneath the metaphoric level. A second check on a typical Joycean *mot-valise* (which, for the variety and polyvalence of its connotations, assumes a metaphoric value) will uncover, here too, a much more vast and articulate network of metonymies that have been wrapped in silence or revealed in another part of the work.

Finnegans Wake, at this point, presents itself as an excellent model of a Global Semantic System (since it posits itself, quite explicitly, as the Ersatz of the historical universe of language) and confronts us with a methodological exigency of the sort found in a study of general semantics proposing to illuminate the ways in which language can generate metaphors. The conclusion is that the mechanism of metaphor, reduced to that of metonymy, relies on the existence (or on the hypothesis of existence) of partial semantic fields that permit two types of metonymic relation: (i) the *codified* metonymic relation, inferable from the very structure of the semantic field; (ii) the *codifying* metonymic relation, born when the structure of a semantic field is culturally experienced as deficient and reorganizes itself in order to produce another structure. Relations of type (i) imply *semiotic judgments*, whereas relations of type (ii) imply *factual judgments*.[3]

The usefulness of such an analysis, which traces each metaphoric substitution back to a metonymic chain founded on codified semantic fields, is as follows: any explanation which restores language to metaphor or which shows that, in the domain of language, it is possible to invent metaphors returns to an analogical (and hence metaphorical) explanation of language and presumes an idealist doctrine of linguistic creativity. If, on the other hand, the explanation of the creativity of language (presupposed by the existence of metaphors) is based on metonymic chains based in turn on identifiable semantic structures, it is then possible to bring the problem of creativity back to a description of language which depends upon a model susceptible to translation in binary terms. In other words, it is possible (even though for experimental purposes and only for limited parts of the Global Semantic System) to construct an automaton capable of generating and understanding metaphors.

A last important qualification: this study is concerned not only with poetic metaphor but with metaphor in general. The majority of our messages, in everyday life or in academic philosophy, are lined with metaphors. The problem of the creativity of language emerges, not only in the privileged domain of poetic discourse, but each time that language—in order to designate something that culture has not yet assimilated (and this 'something' may be external or internal to the circle of semiosis)— must *invent* combinatory possibilities or semantic couplings not anticipated by the code.

Metaphor, in this sense, appears as a new semantic coupling not preceded by any stipulation of the code (but which generates a new stipulation of the code). In this sense, as we shall see, it assumes a value in regard to communication and, indirectly, to knowledge.

What remains to be defined is the particular status of its cognitive function.

This study is centered, therefore, on the semantic aspect of metaphor. The semantic aspect does not explain how metaphor can also have an aesthetic function. The aesthetic nature of a given metaphor is also produced by contextual elements or by the articulation of supersegmental features. This means, then, that, if on the one hand our study considers metaphor capable of segmenting in different ways the substance of content to the point of transforming it into a new form of content, on the other hand it does not explain by what segmentations of the substance of expression a given metaphor can obtain aesthetic effect. In other words, one's interest lies in knowing in what sense the fact of saying that the eyes of Leopardi's Silvia are /*fuggitivi*/ (fugitive) increases (in legitimizing the operation) the adjectival possibilities of the Italian language. It is not my purpose in this text to establish how and why the position of /*fuggitivi*/ (fugitive) after /*ridenti*/ (laughing) or the use of /*fuggitivi*/ instead of /*fuggenti*/ (fleeing) or /*fuggiaschi*/ (runaway) imparts to Leopardi's metaphor the aesthetic impact with which it is generally credited.

Not by chance have I chosen *Finnegans Wake* (hereafter *FW*) as our field of inquiry: as a literary work it produces sufficiently violent metaphors without interruption or reservation; at the same time, in proposing itself as a model of language in general, it focuses our attention specifically on semantic values. In other words, since *FW* is itself a metaphor for the process of unlimited semiosis, I have chosen it for metaphoric reasons as a field of inquiry in order to cover certain itineraries of knowledge more quickly. After this test we will be able to pass on to a more technical discourse that touches on the real linguistic mechanisms outside of the pilot text.

2. *Mandrake makes a gesture*

In part 3, chapter 3 of *FW*, Shaun, in the form of Yawn, undergoes a trial in the course of which the Four Old Men bombard him with questions. The Old Men say to Shaun: "Now, fix on the little fellow on my eye, Minucius Mandrake, and follow my little psychosinology, poor armer in slingslang."[4] James Atherton, who has identified an enormous number of bibliographical references hidden in *FW*, recognizes in this passage a clear reference to a father of the church, Minucius Felix, an author whom Joyce perhaps knew.[5] But as for the meaning of /Mandrake/, he simply gives up: "I do not understand the allusion." The English meaning of /mandrake/ is a clue that only leads us to a dead end.

Probably Atherton had not thought of the world of comic strips (a world which Joyce—as Richard Ellman informs us—knew very well through the daily comics in the newspapers of the time); otherwise, he would have realized that Mandrake could be Mandrake the Magician, the famous character of Lee Falk and Phil Davis. Joyce, who in *FW* resorted to cartoon characters such as Mutt and Jeff, for instance, could not have been ignorant of this character. Let us hypothesize that the Mandrake of the text is the Mandrake of the comic strips and see what comes of it.

Mandrake is a master of prestidigitation, a hypnotist, an illusionist. With a simple gesture (the recurrent phrase is "Mandrake makes a gesture"), his eyes glued to those of his adversary, Mandrake forces him to see nonexistent situations, to mistake the pistol in his hand for a banana, to hear objects talking. Mandrake the Magician is a master of persuasion, a master of diabolic tricks (even if he uses his 'white' magic for good); in short, he is a 'devil's advocate'. In this regard it is interesting to note that Minucius Felix, too, was an advocate, professionally speaking (*Octavius* is a harangue in favor of Christianity), and an apologist father, whose historic function was to convince the Gentiles of the truth of the Christian faith.

From this point on, the relation between the two characters, in the interior of the Joycean context, becomes crystal clear.

At issue in the passage under consideration is the struggle between the ancient Irish church and the Catholic church, and the Four Old Men specifically ask Shaun whether or not he is a Roman Catholic. However, in a typical Joycean pun, they ask him if he is "roman cawthrick." Now, /to caw/ is the crow's cry and, even if we put to one side the fact that Joyce, in Trieste, perhaps learned the anticlerical sense of the word /cornacchia/, 'crow' (used in Italy to designate priests), there is still the problem of this

/thrick/ which deforms (in order to echo one of the phonemes of 'catholic') the verb /to trick/. That Minucius Mandrake (alias Shaun) is a *trickster* is repeated several times in the context; for example, we find /*Mr. Trickpat*/.

Here let us put aside the other fascinating clue, one that could lead us to the character of the 'practical joker' in many primitive sagas, the *Schelm* or Trickster God (and we don't know if Joyce knew about him) that could trace Shaun back to archetypes of the gnome-like joker, such as Till Eulenspiegel. Let us only consider for the moment, without dealing with other problems, that Shaun has been accused of being a *trickster*. When he is called /Minucius Mandrake/ (afterwards we will see why), he—Catholic priest, expert in tricks and other persuasions more or less occult, crafty rhetorician, master of chicanery—must submit to a typical Dantean *contrappasso*. As an advocate he must undergo a trial; as a hypnotist he is asked to fix his eyes on the eyes of his interrogator. In this manner his art is neutralized and turned back against itself. The magical gesticulation (the gesture which presumably accompanies the words "Look at me with your eyes!"), too, is turned against itself, and the following gesticulation is ascribed to him: "Again I am deliciated by the picaresqueness of your irmages"—where the root /arm/ (the arm that makes the gesture) is inserted in the key word /image/, which is found at the base of all illusion.[6]

It is therefore reasonable to consider him, whether Minucius or Mandrake, as a metaphoric substitution in the place of something else, that is, the series of attributes and faults proper to Shaun.

But at this stage it is necessary to verify the credibility of this interpretation and the mechanism of this substitution.

3. *Felix the Cat*

The first version of the passage under consideration dates from 1924. In this version the name Mandrake does not appear.[7] The reason seems (to me) simple enough: the comic strip character appeared for the first time in 1934. And, in fact, the aforementioned passage was revised and expanded between 1936 and 1939. Thus the origin of the metaphoric 'vehicle' is plausible. But why couple Mandrake with Minucius? In other words, from the moment in which they first appear together in the text, they seem to us eminently well matched. But how did the idea of matching them come about? Once matched they seem to cause a short circuit of associations, but we know that for the most part the short circuit arises *a posteriori* and does not motivate the act of association. Minucius is like Mandrake: the coupling institutes between the two an elisional similitude which generates a metaphor (in which vehicle and tenor are exceptionally co-present and interchangeable).

But why specifically Minucius and Mandrake? The comic strip itself supplies the key which allows us to give a new answer (which in turn reinforces our original hypothesis). Minucius is also called Felix. And Felix is another typical comic strip character, Pat Sullivan's cat, appearing in the daily comics from 1923 and thus probably known to Joyce.

Here, then, is the mechanism subjacent to the metaphoric substitution: Minucius refers by contiguity to Felix, Felix refers by contiguity (belonging to the same universe of comic strips) to Mandrake. Once the middle term has fallen, there remains a coupling that does not seem justified by any contiguity and thus appears to be metaphoric. The always possible substitution between Minucius and Mandrake is attributable no longer to the possibility of passing from one to the other through a series of successive choices but to the fact that they seem to possess characteristics which are 'similar' (advocates, rhetoricians, and so on) and thus 'analogous'.

This example explains to us how the metaphor came about, but not why it functions. In point of fact, the reader grasps the analogies between Minucius and Mandrake and does not depend upon the existence of a third term. However, it could be said that he depends upon an extremely long series of third terms that exist in the general context of the book, some of which we have already examined: *trickster, arm, image,* and so on. We should therefore be able to show that each metaphor produced in *FW* is, in the last analysis, comprehensible because the entire book, read in different directions, actually furnishes the metonymic chains that justify it. We can test this hypothesis on the atomic element of *FW, the pun,* which constitutes a particular form of metaphor founded on subjacent chains of metonymies.

4. *Morphology of the meandertale*

The pun constitutes a forced contiguity between two or more words: *sang* plus *sans* plus *glorians* plus *riant* makes 'Sanglorians'.

It is a contiguity made of reciprocal elisions, whose result is an ambiguous deformation; but, even in the form of fragments, there are words that nonetheless are related to one another. This *forced contiguity* frees a series of possible readings—hence interpretations—which lead to an acceptance of the term as a metaphoric *vehicle* of different *tenors*. At this point the lexemes (or the lexematic fragments) thrust into forced contiguity acquire a kind of natural kinship and often become mutually substitutable. However, in the pun the metaphoric substitution assumes a particular type of status: vehicles coexist with tenors—for example, 'Jungfraud messonge': 'Jung' plus 'Freud' plus 'young' plus 'fraud' plus 'Jungfrau'; message plus *songe* plus *mensonge*.

All the terms present stand in a relationship of *mutual substitution*.

This is the case with 'Minucius Mandrake' and also with a pun such as the one mentioned above: the reading 'young message' replaces 'virginal fraud', and vice versa. Each term is at the same time vehicle and tenor, while the entire pun is a multiple metaphor. At other times the forced coexistence does not imply possible substitution; think, for instance, of 'cawthrick'. A shadow of predicability remains, however, since one term appears to qualify the other (the crow is a trickster himself), and thus it can be said that the pun nevertheless decides the fate of future reciprocal substitution affecting the two terms in a position of forced contiguity.

One can object to our discourse that, if Jung and Freud or the crow and the trickster are placed in a position of contiguity, it is because they already stood in a prior analogical (and thus metaphoric) relation to each other.

Just as in the quarrel between analogic and digital, the quarrel between metaphor and metonym can generate a flight to infinity, in which one moment establishes the other, and vice versa.[8]

We can in theory distinguish between two types of puns, in accordance with the reasons that established the contiguity of the terms:

contiguity by resemblance of signifiers: for example, 'nightiness' contains 'mightiness' by phonetic analogy ('m/n'); 'slipping' contains, for the same reasons, 'sleep' and 'slip';
contiguity by resemblance of signifieds: 'scherzarade', for the playful analogies between '*scherzo*' and 'charade' (sememes in which 'game' would be the archisememe); but it is also true that the origin could lie in the simple phonetic similarity between /*cha*/ and /*za*/. One could then ask if the allusion to 'Scheerazade' is born first from the phonetic similarity or from the semantic similarity (the tale of Scheherazade as game and enigma, and so on).

As one can see, the two types refer to each other, even as contiguity seems to refer to the instituting resemblance, and vice versa.

In truth, though, the force of the pun (and of every successful and inventive metaphor) consists in the fact that prior to it no one had grasped the resemblance. Prior to 'Jungfraud' there was no reason to suspect a relationship between Freud, psychoanalysis, fraud, lie, and lapsus (*linguae* or *calami*). The resemblance becomes necessary only after the contiguity is realized. Actually (*FW* itself is the proof), it is enough to find the means of rendering two terms phonetically contiguous for the resemblance to impose itself; at best, the similitude of signifiers (at least in the place of encounter) is that which precedes, and the similitude of signifieds is a consequence of it.

The exploration of the field of *FW* as a contracted model of the global semantic field is at once useful and derisive. It is useful because nothing can show us better than a reading of *FW* that, even when semantic kinship seems to precede the coercion to coexist in the pun, in point of fact a network of subjacent contiguities makes necessary the resemblance which was presumed to be spontaneous. It is derisive because, everything being given in the text already, it is difficult to discover the 'before' and the 'after.' But, before arriving at any theoretical conclusions, let us make an incursion into the text, with all the risks that that involves.

Let us take the lexeme /Neanderthal/ (not found as such in the text) and see what mechanisms led the author to modify it into /meandertale/. Naturally, we could also follow the inverse process: we could take the pun found in the text and trace it back to its original components. But the very fact that we can conceive of two possible courses indicates that, in this case (as opposed to /Minucius Mandrake/), the two moments coincide: it was possible to invent the pun because it is possible to read it; language, as a cultural base, should be able to allow both operations. It should be noted also that, for reasons of a simple operative convention, we will start from one of the component words of the pun in order to deduce the other; probably another one would serve our purposes equally well. But this is the very characteristic of a language considered as the place of unlimited semiosis (as for Peirce), where each term is explained by other terms and where each one is, through an infinite chain of interpretants, potentially explainable by all the others.[9]

Our experiment thus has two senses: first, to see if, from a point outside Joyce's linguistic universe, we can enter into the universe; then, departing from a point internal to that universe, to see whether or not we can connect, through multiple and continuous pathways, as in a garden where the paths fork, all the other points. It will then come down to defining whether or not this entrance and this traversability are based on simple relationships of contiguity. For the moment, however, we will attempt to reason in terms—however imperfectly defined—of 'association' (phonetic and semantic).

Let us take the word /Neanderthal/. In the following schema we will notice how the lexeme generates, through a phonetic association, three other lexemes: /meander/, /tal/ (in German, 'valley'), and /tale/, which combine to form the pun /meandertale/. In the associative course, however, intermediate modes create themselves from terms that are all present in the text of *FW*. Here the associations can be of either a phonetic or a semantic type.

It should be noted that all the lexemes mentioned here are only those which are to be found in the text of *FW*. The same psycholinguistic test might have generated, in another subject, other equally plausible responses. Here we have limited ourselves to this type of response, not only because it is the Joycean one (in which case the experiment would only seek to understand how the pun is born, not how it is read),

but also for reasons of economy and, in addition, because the reader of
FW, controlled by the text, is in fact led into a game of associations that
were previously suggested to him by the co-text (which means that every
text, however 'open' it is, is constituted, not as the place of all possibilities, but rather as the field of oriented possibilities).

The interconnections show, moreover, the way in which every lexeme
can in this turn become the archetype of an associative series which
would lead to the recuperation, sooner or later, of the associative termi-
nals of another lexeme. The whole diagram (Figure 1) has a purely orien-
tative value, in the sense that it impoverishes the associations in terms of
both number and dimension: a bidimensional graph cannot reproduce
the game of interconnections produced when lexemes are brought into
contact with their respective sememes. We should consider as multidimensional, not only the game of interconnections produced in the global
semantic system of real language, but also the game of that Ersatz field—
the literary work, the text (in our case *FW*, more open to interconnections than are many other texts and thus more fit for experimentation).

If we pass from the diagram to Joyce's text, we can see how all the
associations have been developed. They actually produce the puns which
define the book. The book is a /slipping beauty/ (and thus a beautiful
sleeper who, in sleeping, generates lapsus by semantic slippages, in remembering a flaw and so on), a /jungfraud's messongebook/ (where, to
the previously cited associations, is added that of a 'message'), a labyrinth in which is found /a word as cunningly hidden in its maze of confused drapery as a fieldmouse in a nest of coloured ribbons/, and thus at
last a /Meandertale/.

The pun-lexeme /meanderthaltale/ becomes, in the end, the metaphoric substitution for everything that can be said about the book and
that is said by the associative chains indicated in the diagram.

5. The games of the Swedish stall-bars

Once again we can foresee the objection that can be made to the diagram under consideration. The associative sequences, except for the first
quadripartition, have a semantic character. The sememes associate among
themselves through semic identity. Through a componential investigation
it can be proved that all the associated sememes have in common a series
of *semes*.[10] To explain the association by a partial identity of meaning
means once again to explain it by similitude or by analogy. Thus the diagram would confirm the fact that, at the roots of the pun's forced contiguity, previous resemblances are found.

However, in its historic development, semantic theory has provided a
series of explanations capable of capsizing our problem once again. If we
reread the associative sequences, we see that each one of them could be

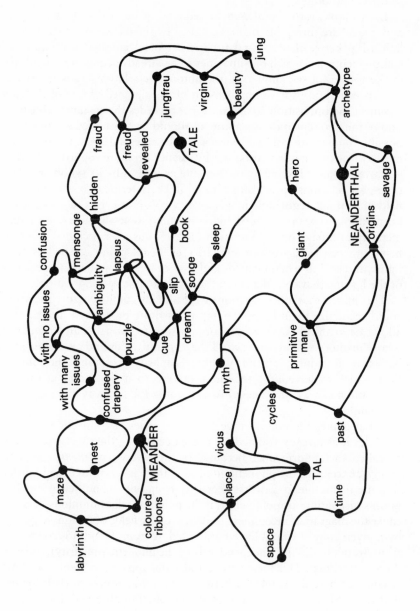

constructed in retracing itself to a 'field of notions' accepted in a given culture or to one of the typical linguistic crossroads theorized by Trier, Matoré, and others.

Let us look, for example, at the sequence generated by /Tal/: 'space' and 'place' are the archisememes codified by the dictionary itself; the relationship between space and time is a typical antonymic relation by complementarity, which one imagines to be already acquired by a culture in the form of a semantic axis (the antonymic relationship is the structural precondition for comprehension of the signified of one of the two lexemes: the opposition /space vs. time/ precedes the semantic constitution of the two sememes; the antonym should be considered as one of the possible immediate connotations of the lexeme and thus as one of its most curious semantic marks; not by chance do more sophisticated dictionaries define a lexeme by its opposite as well as by its synonym). The time-past relationship is also acquired in the interior of a very obvious field of notions, registrable in advance. Vico's past-cycles relationship is born out of a type of classbook-like contiguity, somewhat like one's visual memory of a page out of Monarch Notes. Thus all associations, before being grasped as identity or similarity of meaning, are grasped as contiguity internal to semantic fields and axes or to a componential spectrum of the lexeme that considers even the most peripheral connotations.

This means that all connections were already codified before the artist could recognize them by pretending to institute or discover them. This allows us to affirm that it is in theory possible to construct an automaton whose memory would conserve all the semantic fields and axes which we have just mentioned; it is thus within its capacity to establish the connections which we have indicated (or, as it were, to attempt to make others; this could mean writing a new *FW* or reading *FW* in a way different from our own).

What makes the pun creative is not the series of connections (which precedes it as already codified); it is the decision of the short circuit, the so-called metaphoric one. Because, in fact, between /mensonge/ and /songe/, except for the phonetic similarity, there is no contiguity; in order to unite them, a leap was first necessary from one to another of the diagram's discontinuous points. But, if the points are discontinuous, it is because the diagram is incomplete. A review of the fields of notions acquired by a given culture would have rapidly led us from /Freud/ to /songe/, or from /fraud/ to /Freud/ (independently of the phonetic similarity), or from /Freud/ to /Jung/. This means that, under the apparent metaphoric short circuit (for here the similarity between two senses seems to click for the first time), there is an uninterrupted web of culturalized contiguity that our hypothetical automaton might be able to traverse through a sequence of binary choices.

A metaphor can be invented because language, in its process of unlimited semiosis, constitutes a multidimensional network of metonymies, each of which is explained by a cultural convention rather than by an original resemblance. The imagination would be incapable of inventing (or recognizing) a metaphor if culture, under the form of a possible structure of the Global Semantic System, did not provide it with the subjacent network of arbitrarily stipulated contiguities. The imagination is nothing other than a ratiocination that traverses the paths of the semantic labyrinth in a hurry and, in its haste, loses the sense of their rigid structure. The 'creative' imagination can perform such dangerous exercises only because there exist 'Swedish stall-bars' which support it and which suggest movements to it, thanks to their grill of parallel and perpendicular bars.[11] The Swedish stall-bars are Language [*langue*]. On them plays Speech [*parole*], performing the competence.

6. Rhetoric of the Swedish stall-bars

A semiotic explanation of different rhetorical figures can be attempted through the development of the theory of interpretants as represented in the Model Q.[12]

Suppose a code is formed that posits a system of paradigmatic relations of the following sort:

$$A \quad vs. \quad B \quad vs. \quad C \quad vs. \quad D$$
$$\downarrow \qquad \downarrow \qquad \downarrow \qquad \downarrow$$
$$k \qquad y \qquad z \qquad k$$

where the horizontal line constitutes a paradigm of different sememes and the vertical correlation constitutes relations from sememe to seme or semantic mark (k is a semantic mark of A; obviously, according to the Model Q, k can become in its turn a sememe k to be analyzed through other semantic marks, among which even a could be considered).

To name A by k is a case of synecdoche (the veil for the ship, *pars pro toto*). Since k could even be the seme «crown» characterizing the sememe «king», to name A by k can also be a case of metonymy (in traditional terms; in the terms of our present approach, such a difference tends to disappear). But k happens to be also a seme of another sememe, namely, D. Therefore, by an amalgamation through k, one can substitute A with /D/. This is a case of metaphor. A long white neck being a property both of a beautiful woman and of a swan, the woman can be metaphorically substituted for by the swan. Apparently, one entity is in the place of the other by virtue of a mutual resemblance. But the resemblance is due to the fact that in the code there exist already fixed relations of substitution which, in some way or other, link the substitute entities to those substituted for.

Now suppose that there exists a practice of language in which A is *ha-*

bitually substituted for k. In this case k becomes, by convention, one of the possible connotations of A. The metaphor, once it has become usual, enters as part of the code and in the long run can fix itself in a *catachresis* ('the neck of the bottle', 'the leg of the table'). The fact remains, however, that the substitution took place because of the existence, in the code, of connections and therefore contiguities. This would lead us to state that the metaphor rests on a metonymy. If Model Q is based upon unlimited semiosis, every sign, sooner or later, must depend upon a connection anticipated by the code. Obviously there can be produced connections of which no one had ever thought. We then have an ambiguous message. The aesthetic function of language seeks to create connections which as of yet do not exist; thus it also seeks to enrich the code's possibilities. Even in this case metaphoric substitution can rely upon metonymic practice.

7. *The crown and the white collar*

At this point we need to elucidate the terms 'metaphor' and 'metonymy', since it seems that up to now the latter term has been used in a metaphoric sense.

Every theory of metaphor defines this figure as the substitution of one element of language for another (the operation is completely internal to the semiotic circle), but *by virtue of a resemblance between their referents*. It is this necessary recourse to referents (and to their presumed relations of analogy or resemblance) that has prodded us to criticize the notion of metaphor as something that cannot be founded on autonomously semiotic terms. The risk is now that (reconducting every metaphor to a chain of metonymies) even these will demand to be founded on a recourse to referents. In reality, rhetoric—in having recourse to referents—explains metonymy to us. We name the king by the crown only because there is a *factual* contiguity between king and crown (the fact that the king wears a crown is a fact, not a linguistic phenomenon). But then, again, if the fact of naming the crown refers us by force of analogy to the king, it also retransforms the metonymic explanation into an explanation founded on similarity. There is a natural resemblance, due to the habit of contiguity, that pushes for recognition of the king in the crown.

Notice, however, that if by some chance an employee of the property-tax office whom I know wears spectacles, I cannot name, in a figurative discourse, the employees of the property-tax office by spectacles. This contiguity would not be recognizable and, in any case, even if recognized, it would not be sufficient to found the metonymic substitution. It must be that (by recognized and *codified* habit) all (or a large number of) employees of the property-tax office wear spectacles for it to be possible to operate the substitution by contiguity. Now, there was a time when all (or most) of the employees wore white collars on their shirts. This contiguity was codified, and only at that moment was it possible to designate the employees as 'white-collar workers'; even if today there are no employees wearing white collars, one can recognize that this contiguity is capable of founding a metonymic substitution. This is a sign that the contiguity is no longer factual, but semiotic. What matters is, not that in reality some-one wears white collars, but that in a semantic representation of the lexeme /employee/ there exists the connotation «wears white collars».

The contiguity on which the metonymic transposition is founded is thus transformed from factual (empirical) contiguity to *contiguity of code*. The referent no longer carries any weight, and neither does the pos-sibility of recognizing the metonymized term by a natural kinship with the metonymizing term. The kinship is not natural; it is *cultural*. The two terms refer to each other because they are conventionally situated each in the place of the other. The metonymizing term is already part of the se-mantic representation of the metonymized term, as one of its *interpre-tants*. The rhetorical rule presupposes, then, that one can name a lexeme by one of the semantic components of the corresponding sememe. A study of efficient and comprehensible metonymies would lead to the discovery that they employ, as metonymizing, a semantic component that belongs exclusively to one particular lexeme and not another. The mark «male» is also a semantic component of the lexeme /king/, but no one would use /male/ as a metonymy of /king/. /Crown/ is used because *only the king* wears a crown. We can thus imagine a robot constructed in order to recog-nize metonymies, provided that it has been programmed for the following: "replace the metonymizing term with that sememe, unique among the others (or the only one allowed by the context), which possesses it as a semantic component." The correction between parentheses should serve in such cases as 'i veloci legni' (the swift woods); without a doubt, 'di legno' (of wood) enters into the semantic spectrum of many lexemes, but, in a naval context, it is obvious that the lexeme in question is /*nave*/ (ship).

The extreme traversability of the chains we have called 'metonymic' (and it would be better to say 'of contiguity in the code')—chains that allow metaphoric substitutions with leaps which are apparent ones, but which in fact are short circuits of a preestablished path—results from the fact that these chains are already entirely constituted *inside the code* and do not refer to connections attained in the referents. We can then estab-lish that every metonymic connection refers to one of these three types of contiguity:

contiguity in the code: the most common type, it corresponds to some of the examples given in the preceding pages, such as /crown/, /white-collar/, and so on;

contiguity in the co-text: an example could be as follows: "out of the getaway car came some pistol shots; that car had to be silenced" (where the car is substituted for the pistol, and vice versa);

contiguity in the referent: according to what has already been said, this genre of contiguity should be practically nonexistent. However, since there are some special cases, let us see if it is a question of *contiguity through the referent* or *contiguity through the signified* (and thus it can revert back to the two preceding cases of contiguity in the code or contiguity in the co-text).

Let us examine the case of a particular type of lapsus, also studied by psychoanalysis, which is born not out of the comparison of two words but, rather, out of the comparison of two given facts of experience. That is to say, in a situation of lapsus, I can say 'ho colto il morto' (I have picked up the dead body) in the place of 'ho colto il mirto' (I have picked up the myrtle), because I know that a corpse is buried under the myrtle bush (or because I remember a corpse buried under another bush). In this case the contiguity, which would appear to be linguistic, cannot be explained without recourse to the referent. In the same way, one cannot explain the fact that in seeing a dagger an individual has erotic fantasies, unless one knows for certain that he saw his own mother kill her lover with a dagger during intercourse.

This type of contiguity—imposed by some sort of violence done to the code—remains so inexplicable that the need emerges for an 'interpretation' of dreams, until, once the dream is explained, the contiguity is institutionalized and becomes *part of the culture*. In this sense the hermeneutic work of the psychoanalyst, when applied to the contiguity of the referent, is a case of code making and not of code observing.[13]

8. *Language makes a gesture*

Since we suppose that, in the making and unmaking of particular semantic fields, the entire Global Semantic System is never completely structurable (and even if it were, it would not be structured; and even if it were structured, we could not describe it in its globality), we should assume that *only in theory* does each semantic unit refer to all others. In practice there are millions of empty valences and millions of units that *cannot* be connected to the others. To do so would mean to emit factual judgments (of the type 'A is the same as D') that the Global Semantic System can accept only at the cost of exploding.

Let us imagine that the scheme envisaged in section 6 does not anticipate only four terms (A, B, C, D) and two levels of correlated entities but, rather, an infinite number of terms and levels. And let us also imagine that

D is not segregated from A by only four passages (A→k→k→D), but rather by millions of passages. If culture has never made these passages, A and D have never been connected. We can connect them without any good reason (the bad reason being immediately evident) or for reasons as yet difficult to realize, and we can do this either by disturbing or not disturbing the semantic system we rely upon. Let us try to throw a first and tentative light upon this web of intertwined semiotic problems—our attempt aiming only at being a first approach to a much more complex question.

First, what is a 'good' reason to establish a metaphorical connection? Let us distinguish two kinds of successful metaphor, the merely 'acceptable' and the 'rewarding'. A metaphor is (at least) acceptable when its metonymic foundation is immediately (or only after more mediation) evident. The substitution of /sleep/ for «death» constitutes an acceptable metaphor (many semes or marks in common). No one would say that it is 'beautiful'; it is missing the tension, the ambiguity, and the difficulty which are characteristic of the aesthetic message.

Let us suppose, on the other hand, that there is issued a metaphor whose metonymic foundation is not evident—for example, the 'selva oscura' (dark wood) of Dante. In this case the semantic necessity that connects the vehicle (as the signified), which is of a physico-geographical sort, to the moral entity that constitutes the tenor is quite occult—at least to the extent that it allows a series of hermeneutic games aimed at discovering an interpretation, a reliable reading. What is instead immediately apparent? The rhythmico-phonetic necessity in the order of signifiers—in other words, the necessity caused by meter and rhyme, which makes 'reasonable', for reasons of a 'musical' sort, the occurrence of the signifier /selva oscura/ in relation to the signifiers /dura/ (hard) and /paura/ (fear). Faced with one possible, although still unthinkable, relation on the level of the form of content, a clear relation stands out on the level of the form of expression, so that we are led to believe that a relation *should* exist also on the level of the form of content. This metaphor is 'rewarding' because it prefigures a semantic necessity before that necessity has ever been defined and located.

When, though, does it happen that a metaphor is 'deceiving' or 'defaulting'? Whenever a weak necessity on the level of the form of expression corresponds to the incommensurable distance between vehicle and tenor on the level of content, and despite this distance the amount of new knowledge provided is disappointing. Many Baroque metaphors are of this type.

In Artale's sonnet about Mary Magdalen, the fact that her hair is named /fiumi/ (rivers) without a doubt presents a necessity in terms of the form of expression—the rhyme necessarily links /fiumi/ (rivers) to /lumi/ (lights) and /allumi/ (he lights):

L'occhio e la chioma in amorosa arsura
Se' l bagna e 'l terge, avvien ch'amante allumi
Stupefatto il fattor di sua fattura;
Ché il crin s'è un Tago e son due Soli i lumi,
Prodigio tal non rimirò natura:
Bagnar coi Soli e rasciugar coi fiumi.

But this necessity serves only to induce a search for the metonymic connection between rivers and hair. When it is discovered (thanks in part to a preceding revelatory verse, which prepared the metaphor with a similitude), we see that the seme «fluency», which could unify the two sememes, is rather peripheral to those semes characterizing the two sememes in a mutually exclusive sense, since hair in effect is dry and solid and rivers are wet and liquid. It is nonetheless true that—still in the order of content—the semantic necessity of /fiumi/ (rivers) could be reinforced by its opposition to /soli/ (suns), which has replaced /occhi/ (eyes). But, here too, since eyes seem as 'necessarily' connected to /soli/ (suns) as hair is to rivers, two wrongs clearly do not make a right, and two weak and isolated necessities in the form of metaphors do not reinforce the joint necessity of their chiasmatic and oppositional occurrence. This means that, while we ask the form of expression to guarantee the supposed or proposed semantic necessity, we ask the form of content to insure that the necessity, once discovered, will enrich in some manner the knowledge of either the signifieds of the message or the operational possibilities of the code.

As for Mary Magdalen, the facts that her eyes are suns and that her hair is a river do not help us at all to a better understanding of this woman's personality; thus the expressive artifice that led us to discover metaphoric relations at the semantic level seems wasted to us, or deceptive. From this moment on our possibility of using the code no longer seems enriched, because we will rarely find ourselves in a situation that will allow us to reuse a metaphor of this genre. The poetic effect is recognized as null, since in this case poetry seems 'to serve no purpose'. Dante's 'selva oscura', on the other hand, refers us to an open chain of semantic associations whose roots run deep in a symbolic and theologic tradition and which allows us to speak of life, sin, and man's situation on earth. Here is what some have intuitively called 'the universality of poetry': its capacity to provide, in the order of content, alterations that become operative even beyond the concrete occasion which generated the semantic substitution.

Achillini, another eighteenth-century author, provides a different example of 'defaulting' metaphor (from the point of view of content) which, this time, finds no support on the level of expression. But Achillini does not fail because of a too 'distant' connection; on the contrary, he is matching something that our common knowledge has long since matched, and without exciting results. 'Sudate, o fochi, a preparar metalli' (sweat, O fires, to prepare metals), imposes no expressive necessity that justifies the use of the verb 'sudare' (to sweat). One might very well have said, without detracting from the rhyme or the meter, 'bruciate o fochi' (burn, O fires). The whole discourse then displaces itself to the level of content. And here again, even if the subjacent metonymic chain exists and is visible (fire-heat-sweat, the fire which receives as its own seme the effect that it has on whoever is subjected to its action, and so on), it appears as rather contorted, demanding a pathway, a tiresome short circuit that *does not pay* sufficiently well, so much exertion in order to learn what was already known—that fire causes sweat. The reader refuses the invitation to an adventure without worthwhile results, to a linguistic operation that, with the pretense of making language function in a creative direction, actually creates nothing and succeeds only in the realization of a wearisome tautology.

A different series of judgments might be of the sort, 'The chemical composition of hair is similar to that of water; fire secretes, through glands similar to the sweat glands of humans, a sort of liquid with homeostatic functions . . .'. Here we confront a series of *factual* judgments. As has already been said, it is not up to semiotics to establish whether they are true or false, but it is up to semiotics to establish whether or not they are socially acceptable. Many factual judgments seem unacceptable, not because they are false, but rather because to accept them would mean to impose a restructuration of the Global Semantic System or large parts of it. This explains why, under particular historical conditions, physical proof of the truth of certain judgments could not stand up before the social necessity of rejecting these same judgments. Galileo was condemned not for logical reasons (in terms of True or False) but for semiotic reasons—inasmuch as the falsity of his factual judgments is proved by recourse to contrary semiotic judgments of the type 'this does not correspond to what is said in the Bible'.

Nevertheless, it can be the case that unacceptable factual judgments are enunciated in metaphoric form before being enunciated in referential form. For example, whoever before Copernicus used the metaphor 'the peripheral sphere' in order to describe the Earth would have forced the receiver of the message to face the necessity of inferring substitutibility between two sememes which, on the contrary, presented completely opposite semes: the Earth has a seme of centrality and no semes of periphericity (in regard to the solar system). In this case we would find ourselves before a metaphor which, in a confused way, anticipated a restructuration of the future code and which allowed the inference of the possibility of factual judgments that, however, could not yet be enunciated. In this case the creativity of language would have encouraged a new structuration of semantic fields and axes, without being able to guarantee the necessity of the formulation. Language is full of such metaphoric anticipations, whose hermeneutic value—the capacity to uncover new metonymic chains—is revealed afterwards and whose fortune is determined by historic circumstances not grasped by semiotics.

Another case is that of a metaphoric anticipation which installs a short circuit between two semantic units hitherto foreign to each other and which, however, sustains it by a sort of necessity at the level of the form of expression. Some years before the development of nuclear fission, when /atom/ was still burdened with a seme of «indivisibility» (at least at the level of common knowledge), Joyce spoke in *FW* of the "abnihilation of the ethym." Here we find a substitution between 'atom' and /*etymon*/ (*etym-* = the root of a word) that depends upon something we have called *contiguity by resemblance of signifiers*. Once the substitution is made, we can begin to verify, at the semantic level, a series of inspections into the possible realization of a destructive atomic process which, in regard to the "etyma" (roots), seems to have been completely developed in the text in front of us (and thus a *contiguity in the co-text* develops as a reinforcement); semes that are common to the two sememes (their elementary radicality and their originality that make the atom an 'etymon' of physical events and the 'etyma' a verbal atom; the very structure of the code makes all these associations reasonable ones) begin to lend credibility to a possible factual judgment that would overturn the entire semantic field. The poet anticipates a future scientific and conceptual discovery because—even if through expressive artifices, or conceptual chains set in motion to put cultural units into play and to disconnect them—he uproots them from their habitual semiotic situation.

Here is how and why, to return to our explanatory schema, A and D can be connected *with some reason*. This means that, sooner or later, someone understands in some way the reason for the connection and the necessity for a factual judgment that does not yet exist. Then, and only then, is it shown that the course of successive contiguities, however tiresome, was traversable or that it was possible to institute certain traversals. Here is how the factual judgment, anticipated in the form of an unusual metaphor, overturns and restructures the semantic system in introducing circuits not previously in existence. And thus here is why it is possible to anticipate the creative functions of language which, rather than depend upon the existence of already culturalized courses, take advantage of some of these courses in order to institute new ones. All of this clarifies at last what really separates the inventive metaphor from the true factual judgment, even if both seem to have the same function of establishing new connections in the semantic system.

The factual judgment draws, perceptively or intellectually, the disturbing data *from the exterior of language*. The metaphor, on the other hand, draws the idea of a possible connection *from the interior* of the circle of unlimited semiosis, even if the new connection restructures the circle itself in its structuring connections.

The factual judgment is born from a physical mutation of the world and only afterwards is transformed into semiotic knowledge. The metaphor is born from an internal disturbance of semiosis. If it succeeds in its game, it produces knowledge because it produces new semiotic judgments and, in the final outcome, obtains results which do not differ from factual judgments. What is different is the amount of time spent in order to produce knowledge. Factual judgments as such die as soon as they are transformed into semiotic judgments. Once accepted as true, the factual judgment ('the earth is not the center of the solar system') dies as such in order to generate a stipulation of code ('*earth entails periphery*').

Successful factual judgments are remembered as such only when they become famous ('the famous discovery of Copernicus'; but it is clear that this famous discovery is henceforth part of the codes of a first-grader). On the other hand, metaphors (which, after all, are *metasemiotic judgments*) tend to resist acquisition. If they are inventive (and thus original), they cannot be easily accepted; the system tends not to absorb them. Thus they produce, prior to knowledge, something which, psychologically speaking, we could call 'excitation' and which, from a semiotic point of view, is none other than 'information' in the most proper sense of the term: an excess of disorder in respect to existing codes. When faced with metaphor, we sense that it is turning into a vehicle of knowledge, and intuitively (in surveying the subjacent metonymic chains) we grasp its legitimacy; but until analysis has brought these subjacent metonymic chains to light, we must recognize that metaphors imply additional knowledge without knowing how to demonstrate the legitimacy of the argument.

The coupling between the new vehicle and the new (or old, or unsuspected) tenor is still not a part of our culture. The sense of this still unrecognized codification, nevertheless felt in a confused way to be necessary, confers to metaphor its memorability and exemplariness. When united to other contextual or supersegmental artifices involving operations on the substance of expression and thus aesthetic metaphors, this confused sense becomes exactly that which naive aestheticians choose to call 'poetry', 'lyricism', or 'the miracle of art'. It is the sense of availability, of a valence not yet saturated by culture. It is the moment that new codes *could* (*should*) be born and that the old codes cannot resist the impact. When, finally, metaphors are transformed into knowledge, they will at least have completed their cycle: they become catachreses. The field has been restructured, semiosis rearranged, and metaphor (from the invention which it was) turned into culture.

In any case, in order to arrive at these results, metaphor has had to rely upon possible contradictions of the code. It has obtained subversive value, thanks to the existence of two conditions in the code, one linked to the level of expression and the other to the level of content:

(i) It was necessary for the code's fundamental arbitrariness that there be correspondences between signifying systems and signified systems (not strictly univocal correspondences, not in a single sense, not predetermined once and for all; but, on the contrary, open to slippages of different sorts), by virtue of which we could conceive of the possibility of using a signifier to indicate a signified which, in the current game of couplings, is not its own.

(ii) In the second place, it was necessary—in passing from one semantic field to another and in putting them in relationship to each other—to discover in the interior of the Global Semantic System that it is possible to attribute contradictory semes to a single sememe.

Given once again the schema

$$A \quad vs. \quad B \quad vs. \quad C \quad vs. \quad D$$
$$\downarrow \qquad \downarrow \qquad \downarrow \qquad \downarrow$$
$$k \qquad y \qquad z \qquad k$$

there should be a possibility (and, in fact, it exists) that, once we begin to substitute D for A by metonymic connections, we discover that D has some semes in contradiction with those of A and that, nevertheless, it is possible, once the substitution of D for A is done, to formulate the meta-semiotic judgment A = non-D.

In order for the Global Semantic System to be able to produce creative utterances, *it is necessary* that it be self-contradictory and that no *Form* of content exist, only *forms* of content.

NOTES

1. See U. Eco, "The Code: Metaphor or Interdisciplinary Category?" *Yale Italian Studies* 1, no. 1 (1977).

2. See H. Lausberg, *Handbuch der literarischen Rhetorik* (Munich: Huerber, 1960) and Pierre Fontanier, *Les Figures du discours* (Paris: Flammarion, 1968).

3. See Umberto Eco, *A Theory of Semiotics* (Bloomington: Indiana University Press, 1976), section 3.2.

4. P. 486 (London: Faber and Faber, 1957).

5. See James Atherton, *The Books at the Wake* (New York: Viking, 1960). A further note of interest: Minucius Felix's *Octavius* in the same way as *Ulysses*. A group of young intellectuals talk of Christ while walking by the edge of the sea, whose incessant movement they describe. Meanwhile, in the distance, some children are at play. The analogy is perhaps a causal one, but it would not

be wrong to suspect one further pastiche-reminiscence on the part of Joyce, that insatiable reader.

6. P. 486 (London: Faber and Faber, 1957).

Another clue: The reference to the picaresque might just be a reference to the Trickster as a leprechaun-like jester.

7. See D. Hayman, *A First Draft Version of F. W.* (London: Faber and Faber, 1963).

8. See Umberto Eco, *Le poetiche di Joyce*, 2d ed. (Milan: Bompiani, 1965), where the same mechanism seems to rule the phenomenon of *epiphany*. In effect, this is no different from what happens with the epiphanic relation.

9. See Chapter 7 of *The Role of the Reader*.

10. See Eco, *A Theory* . . . , sections 2.5–2.11.

11. See Ross M. Quillian, "Semantic Memory," in *Semantic Information Processing*, ed. Marvin Minsky (Cambridge: M.I.T. Press, 1968) and *Theory*, section 2.12.

12. The Quillian model (Model Q) is based on a mass of nodes interconnected by different types of associative links. For the meaning of every lexeme, memory should contain a node which has as its 'patriarch' the term to be defined here called *type*. The definition of a type A foresees the use of a series of other signifiers (as its own interpretants) which are included as *tokens* (and which, in the model, constitute other lexemes).

The configuration of the meaning of the lexeme is given by the multiplicity of its links with several 'tokens', each of which becomes, in its turn, a type B. Type B is the patriarch of a new configuration which includes many other lexemes as tokens; some of these lexemes were also tokens of type A. Thus type B can actually take type A as one among its own tokens.

"The over-all structure of the complete memory forms an enormous aggregation of planes, each consisting entirely of token nodes except for its 'head' node" (Quillian, p. 327).

This model therefore anticipates the definition of every sign, thanks to its interconnection with the universe of all other signs that function as interpretants, each of which is ready to become the sign interpreted by all the others: the model, in its complexity, is based upon a process of *unlimited semiosis*. Starting with a sign that is considered as a 'type', one can retraverse, from the center to the extreme periphery, the entire universe of cultural units. Each of these can in turn become the center and generate infinite peripheries.

13. See Eco, *A Theory* . . . , section 3.1.2.

RENÉ THOM

The generality of semiotic reflection and its points of intersection with geometrical, topological, psychological, physical, epistemological considerations are clearly demonstrated in the "sketch" of a theory of symbolism of the French mathematician and semiotician René Thom. Thom's framework is perhaps the most abstract and general of the four texts presented in this volume that deal most explicitly with "foundations"—Peirce, Saussure, and Morris being the other three. Starting out from the Peircean trichotomy of icons, indexes, and symbols, Thom argues that the production of images or icons poses problems, stemming from the dynamic processes intervening in their production, which are fundamental and which lie at the heart of the relation signified $\leftrightharpoons$ signifier, which characterizes the symbolic relation in its complete form. The genesis of the image—or icon—is through the creation of an "isomorphic" spatially extended correlate from a "model," a process which can occur merely physically or, with appropriate modifications, in the biological and psychological realm also.

An image of a physical object disappears when its model or light source disappears, but the imprint of a physical object upon another physical medium obtains a kind of permanence through the "plasticity" of the receptor system. In the case of the plasticity of a receiving medium—foreshadowing the eminent plasticity of symbol systems as artificial, contrived, produced systems—the image becomes memory and the system undergoes an irreversible, temporal interaction, a perfect analogue, in fact, of the phenomenon of life. In short, Thom notes, "the formation of images from a model appears like a manifestation of the irreversible character of a universal dynamics: the model ramifies into an image isomorphic with itself." At the same time, Thom points out, the process also appears as reversible, thus combining the two opposing principles of thermodynamics: conservation and increasing entropy. "It is by means of this subtle balance between two morphologies, by its simultaneous demand of reversibility and irreversibility, that the dynamics of symbolism carries in itself (this under a local and concentrated form) all the contradictions of the scientific vision of the world and that it is the very image of life."

With these considerations as his starting point, Thom proceeds to introduce the central categories, distinctions, and paradigmatic examples of his foundational theory. The distinction between physical and biological "pregnance"—as conditions of structure and form—is manifested in the persistence of certain morphological accidents when a structure is deformed, a process illustrated by the photographs of "deformations" in the original version of the text and by reference to certain central issues of Gestalt theory. Physical pregnance is the capacity to resist the "noise" of communications while "biological" pregnance is defined as "the capacity of a form to evoke other biologically important forms." Now the "signifying character of a form is always tied to its morphological instability" which allows it to ramify, differentiate, be applied to, be adapted to different functions, or suggest an action, while a stable physical form suggests only itself. Further, this distinction between the two kinds of pregnance can be applied to the syntactic—and semantic—differences between "disinterested" and "interested" forms, rooted as they are in the "affectivity"—a Langerian point—of the symbolizing organism. Thom's discussion of indexes retains Peirce's—and the tradition's—principle of physical or existential connection but embeds it more explicitly in the matrix of his catastrophe theory and in a general system of finality, touching upon Peirce's own acceptance of a teleologically ordered universe. An index can be biologically or semantically tied to its source or referent, and both linkages can ultimately be ascribed to learning, involving a relation of order and hence of stipulated ordering. In the choice of an index— with physical or biological pregnance—Thom sees the origin of Saussure's "arbitrary nature" of the sign.

One of the most distinctive of Thom's procedures, taken up again in his essay 'L'espace et les signes,' (*Semiotica* 29-3/4 [1980], 193–208) is the mutual assimilation of "semantic" and "spatial" categories. The location of a physical object in space and the location of a signification in "semantic" space are not only "genetically" connected but analogous in structure and function. Symbolic activity, if it wants to be effective or efficacious, has to rest necessarily on a mental *simulation* of a "catastrophe" to be provoked or avoided, and in this way it takes on the function of a sensorial relay, a notion Barthes takes up in his essay on the rhetoric of the image. Semiotic or symbolic movement is from the imperative pole to the descriptive pole, and the specific distinctiveness of language is found in its ability to simulate, with more internal complexity, the internal complexity of the world. The break with the animal world— a widely discussed and controversial theme—attendant upon the arrival of symbolism in its human form Thom traces through three facets: (1) the organism's immersion in things to the point of self-forgetfulness (aliena-tion), (2) the discontinuity of subjectivity manifested in the lack of a per-manently conceived "ego" in the animal world, and (3) the lack of an integrated and synthetic image of "space." The peculiarly human world, Thom argues, is characterized by the possession of all these three "pow-ers." From such considerations Thom draws a revolutionary conclusion: "since the identity of a thing has its fundamental principle in its spatial localization, all ontology, all semantics, necessarily passes through a study of space—geometrical or topological." Here the study of space and the semiotic study of biopsychological developments fruitfully intersect.

Note, too, how Thom sees the rise of symbolism as inscribed in the formation of an egg in organic life. This is an "icon" of symbolic life wherein is revealed its most primitive and "pregnant" design. Thom's essay both forces us and allows us to see the deep continuity of organic and nonorganic processes and relations when they are looked at from the semiotic point of view. His generalization and radicalization of Peirce's semiotic trichotomy allow us to draw the Peircean conclusion—even if perhaps meant somewhat differently—that the whole universe is per-fused with signs. As such, then, semiotics becomes the effort of reality itself to double back upon itself and thematize itself, revealing in the pro-cess the isomorphism between "real processes" and semiosis. Reflecting on the "meaning" of symbolization, Thom accordingly ends his essay, one of the most provocative and heuristically fertile explorations of the ultimate conditions of sense, with the statement: "the voice of reality is found in the sense of the symbol."

Thom's primary materials on catastrophe theory are found in his *Structural Stability and Morphogenesis* (Reading, Mass.: W. A. Benjamin, 1975) and in his *Mathematical Models of Morphogenesis* (Chichester, England: Ellis Horwood Limited, 1983). See also Thomas A. Sebeok's "Iconicity," *Modern Language Notes* 91:1427–1456, reprinted in his *The Sign and Its Masters* (Austin: University of Texas Press, 1979). Umberto Eco has an extensive discussion of iconism in his *A Theory of Semiotics* (Bloomington: Indiana University Press, 1976), which cites a great deal of the relevant literature.

From the Icon to the Symbol

RENÉ THOM

1. *From the Icon to the Symbol*

Usually we see in symbolic activity, in conceptual thought, the supreme achievement of human capacities. Many philosophers attribute it to the existence of a "facultas signatrix" with which only man could be equipped, and which would be absent in animals. However, we shall see that, when we analyze symbolism into its elementary mechanisms, we do not find any which do not figure either in inanimate matter, or in the humblest forms of life. The appearance of language in primitive man is perhaps not the abrupt discontinuity we are so eager to imagine. There is indeed a great change in the passage from animal into man; but as we shall try to show in Section 7, this change is probably due less to a catastrophic structural innovation in the cerebral organization than to a modification in the stages of individual development, associated with the presence of a social milieu which at the same time protects and educates the newly born.

Any discussion of symbolism must start from the classification of signs, so simple and so profound, which has been left to us by Charles Sanders Peirce. Let us recall that, according to Peirce, there are three types of signs:

(1) Images or *icons*, which are graphic representations, more or less faithful to the object.

(2) *Indices:* these are beings or objects linked to the symbolized object and necessary to its existence, for example, smoke is an *index* of fire.

(3) *Symbols:* these concern an arbitrary form, the relation to the signified object of which, arises from a social convention of limited validity in space and time. For example, a word is a symbol because its phonetic form has no intrinsic relation to that of the object signified ("arbitrariness of sign," according to Saussure).

Philosophers have a tendency to look upon the first category of signs, the icons (or images) as of a banal nature and of little interest for the theory

The paper "De l'icone au symbole" appeared in *Cahiers Internationaux de Symbolisme*, 22–23 (1973), 85–106. The English version is reproduced with permission from R. Thom, *Mathematical Models of Morphogenesis*, copyright ©1983, which was published by Ellis Horwood Limited, Chichester, England.

of symbolism. It is reasonable to believe that they are wrong and that a delicate analysis of the dynamic process involved in the production of the images (the "copy") poses problems of a fundamental nature which are at the very heart of the relation: signified ⇋ signifier ("signifié ⇋ signifiant"), which characterizes the symbol in its complete form.

2. *Genesis of the Image*

In many circumstances images appear naturally: the shadow of a man on the ground, his image reflected in water, the imprint of a foot in the sand, are some simple examples of image forms which are not endowed, except in special circumstances, with symbolic value. It is nonetheless important to analyze the nature of the physical processes which come into play in these examples.

The first remark is that the image A' and its model A are necessarily of forms *extended in space*. We can only speak of "isomorphism," of identity of forms if we have defined an equivalence group operating on the forms of a space, in other words a "geometry." More precisely, let us suppose that the model A is defined in an open set U of Euclidean space (and the image A' in an open set U'). Then the correspondence $A \rightarrow A'$ is induced by a geometric transformation $\tau: U \rightarrow U'$, which in the most perfect case is a metric congruence (in the cases of the mirror image and of the imprint) or an affine projection (in the case of the shadow).

We note that neither of the two aspects U, U' can be said to be subordinate to the other; the correspondence, at least in the first case is reversible. This correspondence is induced by a physical process of interaction, a "coupling" which is expressed by the metric equality $\Phi: U \rightarrow U'$. In the case of the mirror image, or the shadow, the element of interaction is light, the propagation of which is perfectly reversible (invariant under a change of direction of the arrow of time). The very regular character of this correspondence is explained in the last analysis by what the physicist Wigner calls "the unreasonable exactitude" of physical laws.

Technically therefore, if S and S' are two Hamiltonian dynamical systems having a Lie group G as a symmetry group and if we couple them by a Hamiltonian interaction itself G-invariant, then these systems have first integrals (at least local) in the Lie group alegebra L_G. In this coupling these first integrals (kinetic moments) combine vectorially ($X + X' =$ const), so as to allow the identification of the space U relative to S as U' is relative to S'. There is nevertheless in the formation of the image a fundamental irreversibility, even if the physical laws brought into play are reversible. In order that a shadow may form, the model must be illuminated by a luminous source approximating to a point. The light issuing from the source first touches the model then outlines the shadow. It is the same in the formation of the mirror image, the object has to be illuminated and the reflecting surface perfectly flat. Narcissus leaning over his fountain can only see the object of his passion, when lit by the rays of Apollo, and in the perfect liquid shell brought about by the earth's attraction.

In these light dependent examples, the image has no permanence, it disappears if the model disappears (or the solar source). With the imprint of a hand in the sand, we meet a fresh phenomenon; the "plasticity" of the receiver system. This last system allows a great number of forms of equilibrium as it is inadequately controlled. The image is formed by an irreversible stimulus which changes the form of equilibrium of the receiver system by inculcating the imprint of the form of the model: here the image becomes memory. In order that the imprint materialize the receiver system has to possess very special dynamic properties: a Hamiltonian dynamic allowing many first integrals linked to a symmetry group and the possibility of irreversible temporary interaction. We shall designate this very special dynamic state with the word 'competence'. If the shadow is thrown not on to an insensitive screen but on to a sensitive photographic plate, the image will be able to be fixed for all time, thanks to the competence of the system.

With a plastic receiver system, we can see the possibility that images are formed as stable as their model, or even more so, like the dinosaurs' eggs near Aix-en-Provence which are only recognized by their imprint on the rocks. This is a state which is attained by the dynamic of life. A living being V makes at some distance from itself a living being V', which is isomorphic to him, and which will soon supplant him. The plastic aspect of the local dynamics is doubtless a characteristic of the original metabolism (in the 'primordial ooze'). The organism V proceeds by sending localized stimuli (the gametes) which germinate, that is to say explode in a controlled manner in their neighborhood. The controlled character of this local explosion is already apparent in the case of photographic emulsion on a sensitive plate. It appears even more clearly in the embryological development which leads to a structure isomorphic to the parent organism but with a certain time-space translation. At the molecular level this mechanism is manifest in the replication of DNA, a fragment of which goes to make, as its imprint, a dual fragment. Here the competent dynamic is the set of the cytoplasmic milieux containing precursors, enzymes, chemical energy, . . . etc.

Going to the other end of the scale of life, how shall we characterize perception if not as the modification of a competent dynamic under the sensory aspect of external reality? Already Plato in the Theaetetus has compared the impression that perceived objects make on us to the imprint of a solid on wax. We note that here the competent system (for example, retina, visual cortex, etc.) recovers at each instant the pristine virginity indispensable to a total and permanent competence. However, a certain plasticity exists since the sensations perceived are stored in the memory.

To sum up, the formation of images from a model appears as a manifestation of the universal dynamic having irreversible character. There is a self-ramifying of the model into an image isomorphic to itself. But very often this process utilizes an interaction of reversible character. It is there that the dynamic of symbolism is so clearly exemplified. The thermodynamic wavers constantly between two points of view: the conservative point of view which is manifest in the presence of Hamiltonian dynamics, that is by the conservation of energy (the first principle); and the Heraclitean notion of the irreversible flow of time, which expresses itself as increase of entropy (the second principle). Reconciliation of these two points of view has only been possible by introducing the creator and the first snap of his fingers (the *big bang* of ten thousand million years ago. . .). In the interaction "signified—signifier," it is clear that, borne along by the universal flux, the signified generates the signifier in an uninterrupted burgeoning ramification. But the signifier regenerates the signified each time that we interpret the sign. And as is shown by the example of biological forms, for the signifier (the descendant) to become the signified (the parent) again, the time-lapse of a generation is sufficient.

It is through the subtle balance between two morphologies, through the simultaneous demands of reversibility and irreversibility, that the dynamic of symbolism carries within itself (and this in a local and concentrated form) all the contradictions of the scientific vision of the world. And that is the very image of life.

3. Death of the Image: Physical Pregnance

We have seen in the interactions between extended systems that through the "unreasonable" exactitude of the laws of physics an exact copy, complete in every metric detail, can be made from an object taken as model. What will happen if we disturb slightly, by small random perturbations, the working of this perfect imitation. The image becomes deformed, confused and fuzzy. But, in this distortion certain morphological features resist the *noise* of the interaction better than others: these are structurally stable forms, the physically pregnant forms. So, under such perturbations the form has a tendency to break up into locally stable elements, where the more fragile global connections give way more easily. The first stage of this process does not however necessarily lead to a non-recognizable form. On the contrary, frequently enough, the perturbation results in a "stylization" of form which does not hinder its recognition. In fact, to "stylize" a form is to reduce it to its fundamental organizing features which would only have the effect of making it appear more striking.

Given a plastic form, separated from its mold and subject to persistent erosion in time, then it can only follow its proper path of disassociation, a ramifying proliferating decomposition. Such a form is degraded more and more by the proliferation of local random accidents and it soon ceases to be recognizable. Here I may refer to the photographic experiments of Claire Lejeune, who has made the degradation by sunlight treatment of photographic images a wonderful tool of artistic investigation [1].

In biological forms we are concerned with ageing: the vital form severed from its genetic model can only sink by being overloaded with pointless accidents. That a theory of the pregnance of forms be possible was the essential dogma of the Gestalt theory of psychology, a theory which W. Köhler [2] defended with courage and lucidity. The modern ideas of qualitative dynamics (catastrophe theory, structural stability) can provide a justification for this idea, which has been missing up to now. But perhaps the mistake of Gestalt theory was not to distinguish between two closely allied notions. Firstly, *physical pregnance* of a form meaning to have the capacity to withstand communication noise, and secondly, "*biological*" *pregnance* defined as the capacity of a form to evoke other important biological forms and thus to be easily recognized and classified in the field (perceptive or semantic) of enquiry.

We might accept that a biologically pregnant form is necessarily physically pregnant. It is true in general, at least locally. But it should not be concluded, as I once thought, that a theory of symbolism could be built on the physical pregnance of the form of the message alone. The truth is that the form of a sign cannot (at least historically) be dissociated from its motivation. A physically pregnant detail cannot be significant by itself; in fact, it is a consequence of the theory of structural stability that such a detail is a kind of irreducible "atom" in the transmission of forms. It can thus only generate itself. On the other hand, the signifying characteristic of a form is always linked to its morphological instability, a fact which allows it by transmission, to generate, by unfolding, a complex of more simple forms.

One of the factors which makes the distinction between physical and biological pregnance so fine is the following: biological pregnance is linked to the evocation of organs typical of living beings. For an animal, the recognition both of prey and predators is a fundamental necessity: whence a preferential sensitivity for the perceptive apparatus appropriate to these typical forms. Now, the form of an organ is always more or less dictated by its functional efficiency and only the forms defined by the "catastrophic" schema which characterizes their function have the chance to materialize organically. But the functional efficiency of a mechanism called into play in space—time is itself governed by the demands of a structural stability having a dynamically physical character. It follows from this that the biological forms are to a large extent subject to the constraint of a physical pregnance of the same origin, in principle, as the need for stability in communication by spatial coupling. At the very most, the organic release of evolution allows the appearance of forms, more refined, more subtle, more global, metrically characteristic, and by this fact, charged with more meaning. The difference lies in the fact that the biological form suggests an "action," whereas the stable physical form only suggests itself.

To illustrate these considerations, let us take the example of the symbolism of the arrow. The mark ← suggests, in our society, the direction of right to left.

Is this to do with a social convention or, on the other hand, is it an intrinsic effect linked to the very form of the figure? I incline to favor the second hypothesis. According to a theory of perception due to Harry Blum, every perception of an object implies an immediate and implicit search for a better manual grasp of the object. Now if one tries to grasp the two branches of the arrow, the "fictitious" fingers that will try can only slide towards the left, in a vain search for a position of stable hold. This could be a biological explanation of the symbolized direction. We can also consider (as remarked by Guy Hirsch) that a mobile arrow in a fluid milieu will meet less resistance to its movement in its "normal" direction than in the opposite direction: because the "wings" of the arrow model the contours of the wake, when a stick is pushed along the surface of a liquid along its axis. But the contour of a wake confirms certain properties characteristic of unstable forms, according to Blum's theory. Here then is coincidence (by no means accidental) of biological pregnance and of physical pregnance.

Moreover we know that animals themselves are subject to certain "classical" optical illusions, which seems to suggest that we are touching here on mechanisms of a very elementary nature, infra-psychic, if we can say that!

Perhaps one of the most striking experimental proofs of the existence of "archetypal" forms lies in the existence in animal psychology of "supranormal releasers." Thus, in a fledgling, newly hatched, the reflex to open its beak can be more effectively released by the sight of an artificial beak of a red color and pyramidal form (the "archetypal" beak) than by the biologically normal form of the beak of one of its parents. We might possibly think that the determination and theoretical explanation of these "archetypal" forms will disclose the secret of human symbolism. The response to this is, I believe, as follows: it is correct that these forms are going to play an important role in the external morphology of the sign, in the "How" of symbolic activity. But it does not explain the "Why" of the symbol, its initial motivation. As we shall see further on, the source of symbolism is to be found in the complex mechanisms of the regulation of living organisms and of society. We could, I believe, defend the following idea: the more a message is "disinterested," the less strong is the affective thrust that generated it, the more it is subject to the demand of physical pregnance, the more it reveals the formal structure of the archetypal origin. On the other hand, if the message is "interested," if it responds to a biological or immediately urgent sociological necessity, it is then very unstable morphologically. Its "excited" strength convolutes itself locally sometimes to the point of defying all formalism; every rule of good internal organization. The misuse, so often, of rules of syntax in exclamations, orders, interjections and in poetry is a striking example of it. We can in effect accept that the rules of syntax in natural languages are the temporal transcription of archetypal morphologies in space–time, as they owe their origin to the need to preserve physical pregnance.

4. *Indices*

When we consider a being (a) as defined by a noun (A) of a natural language, we shall be able to observe the following fact: in order that the being (a) exist with the same meaning, it must be the seat of recurrent activities which are essential either to its physical permanence or to the spatio-temporal realization of its meaning. For example, an animal must, in order to subsist, be committed to a spectrum of physiological activities: move, eat, drink, breathe, etc. An inanimate object itself participates in a series of movements that we normally expect as a consequence of the function of the object: a broom sweeps, a car moves, a stone falls, the fire burns, etc. So to each noun is attached in a canonical manner a "spectrum" of verbs which specify the activities indispensable to the realization of the meaning. But each verb itself describes an "archetypal" morphology where beings other than the given being intervene. For example, to eat requires a prey, or a food, to drink requires a liquid taken as a drink, and in consequence a receptacle containing the liquid . . . the fire, during burning, emits smoke, etc. Every being intervening in such a morphology, and which linguistically is described by either the direct or indirect object of the verb, will be called an index (α) of the being (a). In classical languages, the relation between a being (a) and its index (α) is usually expressed by the genitive: α of a. For example, the smoke of the fire, the beak of the duck, the tail of the squirrel. Or, alternatively in English: a's α as in "the fire's smoke," "the duck's beak," "the squirrel's tail."

As every verbal morphology describes a process of interaction where the actants enter into contact, the result is that the index is always an actant which is, or has been, in contact with its object, if it is not actually part of it. (In passing I add that in general the index is not in place of the actant subject in a verbal catastrophe; there exist precise morphological criteria for the topology of interaction which enables us in many cases to specify what the actant subject is.) Very often, we replace a being by one of its indices, an act which confers on the latter a symbolic value. In language, this procedure is at the root of many *tropes* (metonymy in particular: taking the part for the whole).

But it is important to see clearly that in the pair (a, α) of a being and one of its indices, the index (α) has no value or symbolic function in itself. It will only be so

(1) if the being (a) is itself an index of an actant (b) taken as subject of reference, and if the catastrophe linking (a) to (b) is of great importance (biologically or semantically) for (b);

(2) if the being (b) comes accidentally into relation with (α), the verbal catastrophe which makes (α) an actant in a catastrophe of (b) is not itself indispensable to the semantic stability of (b). (In other words (α) is not in itself an "index" of (b).)

Example 1. (a) is a gazelle; (b) a tiger. The catastrophe a $\rightarrow$ b is predation and of great biological importance for (b). The index (α) of (a) could be the tracks of the gazelle on the ground, or a dropping. In this case the catastrophe, $\alpha \rightarrow$ a, would be a standard catastrophe of emission. If the tiger accidentally perceives the index (α), it will be apparent that he will be deeply affected, so that it is legitimate to say that (α) is for him a gazelle "symbol." The "rejected" becomes the "projected."

Example 2. (a) is a drink, it might be of wine for example, (α) the bottle that contains it, (b) an inveterate drinker. Here the catastrophes are obvious; note that the empty bottle still has a symbolic value for (b) but not quite so obviously as a full bottle.

Pavlov's well known experiments show that a false index (α') can have a symbolic value for an animate being (b). For that to be it is sufficient that the catastrophe $\alpha \rightarrow$ b is biologically important, such as predation (α being the true index). Then $\alpha' \rightarrow$ a need be no more than a simple spatio-temporal contiguity (the sound of a bell at the arrival of a meal). It will be seen by some that this hypostasis of spatio-temporal contiguity to causality is the index of animals' typical inferiority with respect to man. This would be to forget that according to the empiricism of Hume, or modern elementary particle Physics, it is in practice impossible to dissociate causality and spatio-temporal contiguity.

Finally, we can see in these humble, but real, manifestations of the symbolic function, a kind of smoothness in a catastrophe which has considerable biological, or semantic, importance. That (b) accidentally comes to meet (α) is of little importance in itself, but if (b) knows that (α) is semantically or biologically linked to (a), which is an indispensable index of (b), then (α) has a tendency to become itself also an "index" of (b), as if the relation (α) $\rightarrow$ (b) acquires through the existence of the intermediary

(a) an intrinsic importance. This comes about as if the relation: (α) is an index of (a), becomes an order relation.

This analysis shows that symbolic activity is, in its origin, linked in an essential manner to biological control systems: or more exactly, as said by older thinkers who were not afraid of words, to biological finality (finalité : ultimate purpose). It is so in two ways: on the one hand, it is an extension of the efficacy of complex control mechanisms (an extension of the basin of catastrophes favorable to (b) and a diminution of the unfavorable ones): on the other hand, it postulates the possibility of the actant (b) *simulating* in its own appropriate state of being (psychism), the relation linking (a) to its index (α): thus being a form of intelligence. The fact that initially, as in the Pavlovian schema, this simulation is no more than a simple association, does not stop us from considering that we have here the first tremors in the plastic and competent dynamic of the psychism of (b) of an external spatio-temporal liaison interpreted not without reason, as causal. If the canine race, in order to survive, had had to pass a great number of generations in the Pavlovian laboratories, it would no doubt have finished by reacting differently. . . .

In every case the experimental signal (α'), thanks to a kind of apprenticeship, manages to play the same role as a true index. We can thus see here and now a "symbol", since the intimate relation between the morphology of (α') and that of (a) is arbitrary, and their association has only been established by virtue of an experimental procedure of an artificial nature. The relation $\alpha' \rightarrow a$ is acquired by (b) as the outcome of a process of *apprenticeship*, that is to say, a sequence of events, where the will of individuals other than the subject intervenes; a "social" effect. Hence, from the beginning, the situation is not fundamentally different from that of language. We will note that for every way in which the apprenticeship succeeds, it is necessary to "reinforce" the effect by bringing major biological regimes into play: food, sexuality. Only these fundamental "catastrophes" of biological finality have the power to generate the symbol in animals. This no longer holds true in man, where the smoothness property, this transitivity of the index, spreads, even to objects, and to concepts which are biologically indifferent.

5. Symbolism in Man

In man, as in animals, symbolic activity originates in the need for regulation, homeostasis in the living organism and similarly, stability in the social body. As far as organized systems are concerned, the organism (or the society) reestablishes its equilibrium after an external stimulus by the intervention of "reflexes." That is to say, in terms of the space of the states of the system, there are certain privileged and attracting trajectories (the "chreods" of C. H. Waddington). Each of these attractors has a basin just as each water course has its own basin. However, the control of such a system (organic and social) is never perfect; there exist, as a consequence of constraints of topological nature, weak points in this "figure of regulation." For example the thresholds which are the border-line between the basins of two reflexes. At these points the organism hesitates as to the reflex it must use. In addition there may even be in the space of the states exceptional points, where a catastrophe disadvantageous to the organism but of limited scope, may release itself. Finally the figure of regulation is bounded by catastrophes of lethal and irreversible effect: death. Every biological (or sociological) development consists of a system which exploits to the full its figure of regulation, in such a way that in a given environment, catastrophes favorable to the organism see their basins augmented, and the unfavorable catastrophes have their basins diminished. This extension of the basins is produced through affectivity (pain or pleasure) and through symbolism. Consequently, we see immediately that there will be two types of signs: attractor signs, aimed at increasing the efficacy of favorable catastrophes and repelling signs (inhibitors) aimed at the prevention of unfavorable catastrophes.

Thus from its very genesis any symbol has an imperative characteristic, a characteristic which remains largely unconscious, linked to a feeling of trust and to the original hypostasis of the symbol which will be explained below. There equally we find the syntactical and semantic autonomy of the verb taken in the imperative ($I!$).

This being accepted, it remains, and here in principle is the very aim of "semiology," to explain how the teleological ("*finaliste*") motivation of the sign can generate its true morphology, its rules of internal structure. It is possible in this regard to give a rule, at once simple and of wide generality: *the principle of the inverse path*. Properly speaking this principle does not determine the true form of the sign (icon, index or symbol): but it determines its spatio-temporal localization. It must not be forgotten that above all signs are forms in space–time, and that consequently their spatio-temporal localization is one of the first factors to consider.

To state this principle some vocabulary of differential topology will be necessary. Given a domain of Euclidean space of n dimensions, let U be the space of states of a system. Very frequently, the set of "catastrophe" points (in the usual sense) of the system which lead to a local or total destruction of the system form a space of dimension $(n - k)$, a submanifold of co-dimension k. The appearance of unfavorable or dangerous catastrophes in the development is necessarily relatively rare, without which fact homeostasis could not be preserved.

We express this fact by saying that these catastrophe points form a submanifold J of finite co-dimension: it is a matter of rare, but not exceptional, facts. Then we consider the set Γ_i of the trajectories bordering on J. This set of initial anterior positions to the catastrophe, forms a sort of cone Γ_i. In the same way the set of the possible outcomes of the catastrophe forms a cone of trajectories Γ_0. Furthermore, in general, the final states of the catastrophe constitute a well-defined subset W_0, compact in the space U (which explains the well-known adage: For good or ill, things always work out in the end). An important fact is the indeterminacy in practice of the catastrophe. A very small variation of these initial conditions can bring about a very great variation of the effects, as is the case in the neighborhood of a threshold, of a critical point. . . . Let us suppose two roads cut each other at right angles in a point O of the plane. We take as axes Ox, Oy of the plane the directions of the two roads. Suppose that two vehicles are moving on these two roads each with a coordinate (x, speed x') and (y, speed y'). There will be a collision if at the initial instant t_0 we have $x'_0/x_0 = y'_0/y_0$. The equation $x'_0 y_0 - x_0 y'_0 = 0$ then represents the cone Γ_i of entry into the catastrophe.

The exit cone Γ_0 cannot be simply described because the trajectory of a vehicle after collision cannot be easily calculated. But the set W_0 of the final states will be intuitively well-represented by the set of scattered wrecks in the neighborhood of O after a set of collisions. This being so we consider the set $\Gamma_i + \Gamma_0$ as immersed in the set of trajectories tangent to the catastrophe. This global dynamic allows us to transform in a continuous manner, a neighborhood τ_i of the base W_i into a neighborhood τ_0 of W_0 (see Fig. 1). Suppose $h: \tau_i \to \tau_0$ to be this transformation.

Furthermore, the catastrophe at the origin O involves, in general,

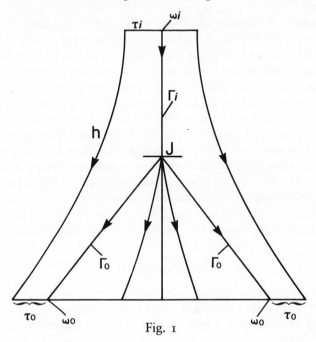

Fig. 1

morphological changes, often irreversible, for the actants that are involved. There are in consequence, indices, actants either issued from the catastrophe, or implicated in its preparation. The principle of the inverse path states:

In order to forestall an unfavorable catastrophe, we consider an index α_0, issued from the catastrophe; final states are then found in a neighborhood of the manifold W_0.

We thus bring back this actant by the inverse transformation

$$h^{-1} \alpha_0 \rightarrow \tau_i$$

into a neighborhood of the initial states where it is realized "iconically." To favor a beneficial catastrophe we realize iconically an actant implicated in the preparation of the catastrophe, equally in the neighborhood of τ_i.

Example 1: The road sign "Danger" is frequently represented, in France, by a death's head: This involves an aesthetic euphemism for the lethal consequence of the catastrophe. The usual Danger sign (an exclamation mark) is a stylization of an unstable situation, like that of a needle resting on a point.

Example 2: The sign "Restaurant" on the motorways is represented by a place setting. In this case it is obviously to do with a preparatory index to the catastrophe of ingestion, localized on the access road to the restaurant.

Example 3: Sometimes we do not even have representation by an index but a simple "potential barrier" with a discouraging effect. For example if there was a hole in the road a light "symbolic" barrier would be placed some yards in front of the hole where vehicles could see it.

In each of these cases, the catastrophe participates in the semantic universe of the users; the authority which installs the signal is aiming to encourage the simulation in the mind of the users of a more severe catastrophe than the somewhat vague and general one which is normally present. It is in terms of this calculated expectation that the warning signal is localized. A catastrophe can have numerous actants, as many anterior as posterior. Also the choice of the representing index is fairly arbitrary. We will be guided simply by the more or less pregnant (physically and biologically) character of the chosen figure. It is in this arbitrariness that we can see the origin of the Saussurean *arbitrariness of the sign.*

6. Localization and Meaning

The number of fundamental catastrophes either to avoid or to provoke, in the control of the organism of society, is relatively limited. Also we can be satisfied with a finite code of signals aiming at forestalling or encouraging these catastrophes. But then we are led very quickly to make the distinction between the intrinsic meaning of the sign (the type of catastrophe evoked) and its spatio-temporal localization, which is the domain of space-time where the sign exerts its imperative effect (or sometimes "performative" according to the terminology of the Oxford School). In order that the effect of the sign is fully realized, its localization must be "reasonable" that is to say governed by the principle of the inverse path. What would be the use of a "STOP" sign in the middle of a field of beetroot?

It follows from this analysis that symbolic activity, if it is to be effective, rests necessarily on a mental simulation of the catastrophe to avoid (or to provoke). We have seen that such a simulation is sketchily present already in an animal subject to a Pavlovian type regime. One of the typical aspects of human psychism is the "open" character of the catastrophes forestalled by symbolism. Although social organization shields man from the danger of immediate biological catastrophes (such as hunger, war, etc.), the mental dynamic is compelled to forestall the rarer and more exceptional catastrophes (of higher co-dimension, according to the above geometric terminology). This necessitates a description by longer and more articulated symbols in so far as we can similarly describe the rare catastrophe as the "accidental collision" (geometrically, the transverse intersection) of the more ordinary catastrophes.

So we have the language, the possibility of a relatively precise description, at least qualitatively of the spatio-temporal processes of our environment. Insofar as the symbol is long, each of its elements loses in imperative value and gains in descriptive power: in fact, the imperative characteristic can be associated only with the global symbol, and is necessarily diluted with each partial symbol. Language thus takes the role of a sensory relay. It allows the speaker A to describe to the hearer B what he sees. Even if B cannot himself see the event described, he can imagine it from the account that A has given. So the possibility of simulation of the psychism, originally developing only on the catastrophes of biological regulation, has ended by extension to all the phenomena of the macroscopic world. This permits a more and more faithful simulation of exterior phenomena by the mind. How has such a leap been effected?

7. From Animal to Man

Of the evolutionary mechanisms which have given rise to the appearance of man we can scarcely conjecture, but it is perhaps possible to give a more precise description of this radical change. For that we must understand animal psychism from "inside." I believe that on three essential points animal psychism is distinguished from human psychism.

7.1. ALIENATION BY THINGS

We may propose that the psychic life of an animal is constantly subject to certain automatisms (certain "chreods") linked to the perception of biologically important objects, such as prey and predators. In fact, an analysis of the mechanisms brought into play in Embryology leads us to think that, in a manner which is only just symbolic, the hungry predator "is" his prey, he identifies physically with it. It is only when he sees a real prey (externally), that the catastrophe of perception materializes. He becomes himself again just as the motor process of capture of the prey is released. From this point of view the primitive symbolism linked to predation is easily explained, therefore, if the predator (B) is identified with prey (A), we can easily see that an index of (A) is *ipso facto* an index of B without the intervention of the property of transitivity of the relation: index of. (Indeed this can be true even at the level of organic morphology: when an animal such as the lamprey has the tip of its tongue like a worm, and uses it as bait to attract small fishes which are its prey, we can say that in this case the bait is a morphological index of the predator.)

7.2. DISCONTINUITY OF SUBJECTIVITY

Owing to the enthrallment (French: "fascination") exercised by objects, the "ego" of the animal is not a permanent entity. The "ego" re-establishes itself only on the initiation of the gross reflexes and perhaps in the satisfaction of instincts. In particular, the animal has not, in general, a permanent consciousness of its body insofar as it is a preferential domain of space. (On the other hand, a permanent internal simulation of the mechanical state of the body is indispensable to the efficacy of movements.) On this basis, the distinction "subject-object" does not exist for an animal in any permanent manner.

In animals, the internal representation of space does not have Euclidean space as image. The space is a union of distinct maps, each associated with a well-defined "ego" and assigned to a well-defined motor or physiological behavior (territories for hunting, for sleeping, for mating, for nesting, etc.) and they pass from one map to another by well-defined spatial references (visual or olfactory). (Of course in certain animals like migratory birds, some of these maps can be very extensive; but it is no less certain that each of these maps is centered on a well-defined point of physiological vocation.)

In man, these three characters have developed as follows:

(1) The enthrallment of things has become merged into human psychism. Very probably, symbolic activity and the appearance of language have played an essential role in this development. Man is freed from the

enthrallment of things by giving them names. Human psychism did unfold in some way: the primitive representation of space, half-conscious, unfolds itself, and creates one or more spaces of the same type: the semantic spaces, where the "actants" are installed: the concepts. The control of these actants in their true semantic space is accomplished by mechanisms of a "reflex" type, analogous to the control of the organism itself. By an unfolding pushed more towards the surface, automatisms of language are created. These are kinds of universal actants which intervene in the control of concepts.

(2) Thus freed from the enthrallment of things, the ego has been able to constitute itself in a permanent manner by taking as support the representation of the true body in space.

(3) Human psychism is capable of integrating the primitive functional maps the one with the other, in order to constitute the global representation of the geometry of space. (For example, the notion of an infinite straight line is made clear by the indefinitely repeated operation of the measure of a length: to place a ruler at the end point of a length, is the refined and free form of the associating of two maps.)

Of the original alienations there remains only a certain feeling of the sacred attached to certain objects (taboos, fetishes, etc.).

A long time after the global mental reconstruction of space, man became capable of perceiving that the foundation of the identity of things is their spatial localization: "Two things occupying simultaneously two disjoint domains could not be identical." This postulation took a long time to establish itself and "primitive" (or magic) thought, participation (in the sense of Lévy-Bruhl), represents the last connection with primitive alienation. From this postulate, of which modern man is hardly conscious, we shall easily deduce that since the identity of a thing has its principle in its spatial localization, *all ontology, all semantics necessarily depends on a study of space—geometric or topological.*

We know that the period of the first three years is critical in a child's development. If the child does not hear his parents (or those around him) speaking during this period, the acquiring of language and intellectual development will be irremediably compromised. The relative immaturity of the newborn human enables him to keep the primitive representation of space very plastic and flexible for a long time. The major motor schemata form only slowly, with the beginnings of language. It is quite reasonable to consider that, according to the law of recapitulation, the child passes through a period of primitive alienation where certain beings and objects exercise a total enthrallment of him. The presence of external verbal stimuli linked to the appearance of these beings plays an *inductor* role (in the embryological sense) in this competent structure, that is the primitive spatial field. These forms find their true space from primitive space, by unfolding, by finding support in the auditory and articulatory schema of the corresponding word, which frees the subject from their enthrallment. Then, the same schema of unfolding, of branching out, continues for semantic spaces, leading eventually to the formation of the semantic space of the adult. For a newborn animal forced to move about while very young, such an immaturity of the primitive spatial field is impossible: motor activities structure and harden it before the inductor effect of a hypothetical exterior language can come into play.

Freed from the tyranny of these alienating forms, the space in human psychism can become the open framework for Geometry and for Mechanics. The group of spatio-temporal translations then operates in semantic space and so human language allows the description of a distant process (in space and time) and frees the mind from the tyranny of the "here and now" to which the animal remains subject.

Perhaps in this, life is only pushing one of its fundamental mechanisms to the limit. As soon as it makes an egg, a living organism initiates the project of colonizing space and time and it is subjected to the "here and now." The essential function of the human intellect, to simulate the laws and structures of the external world, is hardly more than the extension or the making clear of this primitive design.

Perhaps it is not absurd to see in the most elaborate acts of human psychism, for example, in mathematical discovery, a direct extension of this mechanism of symbolic creation. Indeed, while exploring a new theory, while juggling with this new material, the mathematician sometimes sees an expression, or a relation, turning up again and again with an embarrassing insistence. He will then be tempted to introduce a new symbol to condense this expression into a single form and so continue the work on a new basis. This simple procedure may sometimes lead to success. More often he will be struck by the idea of new expressions to condense, new figures to construct and name through suspecting *a priori* their properties. To introduce a new symbol, that is, injecting a new letter on to the paper, promotes a kind of tearing away, with the establishing of a new semantic field which will be the support of the new actant and so free the mental movement from the obsessional presences which impede it.

We know that around 18 months, the newly born child begins his babbling; he becomes aware of articulatory possibilities and, so the specialists say, in this period forms phonemes of all the languages of the world. The parents answer him in their own language, and soon after the baby produces only the phonemes of this language, the vocabulary and syntax of which he will master some months later. I would willingly see in the mathematician a perpetual newborn baby who babbles before nature. Only those who know to listen to the response of Mother Nature will come later to open a dialogue with her and to master a new language. The other will only babble and buzz in the void, *bombinans in vacuo*. And where, you may ask, will the mathematician be able to hear Nature's response? The voice of reality is in the significance of the symbol.

REFERENCES

1. C. Lejeune. Pictures taken from *Mémoire de rien* (Brussels: ed. Le Corcuer, 1972), obtained in the first place from photographs of plants.

2. W. Köhler. See any source book for Gestalt Psychology: for instance D. Katz, *Gestalt Psychology* (London: Methuen, 1951).

THOMAS A. SEBEOK

Semiotics is the study of semiosis in all its forms, and all the texts in this volume thematize, with varying degrees of generality and specificity, some aspect or other of this generative and infinite process. Thom's essay indicated that the essential structures of semiosis are rooted in the essential structures of morphology and morphogenesis. Thomas Sebeok, in the following essay, undertakes, in his inimitably synthetic fashion, to broaden the framework of discussion to include all those systems for exchanging messages that human beings share with living creatures quite generally. It gives us a map for plotting that immense realm and offers us an indispensable guide to discussion and research.

Human communication is admittedly built around the pivotal institution of language and the complex symbolic formations built on top of it. The main line of semiotic research has also been focused on semiotic systems that are anthroposemiotic, in the strict sense, that is, species-specific in man, and in fact has often used linguistics as the paradigm semiotic system, on which all the other systems are modeled or in terms of which they are conceptualized. Sebeok, however, wants to show how focusing on zoosemiotic systems leads us to a vast field of phenomena which enrich immeasurably our perspective on the webs of semiotic exchange which, in the term, constitute the very definition of life itself, a theme which runs throughout Sebeok's essay reproduced here and many others, too. Living and semiosis become identical or at least isomorphic processes.

The specific procedure of the following essay is to pass in review the numerous points of intersection between the various components of zoo-semiotic systems, on the vast scale running from cells to human brains, and to display the crucial categories for thematizing them.

The distinctions around which Sebeok constructs his sketch are clear and heuristically fertile, even if, I think, they will be considered somewhat contentious by some. Sebeok first shows that there is real room for an "endosemiotics," "which studies cybernetic systems within the body." One of the most interesting contentions of this part of the essay, taken up by others, too, is that "the integumentary threshold" is not a rigid boundary and that furthermore, as the proxemics theorists have been exploring, there is in fact a semiotic extension of the body out into "appropriated" space. Semiotics penetrates inward into somatic processes and outward into somatic prostheses. Secondly, it is necessary to delineate the dialectic between vocal and nonvocal exchanges of signs. Sebeok points out "how uncommon [the] prominence of the role of sound is in the wider scheme of biological existence" and indicates that beyond this distinction of the vocal from the nonvocal lies the further one of the verbal from the nonverbal which, in the state of current research and the "conceptual chaos" which is attendant upon this aspect of the total semiotic problem, looks questioningly at the points of intersection between a cultural semiotics and ethology, but still without a conceptual scheme to allow it to be brought under a unitary point of view, a fact which has become, perhaps painfully, obvious in the texts assembled in this volume.

Sebeok also shows how many of the messages exchanged in life are bounded by the two poles of witting/unwitting. In many cases we cannot control the emission of messages, which are nevertheless crucial in a social encounter—no matter what the scale—and, if we accept what Polanyi, for example, has written about the tacit dimension in human knowing, it is often impossible to specify just what cues we are relying on when we grasp the message that is being sent to us, whether wittingly or unwittingly. This topic is taken up, with ample references, in the section witting/unwitting.

After some rapid allusions to the left/right issue in cerebral research Sebeok sketches what promises to be a major theme in future work, the diachronic study of the formation and dissolution of signs and systems of signs in phylogeny and ontogeny. Sebeok points out the need for more detailed work on the differentiated matrix within which human speech is first acquired by the infant and on the twofold processes of decay of semiotic systems attendant upon injury and disease and upon the processes of ageing. This last proposal for a "semiotics of old age" is, I think, one of the most pressing problems of medical semiotics.

Sebeok ends his essay with a claim that in light of the increasingly unlikely fact "that a terrestrial languagelike animal communication system will ever be located under natural conditions" we should turn with increased vigor to the comparative study of zoosemiotic systems in man. His essay marks out the paths and furnishes part of the gear for this research trip.

In light of the extensive cross-referencing contained in Sebeok's essays, which resemble in some respects miniature Alexandrian libraries, I will only mention his last two works, *The Sign and Its Masters* (Austin, Texas: University of Texas Press, 1979) and *The Play of Musement* (Bloomington: Indiana University Press, 1981). The list of references therein will lead one further.

Zoosemiotic Components of Human Communication

THOMAS A. SEBEOK

NOTE: *O. F. Kugelmass has written a brilliant paper about certain tribes in Borneo that do not have a word for "no" in their language and consequently turn down requests by nodding their heads and saying, "I'll get back to you." This corroborates his earlier theories that the urge to be liked at any cost is not socially adaptive but genetic, much the same as the ability to sit through operetta.—Woody Allen, "By Destiny Denied,"* THE NEW YORKER, *February 23, 1976. By permission.*

1. "Zoosemiotics": Notes on Its History, Sense, and Scope

The term *zoosemiotics* was launched in 1963 and initially proposed as a name "for the discipline, within which the science of signs intersects with ethology, devoted to the scientific study of signalling behavior in and across animal species" (Sebeok 1972:61). It obviously satisfied a felt need, for—despite some initial resistance, as to any neologism, especially one with overtones of academic jargon—it rapidly diffused in two criss-crossing directions: multidisciplinary and multilingual. It has since been adopted by scholars in a variety of fields, notably biology; and it has penetrated many of the languages of Europe, East and West, and beyond, including Hebrew and Japanese. Outside of scientific writings, the word has cropped up in well-known newspapers, like *Le Monde*, and magazines, like *Il Mondo*. It was featured in at least one novel by a famous English author, as well as in a balloon emanating from the muzzle of that most distinguished of beagles, Snoopy. Discharging a professional obligation to lexicography, I endeavored until recently to keep track of these migrations, and, on occasion, published at least highlights from the progressive record (Sebeok 1972, ch. 9; 1976a:57, 86ff.).

This chapter incorporates observations delivered in Milan at the concluding Plenary Session, on June 6, 1974, of the First Congress of the International Association for Semiotic Studies, in the course of an invited presentation on the state of the art of "Nonverbal Communication." Responses to the ensuing discussion from the floor by Geoffrey Broadbent, David Efron, Tomás Maldonado, Christian Metz, and Leo Pap have all been blended into the text. The argument, of course, has been greatly expanded, brought up to date, and refocused to fit the overall purposes of this book: *How Animals Communicate*, edited by Thomas A. Sebeok, Bloomington: Indiana University Press. Copyright © 1977. Reprinted by permission of the publishers.

What was originally intended by this term and what it seems to have come to mean to many others is quite another story, and still a bit perplexing. In most instances *zoosemiotics* has been used, roughly, as a one-word equivalent for "the study of animal communication," particularly in explicit or at least implicit contrast with "the study of human communication." This restricted usage is, however, far from what the original definition actually implied. In 1970, in a typology of semiotic systems in general, it was clearly specified that "Human semiotic systems are of two kinds: anthroposemiotic, that is, species-specific systems of man; and zoosemiotic, that is, those component sub-systems of human communication that are found elsewhere in the animal kingdom as well" (Sebeok 1972 : 163). Because of a colossal accretion in semiotic theory and praxis in recent years, accompanied by a well-nigh unmanageable proliferation of literature in animal communication studies, a conceptual cleansing is called for. Is *zoosemiotics* a useful term? What does it cover? How does all this fit into the vaster framework of general semiotics? Some of the difficulties of terminology and classification, which confront everyone who enters the field of study covered in the rest of Sebeok 1977a, have worried the most thoughtful of its practitioners and observers, but the only thing that is absolutely clear is that we are far from having reached consensus in this area (Hinde 1972 : 86–98, 395).

The subject matter of semiotics is, quite simply, messages—any messages whatsoever. Since every message is composed of signs according to some ordered selection, semiotics has been variously identified as the doctrine (Locke, Peirce), or the science (Saussure), or the theory (Charles Morris, Carnap, Eco) of signs. Correspondingly, the study designated semiotics comprises the set of general principles that underlie the structure of all signs, constituting a code, which was defined by Cherry (1966 : 305) as "an agreed transformation, or set of unambiguous rules, whereby messages are converted from one representation to another." Further, semiotics aims to uncover the ways in which such principles are or may be manifested in diverse messages, and to identify the specifics of particular sign systems, with comparative (including cross-taxonomic) as well as typological, synchronic (both structural and functional) as well as diachronic (both phylogenetic and ontogenetic; see section 7, below) ends in view. Semiotics is concerned, successively, with the generation and encoding of messages, their propagation in any sensorially appropriate form of physical energy, their decoding and interpretation. The methods employed by some investigators are more empirical, those by others more analytical. Some prefer to study communication, others signification (Prieto 1975, for instance, makes much of this distinction). Plainly, however, these tendencies are complementary, each implying the other. (Naturalists, as one would expect, by their inclination and training have leaned toward an empirical approach to animal communication, but solid foundations for an analytical approach to animal signification have also been

laid in the classic literature of ethology, notably in von Uexküll's marvelous 1940 monograph, "Bedeutungslehre" [cf. Sebeok 1977a].)

If the subject matter of semiotics encompasses any messages whatsoever, the subject matter of linguistics is confined to verbal messages
only. The fundamental competence underlying verbal messages is generally assumed to be (1) species-specific and (2) species-consistent. Species-
specificity of the linguistic propensity means that the formal principles
we deem sufficient to characterize natural languages (spoken or not) differ radically from those found sufficient to characterize any known system of animal communication, including especially man's so-called nonverbal communication systems. This does not necessarily imply, however,
that the neural substrates and/or psychological processes involved need
be substantially dissimilar—these are surely secondary and tertiary lami-
nations that are each of a distinct order (cf. Dingwall 1975). Moreover,
this conception of species-specificity does not exclude the possibility of
quite sophisticated, though always only partial, code sharing, and hence
communication, between man and animal (Hediger 1967; 1974 generally; Fouts and Rigby, in respect to the man-chimpanzee dyad, Sebeok
1977a, ch. 37). Nor is species-consistency necessarily universal, for se-
verely handicapped children may lack the capacity to master language in
more than rudimentary fashion (Malson 1964; Curtiss et al. 1975).

The situation of the verbal code in a semiotic frame has been considered by almost everybody who has written on the subject since Locke
(1975 [1690]:721). Late in the seventeenth century, he asserted that articulate sounds are the signs "which Men have found the most convenient, and therefore generally make use of. . . ." Linguists—building
upon Locke without attribution—generally flatter themselves by at least
acquiescing in dicta like Bloomfield's that "Linguistics is the chief con-
tributor to semiotic," or persisting in Weinreich's sentiment that verbal
messages constitute "the semiotic phenomenon par excellence" (Sebeok
1976a:11–12)—no doubt a conscious rephrasing of Sapir's (1931) "language is the communicative process par excellence in every known society"—just recently reechoed by Greimas (1976:9) in his remark that
"la linguistique . . . est la plus élaborée des sémiotiques."

It was apparently Saussure who promoted linguistics to the status
of a pilot science, or "le patron général de toute sémiologie" (Sebeok
1976a:12), a programmatic statement which, when pursued blindly, can
lead into many a cul-de-sac (cf. Marcus, in Sebeok 1974:2871ff.; see also
Polhemus, in Benthall and Polhemus 1975:20ff.). I have referred to the
principle that is usually invoked in this connection as one of "intersemiotic transmutability," which may have been first, or was, at any rate,
most insistently enunciated by Hjelmslev (1953:70): "in practice, a language is a semiotic into which all other semiotics may be translated—
both all other languages, and all other conceivable semiotic structures."
Elsewhere, I have questioned whether this *ex cathedra* declaration has ac-

tual support or remains, as I think, although still much cherished by linguists, hardly more than unsubstantiated dogma. In particular, I tried to show that animal sounds are often incapable of being paraphrased: "one gropes in vain for a set of linguistic signs to substitute instead of the significative unit employed by the speechless creature both to refer to his scarcely understood species-specific code and to the context of delivery, or *Umwelt*, through which the message fragment is aligned within the observed sequence of signs emitted" (Sebeok, 1976b). Even the transmutation of certain categories of human nonverbal messages into linguistic expression is, at best, likely to introduce gross falsification, or, like most music, altogether defy comprehensible verbal definition. Sapir (1931) put his finger on a "more special class of communicative symbolism," such as the use of railroad lights, bugle calls in the army, or smoke-signals, in which "one cannot make a word-to-word translation, as it were, back to speech but can only paraphrase in speech the intent of the communication."

Semiotic systems that are species-specific in man are, then, for convenience, categorized as *anthroposemiotic* (Sebeok 1972:163ff., 1976a:3). Language clearly belongs here, not only in its global spoken form but also as a visible means of communication used by a small minority population among a minority of mankind with partial or total hearing impairment and by those associated with such persons (Stokoe 1972, esp. ch. 1). Here are counted also a wide array of speech surrogates (Sebeok and Umiker-Sebeok 1976), mute communication systems preserved in certain monasteries (Barakat 1975), aboriginal sign languages used among native peoples of the Americas and Australia (Umiker-Sebeok and Sebeok 1977b), complex (viz., nonisomorphic) transductions into parasitic or restricted formations, like script or other optical displays of the chain of speech signs (the Morse code, or any of the several acoustic alphabets designed to aid the blind, or sound spectrograms), optionally imposed upon chronologically prior acoustic patterns (Kavanagh and Mattingly 1972), and more or less context-free artificial constructs developed for various scientific or technical purposes (see, e.g., the respective articles by Golopentia-Eretescu, Gross, and Freudenthal in Sebeok 1974).

Over and above such transfers (Sapir 1931), transforms, derivatives, and substitutes, there are those macrostructures that are based, in the final analysis, on a natural language, the "primary system" on which culture is superimposed, "regarded as a hierarchy of semiotic systems correlated in pairs, realized through correlation with the system of natural language" (Sebeok 1975:76–77, 1976:23 n. 38). Particularly, this is implied by the concept of "secondary modeling systems," propagated chiefly by the Moscow-Tartu School of semioticians (Eimermacher 1974; Sebeok 1975:57–83; Ivanov 1976; Winner and Winner 1976). All secondary modeling systems are, therefore, anthroposemiotic by definition.

In a third category that might be reckoned anthroposemiotic are sets

of signs affirmed to be uniquely used by man independently of any linguistic infrastructure (although, of course, unavoidably intertwined with
verbal effects), but one must exercise great caution with respect to this
division. In 1968, I blithely declared that music is "a species-specific, but
not species-consistent form of behavior" (Sebeok 1972: 164–165). There
is ample cause for wonder now if the first part of this allegation is true,
and in what way? The relation between human and avian music was
thoughtfully reviewed by Joan Hall-Craggs (Hinde 1969, ch. 16), with
special regard to the nature of the esthetic content of bird song. She concluded that "the form of music remains the privilege of birds and men"
(ibid.: 380), but suggested that the resemblances between the two varieties of semiosis can best be understood in terms of analogous functional
requirements, such as the need to signal to distant listeners. The philosopher Hartshorne (the same, incidentally, who had served as the se-
nior editor of C. S. Peirce's selected papers) has since reexamined the material in even more detail (1973, ch. 3). He characterized bird song as
"the best of the subhuman music of nature" (ibid.: 39) and declared,
"considering the enormous gap between the anatomies and lives of man
and bird, it remains astonishing how much musical intelligibility the utterances of the latter have for the former" (ibid.: 46).

Investigations in this area have even crystallized into a subdiscipline
called "ornithomusicology" by Szöke (1963), who maintains that since
birds evolved elaborate musical utterances before we appeared on the
scene, it is reasonable to suppose that the development of primitive music
was actually stimulated by hearing and mimicking bird vocalizations
(cf. remarks by Hewes, Livingstone, and Lomax in Wescott 1974). Some
species of Mysticetes, notably *Megaptera novaeangliae*, also "produce a
series of beautiful and varied sounds," likewise called songs, the function
of which is still a matter for much speculation but is usually assumed
to serve communicative ends, possibly over great distances (Payne and
McVay 1971: 597); these prolonged vocalizations are frequently compared to bird songs, the chief difference being that the latter normally last
only a few seconds, whereas those of the humpback whales have a cycling
time of up to thirty minutes, their patterns being repeated by individuals
with considerable accuracy. Whatever the ultimate merits may be of such
cross-taxa comparisons and contrasts between distantly related species
occupying only vaguely similar ecological niches (as considered, e.g., in
terms of quite abstract geometric patterns by Nelson 1973: 299–300,
324ff.), the facile grouping of music among anthroposemiotic systems
appears, in retrospect, to have been premature.

The same can be said, *mutatis mutandis*, about other nonverbal art
forms, for instance, abstract picture-making, a behavior that has been induced in apes (D. Morris 1962; Bourne 1971, ch. 9), and even in capuchin
monkeys, with some success. According to the ethologist Andrew Whiten,

the taste exhibited by apes—their choice of color, brightness, composition—"provides a unique background against which we may try to understand the origins and fundamental nature of visual art in our species . . ." (in Brothwell 1976:40). Nicholas Humphrey's experiments show that apes prefer blues and greens over yellows and reds, leading to speculations that they favor the safety of green trees as opposed to the perils of exposure against red or yellow earth. Whiten "explains" their liking for bright light by assuming that it helps them perceive potential danger and surmises that their predilection for regular pattern might have something to do with an aptitude for handling intricate spatial relationships required to move safely through forests (ibid.: 32ff.). Apes do seem to enjoy what they are doing, but forms of life that are not our direct phylogenetic ancestors, like the bowerbirds, also exhibit significant traces of a visual esthetic sense (von Frisch 1974:244ff.; Waddington, in Brothwell 1976:8; Griffin 1976:76ff.); thus male black woodpeckers chisel out nests that no less a scientist than von Frisch has depicted as architectural "works of art" (1974:189). Other birds build elaborate nests that they continue to improve upon with practice, in the sense of imparting a heavier semiotic charge: their constructions become, at least in our eyes, tidier and more elegant, but not recognizably more useful by strictly biological criteria.

Because I now consider it increasingly doubtful that any sign system that is not manifestly language-related belongs with man's repertoire of anthroposemiotic devices, I provisionally conclude, as a heuristic tactic, that all other systems used by man are to be construed as zoosemiotic until demonstrated to be otherwise. This view represents a radical shift in my position over the last ten years, one that still preserves the established dichotomy but enlarges the biological base as against the cultural superstructure, encouraging the search for true antecedents (homologies), not just the sharing of traits. It also counsels caution about a saltatory "discontinuity theory" in the terms argued for by Eric H. Lenneberg (in Sebeok 1968, ch. 21) and supported to a degree by some notable ethologists (e.g., Klopfer, in Hahn and Simmel 1976:7–21). The strategic anthroposemiotics/zoosemiotics dichotomy will stand just as long as the riddle of the origin of language remains unsolved (Hinde 1972:75ff., 94ff.; Wescott 1974; Lieberman 1975; 1977). Recent concerted efforts at experimentation with various Great Apes notwithstanding (Fouts 1978), no breakthrough is in sight; indeed, Thorpe (in Hinde 1972:174) fears that the solution is likely to elude us forever. It may well be the case, as Julian Huxley (1966:258) once remarked, and as I would very much like to believe, that language "can properly be regarded as ritualized (adaptively formalized) behaviour," but, unfortunately, he did not go on to spell out just how one could apply the essentially comparative methods of ethology to a phenomenon that stubbornly remains a singularity in our known universe. In brief, what zoosemiotics has hitherto failed to provide is a comparative perspective for language (Hinde in Benthall and Polhemus 1975:107–140), particularly with appropriately correlated operational procedures. The importance of a comparative semiotics (called for in Sebeok, 1976a, ch. 3; 1977a) cannot be overestimated, so it is encouraging to know that at least a few animal behaviorists of the first rank are not only commencing to share this long-felt conviction but have actually concluded that "the road now seems open" to realize its goals (Griffin 1976:95–106).

The relation between the mutually opposite categories in man is hierarchical, and can therefore productively be viewed in terms of a notion standard in linguistics, *markedness*. Anthroposemiotic systems are always *marked*, in contradistinction to the zoosemiotic systems that comprehend them. This means that a specific anthroposemiotic sign implies the presence of a certain property X, whereas a genetic zoosemiotic sign implies nothing about the presence of X (it may, but need not, indicate the absence of X). The marked sign is always the negative of the unmarked sign: "statement of X" vs. "no statement of X." Some major controversial issues of long standing can be clarified in this light, such as the much-debated question whether a particular facial expression signifies the same emotion for all peoples or whether its meaning depends on the culture of the expressor and the "expressee." Ekman's carefully wrought theory postulates "culture differences in facial expressions as well as universals" (1972:279). The pancultural expressions are plainly zoosemiotic—they reflect biological bias in human behavior; hence, in the technical sense of the term, they are unmarked. The consequences of social learning, which varies both from culture to culture and according to smaller groupings within a culture, include the acquisition of markedness for every possible transition state in terms of the gain or loss of whatever the feature under consideration.

"The relationships between verbal and nonverbal communication are rather tenuous," Hinde (1974:146) ruefully conceded in his latest excellent survey of human zoosemiotic techniques. Oddly, however, he has overlooked a pivotal article by Gregory Bateson (in Sebeok 1968, ch. 22), which cogently and forcefully set forth the reasons why this must be so. There is a popular belief, Bateson said, "that in the evolution of man, language replaced the cruder systems of the other animals," but he believed this to be totally wrong, because, if "verbal language were in any sense an evolutionary replacement of communication by means of kinesics and paralanguage, we would expect the old . . . systems to have undergone conspicuous decay." Such is manifestly not the case: rather, "the kinesics of men have become richer and more complex, and paralanguage has blossomed side by side with the evolution of verbal language . . . [both of which] have been elaborated into complex forms of art, music, ballet, poetry, and the like, and, even in everyday life, the intricacies of human kinesic communication, facial expression and vocal intonation far exceed anything that any other animal is known to produce." In brief, the two kinds of sign systems, though they are often in performance subtly inter-woven, serve ends largely different from one another, indeed, zoosemiotic devices perform functions that anthroposemiotic devices are unsuited for, and vice versa. An exquisite illustration of the "reconciliation of the human necessity of speaking with the spiritual need for silence . . . within a single behavioral frame in which both components, otherwise contradictory, were indispensable" (Bauman 1974:159–160) is related from the life of Quakers, whose style of preaching, mixing a "bundle of words and heap of Non-sense," evoked astonished comment even in 1653 (ibid.: 150).

2. *Inner / Outer*

Another coined term (Sebeok 1974:213; 1976a:3), albeit proposed no more than half seriously, was *endosemiotics*, "which studies cyber-netic systems within the body." Clearly, man's semiotic systems are char-acterized by a definite bipolarity between the molecular code at the lower end of the scale and the verbal code at the upper. Amid these two uniquely powerful mechanisms (Marcus 1974; Sebeok 1972:62; 1977a) there ex-ists a whole array of others, ranging from those located in the interior of organisms (von Uexküll's *Innenwelt*) to those linking them to the exter-nal "physical world" (his *Umwelt*), which of course includes biologically and/or sociologically "interesting" other organisms, like preys and preda-tors. Semiotic networks are thus established between individuals belong-ing to the same as well as to different species. Jacob, who has more suc-cinctly stated that the "genetic code is like a language," goes further: if they are to specialize, he points out, "cells must . . . communicate with each other," and, at the macroscopic level, "evolution depends on setting up new systems of communication, just as much within the organism as between the organism and its surroundings" (Jacob 1974:306, 308, 312). After the new integrations have occurred, such that the coordina-tion of elements has progressed from molecular interaction to the ex-change of verbal messages, a still more novel hierarchy of integrons is set up: "From family organization to modern state, from ethnic group to coalition of nations" (ibid.: 320), a variety of elevated ("secondary") codes come into play—cultural, moral, social, political, economic, mili-tary, religious, ideological, etc. The genetic conception of integron—called "shred out" in general systems theory, in reference to evolution "from slow, inefficient, chemical transmission by diffusion at the cell level up to increasingly rapid and cost-effective symbolic linguistic transmis-sions over complicated networks at the higher levels of living systems"

(Miller 1976:227)—is equivalent to the semiotic notion of "radius of communication," the progressive widening of which mirrors the history of civilization (Sapir 1931) as much as it marks stages in the maturation of every individual.

There is no absolute boundary where zoosemiotics abruptly turns into anthroposemiotics. Least of all is this a correlate of "the appearance of a new property: the ability to do without objects and interpose a kind of filter between the organism and its environment: the ability to symbolize," which Jacob (1974:319) ascribes to mammals in general. So does Washburn (1973:181), who refers to "the mammalian brain as a symbolic machine." In fact, the groundwork for the mosaic of changes that enable organisms to utilize symbols was prefigured much earlier, as Gordon M. Tomkins (1975) convincingly delineated, and was sketchily reviewed in the framework of Peirce's doctrine of signs in Sebeok (1977c). On the invertebrate side, insects, such as the balloon flies, have evolved a symbolizing capacity in one of their species, *Hilara sartor* (ibid.; for symbolic communication in bees, see Griffin 1976:19–25). Also, John Z. Young has recently shown that the octopus deals with the world in a manner that can only be described as "symbolic." In a lecture given at the American Museum of Natural History in 1976, he said: "The essence of learning is the attaching of symbolic value to signs from the outside world. Images on the retina are not eatable or dangerous. What the eye of a higher animal provides is a tool by which, aided by a memory, the animal can learn the symbolic significance of events." Cephalopod brains may not be able to elaborate complex programs—i.e., strings of signs, or what Young calls "mnemons"—such as guide our future feelings, thoughts, and actions, but they can symbolize at least simple operations crucial for their survival, such as appropriate increase or decrease in distance between them and environmental stimulus sources ("Withdraw" or "Approach": Schneirla 1965). The use of symbols on the part of the alloprimates is, of course, a current commonplace, but it has been apparent to unbiased scientists at least since Wolfe's (1936) experiments with a group of young chimpanzees nearly a half century ago (Wolfe was an excessively timid reader of Charles Morris; ibid.: 70). As Katz (1937:237) then noted in a needless display of the double negative, "It appears that chimpanzees are not completely incapable of using non-linguistic symbols." A recent remark of Lévi-Strauss sums the matter up far more cogently: "Les animaux sont privés de langage, au sens que nous l'entendons chez l'homme, mais ils communiquent tout de même au moyen . . . d'un système symbolique" (Malson 1973:20).

The genetic code and the metabolic code—which intimately couples the endocrine and nervous systems (Tomkins 1975:763)—are obviously at once endosemiotic and zoosemiotic, but other intracorporeal sign processes, notably the phenomenon of "inner speech" (Egger 1904; Vygotsky

1962; Vološinov 1973), may be at least partially anthroposemiotic. Thus memory experiments have convincingly shown that thinking has two richly interconnected components in man: one verbal, the other nonverbal, each with characteristic properties. The imaginal effects in this dual coding system are zoosemiotic. Neurological studies display in extreme form a functional separation between the verbal and nonverbal spatial systems (Bower 1970:509). Further, at least two scholars have independently pointed to the evolutionary intermediacy of man's dreaming, focusing their arguments chiefly on one particular kind of semiotic entity, the icon (Bateson, in Sebeok 1968:623; Thom 1975a:72–73; cf. Sebeok 1976a). Moreover, tests conducted on patients with commissurectomies (in the so-called Bogen [1969] series) have also yielded rather conspicuous clues that the right half of the brain may be primarily responsible for imaging processes in dreaming. If confirmed by current sleep research experiments, these results will be highly interesting in view of the association of the right hemisphere with the normal imaging mechanisms implicated with the handling of visual-spatial tasks criterial of (nonvocal) nonverbal communication (cf. Ornstein 1972:64–65, 235 n. 17; see also section 6, below).

The field of transducer physiology studies the conversion of "outer" signs to their initial "inner" input and considers the relative or absolute contrasts between the pathways of information outside the body and the pathways deep inside it. Although one can but concur with Shands (1976:303ff.) that it is essential to grapple with "the human problem of the greatest moment . . . of so relating the outer to the inner that the minimal information derivable from inner sources comes to be a reliable index of the external situation," and that this bifurcation must eventually be dealt with in semiotic terms, this science, powerfully foreseen by Leibniz, is as yet barely developed. Its modern theoretical foundations were laid in Bentley's spellbinding paper (1941) on the human skin as philosophy's last line of defense, the argument of which rested on the semiotic of Peirce (ibid.: 18). Beck, looking toward "a truly human sociobiology" (1976:157), reviewed recent work with specific regard to nonverbal communication in man.

It is, in fact, hard to ascertain where "inner" ends and "outer" begins. The human skin itself is a rich arena of momentous semiotic events throughout the life of each individual, not only within our species (Moles 1964; Kauffman 1971; Montagu 1971) but, more fascinatingly and almost wholly out of awareness, also in intricate communicative interaction with the teeming faunal and floral inhabitants of that veritable microscopic dermal ecosystem (Marples 1965). Beyond the skin toward the outside, as Hediger (e.g., 1968:83) has incontrovertibly been demonstrating since 1941, every individual, according to its species, moves in the interior of an invisible but nonetheless sharply defined insulating space circumscribed by that animal's "individual distance" (the minimum remove within which it may approach another) and its "social distance" (the maximum separation between the members of any group). These concepts are crucial in the management of animals in zoos and circuses, and in their handling in laboratory experiments, under conditions of domestication, or as pets. In a test in which the density of children was modified in a playroom, a similar process was observed in operation (Hutt and Vaizey 1966). Evidence bearing on the structuring of space and time in animals, or having to do with territoriality, overcrowding, and other sorts of distance regulation, were later extrapolated to man's perception of space and cultural modifications of this basic biological structuration. The branch of anthroposemiotics that studies such behavior is sometimes called proxemics (E. Hall 1959; Watson, in Sebeok 1974:311–344). Its subject matter falls between bodily contact (the most intimate involvement of the *ego* with the *alter*) and patterns of physical appearance such as facial postures and bodily position, eye movements, and the nonverbal aspects of vocal acts. All of these come into play, in the main, beyond the Hediger "bubble," a variably shaped zone of personal space that admits no trespass by strangers and is defended when penetrated without permission (Figure 1).

The distinction between anthroposemiotic and zoosemiotic events is thus not at all demarcated at the integumentary threshold. Both processes have important extensions past the skin, in either direction. These "boundary" communicative phenomena, to which Peirce drew our attention repeatedly (when discussing Secondness) as the shock of reaction between *ego* and *non-ego*, may prove particularly interesting for future semiotic and related researches.

3. Vocal / Nonvocal

Sound emission and sound reception are so much a part of human life that it comes as something of a surprise to realize how uncommon this prominence of the role of sound is in the wider scheme of biological existence. In point of fact, according to Huxley and Koch (1964 [1938]:26–27), "the great majority of animals are both deaf and dumb." Of the dozen or so phyla, "only two contain creatures that can hear or produce functional sound," namely, the Arthropods and the Chordates. Their respective situations are, however, quite different: while practically no members of the lower classes of Chordates are capable of sound production, the "highest three-and-a-half classes of the vertebrates are . . . unique in having all their members capable of sound-production, as well (save for the snakes) as of hearing." The methods of sound production, of course, vary enormously from group to group. Not only does our own method appear to be unusual, but Huxley and Koch (ibid.: 32) confirm

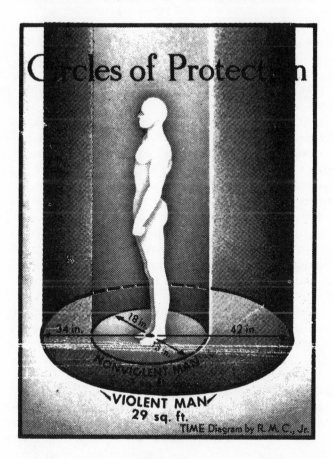

Figure 1

Psychiatrist Augustus F. Kinzel has differentiated violent from non-violent human subjects in terms of their communicative radius: on the average, the former stopped him at a distance of three feet, the latter at only half that distance. The two areas of insulating space differed, as well, in shape, from nearly cylindrical in nonviolent subjects to those bulging to the rear in violent ones—an avenue of approach interpreted as particularly menacing. Reprinted by permission from TIME, The Weekly Newsmagazine; Copyright © Time Inc., 1969.

that it evolved only once in a stream of life. The vocal mechanism that works by means of a current of air passing over the cords and setting them into vibration seems to be confined to ourselves and, with distinctions, to our nearest relatives—the only mammals, the birds (since they possess a syrinx), the reptiles, and the amphibians (although some fish use wind instruments as well, they do so without the reed constituted by our vocal cords). So far as we know, no true vocal performances are found outside the land vertebrates or their marine descendants. Among many, notably ourselves, unarticulated vocalizations are used for status displays or to convey information about age, sex (Guthrie 1976:33), and a host of specific characteristics about the state of the emitter-in-context (Lotz 1956a:212); usually, they are employed in the manner of icons (Sebeok 1976c).

Humans communicate via many channels, only one of which is acoustic. Acoustic communication in man may be somatic (e.g., humming) or artifactual (e.g., drumming: Sebeok and Umiker-Sebeok 1976). Acoustic somatic communication may be vocal (e.g., shouting for a waiter) or nonvocal (snapping one's fingers to summon him). Finally, acoustic somatic vocal communication may be verbal (speech) or nonverbal (Pike 1943:32–41, 149–151 remains by far the best survey of such mechanisms), with the latter being either linked to or independent of speech (Argyle 1975, ch. 18). On the other hand, by no means all verbal systems are manifested in the acoustic medium: Classical Chinese occurs only in written form; the American Sign Language (ASL) is encoded and decoded visually; and the mode in which man communes with himself, his thinking—which, as Peirce taught, "always proceeds in the form of a dialogue . . . between different phases of the *ego* . . ." (Sebeok 1976a: 28 n. 45), and which constitutes one of man's unique uses of language (Bronowski, in Sebeok 1974:2539–2540)—requires audible articulation but facultatively.

These observations, which underline obvious distinctions, are necessary because much conceptual confusion is engendered by the terminological disarray that bedevils the field of human zoosemiotics (Sebeok 1976a:156–164). For example, at least two major books (Hall 1959; Critchley 1975) bear the title *Silent Language*. The attentive reader soon discovers that neither work deals with language, except in a misleadingly metaphoric sense, or even, strictly, with silence: thus Critchley declares in his very first paragraph, "Gesture may sometimes be audible though still unvoiced."

The foregoing is summarily depicted in Figure 2, which substantially develops a single node from a tabular representation introduced in an earlier classification of zoosemiotic devices to illustrate the human production of signs according to the different communicative techniques involved (Sebeok 1976a:30, Table 4; also in Eco 1976:175, Table 34), but which also constitutes a considerable amplification of a clarifying figure with similar intent by Argyle (1975:346, Fig. 18.1).

The superficially similar classification by Wescott (1969:152), possibly the most tireless nomenclator in this field, is both incomplete and at least partially mistaken. He distinguishes, in the acoustic channel, among three communicative systems, which he labels, respectively, *language*, *phasis*, and *strepitus*. "Language and phasis are both vocal," he con-

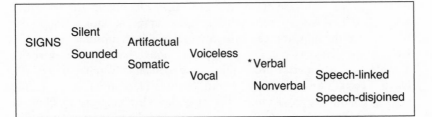

Figure 2

An asterisk indicates the category assumed to be purely anthroposemiotic; the status of speech-linked phenomena, such as singing (i.e.,
a tune plus lyrics), is best reckoned as hybrid, or transitional, if not
downright fuzzy (cf. Crystal 1969:179–194). Terms to the right are
progressively marked. Note that less than 1 percent of the information
conveyed by speech is used for linguistic purposes as such (cf. Lotz
1956:212).

tinues inaccurately (cf. Dingwall 1975:32), the former being articulated,
the latter consisting "solely of grunts and other vocalizations insuscep-
tible to combination." Strepitus is then said to differ from both "in being
nonvocal," e.g., hand clapping or foot stamping. Incidentally, there have
been many efforts to design a system that describes all human movement
in terms of the place and type of articulation of the segments of an
idealized lay figure, that is, to devise a notation for muscular movement.
The model, as construed in a volume of three-dimensional space so
that the behavioral sequences can then be delineated as a syntagmatic
concatenation of volumes, was envisaged by Bouissac (1973) and, in a
measure, actually attempted by Schutz (1976; cf. Kelley 1971, which,
oddly enough, is not cited).

The taxonomic fragment sketched in Figure 2 could be enriched in
various intersecting ways. For instance, one may inquire to what degree
the signs emitted by the source are "wanted," i.e., constitute its message
for the destination, or have become increasingly "unwanted" (i.e., noisy)
in the course of transmission. Or one may focus on whether the emission
and/or the reception of a given string is conscious or out of awareness (a
distinction to be pursued further in section 5, below).

4. Verbal / Nonverbal

The subject matter of linguistics, as we all "know," is communication
consisting of verbal messages and the undergirding verbal code enabling
them. By contrast, the concept of nonverbal communication is one of the
most ill-defined in all of semiotics. No wonder the notion is often nega-
tively formulated: as early as 1888, Kleinpaul (1972) paradoxically desig-

nated the topic of his classic manual as *Sprache ohne Worte*, or "wordless language." This concept recurs over and over in recent book titles, particularly since the appearance of the comprehensive, handsome treatise by Ruesch and Kees (1956), in the shape of "nonverbal" or "non-verbal." Sample listings, merely from this decade, include Bosmajian (1971), Davis (1971), Eisenberg and Smith (1971), Harrison (1974), Hinde (1972), Knapp (1972), Krames et al. (1974), Mehrabian (1972), Pliner et al. (1975), Poyatos (1976), Scherer (1970), and Weitz (1974). Countless monographs, special journal issues, and brief articles insist on viewing nonverbal communication as "communication minus language"; many of them are listed in Part 8 of the Eschbach-Rader bibliography of semiotics (1976:75–87), which is itself headed "Non-verbal communication" in the restricted sense. Such works tend to deepen the gulf segregating the "nonverbal" from the verbal; to paraphrase an amusing observation of Voegelin and Harris (1947:588), one might infer from some of them "that houses are built in sullen silence."

Two further interconnected problems immediately arise. On the one hand, the contents of these works so labeled encompass an astounding congeries of topics. On the other hand, the partial synonyms that have been devised to cope with this massive confusion have all proved unsatisfactory for one reason or another, as has already been adumbrated in Sebeok (1976a:158–162). Such competing though only partially overlapping terms and expressions include bodily communication, body language or body talk, coenetics, gesticulation, gesture, gSigns, kinesics, kinesiology, motor signs, pantomime, proxemics, silent language, tacesics, etc., and, of course, zoosemiotics with extensions thereof. This is not the place to enter the soggy quicksand of usages appropriate to this particular trade, but what about the nature of the traffic itself? What do we know about the commodity purveyed, beyond the presumed barring of what belongs strictly to linguistics?

Mehrabian's definition of what pertains to nonverbal behavior and what its functions are is fairly typical in that it starts out with an equivocation. He distinguishes (1972, ch. 1) between two senses, one narrow "and more accurate," the other broader but, while traditional, allegedly "a misnomer." The former embraces "facial expressions, hand and arm gestures, postures and positions, and various movements of the body or the legs and feet." The latter is equivalent to what has frequently been included under the subcategory of "paralinguistic or vocal phenomena" (also in Argyle 1975, ch. 18). No mention is made of the obvious: that all animals communicate nonverbally, and that, in point of fact, other books, with identical titles, are devoted to just this, to the exclusion of virtually the entire human domain (e.g., Krames et al. 1974; Pliner et al. 1975; and Hinde 1972, which is evenly balanced between the behavior of man and that of the creatures devoid of language). As to the concept of "paralanguage" (Crystal in McCormack and Wurm 1976: 13–27; Laver 1976: 347–354)—which ought, more accurately, to be termed "para-phonation," but which the innocent inquirer may reasonably assume to bear some relation to language—it further confounds the already frustrating jigsaw puzzle. Paraphonetic features may easily be homologized with aspects of animal communication, such as the conveyance of information about sex, age, and individual identity, much as song is assumed to do in many birds. However, in preparation for a state-of-the-art paper on the topic, David Crystal wrote a number of colleagues asking them what they understood to fall under this heading; he then reported his findings: "animal vocalization (or some aspect of it), memory restrictions on language, recallability for language, utterance length, literary analysis, environmental restrictions on language use . . . glossolalia, and emotional expression in general language disturbance—in effect, a fair proportion of socio-linguistics and psycholinguistics" (in Sebeok 1974:269).

It is indeed very difficult, in practice, always to assign unambiguously what segment of a vocal encounter (conversation, state of talk) between people concerns linguists and what segment concerns "nonverbal" inter-actional analysts: "Please remember that the integral role of gesture in speech is quite as important for our understanding of an utterance as the one or two significant movements or indications which actually replace an uttered word," Malinowski (1965 [1935]:26) warned more than forty years ago. The borderline becomes more blurred the closer the focus of analysis gets. Some of the awesome entanglements of verbal re-sponses with other kinds of acts were first heroically wrestled with by Malinowski, but he failed to achieve the integration he had preached be-cause he lacked one indispensable analytic tool, an understanding of Kiriwinian verbal structure. Goffman dealt with them concretely in his masterful working paper (1975) on minimal dialogic units. They amply justify the research strategy increasingly being applied to the organiza-tion of conversations by workers like Duncan (1975), Poyatos (1976: see Fig. 4, p. 66), and others under such labels as speaker synchrony, interac-tional synchrony, interactional equilibrium, and conveyance of indexical information (Laver 1976:354–358).

In Figure 3, the two oppositions Vocal/Nonvocal and Verbal/Non-verbal, as they are realized in a few of the aforementioned phenomena, are condensed into a sample distinctive feature chart. This matrix is merely meant to be illustrative: many other oppositions, as well as many other kinds of sign systems, could be adduced at will. (The assigned val-ues are adopted from standard linguistic usage: + means that the feature is present, − that it is not, ± that both are co-present, and o that the distinction is inapplicable.)

	VOCAL	VERBAL
Language	0	+
Speech	+	+
ASL	–	+
Babbling; paralanguage	+	–
'Fig'	–	–
Song (tune with or without lyrics)	+	±
Whistle	+	0

Figure 3

The "fig" (thumb thrust between middle and ring fingers of fist) is an invitation to sexual intercourse in some cultures (Bäuml and Bäuml 1975:72), a gesture randomly selected for this chart as an example of a soundless movement of the sort Efron (1972[1941]:96), one supposes, might have called an intrinsically coded kinetograph. Whistle is "Verbal O" because it could represent merely a tune or be used as a speech surrogate (Sebeok and Umiker-Sebeok 1976).

But the conceptual chaos does not end there, because "nonverbal" of course subsumes a considerably vaster radius than the sphere of bodily communication as such. (Incidentally, one may well ask, the so-called organs of speech also being parts of the human body, why are the several manifestations of man's linguistic endowment, notably speech itself, generally not comprehended under this or similar rubrics?) Surely, music (Nattiez 1975), the culinary arts (Barthes 1967:27–28), a circus act (Bouissac 1976), gardening (Malinowski 1965 [1935]), a floral arrangement (Cortambert 1833), the application of perfumes (Sebeok 1972:100–101), the choice and combination of garments (Bogatyrev 1971; Guthrie 1976, ch. 18) are only some random means among man's multiform options for communicating nonverbally. Accordingly, it would hardly be an exaggeration to claim that the range of the "nonverbal," thus conceived, becomes coincidental with the entire range of culture exclusive of language yet further encompassing much that belongs to ethology. But this way of looking at "nonverbal" seems to me about as helpful as the Kugelmass theories reported by Woody Allen in the epigraph to this chapter.

5. Witting / Unwitting

People are capable of encoding messages either deliberately or unwittingly, and to decode messages either with the knowledge that they are so engaged or without conscious awareness of what they are about. In a dyadic interaction between organisms, therefore, four possibilities exist in respect to this distinction.

The first possibility is that neither the emitter nor the receiver is able to identify the message, let alone restate it verbally. The pupil response furnishes a nice illustration of this: "While it is evident that men are attracted to women with large pupils their responses are generally at a nonverbal level. It seems that what is appealing about large pupils in a woman is that they imply a strong and sexually toned interest in the man she is with, as well as making her look younger. . . . The enlarged pupils, in effect, act as a 'signal' transmitted to the other person. Several observations made by others have indicated that this is what really can occur in the interpersonal relationship between a man and a woman, and apparently without conscious awareness" (Hess 1975:95).

This state of affairs can, however, be altered either at the source or at the destination, or, of course, at both the input and the output end. For instance, a woman can deliberately dilate her pupils with one of several pharmaceuticals to enhance her appearance: such, indeed, was the custom in Central Europe in the interwar period (the drug used was a crystalline alkaloid derived from belladonna, which means "beautiful woman"). At the other end of the transmission chain, as Hediger (1976) has noted, the best circus animal trainers "haben schon längst erkannt, dass die Pupillenbewegungen z.B. ihrer Tiger wichtige Schlüsse auf deren Stimmung zulassen. . . ."

Signs that are normally unwitting, like the pupil response in man and animals, are regarded by most specialists (e.g., Peirce, Bühler, Jakobson, and American clinical semioticians generally) as constituting a subcategory of indices that, since Hippocrates, has comprehended symptoms and syndromes (Sebeok 1976a:124–128, 181–182). These are of prime concern no less to semiotics than to medicine (Sebeok 1977c). Instead of dwelling on these wide implications here, let us briefly reconsider the story of Clever Hans (Pfungst 1965 [1911]). One is compelled to concur with Katz (1937:5) that at the turn of the century this case was (and is now more than ever: Hediger 1976) "a problem of first-rate importance, not merely of interest to special sciences, like zoology and psychology, but having some bearing on the deepest philosophical questions." Let us add that it is also of interest to the integrated science of communication, semiotics most particularly (cf. Rosenthal, in Pfungst 1965 [1911]:xxxiii, xxxix n. 11). This eponymous horse gave its name to one of the classic errors in the history of psychology after it was finally realized "how fatally the unintentional effect on the animal of the observer can influence the results" (Katz 1937:7), and paradigmatically illustrated "the power of the self-fulfilling prophecy. Hans' questioners, even skeptical ones, expected Hans to give the correct answers to their queries. Their expectation was reflected in their unwitting signal to Hans that the time had come for him to stop his tapping. The signal cued Hans to stop, and the questioner's expectation became the reason for Hans' being, once again, correct" (Rosenthal 1966:138).

It must be emphasized that one is concerned here with what Carl Stumpf (in his original [1907] Preface to Pfungst 1965) described as *minimale unabsichtliche Bewegungen*, or unintentional minimal movements of the horse's questioner, which occasioned the colossal case of self-deception. Máday soon refocused the whole phenomenon in its properly explicit frame, designating the proposition as a *Zeichenhypothese* (1914:12) and enumerating the proofs therefor (ibid.: 13–18). He also described the *unwillkürliche Zeichen*, or unwitting signs in abundant detail (see esp. ibid., ch. 6 and pp. 247–259), dispelling whatever lingering doubts may have existed. To be sure, Pfungst tells of other clever animals, and there have been records of many since—not just "talking" equines but learned canines, reading pigs, and at least one "goat of knowledge." The most fascinating "talking" horse was Berto, which was blind yet gave excellent results when the attendant "thought that the questions had been written on its skin or uttered aloud" (Katz 1937:17–18). All of them were assiduously coached performers intentionally cued by their trainers, who were entertainingly exposed by the prominent American illusionist and historian of conjuration, Christopher (1970, ch. 3; see also Máday 1914, ch. 15). In sum, the Clever Hans phenomenon lies at the very heart of zoosemiotics; the investigators were misled because they sought in the pupil, the horse—or the great spotted woodpecker (Griffin 1976:25–26), or the porpoise (Sebeok 1972:59ff.), or the chimpanzee—what they should have looked for in the teacher, man: covert and unwitting message transmissions from man to man (Rosenthal 1966, ch. 9) as well as from man to animal (ibid., ch. 10).

Much of the mystique that enveloped the Delphinidae in the 1960s is traceable to the Clever Hans delusion (Sebeok 1972:59–60; Wood 1973, ch. 1; Caldwell and Caldwell, in Sebeok 1977b). In the late 1970s, a more lively issue, which has hardly been faced up to yet (but see the inconclusive discussion by D. Premack 1971:820–821; and cf. R. Brown 1973:50–51), is the pervasive, insidious penetration of Clever Hans into all the attempts so far designed to erase the seemingly ineradicable linguistic barrier between man and the Great Apes. (Eccles 1974:106, doubts "if these clever learned responses can be regarded as language even remotely resembling human language.") The possibly insoluble dilemma that experimenters in this area must confront is that man can scarcely be eliminated from any conceivable variant of the requisite training procedures, because, to put it quite starkly, every such animal is critically dependent for emotional sustenance upon its trainer—whether informed or naïve (A. Premack 1976: 101 ff.), even when the system used is computer-enhanced (Rumbaugh and Gill 1976a). Deprived of social contact with a human partner, the home- or laboratory-raised ape perishes, but when given the human contact, the experimenter's expectancy effects must be fully reckoned with (Timaeus 1973).

Of Clever Hans, James R. Angell noted in 1911: "No more remarkable tale of credulity founded on unconscious deceit was ever told, and were it offered as fiction, it would take high rank as a work of imagination" (Pfungst 1965). The lesson Hans tapped out as his legacy for science has not, however, been mastered even today. All efforts, without exception, that aimed to shape linguistic apes, whether the research design was quasinaturalistic or followed an essentially Skinnerian paradigm, not only offered "rich opportunities for drawing the wrong conclusions," in R. Brown's (1973:34) characteristically tactful parlance, but had their focus misplaced to begin with. The really interesting issue has to do with the nature of the communicative coupling between subject and object, hence that is precisely a semiotic problem; it was formulated by Rosenthal (in Pfungst 1965:xxxiii) in the following two sentences (and was expanded by this immensely insightful investigator in many of his other publications, where he drew on social psychological knowledge at large for fruitful hypotheses): "If we knew precisely by what means we unintentionally communicate our expectancies to our animal and human subjects, we could institute more effective controls against the effect of our expectancies. More generally, if we knew more about the modalities by which we subtly and unintentionally influence one another, we would then have learned a great deal that is new about human social behavior." The same point is made in Hediger's (1976:45–46) wide-ranging review of the Clever Hans phenomenon and its consequences, with even more explicit reference to zoosemiotics. The relevant question, he correctly emphasizes, is not how to eliminate human signs from the dyad, but how to—at long last—program a thorough investigation of all channels through which such signs actually are and might be transmitted, and thus to determine what really is happening in man-animal and man-man interaction: "Das ist eine Frage der Semiotik," Hediger insists, and, of course, this has become increasingly clear over the last decade; but the nitty-gritty of the search will also demand an exceptionally broad spectrum of cooperating disciplines.

6. Left / Right

There has been a great deal of agitation lately in the field of brain research about the question of lateralization of at least two modes of mentation in man (Dimond 1972; Ornstein 1972, ch. 3). The yeast that fuels this ferment derives from studies termed, as long ago as the 1870s (Sebeok 1976a: 57–58), *asemasia*, i.e., the impairment of nonverbal communicative functions (Zangwill 1975: 95–106), and, more immediately, from recent split brain experiments (Krashen 1976: 157–191). Some implications of this endeavor—essentially in its infancy—with the aim of moving toward a "true synthesis of biology and culture in the operation of human minds," were recently reviewed by Paredes and Hepburn (1976), giving rise to impassioned debate in ensuing issues of *Current Anthropology* and elsewhere. In general, however, the emerging picture seems to indicate that the left side of the brain processes verbal tasks better, while the right side deals more skillfully with visual-spatial tasks; this is underscored by a demonstration that the two hemispheres are not ontogenetically equal until the end of the first decade of life (Dennis and Whitaker 1976). Another, broader way in which scientists, such as A. R. Luria (e.g., in Sebeok 1974: 2561–2594; cf. Ornstein 1972: 67), prefer to describe the division of labor is to speak of two opposed but complementary ways of thinking, such that the left brain is more likely to deal with tasks seriatim ("logically"), while the right brain manages problems as a whole, perceiving their simultaneous relationships ("holistically").

This line of research has led to the following provisional conclusion, succinctly stated (though immediately, and properly so, hedged in with all sorts of qualifications) by Bogen (1969): "The left hemisphere is better than the right for language and for what has sometimes been called 'verbal activity' or 'linguistic thought'; in contrast we could say that the right hemisphere excels in 'non-language' or 'non-verbal' function." In the current secondary literature, especially on the part of anthropologists and members of the artificial intelligentsia, one finds that this duality of information handling is labeled more starkly as "verbal to nonverbal" (Tunnell 1973: 27), and one encounters such uncompromising assertions as "the appreciation of gestures . . . is the province of the right hemisphere" (Weizenbaum 1976: 220). Psychological tests tend to support the view that the right hemisphere appears somewhat more skillful than the left "in nonverbal reasoning and spatial abilities" (Bower 1970: 509), although both hemispheres are indubitably equipped for language representation in some ways and to some extent, the cerebral dominance seemingly involving, in Kinsbourne's dramatistic phrase, "active competition" between the two, such that "the left hemisphere is genetically destined to win" (1975: 114).

"Dominance" refers to the processing of information by one hemisphere and its ability to control responding. This variable is likely to be independent of "capacity," or the performance of some task when required by the contextual contingencies of a hemisphere. Now, according to Levy (1973: 158), the left hemisphere "simply does not bother to handle information which can be handled by the right," an observation that is in good conformity with the semiotic model espoused here, especially in respect to the hierarchical notion of "markedness" mentioned above (section 1). The pithy formulation of Eccles (1974:92) expresses this best of all by asseverating that the minor hemisphere resembles a very superior animal brain, which is to say that it provides the primary locus for the coding processes we term zoosemiotic but lacks the ability to report mental functions utilizing the verbal (or anthroposemiotic) code, at any rate, vocally (i.e., it is mute). Evolutionary continuities in semiosis from animals to man as well as sudden discontinuities are thus both accounted for, but in grossly different locations in the brain. The corpus callosum serves as the principal channel of intercommunication between the two hemispheres, insuring exact synchrony (unless, of course, the commissures are surgically or otherwise severed). The messages that flow back and forth are presumably all coded neurochemically, but whether the left-to-right commerce is verbal (or digital as was suggested in 1960; see Sebeok 1972, ch. 1; see also Bogen 1969), while the right-to-left traffic is nonverbal (or analog), remains one of many intriguing problems winking at the edge of experimental palpability. It also remains to be seen whether the two opposing schools of belief in regard to the ritualization of man's overall semiotic competence alluded to by the English zoologist Pumphrey (Sebeok 1976a: 67, 142) will be content with some such heuristic model; and, still further down the road, whether a proper characterization of the left hemisphere will require a judicious application of catastrophe theory (Thom 1975a; cf. Sebeok 1976b; 1977c)—since that is the most sophisticated qualitative method designed so far to handle discontinuous phenomena—whereas the right hemisphere's smooth, continuously changing Gestalt configurations will stay amenable to traditional quantitative analysis.

7. Formation / Dissolution: Diachronic Glimpses

Diachronic considerations of two very different sorts are pertinent to zoosemiotic inquiry: one focuses on the evolution of signs and systems of signs in phylogeny (Hahn and Simmel 1976; Marler, in Sebeok 1977b); the other considers their development in ontogeny (Sebeok 1976a: 98–99; Burghardt, in Sebeok 1977b), as well as impairment, leading to their ultimate dissolution in the lifespan of individuals (Zangwill 1975). The former constitutes the principal axis of synthesis in the entire field of the biological study of behavior (Sebeok 1972:135; 1976a:85), or ethology, which has been insistently characterized as "hardly more than a special case of diachronic semiotics" (Sebeok 1976a:156). This identification should disquiet no one who is cognizant of the common historical roots of the comparative method indispensably utilized in branches of both (Lorenz 1966:275–276): they stem from Baron Cuvier, the founder of comparative anatomy (which, in his conception, studied the static interrelationships of immutable species, created and re-created several times over), now transformed into modern phylogenetic behavioral systematics, no less than, albeit indirectly through Friedrich von Schlegel's applications, into comparative grammar (cf. Sebeok 1977c).

Any sensitive and observant caretaker is well aware that a "normal" infant is born with elaborate equipment for interacting with its human surroundings by means of a wide array of vocal and nonvocal signs. Indeed, its success in encoding and decoding vital messages is a most important measure of its very normalcy. Its semiotic growth and differentiation are undoubtedly best conceived of as a series of catastrophes (Thom 1975b). Thom's topological model, following ideas originating in biology and pursued by creative thinkers since the likes of D'Arcy Thompson and C. H. Waddington, could account for successive stages of bifurcation where, much as the development of any cell in an embryo diverges from that of its immediate neighbors, sign functions become ever more specialized and cluster to form particular constellations in a dynamic semiotic system occurring and explicable at any given time. Verbal signs suddenly emerge, superimposed upon babbling—which itself usually functions as an insufficiently explored vocal but, of course, preverbal link between the baby and its caretakers (Bullowa 1970; Bullowa et al., in McCormack and Wurm 1976:67–95). Language then continues to unfold (R. Brown 1973) until the child acquires full mastery over the language of its native speech community along with the culturally appropriate nonverbal systems of signs.

Study of the latter—which also embody the rules of when and how to use the language in accordance with personal needs and social norms—on a scale comparable with the former has barely begun, notwithstanding the pioneering instigation of this sort of research launched by Darwin in a famed segment of the diary he started in 1840 (1877). Surprisingly enough, there exists no definitive treatise of this hardly negligible area comprehending a configuration of attributes in any individual, which Chance calls "primary-group relations," a type of communication that is concerned with associations of an addresser with addressees, a process that Chance further characterizes as the wholly "nonverbal" infrastructure of social cohesion and control (1975:100). There are only a few authoritative survey articles about the state of this art, even the best of which are now getting a bit dated, such as Brannigan and Humphries (1972) or N. G. Blurton Jones (in Hinde 1972:271–296). These should be supplemented by special studies, e.g., of facial expressions in infants and children (Charlesworth and Kreutzer 1973), including tongue showing (Smith et al. 1974:222–227), and the like. The paucity of really robust achievements in this domain of nonverbal infant competences—concerning the sights, sounds, smells, and overall body management appropriate to the survival of the baby in all cultures—is the most startling fact about it. One's sense of wonderment remains far from fulfilled, although the tempo of research has become much livelier of late.

If relatively little is known about the formation of sign systems in the course of a human life, the destructive effects of injury or disease remain hardly understood at all. What Steinthal, in 1881, dubbed *Asemie*, and Jackson, following Hamilton's independent coinage of 1878, then propagated under the accurate label of *asemasia*, comprehending "the loss of gesticulating power," or of pantomime (Critchley 1975, ch. 3; Sebeok 1976a: 57–58) is, alas, too frequently experienced by patients and observed by attending physicians. An example of the extent to which pantomimic movement may be unattainable by victims of severe brain damage was recorded by Luria (1972: 45) from his celebrated patient Zasetsky, who was wounded in war: "I was lying in bed and needed the nurse. How was I to get her to come over? All of a sudden I remembered you can beckon to someone and so I tried to beckon to the nurse—that is move my left hand lightly back and forth. But she walked right on by and paid no attention to my gesturing. I realized then that I'd completely forgotten how to beckon to someone. It appeared I'd even forgotten how to gesture with my hands so that someone could understand what I meant." At one time, Jackson hazarded a tripartite clinical classification of the aphasias, and the third of his categories was the most global, namely, the loss of language when pantomime and gesture as well as speech are annihilated, a tragic condition so devastating as to be tantamount to social extinction.

The communicational problems that beset the aging and the aged typically fall between the two stools of social gerontology and psychosemiotics; in consequence, they have been largely misinterpreted or altogether neglected. Philip B. Stafford (personal communication), for example, has studied closely one dominant sign of senescence in our culture, "repetitiousness," and showed that, contrary to the usual assumption that this tedious habit is simply a symptom of physiological deterioration in old folks, it is rather a semiotic manifestation of an adaptive strategy useful to the elderly in capturing an audience. Nor must one take it for granted that the senescence is accompanied by a mere decrease in semiotic potency: on the contrary, a restocked ambry of nonverbal skills is often required and acquired in course of the aging process to cope with the usually, often dramatically, altered social environment. Just how this is accomplished has hardly been studied so far, but I am convinced that the semiotics of old age is one of the most promising research areas for the immediate future and that it will have great import for both applied gerontology and clinical geriatrics.

Since the application of the principle of ritualization to language was not proving feasible (section 1, above), Koehler (1936: 85ff.) proposed "to seek for roots, initia, precursors" to language and thought he found eleven, but then wisely concluded that "No animal has got all those initia of our language together, they are distributed among very different species, this one having one capacity, that species another. We alone possess all of them . . ." (ibid.: 87). Linguists like Hockett (with Altmann, in Sebeok 1968, ch. 5) and, to a lesser extent, Lyons (in Hinde 1972, ch. 3) later tried similarly to disassemble the verbal code into a quasi-logical roster of components of varying numbers and to examine each function separately from a comparative standpoint, a mechanistic and desperate procedure that turned out to be a largely empty exercise, partly for the reason foreseen by Koehler, partly for others such as are given by Hewes (in Wescott 1969: 4ff.). Unless and until one or more semiotic systems utilizing coding methods comparable with that of language are discovered, this sort of quest seems futile to me. Moreover, it appears increasingly unlikely that a terrestrial languagelike animal communication system will ever be located under natural conditions. The sole alternative lies, then, in the continued scanning—a long, arduous, and costly endeavor, the outcome of which is uncertain—for communicating intelligences on other planets (Arbib 1974).

Zoosemiotic systems in man, on the other hand, are eminently amenable to comparative study (Pitcairn and Eibl-Eibesfeldt, in Hahn and Simmel 1976, ch. 5) and will, no doubt, continue to produce worthwhile findings. An example that shows just how fascinating this line of inquiry can be is Ferguson's (1976: 138) suggestive research proposal that certain verbal routines, such as greetings and thanks, are "related phyletically to the bowings and touchings and well-described display phenomena of other species." The most fertile ground for the application of the methods of ritualization is surely in the domain of interpersonal rituals for which politeness formulas furnish one attractive target.

REFERENCES

Arbib, Michael. 1974. "The Likelihood of the Evolution of Communicating Intelligences on Other Planets." In *Interstellar Communication: Scientific Perspectives*, edited by C. Ponnamperuma and A. G. W. Cameron, pp. 59–78. Boston: Houghton Mifflin.

Argyle, Michael. 1975. *Bodily Communication*. New York: International Universities Press.

Barakat, Robert A. 1975. *The Cistercian Sign Language: A Study in Non-Verbal Communication*. Kalamazoo, Mich.: Cistercian Publications.

Barthes, Roland. 1967. *Elements of Semiology*. New York: Hill and Wang.

Bauman, Richard. 1974. "Speaking in the Light: The Role of the Quaker Minister." In *Explorations in the Ethnography of Speaking*, Joel Sherzer, pp. 144–160. Cambridge: Cambridge University Press.

Bäuml, Betty J., and Franz H. Bäuml. 1975. *A Dictionary of Gestures*. Metuchen, N.J.: The Scarecrow Press.

Beck, Henry. 1976. "Neuropsychological Servosystems, Consciousness, and the Problem of Embodiment." *Behavioral Science* 21: 139–160.

Benthall, Jonathan, and Ted Polhemus. 1975. (Eds.) *The Body as a Medium of Expression*. London: Allen Lane.

Bentley, Arthur F. 1941. "The Human Skin: Philosophy's Last Line of Defense." *Philosophy of Science* 8: 1–19.

Bogatyrev, Petr. 1971. *The Functions of Folk Costume in Moravian Slovakia*. The Hague: Mouton.

Bogen, Joseph E. 1969. "The Other Side of the Brain II: An Appositional Mind." *Bulletin of the Los Angeles Neurological Societies* 34: 135–162.

Bosmajian, Haig A. 1971. *The Rhetoric of Nonverbal Communication: Readings*. Glenview, Ill.: Scott, Foresman.

Bouissac, Paul. 1973. *La Mesure des gestes: Prolegomènes à la sémiotique gestuelle*. The Hague: Mouton.

———. 1976. *Circus and Culture: A Semiotic Approach*. Bloomington: Indiana University Press.

Bourne, Geoffrey H. 1971. *The Ape People*. New York: G. P. Putnam's Sons.

Bower, Gordon H. 1970. "Analysis of a Mnemonic Device." *American Scientist* 58: 496–510.

Brannigan, Christopher R., and David A. Humphries. 1972. "Human non-verbal behavior, a means of communication." In *Ethological Studies of Child Behaviour*, edited by N. Blurton Jones, pp. 37–64. Cambridge: Cambridge University Press.

Brothwell, Don R. 1976. (Ed.) *Beyond Aesthetics: Investigations into the Nature of Visual Art*. London: Thames and Hudson.

Brown, Roger. 1973. *A First Language: The Early Stages*. Cambridge: Harvard University Press.

Bullowa, Margaret. 1970. "The Start of the Language Process." *Actes du Xe Congrès International des Linguistes* 3: 191–198. Bucharest: Academy of the Romanian Socialist Republic.

Chance, Michael R.A. "Social Cohesion and the Structure of Attention." In *Biosocial Anthropology*. New York: John Wiley and Sons.

Charlesworth, William R., and Mary Anne Kreutzer. 1973. "Facial Expressions of Infants and Children." In *Darwin and Facial Expression: A Century of Research in Review*, edited by Paul Ekman, pp. 91–168. New York: Academic Press.

Cherry, Colin. 1966. *On Human Communication: A Review, A Survey, and a Criticism*, 2nd ed. Cambridge: MIT Press.

Christopher, Milbourne. 1970. *ESP, Seers & Psychics*. New York: Thomas Crowell.

Cortambert, Louise. 1833. *Le Langage des fleurs*. 4th ed. Paris: Audot.

Critchley, Macdonald. 1975. *Silent Language*. London: Butterworths.

Crystal, David. 1969. *Prosodic Systems and Intonations in English*. Cambridge, England: Cambridge University Press.

Curtiss, Susan, et al. 1975. "An Update on the Linguistic Development of Genie." In *Georgetown University Round Table on Languages and Linguistics*, edited by Daniel P. Dato, pp. 145–157. Washington, D.C.: Georgetown University Press.

Darwin, Charles. 1877. "A Biographical Sketch of an Infant." *Mind* 2: 286–294.

Davis, Flora. 1971. *Inside Intuition: What We Know About Nonverbal Communication*. New York: McGraw-Hill.

Dennis, Maureen, and Harry A. Whitaker. 1976. "Language Acquisition Following Hemidecortication: Linguistic Superiority of the Left over the Right Hemisphere." *Brain and Language* 3: 404–433.

Dimond, Stuart. 1972. *The Double Brain*. Edinburgh: Churchill Livingstone.

Dingwall, William Orr. 1975. "The Species-Specificity of Speech." In *Georgetown University Round Table on Languages and Linguistics*, edited by Daniel P. Dato, pp. 17–62. Washington, D.C.

Duncan, Starkey D., Jr. 1975. "Language, Paralanguage, and Body Motion in the Structure of Conversations." In *Socialization and Communication in Primary Groups*, edited by Thomas R. Williams, pp. 283–311. The Hague: Mouton.

Eccles, John. 1974. "Cerebral Activity and Consciousness." In *Studies in the Philosophy of Biology, Reduction and Related Problems*, edited by Francisco J. Ayala and Theodore Dobzhansky. Berkeley: University of California Press.

Eco, Umberto. 1976. *A Theory of Semiotics*. Bloomington: Indiana University Press.

Efron, David. 1972. [1941]. *Gesture, Race and Culture*. The Hague: Mouton.

Egger, Victor. 1904. *La Parole Intérieure*. Paris: Alcan.

Eimermacher, Karl. 1974. *Arbeiten sowjetischer Semiotiker der Moskauer und Tartuer Schule*. Kronberg: Scriptor.

Eisenberg, Abne N., and Ralph R. Smith, Jr. *Non-Verbal Communication*. Indianapolis: Bobbs-Merrill.

Ekman, Paul. 1972. "Universals and Cultural Differences in Facial Expressions of Emotion." In *Nebraska Symposium on Motivation 1971*, edited by James K. Cole, pp. 207–283. Lincoln: University of Nebraska Press.

Eschbach, Achim, and Wendelin Rader. 1976. *Semiotik-Bibliographie I*. Frankfurt a/M: Syndikat.

Ferguson, Charles A. 1976. "The Structure and Use of Politeness Formulas." *Language in Society* 5: 137–151.

Fouts, Roger S. 1978. "Capacities for Language in Great Apes." In *Sociology and Psychology of Primates*, edited by R. H. Tuttle, pp. 371–390. The Hague: Mouton.

Frisch, Karl von. 1974. *Animal Architecture*. New York: Harcourt Brace Jovanovich.

Goffman, Erving. 1975. *Replies and Responses*. Urbino: Centro Internazionale di Semiotica e di Linguistica.

Greimas, Algirdas Julien. 1976. *Sémiotique et sciences sociales*. Paris: Seuil.

Griffin, Donald R. 1976. *The Question of Animal Awareness: Evolutionary Continuity of Mental Experience*. New York: Rockefeller University Press.

Guthrie, R. Dale. 1976. *Body Hot Spots: The Anatomy of Human Social Organs and Behavior*. New York: Van Nostrand Reinhold.

Hahn, Martin E., and Edward C. Simmel. 1976. (Eds.) *Communicative Behavior and Evolution*. New York: Academic Press.

Hall, Edward T. 1959. *The Silent Language*. Garden City: N.Y.: Doubleday.

Harrison, Randall P. 1974. *Beyond Words: An Introduction to Nonverbal Communication*. Englewood Cliffs, N.J.: Prentice-Hall.

Hartshorne, Charles. 1973. *Born to Sing: An Interpretation and World Survey of Bird Song*. Bloomington: Indiana University Press.

Hediger, Heini. 1968. *The Psychology and Behaviour of Animals in Zoos and Circuses*. New York: Dover.

——. 1976. "Der Kluge Hans: Möglichkeiten und Grenzen der Kommunikation zwischen Mensch und Tier." *Neue Zürcher Zeitung* 156: 45–46 (July 7).

Hess, Eckhard. H. 1975. *The Tell-Tale Eye: How Your Eyes Reveal Hidden Thoughts and Emotions*. New York: Van Nostrand Reinhold.

Hinde, Robert. 1972. (Ed.) *Non-Verbal Communication*. Cambridge: Cambridge University Press.

——. 1974. *Biological Bases of Human Social Behavior*. New York: McGraw-Hill.

Hjelmslev, Louis. 1953. *Prolegomena to a Theory of Language*. Baltimore: Waverly Press.

Hutt, Corinne, and M. Jane Vaizey. 1966. "Differential Effects of Group Density on Social Behavior." *Nature* 209: 1371–1372.

Huxley, Julian, and Ludwig Koch. 1964 [1938]. *Animal Language*. New York: Grosset and Dunlap.

Ivanov, Vjačeslav V. 1976. *Očerki po istorii semiotiki v SSR*. Moscow: Nauka.

Jacob, Francois. 1974. *The Logic of Living Systems: A History of Heredity*. London: Allen Lane.

Katz, David. 1937. *Animals and Men: Studies in Comparative Psychology*. London: Longmans, Green.

Kauffman, Lynn E. 1971. "Tacesics, the Study of Touch: A Model for Proxemic Analysis." *Semiotica* 4: 149–161.

Kavanagh, James F., and Ignatius G. Mattingly, 1972. (Eds.) *Language by Ear and by Eye: The Relationship between Speech and Reading*. Cambridge: MIT Press.

Kelley, David L. 1971. *Kinesiology: Fundamentals of Motion Description*. Englewood Cliffs, N.J.: Prentice-Hall.

Kinsbourne, Marcel. 1975. "Minor Hemisphere Language and Cerebral Maturation." In *Foundations of Language Development: A Multidisciplinary Approach*, edited by Eric H. Lenneberg and Elizabeth Lenneberg, 2, chapter 7, New York: Academic Press.

Kleinpaul, Rudolf. 1972 [1888]. *Sprache ohne Worte: Idee einer allgemeinen Wissenschaft der Sprache*. The Hague: Mouton.

Knapp, Mark L. 1972. *Nonverbal Communication in Human Interaction*. New York: Holt, Rinehart and Winston.

Koehler, Otto. 1956. "Thinking without Words." *Proceedings of the XIV International Congress of Zoology*. Copenhagen: Danish Science Press, pp. 75–88.

Krames, Lester, Patricia Pliner, and Thomas Alloway. 1974. (Eds.) *Nonverbal Communication*. New York: Plenum Press.

Krashen, Stephen D. 1976. "Cerebral Asymmetry." In *Studies in Neurolinguistics* 2, edited by Haiganoosh Whitaker and Harry A. Whitaker, chap. 5. New York: Academic Press.

Laver, John. 1976. "Language and Nonverbal Communication." In *Handbook of Perception 7: Language and Speech*, chap. 10. New York: Academic Press.

Levy, Jerre. 1973. "Psychobiological Implications of Bilateral Asymmetry." In *Hemispheric Functions in the Human Brain*, edited by Stuart J. Dimond and J. Graham Beaumont, pp. 121–183. London: Elek.

Lieberman, Philip. 1975. *On the Origins of Language: An Introduction to the Evolution of Human Speech*. New York: Macmillan.

Locke, John. 1975 [1690]. *An Essay Concerning Human Understanding*, edited by Peter H. Nidditch. Oxford: Clarendon.

Lorenz, Konrad. 1966. "Evolution of Ritualization in the Biological and Cultural Spheres." *Philosophical Transactions of the Royal Society of London* 251: 273–284.

Lotz, John. 1956. "Symbols Make Man." In *Frontiers of Knowledge in the Study of Man*, edited by Lynn White, Jr., pp. 207–231. New York: Harper and Brothers.

Luria, Aleksandr R. 1972. *The Man with a Shattered World: The History of a Brain Wound*. New York: Basic Books.

McCormack, William, and Stephen A. Wurm. 1976. (Eds.) *Language and Man: Anthropological Issues*. The Hague: Mouton.

Máday, Stefan von. 1914. *Gibt es denkende Tiere?* Leipzig: Wilhelm Engelmann.

Malinowski, Bronislaw. 1965 [1935]. *Coral Gardens and Their Magic II: The Language of Magic and Gardening*. Bloomington: Indiana University Press.

Malson, Lucien. 1964. *Les Enfants sauvages: mythe et réalité*. Paris: Union Générale d' Éditions.

Marcus, Solomon. 1974. "Linguistic Structures and Generative Devices in Molecular Genetics." *Cahiers de Linguistique Théorique et Appliquée* 11: 74–104.

Marples, Mary J. 1965. *The Ecology of the Human Skin*. Springfield, Ill.: Charles C. Thomas.

Mehrabian, Albert. 1972. *Nonverbal Communication*. Chicago: Aldine, Atherton.

Miller, James G. 1976. "Second Annual Ludwig von Bertallanfy Memorial Lecture." *Behavioral Science* 21: 219–227.

Moles, Abraham A. 1964. "Les voies cutanées, compléments informationnels de la sensibilité de l'organisme." *Studium Generale* 17: 589–595.

Montagu, Ashley. 1971. *Touching: The Human Significance of the Skin*. New York: Columbia University Press.

Morris, Desmond. 1962. *The Biology of Art*. London: Methuen.

Nattiez, Jean-Jacques. 1975. *Fondements d'une sémiologie de la musique*. Paris: Union Générale d'Éditions.

Nelson, Keith. 1973. "Does the Holistic Study of Behavior Have a Future?" In *Perspectives in Ethology*, edited by P. P. G. Bateson and Peter Klopfer, chap. 8. New York: Plenum.

Ornstein, Robert. 1972. *The Psychology of Consciousness*. New York: The Viking Press.

Paredes, J. Anthony, and Marcus J. Hepburn. 1976. "The Split Brain and the Culture-and-Cognition Paradox." *Current Anthropology* 17: 121–127. Discussion: ibid.: 318–326, 503–511.

Payne, Roger S., and Scott McVay. 1971. "Songs of the Humpback Whales." *Science* 173: 587–597.

Pfungst, Oskar. 1965 [1911]. *Clever Hans (The Horse of Mr. von Osten)*, edited by Robert Rosenthal. New York: Holt, Rinehart, and Winston.

Pike, Kenneth. 1943. *Phonetics: A Critical Analysis of Phonetic Theory and Technic for the Practical Description of Sound*. Ann Arbor: University of Michigan Press.

Pliner, Patricia, Lester Krames, and Thomas Alloway. 1975. (Eds.) *Nonverbal Communication of Aggression*. New York: Plenum Press.

Poyatos, Fernando. 1976. *Man Beyond Words: Theory and Methodology of Nonverbal Communication*. Oswego: New York State English Council.

Premack, Ann J. 1976. *Why Chimps Can Read*. New York: Harper and Row.

Premack, David. 1971. "Language in Chimpanzee?" *Science* 172: 808–822.

Prieto, Luis J. 1975. "Sémiologie de la communication et sémiologie de la signification." *Études de linguistique et de sémiologie générales*. Geneva: Librairie Droz, pp. 125–41.

Rosenthal, Robert. 1966. *Experimenter Effects in Behavioral Research*. New York: Appleton-Century-Crofts.

Ruesch, Jurgen, and Weldon Kees. 1956. *Nonverbal Communication: Notes on the Visual Perception of Human Relations*. Berkeley and Los Angeles: University of California Press.

Rumbaugh, Duane M., and Timothy V. Gill. 1976. "Language and the Acquisition of Language-Type Skills by a Chimpanzee (*Pan*)." *Annals of the New York Academy of Sciences* 280: 562–568.

Sapir, Edward. 1931. "Communication." In *Encyclopedia of the Social Sciences* 4: 78–81. New York: Macmillan.

Scherer, Klaus R. 1970. *Non-verbale Kommunikation: Ansätze zur Beobachtung und Analyse der aussersprachlichen Aspekte von Interactionsverhalten.* Hamburg: Helmut Buske.

Schneirla, Theodore C. 1965. "Aspects of Stimulation and Organization in Approach/Withdrawal Processes Underlying Vertebrate Behavioral Development." *Advances in the Study of Behavior* 1: 1–74.

Schutz, Noel W. 1976. *Kinesiology: The Articulation of Movement.* Lisse: The Peter de Ridder Press.

Sebeok, Thomas A. 1968. (Ed.) *Animal Communication: Techniques of Study and the Results of Research.* Bloomington: Indiana University Press.

——. 1972. *Perspectives in Zoosemiotics.* The Hague: Mouton.

——. 1974. (Ed.) *Current Trends in Linguistics 12: Linguistics and Adjacent Arts and Sciences.* The Hague: Mouton.

——. 1975. (Ed.) *The Tell-Tale Sign: A Survey of Semiotics.* Lisse: Peter de Ridder Press.

——. 1976a. *Contributions to the Doctrine of Signs.* Bloomington: Research Center for Language and Semiotic Studies.

——. 1976b. "Marginalia to Greenberg's Conception of Semiotics and Zoosemiotics." In *Linguistic Studies Offered to Joseph Greenberg on the Occasion of His 60th Birthday,* edited by Alphonse Juilland. Saratoga, Calif.: Anma Libri.

——. 1976c. "Iconicity." *Modern Language Notes* 91 (6).

——. 1977a. "Semiosis in nature and culture." In *Proceedings of the International Symposium on Semiotics and Theories of Symbolic Behavior in Eastern Europe and the West,* edited by Thomas G. Winner. Lisse: Peter de Ridder Press.

——. 1977c. (Ed.) *How Animals Communicate.* Bloomington: Indiana University Press.

——, and Donna Jean Umiker-Sebeok. 1976. (Eds.) *Speech Surrogates: Drum and Whistle Systems.* The Hague: Mouton.

——, and Donna Jean Umiker-Sebeok. 1977b. (Eds.) *Aboriginal Sign Languages: Gestural Systems Among Native Peoples of the Americas and Australia.* New York: Plenum.

Shands, Harley C. 1976. "Malinowski's Mirror: Emily Dickinson as Narcissus." *Contemporary Psychoanalysis* 12: 300–334.

Smith, W. John, et al. 1974. "Tongue Showing: A Facial Display of Humans and Other Primate Species." *Semiotica* 11: 201–246.

Stokoe, William C. 1972. *Semiotics and Human Sign Languages.* The Hague: Mouton.

Szöke, Peter. 1963. "Ornitomuzikológia." *Magyar tudomány* 9: 592–607.

Thom, René. 1975a. *Structural Stability and Morphogenesis: An Outline of a General Theory of Models.* Reading, Mass.: W. A. Benjamin.

——. 1975b. "Les Mathématiques et l'intelligible." *Dialectica* 29: 71–80.

Timaeus, Ernst. 1973. "Some Non-Verbal and Paralinguistic Cues as Mediators of Experimenter Expectancy Effects." In *Social Communication and Movement: Studies of Interaction and Expression in Man and Chimpanzee,* edited by Mario von Cranach and Ian Vine. New York: Academic Press, chap. 11.

Tomkins, Gordon M. 1975. "The Metabolic Code." *Science* 189: 760–763.

Tunnell, Gary G. 1973. *Culture and Biology: Becoming Human*. Minneapolis: Burgess Publishing Co.

Uexküll, Jakob von. 1940. "Bedeutungslehre." *Bios* 10.

Umiker-Sebeok, Donna Jean, and Thomas A. Sebeok. 1978. (Eds.) *Aboriginal Sign Languages of the Americas and Australia*. 2 vols. New York: Plenum Press.

Voegelin, Charles F., and Zellig S. Harris. 1947. "The Scope of Linguistics." *American Anthropologist* 49: 588–600.

Vološinov, Valentin N. 1973. *Marxism and the Philosophy of Language*. New York: Seminar Press.

Vygotsky, Lev Semenovich. 1962. *Thought and Language*. Edited and translated by E. Hanfmann and G. Vakar. Cambridge: MIT Press.

Washburn, Sherwood L. 1973. "The Promise of Primatology." *American Journal of Physical Anthropology* 38: 177–182.

Weitz, Shirley. 1974. (Ed.) *Nonverbal Communication: Readings with Commentary*. New York: Oxford University Press.

Weizenbaum, Joseph. 1976. *Computer Power and Human Reason*. San Francisco: W. H. Freeman.

Wescott, Roger W. 1969. *The Divine Animal: An Exploration of Human Potentiality*. New York: Funk & Wagnalls.

——. 1974. (Ed.) *Language Origins*. Silver Spring, Md.: Linstok Press.

Winner, Irene Portis, and Thomas Winner. 1976. "The Semiotics of Cultural Texts." *Semiotica* 18: 101–156.

Wolfe, John B. 1936. "Effectiveness of Token-Rewards for Chimpanzees." *Comparative Psychology Monograph* 12(5).

Wood, Forrest G. 1973. *Marine Mammals and Man: The Navy's Porpoises and Sea Lions*. Washington, D.C.: Robert B. Luce.

Zangwill, Oliver L. 1975. "The Relation of Nonverbal Cognitive Functions to Aphasia." In *Foundations of Language Development: A Multidisciplinary Approach*, edited by Eric H. Lenneberg and Elizabeth Lenneberg, 2, chap. 6. New York: Academic Press.

INDEX OF NAMES

INDEX OF SUBJECTS

Robert E. Innis, Professor of Philosophy at the University of Lowell, has published many articles in philosophy, semiotics, and social and cultural theory and is the author of *Karl Bühler: Semiotic Foundations of Language Theory* (Plenum) and the translator of *The Central Texts of Ludwig Wittgenstein,* by Gerd Brand (Basil Blackwell).